‘Iffat Al Thunayan

AN ARABIAN QUEEN

To Princesses
Sarah, Latifah, Lulwah, and Hayfah al-Faysal,
who followed in their mother's footsteps.

'Iffat Al Thunayan

AN ARABIAN QUEEN

JOSEPH A. KÉCHICHIAN

sussex
ACADEMIC
PRESS
Brighton • Chicago • Toronto

2 4 6 8 10 9 7 5 3 1

First published in 2015 by
SUSSEX ACADEMIC PRESS
PO Box 139
Eastbourne BN24 9BP

and in the United States of America by
SUSSEX ACADEMIC PRESS
Independent Publishers Group
814 N. Franklin Street, Chicago, IL 60610

and in Canada by
SUSSEX ACADEMIC PRESS (CANADA)
24 Ranee Avenue, Toronto, Ontario, M6A 1M6

British Library Cataloguing in Publication Data
A CIP catalogue record for this book is available from the British Library.

Library of Congress Cataloging-in-Publication Data
Kéchichian, Joseph A.
'Iffat Al Thunayan : an Arabian Queen / Joseph A. Kéchichian.
pages cm
Includes bibliographical references and index.
ISBN 978-1-84519-685-1 (hb : alk. paper)
1. Thunayyan, 'Iffat, 1916–2000. 2. Queens—Saudi Arabia—Biography. 3. Spouses of heads of state—Saudi Arabia—Biography. 4. Women—Saudi Arabia—Biography. I. Title.
DS244.526.T58K43 2015
953.805'3092—dc23
[B]

2014025651

Typeset and designed by Sussex Academic Press, Brighton & Eastbourne, UK.
Printed by TJ International, Padstow, Cornwall, UK.

Contents

2 A PILLAR OF THE AL SA'UD

3 EDUCATION FOR A RE-BORN NATION

Preface

When the writer Robert Lacey asked Queen 'Iffat's sons about their mother, they apparently fell "silent, for, tuned to the same fine tension between ambition and caution as their parents, they still judge[d] it imprudent in the Arabia of the 1980s to make too much fuss about the achievement of a woman."[1] Times have changed, and for this book not only 'Iffat Al Thunayan's sons but her four daughters and countless grandchildren have openly discussed their mother and grandmother to better acquaint readers with her personality. The late Queen was, by all accounts, one of the key figures in the contemporary history of Sa'udi Arabia. As Lacey writes:

> Everyone knows about Iffat. People chuckle over the sleight of hand with which she infiltrated her ideas into the Kingdom. They tell stories of the battles she fought in the early years of her marriage to flush away Faisal's other wives and women. But public tribute there is none: no newspaper interviews or profiles, no television documentaries, and those that are devoted to her husband seldom even mention her existence. It is as if the greatness of a great man would somehow be impugned if the strength and inspiration that he drew from his wife were to be acknowledged, so, though Iffat's efforts for one-half of Sa'udi society stand comparison with the achievement of any male member of her family now alive, she is, in her own way, if for different reasons, as much a non-person as her brother-in-law Sa'ud.[2]

Anyone who has read about the late King Faysal bin 'Abdul 'Aziz bin 'Abdul Rahman Al Sa'ud, wrote about him and his accomplishments, and otherwise thought about the dramatic transformations that have occurred in the Kingdom cannot, even for a brief moment, overlook the role that 'Iffat Al Thunayan played in the contemporary history of the

---

[1] Robert Lacey, *The Kingdom: Arabia and the House of Sa'ud*. New York: Harcourt Brace Jovanovich, 1981, p. 366.

[2] *Ibid.*, pp. 366–367.

country. To claim otherwise would be to deny justice to a remarkable woman, and while similar figures have marked the contemporary history of the Al Sa'ud, none have matched Queen 'Iffat in the depth of their accomplishments. That is not to say that she single-handedly accomplished all of the achievements discussed in this book, but that she inspired countless others with her generous vision of selfless contribution to the prosperity of the nation.

In the course of writing this study, I have had Sa'udis and non-Sa'udis alike ask me what is the primary audience that would benefit from reading it. Beyond social scientists and political analysts with an interest in the Kingdom of Sa'udi Arabia, several colleagues focused on young Sa'udi girls and women as the principal audience, although my wish and hope is that Sa'udi males, both boys and men, will also read it, if for no other reason than to know who Queen 'Iffat Al Thunayan was and what she represented for the country. Above all, by doing so I hope they would learn what it means to be a real Sa'udi woman.

A Note on Interviews

This book is primarily based on interviews conducted with members of the al-Faysal family, as well as friends and acquaintances of the late Queen 'Iffat Al Thunayan. Fifty-three individuals were kind enough to open their doors, several of them on more than one occasion, to share their recollections. With the exception of an introductory session at Effat University that brought together six members of the family attending a Board of Trustees session, and who graciously agreed to spend two additional hours discussing this project, all of the following interviews, listed exhaustively in Appendix I, were held on a one-to-one basis in the individual's home or office. A few interviews were held in public spaces—a hotel lobby or café—and these are noted as appropriate. Several were held at Effat University in Jiddah simply because of its convenient location and, equally important, because the institution was my official host in the Kingdom during the course of this research effort. There were never any restrictions on the types of questions I could ask or on whether I could tape-record conversations. Some were indeed taped and transcribed. Most of the time I took extensive handwritten notes, double-checking quotations as necessary with the interviewees. Several e-mails were exchanged with those family members who maintain this method of correspondence, and I saved a complete database to back up whatever assertions were attributed to any particular individual. At no time did I refrain from asking intrusive questions about the late Queen or her relationships, although I chose not to write about everything I was told. There were several private conversations that helped me better understand various matters whose contents would be considered invasive if made public. Since none of these were existential in nature, to respect ‘Iffat Al Thunayan’s memory they were left out. Suffice it to say that such knowledge, most of which dealt with the way she was received when she arrived in the Kingdom, strengthened my own appreciation of the remarkable woman that is the subject of this historical biography.

Most of the interviewees wanted to tell their stories of Queen ‘Iffat, aware that time and memory were not their best allies and conscious that a new generation of Sa‘udis would barely remember her in a few years’ time. They wanted her life story to be told in as much detail as possible, recollecting many anecdotes and critical events that occurred, both to cherish her memory and emphasize her accomplishments. They wanted everyone to know who this woman really was and what she actually did over the span of her life. Thus it may be accurate to state that the book is partially a collective story by some of the many individuals who knew, loved, and respected ‘Iffat Al Thunayan. Of course, this was a challenging book to compose, but every effort was made to avoid a hagiography. Because I did not know the Queen and never met her, I could only see her photographs, read a few letters she composed, and in one case hear her voice over a family session mischievously recorded by one of her grandchildren. Her laughter came through and one could easily tell that this was a rather happy woman who accomplished much more than most.

A Note on Methodology

As stated above, the Queen passed away long before I embarked on this project, and because I did not know her, it was logical to assume that I would rely on those who had, principally family members and friends. While there may be Sa‘udis who hold critical views of the Queen, I would wager that there are not too many, even if such an assertion should not be misconstrued as saying that Queen ‘Iffat was perfect. In fact, she was a perfectionist and did not tolerate fools. She was incensed as necessary—and this aspect of her personality is addressed in the book—though I was far more interested in portraying how she channeled her opprobrium to get things done. Critics may even imagine that ‘Iffat’s role in the field of education was tangential, arguing that it was the late King Fahd, during his time as Minister of Education, who actually launched both the ministry and a national education system that included women. While the then Prince Fahd was indeed the official responsible for that endeavor, the ideas pertaining to women’s education on which it was founded originated with ‘Iffat—ideas shared at frequent family gatherings in the Faysal home. Fahd was a regular attendee of Faysal’s *majlis* (meeting room or council)—where ‘Iffat was also habitually present—and was considered to be one of the King’s supporters within the family long before Faysal assumed rulership. Likewise, while King ʻAbdallah bin ʻAbdul ʻAziz has also played a huge role in expanding education for women and in widening the curriculum to include the sciences, business, and information technology, his priorities in the 1950s and 1960s were the National Guard, not education, and especially not women's education. Of course, King ʻAbdallah has been a major promoter of women's education in his own right, and one of his most important achievements—the Princess Nurah bint ʻAbdul Rahman University—merits attention and is also discussed in the chapters that follow.

Although this study is my eleventh book and fourth on Saʻudi Arabia, it is important to state what it is not: it is not a book about contemporary feminism in the Kingdom. I do not consider myself qualified to tackle that task, even if I am an observer of events in the country. Readers will note that I only tangentially touch on segregation, the ban on driving, and other contemporary concerns. That is effectively the case because the book is about a remarkable woman who had a major influence on her country and people. The prime purpose of this volume is to portray her legacy for a rapidly changing society, which is partially addressed by discussing key issues with dozens of young women graduates who attended her university. Moreover, because Queen ʻIffat was not a feminist in the contemporary meaning of the word, even if she expressed her opinion loud and clear on several fronts when she was alive, I concluded that such fare did not belong here. While I do endeavor to assess some of the gains traceable to Queen ʻIffat's work, I have not set out to compose a study on the Saʻudi feminist movement—where it stands today, and where it is going as the Kingdom absorbs hundreds of thousands of students, including thousands of women, into the labor force.

Equally important are references to the late Queen as the "*Turkiyyah*" on account of her birthplace. How a Saʻudi woman who spoke no Arabic—only Turkish—when she returned to Arabia succeeded in integrating herself into the royal family, and how she overcame strong prejudices against her as a foreigner, are not the easiest of circumstances to convey. Indeed, the chief reason why so much attention is devoted to this specific issue throughout the text is not because of any alleged prejudices against non-Arabic-speaking members of the Al Saʻud—which would be a strange declaration given that true Saʻudis cannot, by definition, discriminate against "other" Muslim members of their own family even if these individuals are ostracized—but because I intend to illustrate how Queen ʻIffat managed to overcome latent prejudices. She certainly differed from more recent ultranationalist elements that have skewed this language issue as well as the more relevant national origin question. As a multilingual American of Armenian extraction who grew up in the Arab world, I am amply aware of Queen ʻIffat's "Turkish" background and the language barrier she confronted. What I hope to show in this book is how 'Iffat's Sa'udi credentials went beyond her being born in the Ottoman Empire. In fact, and like all "others" with connections with the Ottomans (of which I am one, too, since my ancestors hailed from Marash, Anatolia, today Kahramanmaraş in Turkey), it may be safe to conclude that she had triumphed over chauvinism long before she returned to her ancestral home. In her case, she did not deride the Ottomans or their Turkish successors, an even-handedness that epitomizes the poise and dignity with which she carried herself, though there is little doubt that she also withstood the heavy weight of her early years throughout her life.

Finally, it is worth repeating that while this is primarily a book about Queen 'Iffat Al Thunayan and her family, it is also about two different Sa'udi Arabias that existed during her lifetime: the one she discovered when she arrived in January 1932 and the one that had emerged—as a leading regional and international power—by the time of her death in 2000. Queen 'Iffat neither invented the Kingdom nor did she found the monarchy, but she played a critical role in strengthening the country and, especially, the ruling Al Sa'ud family. She imparted a vision of what both were capable of and also led the way in education and health matters. It is not surprising, therefore, that her fellow citizens remember her as a genuine "Arabian Queen."

Acknowledgments

The idea for this book germinated during the two years I devoted to researching and composing my 2008 book on King Faysal, which was translated into Arabic and was widely read in the Kingdom. At the height of my research efforts on that volume, I came across various references to 'Iffat Al Thunayan, and determined that her story needed to be told in detail. That was easier said than done. Simply stated, no precedent existed for such an endeavor, and it took me some time to persuade her youngest son, HRH Prince Turki al-Faysal, to assist with the initiative. At the time, His Royal Highness was Ambassador of Sa'udi Arabia in the United States, and I was the CEO of a consulting firm that focused on the Arabian Peninsula. After several conversations, Prince Turki approved my proposal and, more important, made the necessary arrangements for me to meet with his brothers and sisters. In time, Prince Turki invited me, and I accepted, to join the King Faysal Center for Research and Islamic Studies as a Senior Fellow in October 2013, though I hasten to add that this volume was completed before I took up this appointment. I thank His Royal Highness for his support.

The individual who proved to be the lynchpin of this book was HRH Princess Lulwah al-Faysal, who approved my research affiliation with Effat University, and who authorized Dr. Hayfah Jamal al-Layl, its President, to extend a formal invitation for a two-year-long research appointment. I thank Princess Lulwah for her encouragement and for welcoming me at the university, as well as on several occasions at her home, where she answered my numerous questions. Likewise, Dr. Hayfah and her staff went out of their way to follow up on my queries and, especially, to facilitate my appointments with senior members of the ruling family and others. One individual on her staff, Nisrin Ghunaym, deserves particular praise. Nisrin's administrative assistance made for a happy experience and I am grateful to her in more ways than I can express because she made sure that my appointments were all lined up before I even left Los Angeles on the long trips to Jiddah. Likewise, 'Abdallah al-Ghamdi ensured that my residency papers were always in order and, since he worked for the Queen for over three decades, I am equally grateful for his anecdotal snippets. I would be remiss if I did not also single out the Director of Buildings and Grounds at the university, Rushdy M. Al-Azzah, who placed a car at my disposal, along with two alternating and equally congenial drivers, Bandar A. Al-Atiq and Mansur Othman Salih. Although Ms. Ghunaym was meticulous, since she always gave me a map for finding an addressee's office or home, it would have been impossible to reach our destinations without Bandar or Mansur. Sometimes, the smallest details they offered about the late Queen enlivened my numerous journeys through heavy traffic, which both drivers naturally took in their stride.

As listed in Appendix I, scores of individuals extended a welcome mat. I thank each and every one at Effat University, Dar al-Hanan School, the Al-Nahdah Philanthropic Society for Women in Riyadh, the Woman's Charitable Society in Jiddah, the Maharat Center, the Help Center, the King Faysal Specialist Hospital, and the King Khalid Eye Hospital for their assistance. Personnel at all levels spent countless hours with this curious male researcher who was writing about their "Queen." It was truly rewarding to visit all of these institutions and to meet with the many individuals who took time out from their busy schedules to answer my questions. Often, Sa'udi women I interviewed wore a *niqab* in my presence, though many either donned a *hijab* or were uncovered. At the hospitals, I spoke with Sa'udi and foreign physicians and nurses working side by side and, frankly, I could not tell the difference. One of my most memorable visits was at the King Khalid Eye Hospital where I saw how artificial eye sockets were prepared for patients who had been involved in major accidents or had succumbed to disfiguring cancers. It was doubly rewarding to gain insights from indigenous staff members caring for their patients, which, without exaggeration, confirmed the impression that significant strides in health care were being made across the Kingdom, even if this particular institution stood out.

Equally rewarding were my numerous conversations with Dr. Ghazi Faysal Binzagr, an Effat University Board of Advisors member, and Dr. Ahmad Sa'ad Gabbani, the Director of the Human Resources Center of Excellence at Xenel-Expansis in Jiddah (as well as being Dr. Al-Layl's spouse), who were always available to keep me company. Others rose to the occasion as well, and, indeed, I am honored to have made true friends in the Kingdom during the past several decades. It is difficult for a foreign researcher to function in Sa'udi Arabia; personal contacts are critical for success.

For this project, a special note of appreciation must be extended to HRH Princess Albanderi bint 'Abdul Rahman al-Faysal, one of the Queen's granddaughters and now the Director of the King Khalid Foundation. Princess Albanderi shared the tape recording that was made in Paris so that I could hear the late Queen's voice, listen in on an intimate family conversation, and gain insights into her wit. She also showed me countless photographs in family albums, some of which are included in this volume. Few Sa'udis can boast two monarchs as grandfathers, and Princess Albanderi honors them both, confident that she will also contribute to the welfare of the Kingdom.

Finally, I thank Editorial Director Anthony Grahame and the publications team at Sussex Academic Press for their professional assistance in bringing this book to fruition.

A Note on Transliteration

As in all of my work, a modified version of the Library of Congress transliteration system is adopted throughout this book, even if rendering Arabic words and names into English is a nearly impossible task. Still, the style used by the *International Journal of Middle East Studies* has been relied upon and, for practical purposes, all diacritical marks for long vowels and velarized consonants have been eliminated, except for the hamza (') and ayn ('). A name that is commonly rendered one way in English is thus altered under this system; so, for example, Mohammed becomes Muhammad, and Mecca becomes Makkah. Quotations that refer to Mecca or Sheik have not been tampered with, though the late Queen's name was changed if for no other reason than to remain consistent. Thus, 'Iffat Al Thunayan was adopted throughout the text, even if some sources use the Turkish spelling of Effat. Naturally, because the university that bears the Queen's name uses the Turkish spelling as well, references were kept in the original whenever I referred to that Jiddah-based institution of higher learning.

In modern Arabic, even when using standard pronunciation, the feminine -ah is often ignored, with the -h usually silent and unrecorded. Consequently, we see it as -a, as in fatwa, Shia, Sharia, or even Ulama. Strangely, however, the -h is kept in other circumstances, including Riyadh or Jiddah, or even Shaikh when it is not written as Sheikh. Throughout this book an effort has been made to be both uniform and accurate, which is why the -h is recorded in all instances. Therefore, all transliterated words that qualify include the silent h, including when it refers to the *ta' marbutah*, the *alif* (Abhah, Hasah), the *alif maqsurah* (Shurah, fatwah), or even the *hamza* ('Ulamah, Fuqahah). Although special care was devoted to standardizing the spellings of as many transliterated words as possible, there are—inevitably—inconsistencies and anomalies. I trust that readers will understand and forgive any linguistic transgressions.

An effort has also been made to clarify family names. When referring to the proper appellation of ruling families, the Arabic word "Al," which means "family," precedes the name of the eponymous founder. In Sa'udi

Arabia, the founder imparted his name to the family, thus the Al Sa'ud. A lowercase "al-"often refers to a sub-branch of the ruling family. In this instance, Turki al-Faysal is the son of the late King Faysal bin 'Abdul 'Aziz Al Sa'ud. Furthermore, and although the transliteration of 'Abd (servant or slave in Arabic) is rendered as 'Abdul, I am aware that the "ul" (al) is really the article of the succeeding word, as in 'Abdul Allah, and that together they mean "servant of God." In that regard the family of Muhammad 'Abdul Wahhab is not simply Al Shaykh, but Al al-Shaykh, or "House of the Shaykh," as his descendants are called. Yet I use 'Abdallah rather that 'Abdullah throughout this text because it comes as close as possible to Library of Congress and *International Journal of Middle East Studies* protocols.

Finally, while common English spellings for proper names are used whenever they are known, as well as for names of countries, the hamza or ayn are included as applicable. Thus Sa'udi Arabia rather than Al-Mamlakah al-'Arabiyyah al-Sa'udiyyah. Arabic speakers will know the correct references for transliterated words throughout the text and will understand how difficult transliteration can be. I urge patience and understanding, as well as forgiveness, wherever I may have digressed.

List of Illustrations

The color plates (after page 168) include photographs courtesy of The King Faysal Center for Research and Islamic Studies, the Al-Nahdah Philanthropic Society for Women, Dar al-Hanan School, The King Faysal School / Al Faysal University, Effat University, The White House and U.S. State Department, the International Center for Interreligious and Intercultural Dialogue, and the al-Faysal Family photo archive.

0 100 200 300 kilometres
0 100 200 miles
Saudi Arabian borders
Other country borders
SYRIA
ISRAEL
IRAQ
JORDAN
EGYPT
IRAN
KUWAIT
Tabuk
Hafr Al Batin
Gulf of Oman
Hail
Al Jubayl
BAHRAIN
Dammam
Dhahran
Al Khobar
Buraydah
Arabian/Persian Gulf
QATAR
NAJD
Riyadh
Madinah
UNITED ARAB EMIRATES
HIJAZ
SAUDI
ARABIA
EASTERN
PROVINCE
EGYPT
Jiddah
Makkah
Taif
THE EMPTY QUARTER
Red Sea
SUDAN
OMAN
Khamis Mushayt
Abhah
Najran
Jizan
ERITREA
YEMEN
Arabian Sea
ETHIOPIA
Gulf of Aden
Boundary representation is not necessarily authoritative

Introduction

In a recent popular history that offers a broad overview of Muslim women and their great accomplishments, the observer draws sharp links between the roles played by several extraordinary women—from the 7th century to the 19th—including the Prophet Muhammad's wives Khadijah and 'Ayshah.[1] In addition to these two exceptional women, the book provides details on warriors such as Shajarat al-Durr—a Mamluk of Armenian descent who married Salih Ayyub, and who was "the most cunning woman of her age, unmatched in beauty among women and in determination among men"—as well as several rebels and concubines, including Khayzuran, Amat al-'Aziz and Roxolana/Khurrem.[2] A number of musicians and dancers, rulers, queen mothers, and philanthropists, like Jamilah al-Madinah, 'Ulayyah bint al-Mahdi, Sitt al-Mulk, and Nur Jahan receive their dues as well. Even Nanah Asmau, a learned Fulani lady [from Northern Nigeria] who became a successful business entrepreneur, garners rare accolades. Countless poets—among them, Al-Khansah, Maysunah, Hafsah bint al-Hajj, and Laylah Khanum—are recognized for their numerous contributions. Although little was known about many of these renowned ladies, Arab and Muslim societies recognized their deeds, even if traditional norms stood in the way. In all, the achievements of fifty prominent women who played a hand in shaping Muslim history are thus acknowledged.

Renowned Western women ranging from European royalty to commoner officials including prime ministers and ministers, as well as numerous prominent thinkers, researchers and writers, have also received attention throughout history in political and academic circles. Scores of distinguished women added value to their respective societies that, over time, raised the bar quite high. In 2010, *Time* published a list of the 25 most powerful women of the 20th century, which included the likes of Jane Addams (1860–1935), Indira Gandhi (1917–1984), Golda Meir

---

1 Jennifer Heath, *The Scimitar and the Veil: Extraordinary Women of Islam*, Mahwah, New Jersey: Hidden Spring, 2004.

2 *Ibid.*, pp. 218, 251–285.

(1898–1978), Angela Merkel (1954–), Eleanor Roosevelt (1884–1962), and Margaret Thatcher (1925–2013).[3] England's medieval queens, from Eleanor of Aquitaine to Elizabeth of York, mesmerized an entire people over centuries.[4] In the epoch that followed, six towering figures from the Houses of Tudor, Stuart and Hanover—Mary I (r. 1553–1558), Elizabeth I (r. 1558–1603), Mary II (r. 1689–1694), Anne (r. 1702–1714), Victoria (r. 1837–1901) and Elizabeth II (r. 1952–)—have presided over some of the most significant eras in British history.[5]

Like its neighbor across the Channel, France lived through equally momentous periods, in which women played critical roles in the country's affairs. Perhaps the most influential was Anne-Marie Louise d'Orléans, a cousin of King Louis XIV who dramatically changed court politics and is known to posterity as "La Grande Mademoiselle."[6] Of course, other French women, including Pauline Bonaparte [the sister of Napoleon who married Prince Camillo Borghese] and Joan of Arc, the peasant heroine who led France to several important victories against England during the Hundred Years' War and who famously declared at Vacouleurs: "I fear them not . . . I have God with me . . . I was born to do this," marked their times too.[7] Of course, women are also recognized for significant contri-

---

[3] Rachelle Dragani, "The 25 Most Powerful Women of the Past Century," *Time*, 18 November 2010, at http://content.time.com/time/specials/packages/article/0,28804,2029774_2029776_2031847,00.html.

[4] Lisa Hilton, *Queens Consort: England's Medieval Queens*, New York: Pegasus Books, 2010.

[5] Maureen Waller, *Sovereign Ladies: The Six Reigning Queens of England*, New York: St. Martin's Press, 2006.

[6] Anne-Marie Louise d'Orléans was an active participant in the factional struggles that marked French history as she sided with those who wished to depose Louis XIV's Prime Minister, the Cardinal Mazarin. She was arrested and imprisoned for five years after losing her cousin's trust though her knowledge of court politics, of Mazarin as well as the Prime Minister's predecessor, the immensely powerful Cardinal Richelieu, remained unequaled. Her memoirs and rich correspondence reveal a *femme engagée* who stood out in 17th century France. She recounted the dynamics of the Bourbon monarchy and its quest to centralize power at the Palace, as well as the rich debates that occurred which evaluated the role of women in private and public life. She is still discussed in the 21st century, despite being an aristocrat herself, because she challenged the establishment and sought justice for the people. For a solid assessment, see Vincent J. Pitts, *La Grande Mademoiselle at the Court of France: 1627–1693*, Baltimore and London: The Johns Hopkins University Press, 2000.

[7] Flora Fraser, *Pauline Bonaparte: Venus of Empire*, New York: Alfred A. Knopf, 2009. See also the quote from original trial transcripts, "Vaucouleurs and Joinery to Chinon," in *The Trial of Nullification or Rehabilitation* [Le procès de condamnation et le procès de réhabilitation de Jeanne d'Arc], at http://www.jeanne-darc.info/p_trails/trial_03_nullification/04_vaucouleurs.html.

butions made to the history and societies of Europe, Asia and Africa, ranging from Cleopatra to Mother Teresa and from Marie Curie to Indira Gandhi.[8] The names listed above represent dramatic personalities that stood out for their skills, ambitions, and achievements.

Like many Western societies until just a few decades ago, contemporary Sa'udi Arabia is confronted by socio-economic and political

---

[8] Cleopatra, the last Pharaoh of Egypt and lover to both Julius Caesar and Mark Antony, was an immensely intelligent woman despite many flaws in her character. Her determination to sew so much mischief within the highest levels of the then dominant Roman Empire, and the charm she exerted in getting equally powerful leaders to agree to the most extraordinary things, has few parallels. By the time she was a mere 35 years old, she ruled over an empire that stretched from the Atlantic Ocean to the Asian subcontinent, though her actions brought tragedy on both her and her nation.

Mother Teresa, a Macedonian woman whose real name was Agnes Gonxha Bojaxhiu, became a Roman Catholic nun who learned English in Ireland before being sent as a missionary to India, where she taught at the Loreto convent school in Calcutta. In 1948, she began her missionary work with the poor, replacing her traditional Loreto habit with a simple white cotton *sari* decorated with a blue border. She received Indian citizenship and, after a few months in Patna to receive basic medical training, ventured out into the slums. Her organization, the Missionaries of Charity, was established in 1950 with just 13 members but grew into a global institution with nearly 5,000 nuns operating dozens of orphanages, AIDS hospices, and charity centers worldwide. In 1979, her establishment of a hospice for the impoverished won her a Nobel Peace Prize and made her not only a household name, but one that was synonymous with compassion and charity. Pope John Paul II beatified her in 1998, giving her the title "Blessed Teresa of Calcutta."

Born Maria Składowska in Warsaw, Poland on 7 November 1867, Marie Curie tested the old adage that a woman's place was in the home. As a penniless governess and tutor while pursuing her studies to become a physicist, she reached Paris in 1891 where she found work at the laboratory of physicist Gabriel Lippman, while studying at the Sorbonne. It was on the "Left Bank" that she met Pierre Curie, a physics and chemistry instructor, whom she married in 1895. The couple's work earned them two Nobel Prizes, a joint Physics Prize in 1903 (shared with the equally brilliant Henri Becquerel) and, remarkably, a solo Chemistry award in 1911. More important, Marie Currie became the first female head of Laboratory at the Sorbonne University in Paris after Pierre passed away. Her accomplishments served as a source of inspiration to thousands of women scientists and researchers who followed in her footsteps.

Indira Gandhi was one of India's most powerful political figures. Loved as well as despised, Prime Minister Gandhi (who had no family ties to the spiritual and political leader Mahatma Gandhi) ruled intermittently for almost two decades until her 1984 assassination at the hands of Sikh extremists. Although she was accused of being a devious and corrupt politician—critics resented her doctrinaire approach (i.e. Delhi's forced sterilization program to control India's burgeoning population)—Gandhi transformed the country into the modern democracy it became. Her son Rajiv, who became Prime Minister after her assassination, met the same fate as his mother in

problems arising from the partial exclusion of women from public life, problems to which the country's inherent gender segregation inevitably draws attention. In 2014, heated debates over this state of affairs have taken place within Sa'udi society, across the rest of the Muslim World, and even in major Western countries interested in the Kingdom. In fact, Western observers almost always leave the impression that conditions are dire, that changes to the status quo for women are nearly impossible, and that, as a result, the end is near for both the country and its inhabitants.[9] However, their segregated status notwithstanding, it is accurate to say that Sa'udi women made serious inroads into various areas of public life during the past few decades, with many achieving remarkable successes

---

1991 when a Tamil Tiger woman detonated a bomb in a village near Chennai that he was visiting in support of a congressional candidate [at least 14 other people were also killed that day]. Rajiv's wife, the Italian-born Sonia Gandhi (Antonia Edvige Albina Maino), became President of the Indian National Congress Party in 1998, when she was elected leader. In many ways, Sonia Gandhi was the power behind the Prime Ministership until 2014 when her party lost elections to nationalist forces.

See Stacy Schiff, *Cleopatra: A Life*, New York: Little, Brown and Company, 2010; Kathryn Spink, *Mother Teresa: A Complete Authorized Biography*, New York: HarperCollins, 1997; and D.R. Kaarthikeyan and Radhavinod Raju, *Triumph of Truth: Rajiv Gandhi Assassination—The Investigation*, New Delhi: New Dawn Press, 2004.

[9] The most recent writer to address women's issues in the Kingdom was Karen Elliott House in a pessimistic book, *On Saudi Arabia: Its People, Past, Religion, Fault Lines—and Future*, New York: Knopf, 2012, pp. 72–101. The trend started a while ago, most famously under the pen of Jean Sasson, in a niche market that includes dozens of books developed around this theme. For her popular trilogy, see Jean Sasson, *Princess: A True Story of Life Behind the Veil in Saudi Arabia*, New York: William Morrow & Co, 1992; idem, *Princess Sultana's Daughters*, New York: Doubleday, 1994; idem, *Princess Sultana's Circle*, Atlanta, Georgia: Windsor-Brooke Books, LLC, 2002. For other interesting additions to this type of literature, see Qanta A. Ahmed, *In the Land of Invisible Women: A Female Doctor's Journey in the Saudi Kingdom*, Naperville, Illinois: Sourcebooks, Inc., 2008; Sami Alrabaa, *Veiled Atrocities: True Stories of Oppression in Saudi Arabia*, Amherst, New York: Prometheus Books, 2010; Kristin Decker, *The Unveiling: An American Teacher in a Saudi Palace*, College Station, Texas: Virtualbookworm.com Publishing, 2006; Jeanette M. English, *Infidel Behind The Paradoxical Veil: A Western Woman's Experience in Saudi Arabia*, Bloomington, Indiana: AuthorHouse, 2011; Jan Goodwin, *Price of Honor: Muslim Women—Lift the Veil of Silence on the Islamic World*, New York: A Plume Book [Penguin], 1994 and 2003; Patrick Tom Notestine, *Paramedic to the Prince: An American Paramedic's Account of Life Inside the Mysterious World of the Kingdom of Saudi Arabia*, Lexington, Kentucky: BookSurge Publishing, 2009; Homa Pourasgari, *The Dawn of Saudi: In Search for Freedom*, Beverly Hills, California: Lindbrook Press, 2009; and Deckle Edge, *In the Kingdom of Men*, New York: Knopf, 2012. For a more sober assessment, see Marianne Alireza, *At the Drop of a Veil*, Boston: Houghton Mifflin Company, 1971.

against the odds. Many of these gains are due to the work of one remarkable woman, Queen 'Iffat Al Thunayan (1916–2000), who, along with her husband, King Faysal bin 'Abdul 'Aziz Al Sa'ud (1906–1975), established solid socio-political foundations in Sa'udi Arabia that permitted undeniable advances. The late queen's critical advisory role to a prescient ruler added significant value to improve socio-economic conditions even if few ever learned of the major contributions she made. How this unique woman reached a position of influence—even if behind the scenes and in complete discretion—is a story worth elaborating. Indeed, measured against the challenges that she confronted in what was and still is a paternalistic society, her accomplishments gain additional meaning in any analysis of the Kingdom. A pious woman, Queen 'Iffat Al Thunayan displayed a quintessentially Muslim characteristic: her deeply held religious beliefs inspired sincere hopes that she might live a morally correct life that also allowed for intellectual growth. She was, in short, a modernizer par excellence—someone who harvested strength from her faith but who seldom refused an opportunity to dirty her hands to get the job done. Unafraid of change, she never looked back, dreaming only of a better life for her family and her nation.

Political Awareness and Relationship with the King

Prince Faysal bin 'Abdul 'Aziz bin 'Abdul Rahman Al Sa'ud, who became the Kingdom's third ruler in the 20th century, first met his future spouse in 1932, after she arrived in Makkah to perform the pilgrimage with her paternal aunt, Jawharan bint 'Abdallah Al Thunayan. Although 'Iffat was apparently destined to marry the founder of the third Sa'udi monarchy, King 'Abdul 'Aziz bin 'Abdul Rahman Al Sa'ud, Faysal was immediately smitten with her and sealed the betrothal. It was true love at first sight, especially since 'Iffat spoke little or no Arabic and Faysal knew only a few words of Turkish. Remarkably, 'Iffat and Faysal taught each other their respective native languages, while four of the nine children they had together became bilingual as they couldn't help but learn Turkish and Arabic simultaneously at home. The younger ones concentrated on European languages though all have basic understanding of Turkish. Although she eventually became fluent in Arabic, the future queen always retained traces of a Turkish accent, which further distinguished her in the multinational Hijaz region, on the Western part of the Arabian Peninsula, home to Islam's holiest cities to which pilgrims from all over the world have gravitated for centuries. This linguistic particularity was valuable as she imparted her interest in other cultures not only to her children but, over the years, to many Sa'udis, too. Though she was soon labeled the "*Turkiyyah*," the young princess and future queen gradually overcame existing prejudices and thrived.

According to those who knew 'Iffat Al Thunayan, she was extremely well organized. She sowed, with her mother's assistance, the curtains of their new home in Makkah, and insisted on family lunches or dinners, depending on where they happened to be at the time. Her table was a unique platform for discussions of myriad subjects, as she encouraged family members to share insights and offer intelligent commentary. She listened carefully, joined in conversations as appropriate, only spoke with moderation but always with authority, and was fully conscious of her role as the spouse of the Viceroy of the Hijaz. Above all, she was an avid reader, her appetite fed by the many books Faysal brought back for her from his travels, and the foreign magazines to which they subscribed, which were always delivered to the "Palace." Throughout her life, but especially after she became queen, 'Iffat Al Thunayan played the leading role in Sa'udi female society, attended many state functions, including graduations, and received female state guests. She was an invitee at various official functions, and traveled extensively on a private basis, especially in Europe.

To say that Queen 'Iffat shared everything with her husband would be an understatement even if she fully appreciated the tightly constrained parameters of the society in which she moved. Her doors were open to everyone, as she tried to keep abreast of developments and assist her husband by acting as a well-attuned source of information, initially within the Hijaz and then later in the Najd, the Al Sa'ud stronghold located in the central part of the Kingdom. (See the map on page xxxiii.) Faysal valued what his wife heard from visitors, not only because he relied on her for rare insights that helped formulate appropriate state policies, but because he intuitively trusted her judgment. Consequently, and perhaps like many astute wives married to imposing leaders, her influence on Faysal increased as she began to share with him her ambitions and ideas both for the Al Sa'ud and the entire country. Faysal and 'Iffat complemented each other, an exceptional quality in Sa'udi Arabia at the time, and one that distinguished the prince and princess from many of their contemporaries. Thus, even in a patriarchal society like Sa'udi Arabia the future queen played a key role in shaping her ruler's vision of excellence, something that is neither well-known nor appreciated, and that therefore merits close attention.

Role in Education

Because Faysal considered education to be the founding investment in each member of society, he was quite receptive to 'Iffat Al Thunayan's ideas to improve what was a very underdeveloped provision when the country declared its independence in 1932. Toward that end, and given the dearth of citizens sufficiently well qualified to assume nation-building burdens, Riyadh devoted significant resources to primary and secondary schools. Available statistics from the period are dizzying and reveal that the numbers of primary and secondary schools went literally from zero in 1932 to 316 twenty years later, for a total enrollment of 39,920 pupils; by 1973, the number of schools stood at 6,595 for a total of 707,318 enrollees. Naturally, these dramatic increases required faculty, whose numbers went from 1,605 in 1952 to 15,232 in 1973, most of them coming from Egypt, Jordan, Palestine, and Lebanon. Faysal made sure that education was free for girls as well as boys after religious figures were persuaded of its added value to have educated youngsters. Few realized the efforts that went into these accomplishments, or the depth of discussions devoted to enlarging parameters, as well as the critical role that Queen 'Iffat played in ensuring their realization.

Twelve years after her "return" to Makkah, Prince Faysal and Princess 'Iffat inaugurated the Ta'if Model School for Boys in 1944, where the student body included their own children, other Al Sa'ud offspring, and other children from leading families who consented to attend. Between 1943 and 1953, when a similar experiment was conducted at the Ta'if Model School for Girls, mentalities evolved so that education was no longer frowned upon. Still, the very idea of a boarding school, with Egyptian and Yemeni female nurses (along with a sole Sa'udi) attending to the youngest students, did not sit well in the conservative environment that considered family life to be both perfect and inviolable. Indeed, despite the couple's two eldest daughters attending, the Model School turned out to be a premature effort. Undeterred by this first failure, Princess 'Iffat inaugurated *Dar al Hanan* ["The House of Affection," a name that was inspired from a passage in the Holy Qur'an] in Jiddah in 1954, where her youngest daughters went to school, with a total of 15 youngsters that initial year. She further inaugurated the first girls' college in Riyadh in 1967, the *Quliyyat Al Banat* [Girls' College], whose purpose was to train local teachers, and as part of her popular efforts started the *Jam'iyyah al-Nahdah al-Sa'udiyyah* in 1968, a philanthropic society that provided free classes for illiterate Riyadh women, along with instruction on hygiene and childcare, foreign languages, typing, and other useful subjects.

Finally, in 1999, Queen 'Iffat inaugurated a college that bears her name where students could earn a degree from among nine majors, including business administration, psychology, architecture, and engineering, though she did not live to see its first graduates don their instantly recognizable gowns bearing the first letter of her name. Taught in English with a curriculum designed around the American liberal arts model, the College added "electrical" and "computer engineering" majors, which were the first such offerings to women in Sa'udi Arabia. In line with significant advances in the education sector, the college became a full-fledged university in 2009, and was the first privately funded higher education institution in the Kingdom. These initiatives illustrated that no educational goals would be unattainable if the will was there to excel.

One of Queen 'Iffat's daughters, Princess Lulwah al-Faysal, has since reflected on the many challenges her mother faced and the incredible ability she displayed in overcoming them, acknowledging in a 2007 interview to *Saudi Aramco World* that she prevailed largely because "she had to deal with things that were completely foreign to her."[10] 'Iffat's youngest daughter, Princess Hayfah al-Faysal, described her mother in more personal terms: "Everybody called her beautiful, but I think her inner beauty came out more than her outer beauty. She was a dark blonde, with very bright, honey-colored eyes. She had great character and was very strong. She had to be strong to live the life she lived. She was just a giant of a woman, really. She was also wise, beyond anything you can think of. You had to run to keep up with her. She had so much energy. When she was going somewhere, she went somewhere. And when she was doing something, she did it."[11] As intimate family members can only know, Queen 'Iffat bequeathed her daughters many different qualities, including a vitality that was certainly not popular in the Kingdom at the time. "She used to laugh uproariously," Princess Lulwah recalled, asserting that her mother "was vivacious and alive, vibrant and quick in her laughter. When she laughed, she laughed from the heart. If she got angry, she really got angry and showed it, and then it was over. You knew you could not go beyond a certain point. One look was enough."[12]

Beyond her own family conditions, 'Iffat Al Thunayan was interested in an educated class in Sa'udi Arabia, and she worked tirelessly to promote women in all fields. Indeed, and somewhat at a distance from politics, she concentrated on education, health services, and philanthropy as fields where the employment of women could be promoted and encouraged because she quickly appreciated that those were the areas where the need was greatest. Together, 'Iffat and Faysal understood the value of education as a way out of an ossified system, and she set out to promote her ideas by encouraging their own sons and daughters to excel and further change ingrained Sa'udi mentalities.

---

[10] Kay Hardy Campbell and Nicole LeCorgne, "Effat's News Roses," *Saudi Aramco World* 58:1, January/February 2007, pp. 2–7.

[11] *Ibid*. Interview with HRH Princess Hayfah al-Faysal, Jiddah, 25 October 2010.

[12] Interview with HRH Princess Lulwah al-Faysal, Jiddah, 17 October 2010.

A Queen's Legacy

If 'Iffat Al Thunayan was a very determined Sa'udi woman, she was also admired for her leadership as an early advocate of education for women and young girls. For Effat University's Dean, Hayfah Jamal al-Layl, the then princess "was focused." Speaking with reporter Kay Hardy Campbell, Dr. al-Layl underscored that the late Queen "used to come and attend school ceremonies. She was always humble and always came to talk to the students. She'd pat them on the shoulder if they did well and, if not, she encouraged them to do better."[13] Tireless as well as determined, King Faysal's spouse encouraged education for girls in one of the most conservative societies in the Muslim world and, towards that end, devised the establishment of specialized schools. More conservative Sa'udis frowned on the idea of sending their daughters for such instruction, and as discussed below it took the Queen and King a good deal of effort to gently persuade them. The couple sent their own children to school, sometimes in foreign countries, offering a model which others could emulate. Whenever they faced resistance, Faysal would ask whether there was anything in the Holy Qur'an that prohibited women's education, and declared: "We have no cause for argument, God enjoins learning on every Muslim man and woman." Over time, the archetype presented by 'Iffat and Faysal found a steady audience among all Sa'udis. For Princess Lulwah al-Faysal, the late queen's motto would probably be the same today as it was during her lifetime: "Educate yourself. Be good mothers. Bring up perfect Sa'udis. Build your country." In her own particular way, 'Iffat Al Thunayan left her mark on contemporary Sa'udi history by bravely espousing ideas that were nevertheless larger than her own personal capabilities. Her own story is a modern-day legend that saw her swap the shores of the Bosphorus for the gentle Red Sea coast, while she remained admirably alert to her goals. Subjecting her dreams to her own formidable will, she propelled her immediate family and, through that intimate paradigm, her nation to new heights.

Methodological Approach

To better acquaint the reader with this fascinating woman, this book first traces the late Queen's roots, as the descendant of a branch of the Al Sa'ud that was forcefully removed to the Ottoman Empire in the 1800s. Chapter 1 provides a background on the Al Thunayan, especially 'Iffat's grandfather, 'Abdallah bin 'Abdallah bin Thunayan, the youngest son of 'Abdallah bin Thunayan, who ruled Riyadh when Faysal bin Turki (r. 1834–1838 and 1843–1865) was captured by the Egyptian vassals of the Ottoman Empire in 1838. In 1840, 'Abdallah bin Thunayan bin

13 Campbell and LeCorgne, *op. cit.*, pp. 6–7.

Ibrahim became ruler, albeit that his reign was short-lived. Faysal bin Turki escaped from his captors and returned to Riyadh in 1843, and when 'Abdallah bin Thunayan refused to concede his leadership, Faysal overcame him and imprisoned him in al-Masmak [the name of the stronghold he occupied near Riyadh] where he eventually died. Ironically, his wife bore him a son on the same night he died, thus explaining why he bore his father's name. When 'Abdallah bin 'Abdallah bin Thunayan grew older, he sought his fortune in India, where, upon his arrival in Bombay [today Mumbai], he was duly arrested and shipped off to Constantinople [today Istanbul] by the British Raj—who thought he was his father on account of the name—ostensibly because Ottoman authorities wanted him.

In Constantinople, the Sultan married 'Abdallah bin 'Abdallah bin Thunayan to a local lady and later appointed him a member of the *Majlis al-'Ayan* [notables]. This relationship produced five sons and a daughter, including Muhammad Sa'ud, 'Iffat's father, who was inducted into the Ottoman Army as a physician and died in the campaign to drive out British, French, and Greek troops from Turkey in 1921. In addition to 'Iffat, Muhammad Sa'ud fathered a son, Zaki, who was the future queen's only full brother. When the doctor was killed in battle, fighting Kurdish rebels most probably in what today is Northern Iraq, his widow married Ibrahim Adham, with whom she had Mawarah Muzaffar and Kamal, 'Iffat's half-sister and half-brother. 'Iffat herself was born in 1916 and lived the first few years of her life in Constantinople. Her uncle, Ahmad, came to Riyadh in 1917, and looked after the family for several years until the second marriage. Funds were scarce but the extended family ensured that the offspring were looked after properly. Ahmad accompanied Prince Faysal bin 'Abdul 'Aziz on his first European trip, to London and Paris, in 1919, when the two men became better reacquainted. Eventually, in 1932 and barely sixteen, 'Iffat accompanied her aunt to Sa'udi Arabia, and soon afterwards she married Faysal. In an interesting twist, Faysal sent a telegram to 'Abdul 'Aziz informing him that he had married 'Iffat bint 'Abdallah Al Thunayan, and that they were on their way to Riyadh to meet him.

In an effort to better assess the impact that the collapse of the Ottoman Empire must have had on the life of the young woman, Chapter 1 also provides essential background on Constantinople, certainly one of the most important cities throughout Muslim history and 'Iffat Al Thunayan's first home. It also provides details on her family life, including ties with members in her reconstituted family unit, before she embarked on the trip that changed her life. It closes with details of her arrival into the harsh environment that was Makkah of the early 1930s, reputed for its tremendous aridity and by all accounts unbearable in the summer. Fortunately, her growing ties with Prince Faysal made the transition supportable as the princely couple sought refuge in Ta'if, about 110 miles to the northeast. At 1,700 meters Ta'if, the "Garden of the Hijaz" which so pleased the young woman, sat high up on the slopes of the *Al-Sarawat* Mountains. The "house" she moved into was made of mud, straw, and rocks, and required communal living arrangements given the scarcity of housing. It must have horrified the young woman to notice the utter lack of essentials, but even worse was the absence of schools—the occasional tutor notwithstanding—with the little teaching that was imparted being focused on learning the alphabet and memorizing the Holy Qur'an.

Chapter 2 discusses the personality of the late queen, starting with her known biography, before concentrating on her nascent educational vision. Although the status of the Viceroy's spouse was certainly a major asset, the early going was difficult, especially as some members of the elite perceived her ambitious programs as being non-adaptable to local traditions. Many doors opened in front of her though a few were also closed. Conditions on the ground were difficult and 'Iffat learned to adapt. Slowly, she tackled the problems that confronted her, and some of the initiatives discussed illustrate how she worked within the system. Wisely, she consulted often with the Viceroy but not only him, as 'Iffat invested the necessary time and money to create a working support system around her that empowered family members, friends, and even acquaintances. The way she went about developing a network of contacts is a facet of her character that also deserves close scrutiny. As an outsider, the princess learned local traditions and adopted them as her own, even when exposure to far more sophisticated norms in Constantinople would have precluded servile deference. 'Iffat Al Thunayan therefore paid her dues like few have, and for this reason the founder-monarch, King 'Abdul 'Aziz bin 'Abdul Rahman, and most of his sons seldom turned her down. As discussed in this chapter, Princes Sa'ud, Khalid, Fahd, and 'Abdallah—all of whom became rulers—along with Princes Sultan, Nayif, and Salman—all heirs apparent—and even Princes Muhammad, Bandar, Musa'id, Mish'al, 'Abdul Rahman, Mit'ab, Talal,[14] Nawwaf, Turki, 'Abdul Ilah, Ahmad, Mamduh, and Muqrin, among others—all

[14] Although not formally interviewed for this book, HRH Prince Talal bin 'Abdul 'Aziz displayed a deference and admiration towards the late Queen that speaks volumes of the esteem in which she was held by the ruling family. When Prince Talal found out that this biography had been completed, he affirmed: "Christians have the Virgin Mary and I have 'Iffat Al Thunayan. She was truly unique and I have no adequate words to describe what she meant to me." Conversation with HRH Prince Talal bin 'Abdul 'Aziz Al Sa'ud, Riyadh, 19 February 2013.

her brothers-in-law—showed her the utmost admiration and unlimited respect. Importantly, she forged excellent relations with the women of the family, including the wives of both her father-in-law and his sons, as well as her husband’s sons and daughters from other marriages. She prized most of these relationships and was, in turn, truly respected. This chapter also assembles useful details on the queen’s offspring, on other family members, and on friends and acquaintances. By forging exceptional ties within the Al Sa‘ud, ‘Iffat became the pillar of the ruling family, someone who understood its essential role in Sa‘udi society and, equally important, the key character in ensuring its longevity by creating socio-economic and legitimizing links with the nation at large.

Chapter 3 concentrates on education, ‘Iffat Al Thunayan’s cherished agenda for the Kingdom and its youngsters, both boys and girls. It first describes what conditions were like before 1932, when whatever learning that go on was almost always associated with religious institutions, thus inevitably excluding most girls. The conversation then turns to the various State-sponsored initiatives that were introduced under the founder-ruler. Gargantuan efforts were deployed to create effective education institutions where hardly any modern facilities existed. Although few Sa‘udis alive today remember what conditions were like back in the 1940s and 1950s, even fewer know of the critical roles ‘Iffat Al Thunayan played in establishing today’s “education system.” Of course, many take it for granted today that young girls attend school, but that was not always the case, as a detailed discussion of the early efforts at *Dar al-Hanan* demonstrates. Others may have concluded that elementary, primary, and secondary education would form the complete cycle of learning for Sa‘udi girls, but Princess ‘Iffat aimed higher. Her push to create the country’s first women’s college, which carried her name, is discussed in detail to show what can really be achieved if the will is there. The chapter then moves to an examination of the critical role that philanthropy played in the queen’s life by providing an in-depth look at the King Faysal Foundation and its primary focus on education. It closes with an evaluation of the many challenges that education in general, and women’s education in particular, posed in the conservative country. What were the many restraints imposed on educators then as now? How did Sa‘udi educators confront the multiple challenges of illiteracy that weakened the country? Remarkably, Sa‘udi fathers, especially those who tirelessly championed literacy and worked to create opportunities for their daughters, certainly deserved a lot of credit, although most were motivated by ‘Iffat Al Thunayan, who simply led the way in articulating a vision of women as potential achievers.

Chapter 4 deals with health priorities for a growing population, and tackles three interconnected questions: the necessity of creating a benevolent society, the various needs of the disabled, and the institutional infrastructure that must be in place in order to provide health care for one and all. Of course, 'Iffat Al Thunayan did not single-handedly dream of everything, but the many small items on her agenda led to the creation of various Sa'udi philanthropic societies to meet multiple social needs. One area to which she gave specific personal attention was the needs of the disabled, perhaps colored by her own experience, the young Princess 'Iffat having arrived in Makkah with her disabled aunt, Jawharan. Moroeover, as discussed in this chapter, her efforts eliminated the huge taboos that existed around disabled individuals in Arabia, as she gradually persuaded people to reject the established norms that neglected the physically impaired. Special emphasis is also placed on how the queen altered prevailing values by encouraging the creation of specialized institutions for disabled children. The chapter then looks at the country's health institutions, most of which emerged after the mid-1970s, and contrasts them with what passed for health care in the early 1930s. It closes with an assessment of what the disability of the queen's aunt, Jawharan Al Thunayan, meant to her.

In Chapter 5, which concentrates on the sensitive topic of the role of women in Sa'udi Arabia, three sets of issues are tackled. First, the discussion places women within the religious context and provides an assessment of how Islam perceives the gender. Because 'Iffat Al Thunayan was a practicing Muslim who took her religious duties seriously, and since she did not waver from her core beliefs, what took place in this segregated society mattered. The queen pushed her daughters and all Sa'udi girls and women to excel, and though extremist elements have hijacked much of this discussion in recent years, her modernizing influence cannot be overlooked. Her progressive instincts and her refusal to see Islam as a faith that shackled women to subservience were critical aspects of her beliefs and character. In particular, the queen's views on the customary veiling of Sa'udi women and the quest for gender equality are especially worthy of analysis in the light of her own faith and submission to God. The investigation then moves to a detailed assessment of Sa'udi women, focusing on judicial restrictions and the putative changes that have now been introduced, along with an evaluation of the sociocultural limitations that delayed reforms. Finally, an attempt is made to assess the roles that women played in key sectors of the economy as the country prepared for the future. The chapter closes with an evaluation of what was Queen 'Iffat Al Thunayan's vision for Sa'udi women.

The final chapter closes the circle, as the queen dealt with the tragic death of her husband and was relegated to a secondary role in the paternalistic society that is Sa'udi Arabia. Although devastated by her loss, 'Iffat Al Thunayan continued to preserve the Al Sa'ud legacy, as she healed her personal wounds. Faysal's legacy and her own merged rather well in the work that their sons and daughters continued, although she herself concentrated on what she knew best: the improvement of women's education in the Kingdom. Towards the end of her life the queen emphasized family contacts, enjoyed the company of her grandchildren and finally submitting to her Maker.

Because Queen 'Iffat was a towering figure in contemporary Sa'udi history, a woman truly endowed with an innate sense of responsibility towards crown and country, this book goes a small way toward providing an assessment of her many contributions, whilst recognizing that she was unable to resolve all the concerns that confronted women in the country. She was a multicultural person, ambitious, and ready to serve her nation. Astonishingly, she refused to be a mere princess, as she worked to create in the Kingdom a mindset that applied to all, which underscored work ethic and accomplishment. It is worth repeating that, as a devout Muslim who understood and practiced her faith, 'Iffat Al Thunayan rejected extremist interpretations, called for tolerance, and implored her nation to rise above pettiness. All those who knew her testified that she displayed impeccable manners, was generous to family, friends, and acquaintances as well as complete strangers, and displayed the utmost modesty. She was unlike most European queens, many of whom reigned with fury and left their mark on history through violence or power struggles. That was not 'Iffat Al Thunayan, who was neither a cunning power-hungry princess desperately climbing to the highest echelons of power, nor a pretentious *parvenue*. The Al Thunayan were noble and her marriage with the ruling Al Sa'ud family further strengthened her intrinsic credentials. She was no Joan of Arc because, while she certainly believed in God, the Sa'udi Queen never pretended that she was born to become one. Neither was she a Cleopatra nor an Indira Gandhi, for 'Iffat Al Thunayan was inconspicuous, and in no way did she compare herself to Khadijah or 'Ayshah. Rather, she was an Arabian Queen who marked the 20th century—a quintessential Sa'udi woman whose dreams matched inherent aspirations to give meaning to her life.

1

From Constantinople to Makkah

When the future matriarch of the Al Faysal family first set eyes on Sa'udi Arabia, it was shock at first sight, a sensation that she could only express to her ailing aunt, Jawharan, her sole companion on the roughly 2,000 nautical-mile sea voyage from Turkey. The trip took nearly a month, with several stops along the way, and although 'Iffat bint Muhammad Sa'ud Al Thunayan was anxious to return to her roots, few appreciated the incredible sacrifices such a journey entailed. Beyond the natural fear the marital engagement must have generated, the teenager was leaving behind her native Constantinople, the ancient city which had taken on a new name, Istanbul, in 1930, barely a year before the decision was made to return home. By all accounts, that step was neither taken hastily, nor was it made for whimsical reasons. Rather—and in the aftermath of World War I, which led to the collapse of the Ottoman Empire, two events that marked 'Iffat for life—the young lady had been destined to a bourgeois life as a teacher in the largest city in the nascent Republic of Turkey. Her father, Muhammad Sa'ud Al Thunayan had always assumed that the Ottoman Army, in which he served with distinction, would provide his family with a stipend in case of his death, but what followed after 1918 was sheer chaos.[1] Officer Muhammad Sa'ud Al Thunayan was a physician drafted in to serve the Empire. He was a devoted husband to Asia, a Circassian lady he married in 1913 or 1914, and a doting father to Zaki and 'Iffat, born respectively in 1915 and 1916. But the family's future happiness was sundered when he failed to return from the front, presumed dead in battle sometime between 1918 and 1923.

1 An effort was made to identify military records for officer Muhammad Sa'ud Al Thunayan in the Turkish Archives. Regrettably, no records could be located, despite repeated efforts made by HE Hakan Tekin, now attached to the Ministry of Foreign Affairs in Ankara. Mr. Tekin placed a formal request with the appropriate authorities, and though the search was unsuccessful, I am grateful for his kind follow-up.

Inasmuch as economic conditions deteriorated after the war, Asia, her two toddlers, and her handicapped sister-in-law Jawharan were barely surviving by the mid- to the late 1920s. As discussed below, Jawharan mustered the courage to write a detailed letter to the founder of the Third Sa'udi Kingdom, 'Abdul 'Aziz bin 'Abdul Rahman, in which she described her family's situation. Though the ruler learned of the fate of his distant relative from this letter, he also knew what the Al Thunayan had endured after the Ottoman authorities carted several members to Constantinople in the mid-1800s. More importantly, between 1914 and 1921 the monarch had been briefed on conditions in the Ottoman Empire by 'Iffat's uncle, Ahmad Al Thunayan, one of his closest advisors.[2]

An Al Thunayan through and through, which meant that she belonged to the Al Sa'ud dynasty, Jawharan's deftly composed communication brought about the desired outcome, as 'Abdul 'Aziz issued a formal authorization that assumed travel expenses for 'Iffat and her aunt from Istanbul to Makkah (via the port city of Jiddah).[3] In fact, the founder of the contemporary kingdom intended to marry 'Iffat, even if the young lady merely asked to perform her pilgrimage or meet members of the family that might wish to know of their distant relatives. There were no indications that she would be greeted by Faysal bin 'Abdul 'Aziz, by then a promising young leader and the Viceroy of the Hijaz, nor that he would sweep her off her feet. Of course, Faysal knew of 'Iffat, and was probably informed of the family's economic circumstances by Ahmad Al Thunayan, especially since the latter was the young man's traveling companion in 1919 when the future monarch represented his father at post-World War I settlement negotiations at Versailles. In the event, the young prince wasted no time and, after a short courtship that was handicapped by serious language problems—she spoke but a few words of Arabic and he could utter barely a few sentences in Turkish—Faysal formally proposed marriage and 'Iffat accepted. It was the beginning of a lifelong love story that marked the couple, their family, their many acquaintances, the Al Sa'ud, and the Kingdom. Yet few appreciated the hurdles that 'Iffat was called upon to jump, especially as she was labeled the "*Turkiyyah*" [the Turkish woman] by less sophisticated

---

2 Sabri Falih al-Hamdi, *Al-Mustasharun al-'Arab wal-Siyasah al-Kharijiyyah al-Sa'udiyyah Khilal Hikm al-Malik 'Abdul 'Aziz bin Sa'ud (1915–1953)* [The Arab Advisors and the Foreign Policy of Sa'udi Arabia under the Rule of 'Abdul 'Aziz bin Sa'ud (1915–1953)], London: Dar al-Hikma, 2011, pp. 11–22.

3 For genealogies of the Al Sa'ud and most of the cadet branches, see Brian Lees, *A Handbook of the Al Saud Family of Saudi Arabia*, London: Royal Genealogies, 1980. An equally useful scholarly source, with several additions and clarifications, is Alexander Bligh, *From Prince to King: Royal Succession in the House of Saud in the Twentieth Century*, New York: New York University Press, 1984.

members of the small but tightly knit, ultraconservative Hijazi society in which she now lived. Remarkably, she overcame the discrimination, and even bonded better than most with the Al Sa'ud and the very few elite families that then made up the Makkah community. To be sure, Faysal helped her, was her rock—a prince who admired his spouse and appreciated her contributions to the ruling family. Over the years, those who knew the couple and interacted with them detected a conspiracy between husband and wife, a scheme that was meaningful, as Faysal and 'Iffat added value to their nation. Indeed, this was possible because of the couple's competence, 'Iffat's undeniable Al Sa'ud credentials, and her determination to do all that she possibly could to improve living conditions for fellow Sa'udis, no matter what their station in life. Early on, she behaved like the spouse of a viceroy, aware that her unique position granted her the flexibility to introduce meaningful changes as long as she didn't upset traditional norms.

Equally important, and although the Al Thunayan aura belonged to an earlier period, 'Iffat seldom insisted that her side of the family ought to receive its share of attention, even if her presence within the Al Sa'ud rekindled interest in giving everyone their dues. 'Abdul 'Aziz was a strong ruler but he was fair, recognizing over time that cadet branches of the family should also play critical roles in the governance of the country. Gradually and painstakingly, the ruler united Arabia's competing tribal confederations that, as expected, catapulted the Al Sa'ud into a preeminent position. Still, the monarch's style was inclusive, as everyone was welcome to contribute to the nascent Kingdom even if circumstances did not allow for everyone's preferences to be satisfied. 'Iffat was no exception to this rule. Notwithstanding the undeniable fact that her journey started in majestic Constantinople—a city which at the time was the envy of civilized nations throughout the Mediterranean but was so different from Makkah—the young woman was determined to live among her people and do the best she could. Indeed, although she left behind a war-torn city and traveled to Sa'udi Arabia out of necessity, this was only a partial reason for making the trip. She was also curious to reconnect with her roots, aware that the Al Thunayan belonged in Arabia, not in Turkey, even if her own father had served the Ottoman Empire and sacrificed his life for Sultan 'Abdul Hamid.

'Iffat's dramatic story was thus linked to the Al Thunayan and the fate that befell them. But who were they and what was their role in the history of Sa'udi Arabia? How did 'Iffat's extended family reach Constantinople and what were the reasons for their leaving Central Arabia in the first place? What was life like in one of the most urbane cities in the world and how did the young lady see her future before contemplating a return to Makkah? What were conditions like for her mother, Asia, after her husband failed to return from the front? Was Asia’s Circassian ethnicity grounds for discrimination in her Ottoman milieu? How efficient was the family support system that looked after the widow and her children after her officer husband was killed in battle? Was Asia on the brink of destitution and was the financial support allocated by the authorities truly insufficient? Why did the attractive young widow settle on a neighbor, the caring Ibrahim Adham, who was not particularly wealthy? Was it for love or because the police officer of Albanian origins had a secure position and could protect her in an increasingly atomized atmosphere? Was Ibrahim Adham’s meager income sufficient to feed everyone? What were ‘Iffat’s relationships with her half-brother Kamal and half-sister Muzaffar? Why was she burdened with the responsibility to care for her ailing aunt Jawharan? More critically, what was the impact of Jawharan’s physical disability on ‘Iffat’s personality, which surely evolved in ways that few attempted to understand? Was that experience of having to care for a disabled individual a determining factor in driving the future queen to push for heavy investment in the Kingdom’s health care system later on in her life?

Obviously, it is impossible to know what the late Queen thought at the time, but a few of these concerns may well have crossed ‘Iffat’s mind when the small boat docked in Jiddah and she first set foot on Sa‘udi soil. For the young teenager who spoke little or no Arabic, the arrival was surely meaningful, and though she left behind modest conditions, what mattered at the time was the pilgrimage to the Holy City of Makkah. In testimonies to her grandchildren, she repeated that her sincere desire to perform pilgrimage—a sacred duty required of every Muslim—had been the sole objective of this trip, which seems to illustrate that there was little else on her mind at that stage. The fact that ‘Iffat started her Sa‘udi journey in Makkah was a genuine blessing for it defined her ties with the country. Her “passage” from her native Constantinople to the Hijaz allowed the young woman to reconnect with her roots in ways that even she could not have foreseen. Indeed, what transpired after those first few days changed her life and those of many more, as the lady shone and helped to change the Kingdom. She became Queen in a country where the ruling family did not sit on a formal throne and where the “crown” was a topic of conversation not a tangible artifact. That accolade, to be known as a queen, would provide further testimony as to the strength of her character, even if the wives of Sa‘udi monarchs were all called princesses. A cosmopolitan with the temperament of a true Al Thunayan, a loyal Al Sa‘ud, and a visionary Sa‘udi, all these traits were woven together with her genuine religious beliefs.

THE AL THUNAYAN

In the turbulent history of the Kingdom of Sa'udi Arabia, which witnessed violent clashes among various tribal confederations that lived throughout the vast expanses of the Arabian Peninsula between the 17th and 20th centuries, one of the most influential branches of the ruling Al Sa'ud family were the Al Thunayan, direct descendants of Thunayan, a full brother of Muhammad bin Sa'ud (1691–1787). The latter, who founded the dynasty in the 18th century and forged the 1744 alliance between the Al Sa'ud and the Al al-Shaykh, relied on Thunayan in his many military as well as political battles. Such a pedigree meant that the Al Thunayan were, in fact, part of the Al Sa'ud family. Yet, the reason why they evolved into a cadet branch of the ruling dynasty was due, in part, to an Ottoman refusal to acknowledge their rightful tribal station. At a time when the Ottoman Empire dominated both shores of the Peninsula, the British Empire appeared over the horizon, effectively boxing in the Al Sa'ud in Central Arabia. In the absence of additional landholdings, the instinct to survive aggravated dynastic rivalries, as the Al Sa'ud once again fell prey to internecine conflict.[4] In 1831, Turki bin 'Abdallah survived a challenge from his cousin Mish'ari bin 'Abdul Rahman but was finally assassinated by Mish'ari's agents in 1834 in

[4] There are a variety of books on Sa'udi Arabia worth consulting, and what follows, alphabetically by author, is but a sample: Harold C. Armstrong, *Lord of Arabia: Ibn Saud, An Intimate Study of a King*, London: Arthur Barker Ltd., 1934; Benoist-Méchin, *Fayçal, Roi d'Arabie: L'Homme, Le Souverain, Sa Place dans le Monde 1906–1975*, Paris: Albin Michel, 1975; idem., *Le Loup et le Leopard: Ibn-Seoud ou la naissance d'un royaume*, Paris: Albin Michel, 1955; John S. Habib, *Ibn Sa'ud's Warriors of Islam: The Ikhwan of Najd and Their Role in the Creation of the Sa'udi Kingdom, 1910–1930*, Leiden, the Netherlands: E.J. Brill, 1978; David Holden and Richard Johns, *The House of Saud: The Rise and Rule of the Most Powerful Dynasty in the Arab World*, New York: Holt, Rinehart and Winston, 1981; David Howarth, *The Desert King: The Life of Ibn Saud*, London: Quartet Books, 1965, 1980; Joseph A. Kéchichian, *Succession in Saudi Arabia*, New York: Palgrave, 2001; idem, *Faysal: Saudi Arabia's King for All Seasons*, Gainesville: University Press of Florida, 2008; idem, *Power and Succession in Arab Monarchies: A Reference Guide*, Boulder and London: Lynne Rienner, 2008 [Chapter 7]; Muhammad Jalal Kishk, *Al-Sa'udiyyun Wal-Hal Al-Islami* [The Saudis and the Islamic Solution], Jeddah: The Saudi Publishing and Distribution House, 1982; Joseph Kostiner, *The Making of Saudi Arabia, 1916–1936: From Chieftancy to Monarchical State*, New York and Oxford: Oxford University Press, 1993; Robert Lacey, *Inside the Kingdom: Kings, Clerics, Modernists, Terrorists, and the Struggle for Saudi Arabia*, New York: Viking, 2009; idem, *The Kingdom: Arabia and the House of Saud*, London: Hutchinson, 1981; H. St. John B. Philby, *Sa'udi Arabia*, London: Ernest Benn Ltd, 1955; Madawi Al Rasheed, *A History of Saudi Arabia*, 2nd edition, Cambridge: Cambridge University

what was the foremost political murder to have been recorded since the 1744 alliance that established the first Sa'udi state. As fate would have it, Mish'ari's tenure on the throne was very short, since he too was soon killed by Turki's son, Faysal, who captured Riyadh that same year, 1834, and proclaimed himself ruler.[5]

In turn, Faysal's rule was cut short in 1838 by the return of agitated Egyptian forces, concerned with the rising influence of the British in and around the Peninsula. The Egyptians expelled and replaced Faysal bin Turki with a puppet ruler, Khalid bin Sa'ud, who, at least theoretically, restored the original dominant branch of the family to power. Nevertheless, in 1840 the British pressured their Egyptian suzerain, Muhammad 'Ali, to withdraw his forces and soon afterwards, Khalid was overthrown by a distant cousin, 'Abdallah bin Thunayan bin Ibrahim. For the first time in contemporary Sa'udi affairs, a member of the Al Thunayan branch of the family had assumed power, even if his tenure would be typically short.

'Abdallah Al Thunayan

'Abdallah Al Thunayan ruled Najd from 1841 to 1843 though few welcomed his decision to impose fresh taxes that, naturally, displeased his original supporters. He was deposed in 1843 by Faysal bin Turki, who successfully escaped Egyptian captivity and returned to power after laying siege to Riyadh. A popular ruler, Faysal bin Turki assumed authority for the second time as he ushered in by far the most stable period in the history of the Peninsula up to that point. Regrettably, Central Arabia was further isolated and fell into oblivion as Ottoman forces occupied Hasah in 1871. In the decade that followed this key engagement, several Al Sa'ud family members competed with each other to earn Ottoman approval. In 1878, an internal uprising prevailed, but failed to mature given the existence of multiple allegiances and thus divided loyalties.[6] What transpired was common practice in the harsh conditions that defined the hinterland of Arabia where allegiances were ephemeral and loyalty was subject to internecine confrontations.

Press, 2010; idem, *Politics in an Arabian Oasis: The Rashidi Tribal Dynasty*, London and New York: I.B. Tauris & Co. Limited, 1991; Alexei Vassiliev, *The History of Saudi Arabia*, London: Saqi Books, 1998; and Robert Vitalis, *America's Kingdom: Mythmaking on the Saudi Oil Frontier*, Stanford, California: Stanford University Press, 2007.

[5] Fuad Hamzah, *Al-Bilad al-'Arabiyyah al-Sa'udiyyah* [The Kingdom of Saudi Arabia], 2nd edition, Cairo: Maktabat al-Nasr al-Hadithat, 1968.

[6] Much of the information on the Al Thunayan was gathered from several conversations with a leading member of the family. Interviews with HH Mansour Al Thunayan, Jiddah, 22 October 2010, 19 March 2011, and 14 March 2012.

A year after this uprising, however, a new claimant to power emerged in ʻAbdallah bin ʻAbdallah Al Thunayan. ʻAbdallah the son [confusingly both son and father shared similar first names], who had resided in Basrah (Iraq) since 1876, went to Constantinople with the object of obtaining for himself a grant of Najd [comprising central Arabia] and Hasah [virtually all of Eastern Arabia] from the Porte, or perhaps to recover his share of the property of the Al Saʻud in Hasah, which the Ottoman authorities had confiscated earlier. On his way to Constantinople, ʻAbdallah bin ʻAbdallah stopped in Bushire, Jiddah, Cairo, and Damascus, approaching various British officials to seek support for his plan, ostensibly arguing that his scheme would benefit British and Ottoman interests jointly. The British Government refused these advances and, after his arrival in Constantinople in August 1880, nothing further was heard of him or of his proceedings although he did become known as *ʻAbdallah Basha* [Pasha] at *Dolmabahçe*, the Sultan's official residence.

ʻAbdallah Basha's Offspring

In effect, successive Ottoman rulers kept ʻAbdallah Al Thunayan as a well-looked-after hostage, jealous of the rising influence of the British in Arabia and anxious to use their prey should the opportunity arise.[7] That was not to be, as dramatic events saw the Al Saʻud reclaim what was rightfully theirs, and as an ailing Ottoman Empire quickly collapsed in the aftermath of World War I both for internal and external reasons.[8] It was in the Ottoman capital, however, that ʻAbdallah Basha married Taza Ruh, a Circassian woman who bore him four children: Muhammad Saʻud, Ahmad, Jawharan [Ahmad's twin], and Sulayman. A second marriage produced two more sons, ʻAbdul Rahman and ʻAbdul Qadir. In turn, Muhammad Saʻud, the eldest, married another Circassian by the name of Asia and was inducted into the Ottoman Army. He was killed between 1918 and 1923 though no information was available in which battle or on what date. Muhammad Saʻud and Asia had two children before he went to war, ʻIffat Munirah and Zaki, though Asia remarried when he failed to return from the front, presumed dead along with count-

[7] Though individual details are difficult to verify, conditions for Arab princes within the vast Sultani realms in and around Constantinople allowed many to enjoy relatively comfortable lives. Still, their situations deteriorated as the Ottoman Empire weakened, and a full-fledged Arab revolt altered the reality of those who rejected Ottoman suzerainty. See George Antonius, *The Arab Awakening: The Story of the Arab National Movement*, New York: G.P. Putnam's Sons, 1946, pp. 61–100.

[8] For anecdotal evidence on the chaos that enveloped the fall of the empire, see David Fromkin, *A Peace to End All Peace: The Fall of the Ottoman Empire and the Creation of the Modern Middle East*, New York: Holt Paperbacks, 2009.

less Ottoman soldiers in what became known as the Turkish War of Independence.[9] Asia's new husband, Ibrahim Adham, was an Ottoman police officer of Albanian origin with whom she had two other children: Kamal and Muzaffar.

Meanwhile, from around 1906 the Ottoman presence in Arabia became dangerous and the Porte evacuated its troops from Qasim. Simultaneously, 'Abdul 'Aziz bin Abdul Rahman prepared his return to Dir'iyyah and Riyadh, in the process mobilizing many members of the dispersed family. Ahmad bin 'Abdallah Al Thunayan (1889–1921) heard of 'Abdul 'Aziz's exploit and escaped his golden Ottoman cage at a time when the Porte was experiencing serious financial cutbacks and was no longer in a position to retain a large presence around the Sultan, 'Abdul Hamid. The circumstances of his departure are not clear, although the chaos that enveloped the Ottoman throne was relatively significant, meaning that many who could bail out did so with relative ease. In the event, and as the future Sa'udi monarch intended to restore the cadet branches of the family to their rightful stations, especially those that were lured to Constantinople, his decision to welcome its leading members clarified the way he intended to correct past Ottoman maneuvers. 'Abdul 'Aziz reasoned that although the Porte might have weakened the Al Sa'ud ruling family in the past, the time was now ripe for Arabs to set in motion the necessary changes that would restore matters to their natural order, and allow Sa'udis to return home. Ahmad Al Thunayan, who had a Turkish wife, arrived in Riyadh and offered his services to the liberator at the head of the Al Sa'ud dynasty, took part in various military campaigns, was wounded—thus the later limp, which he said came from an injury he'd received —and quickly became indispensable to his cousin for several other reasons. In addition to Arabic and Turkish, the Amir Ahmad spoke fluent French and German, a feat unprecedented among the Al Sa'ud at the time. To be sure, these linguistic skills further endeared Ahmad to his cousin, though 'Abdul 'Aziz was delighted to welcome his

[9] The Turkish War of Independence is known as the *Istiklâl Harbi* or the more literal *Kurtulus Savası,* meaning "Liberation War," and was waged by nationalist forces led by Mustafa Kemal Pasha, later Mustafa Kemal Atatürk, against Allied occupation. At least 13,000 Turkish officers and soldiers were killed, with an additional 23,000 dying of various diseases, while 35,000 were wounded and between 7,000 and 22,000 were taken as prisoners of war. For details, see Resat Kasaba, *The Cambridge History of Turkey*, Volume 4, Cambridge: Cambridge University Press, 2008, p. 159; Ergün Aybars, *Türkiye Cumhuriyeti Tarihi I* [History of the Republic of Turkey, Volume 1] (in Turkish), Bornova-Izmir, Turkey: Ege Üniversitesi Basımevi, 1984, pp. 341–348; and Ahmet Özdemir, "Savas Esirlerinin Milli Mücadeledeki Yeri" [Prisoners of War in the National Struggle], Ankara University, *Türk Inkılap Tarihi Enstitüsü Atatürk Yolu Dergisi* 2:6, 1990, pp. 325–333.

relative for yet another reason, namely to buttress his legitimacy against tribes competing for leadership of Arab dynasties throughout the Arabian Peninsula. For all practical purposes, Ahmad Al Thunayan became 'Abdul 'Aziz's *na'ib* [deputy], a position with considerable power.

Valuable Services between 1914 and 1921

'Abdul 'Aziz faced unmistakable internal foes but it was Britain that delayed his conquests, and Ahmad Al Thunayan understood why. When the Najdi ruler set out to conquer the Lower Gulf Shaykhdoms, London protested and, in the case of the Buraymi Oasis on the Oman–Abu-Dhabi–Sa'udi Arabia border, it warned 'Abdul 'Aziz before opposing him. Doubtless the British veto disappointed him, even if the decision taught the ruler an invaluable lesson in the ways that major powers behaved: he would henceforth cooperate with others but only rely on himself.[10] As Ahmad and other senior members of the family witnessed how British and Ottoman leaders conducted themselves with the undisputed Najdi ruler, it was not unreasonable to infer that he sharpened his tactical initiatives, too. When Britain sided with the Hashimites in World War I, for example, 'Abdul 'Aziz turned his attention inward, and Ahmad honed his next moves. The two men waited for the conflict to end to observe the repercussions of the secret 1916 Sykes–Picot agreement—whereby Britain and France carved up the Middle East to serve their particular interests—as they rose to the surface. In the event, British machinations against the Hashimites drew severe criticisms, particularly during the post-World War I Versailles conference then meeting near Paris, when London extended a separate invitation to 'Abdul 'Aziz to discuss the best mechanisms to defuse tensions. The Najdi accepted the invitation but opted to delegate his thirteen-year-old son Faysal to represent him. Ahmad Al Thunayan, who was by then the founder's principal advisor, chief clerk, and foreign affairs executive, seconded Faysal.[11]

'Abdul 'Aziz relied on Ahmad to test the waters. Preoccupied with events in the Hijaz, where the Sharif Hussayn was well entrenched, he assigned Ahmad with a semi-secret mission to see whether London would change its policies. According to Robert Lacey, Ahmad "was fiercely

---

[10] This was a lesson that his children learned as well, though Faysal was the one who truly applied it, trusting no one and nothing—except God. See Kéchichian, Faysal, *op. cit.*, pp. 3–4.

[11] Leslie McLoughlin, *Ibn Saud: Founder of a Kingdom*, Basingstoke and London: Macmillan Press, 1993, pp. 62–63, 115. For the classic perspective on how the British maneuvered their allies in the area, see T. E. Lawrence, *Seven Pillars of Wisdom: A Triumph*, New York: Anchor Books, 1991 [Originally published by Doubleday in 1926].

boastful of the new Saudi-Wahhabi empire that Abdul Aziz was creating, and he alarmed Humphrey Bowman [an English official accompanying Prince Faysal's delegation] during the voyage down the Persian Gulf [on their way to Bombay, their first stop on the long trip to Europe] by hinting darkly at a 'much vaster kingdom' which, [Ahmad Al Thunayan insisted], the Al Saud would be building in the future." This was no idle chitchat but a clear illustration of what Ahmad perceived to be a rightful Al Sa'ud goal.[12]

Because 'Abdul 'Aziz knew the itinerary and the list of passengers on the vessel that sailed to Europe, the ruler charged Ahmad Al Thunayan to uphold his son's dignity, if for no other reason than to underline those features that clarified relations between the Shaykhdoms of Kuwait and Najd. As these ties had deteriorated ever since the Sa'udi conquest of Hasah, the Al Sa'ud leader was anxious to challenge the preeminence of Kuwait in northeastern Arabia. On board the RIMS *Lawrence* paddling down the Arabian/Persian Gulf, feelings were exacerbated by religious differences: the Najdis stuck strictly to their prayer times, but the Kuwaitis were less conscientious—and they smoked the occasional cigarette.[13] Reserved but also attentive, this was the first time the young Faysal had interacted with Kuwaitis, though his cousin made sure that the young man did not fail to observe the necessary protocol. On the vessels that sailed them to India and England, Ahmad Al Thunayan continually pestered Bowman with "complaints that his young charge Faysal was not being accorded equal dignity with the other Arab guest traveling to England in the same party, Ahmad bin Jabir, grandson of the late Mubarak and shortly himself to become Shaykh of Kuwait."[14] This was vintage Ahmad Al Thunayan, probably around thirty years old at the time and entrusted with the mission of his life. In contrast to 'Abdul 'Aziz—unfamiliar with Western ways of thinking but whose skill in desert politics nonetheless made him a formidable negotiator—Ahmad knew how to leave an impression with Westerners. 'Abdul 'Aziz's skills enabled him to strike a fine balance between loyalties and affiliations, yet he also knew his limitations. That was why Ahmad Al Thunayan was so indispensable. Still, it would be a mistake to assume that he had single-handedly devised all the critical negotiating steps between British and Ottoman officials, as 'Abdul 'Aziz had also given his young relative specific instructions. Well briefed and confident that he spoke for his sovereign, Ahmad Al Thunayan distinguished himself with contributions

---

[12] Lacey, The Kingdom, *op. cit.*, pp. 154–157.

[13] The RIMS *Lawrence* was part of the Royal Indian Mail Steamer service, thus the RIMS title.

[14] Lacey, The Kingdom, *op. cit.*, p. 154.

that proved to be immensely valuable. More often than not the founder relied on his cousin, with his precious Constantinople education, to test the waters or to carry out highly confidential missions.

With Faysal in Europe

The young Faysal was a good student of international politics, though it is also true that 'Abdul 'Aziz instructed his son to be careful. In fact, the wily future ruler was already fully mistrustful of the British, who had betrayed and disappointed the Al Sa'ud by preventing a full conquest of Arabia. British officers on the dedicated transport warship quickly noted Faysal's demeanor—a young man who stood his ground—especially when contrasted with the Kuwaiti delegation also making the trip. Throughout, they also noted how Ahmad looked after his protégé with tender loving care in what was a rare opportunity to tutor a future monarch, in the process helping to shape his resolute character. After a brief stop in Bombay, Faysal and his small retinue set sail for Plymouth, England, where they arrived on 14 October 1919. Harry St. John Philby, later an advisor to 'Abdul 'Aziz, welcomed the delegation when it arrived in London, although the reception at Paddington Station was somewhat wanting and drew a sharp rebuke from Ahmad Al Thunayan. If Faysal was displeased with the reception or the mix-up in their accommodations—these were only addressed after Philby intervened with the Lords Cromer and Nathaniel Curzon—he never shared them with anyone. The crafty Curzon quickly repaired the diplomatic faux pas, designating the group as the "Central Arabian Delegation" and Prince Faysal as his "Royal Highness." On the sidelines of multilateral negotiations, Faysal encountered classic but tactful British arm-twisting, as key officials pressured him to end Al Sa'ud–Hashimite feuds which were then reaching their peak. Despite the honorific bestowed on the young prince, the visit to the Foreign Office was a disaster, as Lord Curzon allegedly treated his guests "like children and so patronizingly that they left England enraged," swearing never to return. More important, London was eager to secure a new agreement that would clearly delineate the Hijaz–Najd border and, not surprisingly, called for a reassessment of British financial subsidies to the Al Sa'ud for their various services.[15]

The visit, of course, had a hidden political feature, entrusted by 'Abdul 'Aziz to Ahmad Al Thunayan, who was instructed simply to ask the Foreign Office for safeguarding of Najdi independence and non-interference in its internal affairs. Moreover, Prince Ahmad demanded that the Najd's boundaries include Khurmah and Turabah, strategic locations

[15] Joseph A. Kéchichian, *Faysal: Saudi Arabia's King for All Seasons*, Gainesville: University Press of Florida, 2008, pp. 33–37.

that opened the road to Makkah, and invited a British Commission to delimit them.[16] Finally, the ruler called on London to remove the embargo on pilgrims that the British had applied during the war, since 'Abdul 'Aziz recognized how valuable pilgrimage-generated income could be to his meager financial resources. According to British documents, Ahmad also requested the grant of a subsidy in perpetuity and for the appointment of H. St. John Philby as Political Agent in Najd. Of course, the British were taken aback by these requests, as well as Amir Ahmad's expert presentation. Were they to apply them, several of London's standing policies would be compromised, including existing commitments to the Hashimite Sharif Hussayn. Lord Curzon, the Foreign Secretary, informed Amir Ahmad that London—that is, Curzon himself—would be in a better position to handle Arabia once Britain had defeated the Ottoman Empire, and proposed to meet 'Abdul 'Aziz in person. Inasmuch as this was a major victory for the Amir Ahmad, who secured legitimacy for his master, the trip was judged a huge success.[17]

What Ahmad actually managed to achieve, through careful negotiations and occasional complaints that the delegation was not receiving due respect, was an impeccable demonstration of diplomatic skill. British officials took note and King George V welcomed Faysal at Buckingham Palace on 30 October 1919 to make up for the lapses, before the young Sa'udi visited the House of Commons and other prominent British institutions. In what turned out to be a comical moment, Faysal gave King George an ornamental sword inlaid with pearls, while the British sovereign presented two signed photographs—one of himself and one of his wife. Inasmuch as photography was then a novelty, the British sovereign's calculated gifts, which he knew would be prominently displayed in 'Abdul 'Aziz's office, were intended to remind the Najdi of how the head of an empire looked. In the event, and beyond its symbolism, both Faysal and Ahmad Al Thunayan saw the difference between two photographs and an ornamental sword inlaid with pearls. Few recalled ever seeing the photographs displayed in any of 'Abdul 'Aziz's *majlises*, much less positioned in a prominent place that might conceivably suggest obeisance to a foreign potentate—one, moreover, that was neither Arab nor Muslim. Simply stated, it was not an Arabian custom to display photographs and thus the snaps were for all practical purposes lost.

The "Central Arabian Delegation" ended its visit with no accords on Al Sa'ud–Hashimite differences as neither Faysal nor Ahmad bin

[16] Clive Leatherdale, *Britain and Saudi Arabia, 1925–1939: The Imperial Oasis*, London: Frank Cass, 1983, pp. 22–24, 42–43.
[17] Vassiliev, *op. cit.*, pp. 239–250.

Thunayan were empowered to concede, though their points had been well made.

As soon as the delegation returned in February 1920, 'Abdul 'Aziz received a full briefing from Amir Ahmad, who, despite expressing broad satisfaction with what had been achieved, painstakingly explained to his ruler that Britain continued to support the Hashimites. The monarch called in Harold Dickson, then the Political Agent in Bahrain, and told him that London was backing "a broken pillar." "As sure as I hold this [camel] stick," he emphasized, "so surely do I know the Shareef's days are numbered." In his memoirs, Norman Bray, an Indian Army officer on "special duty" in Arabia at the time, reported that the Amir Ahmad may have given assurances at the Versailles Conference on behalf of 'Abdul 'Aziz, "that no matter what the provocation there shall be no war for three years."[18] Ahmad Al Thunayan understood that, since London was enmeshed with the Hashimites, no assaults would be forthcoming, and concluded, mistakenly as it turned out, that the "Muslim World was not ready to accept the Wahhabis in charge of the Holy Places." Yet according to Khan Sahib Sayyid Siddiq Hasan, the Indian Assistant to the British Political Agent in Bahrain in 1920, Ahmad Al Thunayan, who is referred to in this revealing document as 'Abdul 'Aziz's *na'ib* (deputy), was "distinctly better or more sober in his talk or opinions about the Sharif [of Makkah]." "He is," underscored the British minion, and "if I am not mistaken[,] fairly promising and reasonable and will, it is hoped, make matters smooth" for the English.[19] This turned out to be a false reading of what the Amir Ahmad thought, or what 'Abdul 'Aziz envisaged, or indeed how both of them intended to proceed—but such were the common misreadings in which foreign diplomats excelled.

Death and Legacy

Notwithstanding his invaluable contribution to Sa'udi Arabia, Ahmad Al Thunayan returned to Constantinople for health reasons, perhaps because the *badu* (Bedouin) lifestyle was too difficult for him to endure. During his short tenure as the founder's *na'ib*, he insisted that 'Abdul 'Aziz negotiate from a position of self-assurance if not necessarily of force, and influenced his younger cousin Faysal far more than many

---

[18] Norman N. E. Bray, *Shifting Sands*, London: Unicorn Press, 1934, p. 297; see also Priya Satia, *Spies in Arabia: The Great War and the Cultural Foundations of Britain's Covert Empire in the Middle East*, New York: Oxford University Press, 2008, pp. 28–56.

[19] See "Letter from Siddiq Hasan to Major H.R.P. Dickson, Political Agent in Bahrain, 6 August 1920," R/15/1/557, in A. de L. Rush, *Ruling Families of Arabia, Saudi Arabia: The Royal Family of Al-Sa'ud, Volume 1*, London: Archive Editions, 1991, pp. 299–300.

assumed. In the course of their months-long travels in 1919 and 1920, Ahmad Al Thunayan presumably briefed Faysal on the conditions of the surviving family in Constantinople, which is how the young Prince knew of Ahmad's niece—and not his daughter as it is often surmised—'Iffat bint Muhammad Sa'ud Al Thunayan. That was an equally valuable aspect of his legacy when one considers the 'Iffat–Faysal story. Amir Ahmad died of illness in 1921 while Jawharan, his twin sister, became incapacitated about the same time for lack of medical attention. 'Iffat looked after Jawharan until such time as 'Abdallah Basha's only daughter and her niece, along with several other members of the Al Thunayan family, returned home to Sa'udi Arabia. True to his Al Thunayan heritage, Ahmad defined unfamiliar political parameters for his ruler, and illuminated the future monarch's vision. More than any other of his contemporaries, Prince Ahmad defended the founder's legitimacy with world powers, and inspired as well as reinforced his ruler's vision, as 'Abdul 'Aziz restored Al Sa'ud rights across the entire Arabian Peninsula. A fitting recognition of the family's legacy was the dedication in the mid-1980s of a major Riyadh street named Al Thunayan, off Al Madinah Al Munawarrah Boulevard.

CONSTANTINOPLE

In the chaotic environment that was Constantinople when Ahmad Al Thunayan returned to the last capital of the Ottoman Empire, little was recorded of the conditions that befell his family shortly before his death in 1921. Family members recalled Queen 'Iffat speaking in later years of reunions as well as the insights she shared with them of life in general in Arabia and in particular in Najd. It would have been uncharacteristic of the great diplomat not to impart news received from other members of the family, especially since the Amir Ahmad was Prince Faysal's escort to Europe, knew the young man better than most, and probably anticipated what a match he might make for his "Turkish" niece. This is, of course, mere speculation, for no records confirm what might have occurred. Irrespective of such conjecture, what cannot be disputed is Ahmad Al Thunayan's larger-than-life presence in the Al Sa'ud community in Constantinople, a city he loved and where he was at ease. So was 'Iffat Al Thunayan as she attended school, earned a teacher's certificate, and prepared for a life working to support the family. Even if the Al Thunayan were looked after rather well, as were most Arab royals who had been forcefully and unceremoniously carted off to Constantinople from Jiddah, Cairo, and several North African cities, dramatic changes within the Ottoman Empire had forced the Porte to sharply reduce the privileges they received. 'Iffat, aware of the changes visible all around her, might well have begun to imagine what an alternative future might look like. As the Empire collapsed and the powers of the Sultan steadily dwindled, the fact that she and members of her family were obliged to move to modest dwellings in the city must have awakened her to what was afoot. Moreover, her lively personality responded quickly to developments that affected life in the city, a sensitivity that never deserted her. Sensing the fragility of the world she had grown up in, she focused on her own education, securing a teacher's certificate, cognizant that the city she loved so dearly afforded her that last opportunity. But if its influence on the curious and intelligent young woman was deep and long-lasting, what was Constantinople like around the turn of the century and how did it mark not only its native citizens but many of the outsiders who lived there?

The Ottoman Capital between 1876 and 1915

Constantinople dominated the Ottoman Empire and was the seat of a long line of powerful sultans. Aside from several large cities spread over a vast territory, it would not be ungenerous to describe the remaining centers of population as rural settlements, with surprisingly little development considering the immense land holdings over which successive rulers presided. Located in the northwestern corner of contemporary Turkey, Constantinople was a heavily urbanized city, mimicking European capitals while retaining its oriental charms. For nearly five decades, internal and international tensions heaped significant pressures on the Porte, as the empire experienced simultaneous declines in economic and military power.[20] Confronted by the Prussian, Austro-Hungarian, Russian, French, and British Empires, among others, Sultan 'Abdul Hamid II (r. 1876–1909) introduced expedient political measures to buttress his increasingly weak rule.[21] In 1876, the Sultan promulgated the relatively liberal Ottoman Constitution, which was intended to pioneer democratizing institutions that would guarantee political freedoms. Within two years, this ideal solution had been left in abeyance as the cunning Sultan suspended his own opus. Consequently, none of the promised reforms that might have swayed public opinion—and presumably would have strengthened the Sultan's rule over the many nations

---

[20] Philip Mansel, *Constantinople: City of the World's Desire, 1453–1924*, London: John Murray, 2006. See also John Freely, *Istanbul: The Imperial City*, New York: Penguin Books, 1998.

[21] Carter Vaugh Findley, "The Tanzimat," in Kasaba, The Cambridge History of Turkey 4, *op. cit.*, pp. 11–37.

that comprised the empire—were implemented.[22] A series of wars followed, including the 1877–1879 Russo-Turkish confrontation that ended with the harsh Treaty of San Stefano, inviting Russia to supervise Ottoman reforms. Although Constantinople managed to wiggle out of this straitjacket by coordinating and accepting a new pact under the 1878 Treaty of Berlin—which stripped Russia of its exclusive mandate and replaced it with a collective European responsibility—Ottoman authorities were not inclined to introduce civil and administrative changes under those circumstances. Simply stated, the Sultan regarded modernization with a dubious eye, and liberalization with even more suspicion, even if both renewal and broadmindedness crept into the body politic and, more importantly, the capital city's socio-economic activity. For all practical purposes, Ottoman officials concluded that alleged European interferences favored the empire's minority populations—Armenians, Arabs, Assyrians, and Greeks, among others—even if political reforms were meant to improve conditions for the majority. Inasmuch as radicalized movements emerged when oft-promised transformations were ignored, Constantinople threatened to boil over with secret activities, with a number of "societies" organizing against the state. Of course, these movements quickly spread elsewhere, but meaningful opposition first blossomed in Constantinople as well as in Macedonia and Thrace, traditionally both significant centers of fresh ideas that challenged the Porte.[23]

Greeks and Armenians were in the vanguard of such activist movements, but so were Circassians and other Muslim minorities whose assimilation posed problems of its own. Between 1894 and 1896, between 100,000 and 200,000 Armenians were massacred, galvanizing global public opinion against the ruler.[24] A number of Greek subjects were expelled from the empire and Circassians were forbidden to speak their own language.

Arabs were not spared as a groundswell of opposition forces mobilized against Ottoman authorities throughout the Muslim World. In fact, Arab nationals in the Levant were handled with equally devastat-

[22] Benjamin C. Fortna, "The Reign of Abdülhamid II," in Kasaba, The Cambridge History of Turkey 4, *op. cit.*, pp. 38–61.

[23] Similar secret societies emerged in Ottoman-occupied Arab cities like Beirut and Damascus. See Antonius, *op. cit.*, pp. 79–100.

[24] For two solid background books see Lord Kinross, *The Ottoman Centuries: The Rise and Fall of the Turkish Empire*, New York: Morrow Quill Paperbacks, 1977. See also Sean McMeekin, *The Berlin–Baghdad Express: The Ottoman Empire and Germany's Bid for World Power*, Cambridge, Massachusetts: The Belknap Press of Harvard University Press, 2010.

ing severity, the beginning of what would later be seen as a nadir of discrimination in Palestine, Syria and Mount Lebanon. From Egypt to the Hijaz and from Jerusalem to Lebanon, Arab thinkers honed their nationalist arguments, rejecting Ottoman control over their lives. Men like 'Abdul Rahman Kawakibi and Najib 'Azuri, among others, galvanized an entire generation to relearn their own language, Arabic, rekindle their faiths, and reinvent their societies.[25] Kawakibi, a Syrian writer from Aleppo, achieved genuine fame as his books were widely read and discussed.[26] Courageously, he identified the decrepitude of the Muslim world under Ottoman rule, and called for an end to the theological obscurantism into which Islam had descended, which served the Porte, while insisting that Arabs assume their traditional responsibility for interpreting and propagating the religion. Importantly, Sultan 'Abdul Hamid surrounded himself with Muslim luminaries like Jamaluddin Al Afghani, to preach pan-Islamism. Of course, Kawakibi saw through the ploy, for he understood—perhaps better than most—that the Sultan was only relying on Al Afghani and other pan-Islamist theologians to advance Ottoman interests. Likewise, 'Azuri wished to free Syria and Iraq from Ottoman tutelage, and this also did not please the Sultan. A Christian, 'Azuri was an Arab nationalist first, someone who foresaw the decline and ultimate demise of the Ottoman Empire.[27] Remarkably, while many Ottoman subjects distanced themselves from the Sultan's brutal rule, most thrived in Constantinople, a rare cosmopolitan environment where so many gathered and intermingled. Intellectuals, working as writers and journalists, artists and musicians, poets and teachers from all over the Arab world, flocked to Constantinople to participate in the latest conferences, watch plays, or publish books that rivaled the outputs of leading European capitals. As a result, there was an enlightenment of sorts that further polarized Ottoman society. Sadly, and because of the Sultan's obscurantism, whatever aspirations existed were soon transformed into disappointments, especially after the 1908 Young Turk revolution ushered in one of the most confused groups of politicians to appear even in the lamentable annals of the 20th century.[28]

---

[25] Michael Provence, *The Great Syrian Revolt and the Rise of Arab Nationalism*, Austin, Texas: The University of Texas Press, 2005.

[26] Caesar E. Farah, "Nationalist Concerns for Syria: The Case of Farah Antun, Mayy Ziadah and al-Kawakibi," in Adel Beshara, *The Origins of Syrian Nationhood: Histories, Pioneers and Identity*, London: Routledge, 2011, pp. 210–222.

[27] Antonius, *op. cit.*, pp. 95–99.

[28] Şükrü Hanioğlu, *Preparations for a Revolution: Young Turks, 1902–1908*, New York: Oxford University Press, 2001, and idem, *The Young Turks in Opposition,*

Sultan 'Abdul Hamid abdicated his throne in 1909, but, ironically, it was the Committee of Union and Progress (CUP) that replaced him which spelled the end of the empire. Whether a consequence of the Italian victory in the 1911–1912 war over Libya, which saw the Young Turk government lose Tripolitania, Fezzan, and Cyrenaica along with the Dodecanese Islands in the Aegean Sea, or whether as a direct result of the tremendous losses in the 1912–1913 Balkan Wars, Constantinople experienced a series of cataclysmic events that scarred it for decades to come. In January 1913, another palace coup guaranteed mobilization as opponents of the Sultan prepared for a major undertaking, which would drag the empire into World War I. As in the past, opportunities emerged for several Balkan countries to pounce on the Ottoman Empire, not only to expand but also to cleanse their societies of "undesirable" ethnic communities. The Balkan States were prodded into action by foreign powers, most notably by Russia, which concluded, along with its European allies, that their long-term interests required a near total collapse of the Ottomans. Towards that end, Russian goading prompted Serbia and Bulgaria to conclude several agreements in March 1912, to coordinate whatever actions were launched by both governments against the Porte. Likewise, Bulgaria and Greece signed an important agreement in May 1912 whose terms would prove critical in any military confrontation with Ottoman forces, since Athens was called upon to mobilize its navy in the Aegean Sea to prevent the arrival of putative reinforcements.[29] No one pretended that war was not imminent, but the ethnic cleansing of Ottoman subjects in the Balkans, in which thousands of villages were destroyed and hundreds of thousands were massacred, left an unmistakable mark on Constantinople. Nearly a million refugees reached the capital city, but few were welcomed.

After 1909—that is, after euphoric anti-'Abdul Hamid demonstrations had ended—intra-Ottoman clashes could no longer be squarely blamed on the devious Sultan.[30] On the contrary, the evidence that emerged suggested the CUP's parliamentary democracy was a sham and that only ethnic Turks would be empowered to make key decisions that affected the lives of millions throughout the empire. Of course, this is not

New York: Oxford University Press, 1995. See also Ernest Edmondson Ramsaur Jr., *The Young Turks: Prelude to the Revolution of 1908*, New York: Russell & Russell, 1957.

[29] Richard C. Hall, *The Balkan Wars 1912–1913: Prelude to the First World War*, London and New York: Routledge, 2000, pp. 1–21.

[30] For a sample of views prevalent at the time, see Christopher J. Walker, *Armenia: The Survival of a Nation*, Revised Second Edition, New York: St. Martin's Press, 1980, pp. 181–182.

to say that noticeable improvements were not recorded in the post-1908 period, but that one needed to be careful not to exaggerate the impetus toward democratization. Negative news from the Balkans—Slavs never missed an opportunity to humiliate their ailing rulers—seeped through the Constantinople elites, giving rise to understandable revulsion. Indeed, after 1910 a CUP view of various minority nationalities—but especially perceptions of Armenians due to the latter's critical governance roles throughout the Ottoman administration—also changed dramatically. Increasingly, pan-Turkism was promoted within CUP ranks, with a Tatar member—thus, someone from outside the empire—joining the central committee.[31] To say that fanatics were gaining influence would, indeed, be an understatement. What motivated central committee members to bring in extremists like Nazim Pasha or Dr. Behaeddin Shakir could only be explained in terms of the renewed zeal that often erupts when people believe the whole world is against them. Not only were CUP leaders motivated by skewed racial beliefs—and, one can categorically declare, anti-Islamic ones too—but individuals like Enver, Tala'at and Jamal [Djemal] Pashas were victims of the kind of modernization that went over their heads and thus stoked their resentment.[32]

Against a chaotic backdrop of foreign interferences in the internal affairs of the Porte, the Ottoman Parliament passed its "Law of Associations," which targeted every ethnic community—save for Turks—denying them the right to organize politically, operate social clubs, or even practice religious services unless these were carefully vetted.[33] By the time of the second general election in 1912, a noticeable break had occurred between the CUP and the smaller ethnic parties, meaning that the constitutional monarchy, now under the apparent leadership of the overrated Sultan Mehmet V, was not anxious to make any concessions.

In this context, it may also be useful to note that Constantinople not only feared the consequences of the Balkan wars but thoroughly resented interferences by the Great Powers. Sensing dangers looming over the

---

31 *Ibid.*, p. 191.

32 Ayhan Kaya in collaboration with Ayse Tecmen, "IME Identities and Modernities in Europe, SSH-CT-2009-215949: Work Package 4, 'The state of the art: various paths to modernity' Turkish Case Report," Istanbul Bilgi University, December 2009, at http://eu.bilgi.edu.tr/docs/WP4_Turkey.pdf, especially pages 3–15.

33 Sanderson Beck, "Ottoman Fall and Turkey 1908–1950," *Ethics of Civilization, Volume 16: MIDEAST & AFRICA 1700–1950*, at http://www.san.beck.org/16-2-OttomanFall%26Turkey.html#a3. See also Handan Nezir Akmese, *The Birth of Modern Turkey: The Ottoman Military and the March to WWI*, London: I.B. Tauris, 2005, pp. 93–96.

horizon, the government pushed an ill-advised bill through parliament that conscripted *dhimmis*—non-Muslim subjects of the empire—into the army, as it planned to fend off fresh aggressors. A few weeks after the "Law of Associations," the government rushed through parliament an equally obtuse bill, inadvertently named the "Law for the Prevention of Brigandage and Sedition," which was meant to prevent domestic uprisings.[34] Regrettably, challenged CUP leaders assigned the duty to prevent insurgencies to freshly created paramilitary formations that fell under the control of the *Teskilat-i Mahsusa* [Special Organization] whose primary writ was to suppress Arab separatism and Western imperialism. Few bothered with parliamentary affairs or rights and responsibilities and it was this CUP machination, more than any other motive, that wrestled the Porte away from the Grand Vizier, Mehmet Kamil Pasha, and his minister of war, Nazim Pasha. Both men became CUP targets, as the 23 January 1913 military coup d'état ended whatever constitutional government had existed until that time.[35]

It was at this time that the ambassadors from the six major powers, led by Russia, discussed—or, more likely, insisted on—political reforms for the Ottoman Empire in the heart of the capital city. The Triple Entente of Britain, France, and Russia attempted to push through a series of reforms—ostensibly to protect minorities but in reality to promote their narrower interests—while Germany and the Austro-Hungarian representatives slowed the process down.[36] Russia, in particular, played a notoriously underestimated role in these interferences in domestic affairs. As the power that helped crush the 1905–1906 and 1909 constitutional revolutions, and as the country—along with Britain—that opposed the 1911 reform proposals, Russia wanted subservience above all else. In the event, its strategists failed to factor in the critical rise of Turkish nationalism.

Ironically, CUP leaders naturally opposed to foreign intervention in the country's internal affairs actually endorsed in April 1913 a British offer of assistance in the administration of the Eastern Provinces, a move that further irritated Russia. Whether the assassinations that followed in June that year—especially those of Nazim Pasha and Mahmut Sevket Pasha—pushed CUP leaders to further hone their distrust of minority subjects was a secondary consideration. What mattered was the sense of

---

[34] Akmese, *ibid.*, p. 96.

[35] Hanioğlu, The Young Turks in Opposition, *op. cit.*, pp. 33–40. See also Taner Akçam, *The Young Turks' Crime Against Humanity: The Armenian Genocide and Ethnic Cleansing in the Ottoman Empire*, Princeton, New Jersey: Princeton University Press, 2012, especially pp. 125–140.

[36] Akmese, *op. cit.*, p. 155.

powerlessness requiring tough responses—the main reason why parliament quickly passed new legislation that made the CUP the empire's only legal political party. Centralization followed as the CUP concentrated power in its own hands. The authority of provincial and local officials was drastically curtailed, with Constantinople anxiously counting on existing tensions throughout the provinces to accelerate its long-term goal, to restore what its leaders saw as sullied Turkish honor.

The Ottoman Capital Between 1915 and 1923

Given the above, 'Iffat Al Thunayan was born at a time of great turmoil in the empire. She grew up in a capital that witnessed its share of horrors, both before and after 1915, and was present during the empire's final days. In November 1918, the victory of the Allied Powers resulted in an occupation of Constantinople, and though many returned to reclaim lost properties and lofty positions in the interim government that emerged, the wounds that split the city ran deep. By the end of the war the total population of the Ottoman Empire—estimated to hover around 35 million in the mid-1800s, of whom less than 10 million were Turks—had dwindled to approximately 15 million. Of that number, the population of Arabs stood at over 6 million, while around 1.5 million Kurds and an equal number of Greeks also called the empire home. Moreover, until 1915 between 1.5 million and 2 million Armenians also lived in the empire, though the vast majority perished in the genocide, directed by the Ottoman government, which wiped out most of that nation.

Many survivors who made it to the Syrian Desert at spots such as Dayr al-Zur or Qamishli, as well as the cities of Aleppo and Homs, were saved from death by humane Muslims. Ironically, while Syrians welcomed these escapees, an estimated two million Turkish refugees from Bulgaria, Romania, and Serbia who resettled in Anatolia between 1878 and 1913 lived among the large minority populations destined for annihilation. Anatolia's landscape changed, and while immigration from Russia and the Balkans increased during the war, and an estimated half million Ottoman soldiers died on battlefields, Constantinople retained its heterogeneity both in practiced religions and spoken languages, the factors which had always made the city such an eclectic place.

The Ottoman defeat left the victors free to write post-war histories that tended to diminish the dying empire's final accomplishments, but in fact the Porte made a significant contribution to the Central Powers' war efforts.[37] At various fronts in Europe and the Middle East, but especially at Gallipoli and in Syria and Palestine, the idea that Entente

[37] Edward J. Erickson, *Ordered to Die: A History of the Ottoman Army in the First*

troops could fight on several fronts was severely challenged. It would be fair to conclude that the Ottoman Army dominated Transcaucasia in 1918, though the Young Turks seldom recognized any need to curb their misguided actions, which also led to enormous mistakes that resulted in the Armenian Genocide and, in the case of Arabs, to military confrontations during the Arab Revolt. Between 1915 and 1918 Constantinople abolished various laws, ended autonomous status for Lebanon, executed a number of Arab nationalists in Beirut and Damascus (especially between August 1915 and May 1916), and massacred or deported entire communities in Eastern Anatolia, ostensibly to eliminate domestic support for the Russian foe. At the height of the war, and starting in 1916, the Ottoman Army experienced massive desertions, even if details were never acknowledged in full—or, for that matter, seen for the disasters they were—simply because that was the way most soldiers behaved until modern warfare instilled an *esprit de corps* that frowned on desertion.[38]

Still, the war to end all wars was horrific for survivors, too, as economic pressures became acute, with shortages in every conceivable area. Once-prosperous urban dwellers ran out of basic necessities as hoarding became widespread in the capital city. Luxury goods, including soap and other hygiene supplies, vanished from most markets. By the end of the war, Bulgaria had fallen, severing direct links with Germany, the Ottoman Empire’s sole remaining ally. The CUP cabinet resigned on 7 October 1918 and two days later a new government was formed under Ahmed Izzet Pasha; on 30 October Ottoman officials were forced into signing the Mudros Armistice.

The Entente’s proposals, which carved up Ottoman territories according to specific wartime agreements, further emasculated the capital city. Between March and April 1915 a series of agreements prom-

---

World War, Westport, Connecticut: Greenwood Press, 2000, especially pp. 119–158. See also Peter Hart, *Gallipoli*, New York: Oxford University Press, 2011, pp. 180–274.

[38] By December 1917 some 300,000 soldiers had deserted, and the chief of the German military mission in the Ottoman Empire, cavalry general Otto Liman van Sanders, sounded the alarm. In a report on “the present condition of the Turkish army” he had the following to say: “The Turkish army now has far more than 300,000 deserters. These are not people who go over to the enemy but in the main deserters to the hinterland in their own country, where they pillage, plunder and generally make the land unsafe. Everywhere troops have to be raised to pursue these deserters.” Quoted in Erik-Jan Zürcher (Leiden) “Refusing by Other Means: Desertion in the Late Ottoman Empire,” at http://edoc.bibliothek.unihalle.de/servlets/MCRFileNodeServlet/HALCoRe_derivate_00003228/refusing_other_means.pdf.

ised Constantinople as well as the Dardanelles Straits to Moscow, while Paris secured *de facto* and *de jure* control over Syria and Cilicia. Then on 3 January 1916, London and Paris entered into the then secret Sykes–Picot Agreement, after Britain had successfully declared a protectorate over Egypt and annexed the strategic island of Cyprus. Conveniently, the two leading Western powers allocated themselves choice real estate in the Middle East, while Russia was compensated with the Ottoman provinces of Trabzon, Erzurum, Van, and Bitlis in eastern Asia Minor. Italy was promised the Dodecanese as well as a large area of southwestern Anatolia, including Izmir and other territories. Caught up in the strategic complexities of fighting a war on several fronts, Britain made various promises of independence to Arab leaders and voiced its approval for the establishment of a national home for the Jewish people in Palestine in the Balfour Declaration of 2 November 1917, thus alarming Ottoman officials who nevertheless could do nothing to prevent this systematic dismemberment of their empire.

Whether by design or sheer exhaustion, internal upheavals in Russia essentially meant that Moscow would quickly withdraw the remaining forces it had stationed on Ottoman territories. Starting in 1917, Russia renegotiated existing agreements, though nothing concrete was finalized until 1920. On 10 August 1920, the victorious Allies imposed on the remnants of the Ottoman leadership the Treaty of Sèvres, which stripped it of all Arab provinces while conceding Constantinople and a part of Thrace. According to the terms of this critical accord, two independent national homelands were also envisaged: a landlocked Republic of Kurdistan as well as a Republic of Armenia with access to the sea. Sèvres granted Greece the islands of Gokce and Bozca, and even envisaged Izmir becoming part of Hellas. The Dardanelles Straits were presumably internationalized, strict European control of Ottoman finances was established, and a tripartite agreement between Britain, France, and Italy defined extensive spheres of influence for the latter two powers. Given these strict measures, Constantinople refused to ratify the treaty, which was only accepted by Greece. Although Allied powers acted as if surprised, a determined struggle for independence was waged by the Ottoman wartime general Mustafa Kemal Pasha—later to be known as Atatürk [Father of the Turks]—whose actions on the battlefield alarmed the Western Powers. The Treaty of Lausanne conveniently abrogated the Treaty of Sèvres on 24 July 1923, as Atatürk consolidated his power, sealed the overthrow of the last Ottoman Sultan, and moved the capital city of a nascent Republic of Turkey to Ankara that same year.

Constantinople was occupied between 13 November 1918 and 23 September 1923, by British and French troops who finally departed the city after Atatürk's independence victory. It was a grand moment in contemporary Turkish and even Muslim history for it highlighted the defeat of Allied forces unaccustomed to such losses. Atatürk's forces entered the city on 6 October 1923, and imposed a strict purge that cleansed various neighborhoods of pro-Allied elements. For it must be acknowledged that the nearly five-year-long presence of so many British and French personnel left a noticeable impact, enhancing the pre-existing image of a thriving cosmopolis. The reputation was well deserved: at the time, while less than a million inhabitants called Constantinople home, only half, or even less, were Muslim, while the remainder included Greeks, Armenians, and Jews.[39]

Sultan Mehmet VI, who acceded to the throne on 4 July 1918 and abdicated on 1 November 1922 (though he fled the city on 17 November 1922), never accepted the nationalist movement led by Mustafa Kemal Pasha. He seldom envisaged a military campaign for removing the occupying powers and may also have failed to realize that the end of his empire was a reflection of his own captivity. For all practical purposes, Mehmet VI represented "Turks" even if Constantinople was less Turkish under his rule than under any of his predecessors. In a rare moment of honesty, the Sultan asserted that Mustafa Kemal was a Macedonian revolutionary of unverified origin, which did not qualify him as a Turk. This was tangential at best since Kemal was an Ottoman officer, one who managed to focus on nationalism and who fought for the soul of what was left of the empire. Ironically, the Sultan feared Bolshevism, preferring to accept Western diktats, though this was a technical consideration because the country was occupied and thus he had no choice but to accept commands at the time. In the event, the ideological concerns behind the Sultan's logic did not prevent Enver Pasha from trekking to Moscow and eventually to Kyrgyzstan, from where he intended to regain power against the Allies precisely by relying on the same Bolsheviks, ostensibly through the Union of Islamic Revolutionary Societies. But Mustafa Kemal and his army rejected Bolshevik machinations and Enver Pasha was killed fighting the Red Army. Kemal fought both the Sultan and the allies, abolished the Caliphate, and struck Constantinople from the empire's political map.[40]

Life in Constantinople returned to its carefree pace as city dwellers regrouped, rebuilt destroyed businesses, and rekindled broken ties.

---

39 Sina Aksin, *Turkey: From Empire to Revolutionary Republic—The Emergence of the Turkish Nation from 1789 to Present*, New York: New York University Press, 2007, pp. 113–197.

40 Walter Duranty, "Enver Pasha Slain by Soviet Force; Turks' War Leader is Left Dead on the Field after Desperate Fight in Bokhara. Last of the Triumvirate. His

Foreign occupiers were replaced with republican elements, but the mere fact that Constantinople ceded the honor of being a capital city to Ankara meant that its leisurely way of life returned. Aware of fundamental changes all around them, foreigners accustomed to relatively privileged lifestyles either left the city or accepted much lower standards of living, as most residents were forced to fend for themselves. The imperial palace at *Dolmabahçe*, which stood majestically on the Bosphorous as testimony to its renowned Armenian builder Krikor Balyan, no longer welcomed the Sultan's foreign guests.[41] The sovereign was long gone as were his court members and the assorted acolytes who benefited from his largesse. Even those who were forced to serve the Ottoman Empire, like the Al Thunayan, saw their fortunes disappear. Meager retainers evaporated and, in the case of 'Iffat's parents, the death of a soldier-father on the battlefield did not even ensure a modest pension for the widow and her offspring. 'Iffat Al Thunayan was seven years old when these epochal changes occurred, raised by a mother forced to work, and increasingly destitute. In fact, devastating conditions all around her soon took on severe proportions, as Asia Al Thunayan became amply aware that in order to survive in this new environment, she and her two children needed a more stable home. But who was Asia Al Thunayan and how did she mark her children?

The Circassian Matriarch

Asia was a Circassian, or Cherkess, whose correct ethnic appellation is the Adyghe (or Adygs) people, Sunni Muslims originally hailing from the North Caucasus in what today would be a region spreading along the eastern shore of the Black Sea, north to south across the current border of Russia and Georgia, including the Abkhazia enclave.[42] Most of the Adyghe people were forcefully displaced through the course of the 19th century by Russia, whose leaders concluded that Muslim inhabitants

Colleagues Talaat and Djemal Assassinated by Armenians after Fleeing from Constantinople," *The New York Times*, 18 August 1922, at http://query.nytimes.com/gst/abstract.html?res=F50C17F63B5D14738DDDA10994D0405B828EF1D3.

41 Philip Mansel, *Sultans in Splendour*, London: Parkway Publishing, 1988, p. 15.

42 A common exonym for the Adyghe is Circassian—a term of Italian origin that came from the medieval Genoese merchants and travelers who first gave currency to the name—while the exonym *Cherkess* is applied to the Adyghe by the Turkish peoples of Central Asia. The name Cherkess is usually explained to mean "Warrior Cutter" due to the speed with which they were able to cut down Russian and Turkish forces. The name is also supposed to refer to the predatory habits among Adyghe tribes even if Russians gave the collective name of Cherkess to all the mountaineers of Circassia in the North Caucasus. Although several Mamluk Sultans were of

could not co-exist with victorious Slavs, a common observation at the time.[43] A series of bloody confrontations between 1763 and 1864 resulted in the systematic expulsion of over half a million Circassians from their native lands, many of them seeking and receiving shelter within the Ottoman Empire, others moving further east into today's Kazakhstan and Uzbekistan. While a small administrative division [*oblast*] survived successive Russian pogroms, the Karachay-Cherkessia Autonomous Region included no more than a quarter of a million native speakers of Adyghe, though twice as many speakers profess the language in the 21st century in various localities throughout Central Asia. Circassians receiving sanctuary in the Ottoman Empire spoke the language for a while, although most reverted to Turkish after Atatürk insisted on a full Turkification of all citizens beginning in 1923. Interestingly, many Circassians not only settled in Constantinople throughout the 19th century, but opted for Anatolia where Kurdish and Armenian communities, far more tolerant of outsiders, openly welcomed them into the heart of the Ottoman Empire. Others spread to Palestine, Syria, and Iraq. In time, and after the British created Trans-Jordan, a significant number, formally known in Jordan today as the Cherkess, settled near and around Amman where many members performed important functions as military officers and businessmen.

Asia Al Thunayan's grandparents and parents most probably reached Constantinople around the turn of the 19th century, though little is actually known about them. Like most fellow Adyghes, they assimilated with relative ease, probably because of family connections as well as religious affiliations. Yet, like many Circassians, they would not openly have professed their ethnic credentials for fear of attracting attention or offending bourgeois sensibilities. To say that Ottoman society discriminated would indeed be an understatement, and just as Kurds quickly lost their separate identities—miraculously becoming *Dagh Türkler* [Mountain Turks]—Circassians were labeled *Dıs Türkler* [Outside Turks]. Of course, such labels proved to be ineffective, since Kurds held

---

Adyghe origin, many of them ruling until the Ottoman conquest of Egypt, the Adyghes gave way to Muhammad 'Ali Pasha, who wiped out almost all senior Mamluk officials with a few survivors fleeing towards the Sudan. Mamluk descendants in Egypt formed a distinguished elite though their numbers were too small to stand out. In Russia, the Adyghe people converted to Christianity around the 5th century, though under Tatar influence most accepted Islam. Of course, there are also Cherkess Christians, even if their numbers are relatively small.

43 This section draws on Paul B. Henze, "Circassian Resistance to Russia," in Marie Bennigsen Broxup, ed., *The North Caucasus Barrier: Russian Advance Towards the Muslim World*, London: Hurst & Co., 1992, pp. 62–111.

on to their distinctiveness with rare ferocity, and while circumstances required that most Kurds, Adyghes, and other minorities should learn Turkish, most also retained their separate languages and ethnic characteristics. Miraculously, Cherkess societies in Turkey, Syria, Jordan, Sa'udi Arabia (in the Hijaz region), and other countries—all of which formed part of the Ottoman Empire at one point or another—survived and thrived.[44]

Like most Adyghes in the Ottoman Empire, Asia's male relatives joined the army and participated in the Turkish War of Independence, all loyal subjects of the Sultan. In fact, because Ottoman Sultans always recognized the Al Thunayan as part and parcel of the Al Sa'ud, treated them with deference, and even allocated specific retainers for several years, it may be safe to conclude that all of Asia's male relatives—Sa'udis as well as Circassians—were loyal subjects of successive Sultans.[45] Under the circumstances, the mere fact that Asia and her children were destitute by the end of World War I highlighted both the dire conditions for everyone in the rapidly crumbling empire as well as a lack of precautionary steps taken to look after those who might need assistance. Still, though understandably dejected because she had become a widow at a relatively young age, Asia somehow managed to survive the loss of her first husband, accepting her fate with a remarkable courage that was passed on quite naturally to her offspring. Was the source of this strength her Circassian background? Was it the unwavering support of her mother, Taza Ruh, who imparted age-old stoicism to her daughter? Was her force the result of her relationship, limited as it was, with her husband 'Abdallah, from whom she drew succor and whose memories she carried proudly? Given that she and 'Abdallah had spent so little time together, what was the impact of that relationship on the offspring beyond being an impeccable role model?

By all accounts, like most individuals in her situation in a rapidly decaying society, Asia turned to family for encouragement as well as sustained backing. Seeing the plight of the young Al Thunayan bride,

[44] For useful background details on the Cherkess, see Amjad Jaimoukha, *The Circassians: A Handbook*, New York and London: Palgrave Macmillan, 2001. See also Svante Cornell, *Small Nations and Great Powers: A Study of Ethnopolitical Conflict in the Caucasus*, London: Routledge, 2000; as well as a magisterial study that discusses struggles past and present in Oliver Bullough, *Let Our Fame Be Great: Journeys Among the Defiant People of the Caucasus*, New York: Basic Books, 2010.

[45] Naturally, allocating largesse was part and parcel of Ottoman custom, and lasted until well into World War I. See Şevket Pamuk, *A Monetary History of the Ottoman Empire*, Cambridge: Cambridge University Press, 2000; and Donald Quataert, *The Ottoman Empire, 1700–1922*, 2nd ed., Cambridge: Cambridge University Press, 2005, pp. 93–99.

other family members extended real assistance, but though she hunkered down, life was far from easy by the time the Ottoman Empire was collapsing in 1923. Her brother-in-law, Ahmad, was gone for several years and though he returned from Riyadh after he had served 'Abdul 'Aziz bin 'Abdul Rahman, he died soon after his return. It might well have been an entirely different scenario that unfolded had Ahmad lived, but that was not to be. Luckily, a suitable neighbor, Ibrahim Adham, extended a helping hand.

Life with Ibrahim Adham

Ibrahim Adham was the attentive Albanian-born police officer who lived next door to Muhammad Sa'ud and Asia Al Thunayan, watching over the family with the utmost care. Like other neighbors, he would periodically ask Asia about news she might have received from her husband after the latter went to war, and insisted on helping with basic chores around the house. In the tightly knit Constantinople neighborhood, such were the norms practiced for centuries, which saw people living next door help in any way they could. Several years passed during which it became increasingly apparent that Muhammad Sa'ud would not return. Impoverished and barely able to meet her young children's basic requirements, Asia looked favorably on her neighbor's kindness and considered his marriage proposal. A short courtship followed during which Ibrahim Adham used to visit nearly every day, though always in Jawharan's presence, according to the testimonies of several family members. Concerned that her reputation would be tarnished were she to drag out the courtship further, Asia agreed with her sister-in-law and accepted Adham's formal proposal. A low-key marriage followed, probably sometime in 1927, when Zaki was 12 and 'Iffat 11 years old. Both Zaki and 'Iffat stayed in their paternal homes with their aunt Jawharan, while their mother moved next door with her new husband, although living in adjacent dwellings effectively meant that the family was for all practical purposes living together. In 1929, Asia gave birth to Kamal Adham and, within two years, to a baby girl named Muzaffar. 'Iffat doted on her siblings though she rarely spoke of her mother's decision to remarry, which she certainly understood was necessary. As things turned out, 'Iffat's relationships with her brothers and sister were close, especially with Kamal who adored his older sister.[46] As discussed in the next chapter, much has been written on the role that 'Iffat Al Thunayan played in Kamal Adham's life in Sa'udi Arabia, though what has been published could be called speculation, even if few would deny that

---

[46] Interview with Shaykh Faysal Kamal Adham, Jiddah, Sa'udi Arabia, 9 December 2011.

brother and sister were incredibly close to each other. What was even stronger was Kamal Adham's ties with Prince Faysal who, and this must be openly acknowledged, the future monarch treated more like a son than a brother-in-law. Still, when 'Iffat traveled to Makkah in Sha'ban 1349, which was roughly around mid-January 1932 [as Ramadan fell in February that year], she was only accompanied by her aunt Jawharan, though she would see to it that all of her surviving relatives would join her within a few years.

THE ROAD TO MAKKAH

When 'Iffat arrived in Makkah, it was not a city in the proper sense of the term and, more importantly, it hardly resembled Constantinople. For the cosmopolitan young woman, the Hijaz and its capital were disappointments, not because she looked down at the lack of services but because she was truly shocked to see for herself the poor living conditions its residents were forced to endure. Makkah, which is barely 45 miles (72 kilometers) inland from the port city of Jiddah, was then not more than a small hamlet with narrow alleys around the main mosque, the site of the Holy Qa'abah [Ka'abah]. No more than a few thousand inhabitants called it home, in contrast to its contemporary version which has more than two million permanent residents, with an additional three million at the height of the annual Hajj (pilgrimage). Still, Makkah was the Prophet Muhammad's birthplace and a site of the revelation of the Holy Qur'an, transforming it into Islam's holiest city. Equally important, and from a purely political perspective, Makkah was the spiritual capital of the Al Sa'ud ruling family, hailing from Najd, who liberated the Holy City from the Hashimite Sharif Hussayn on 8 January 1924. Prince Faysal, who became Viceroy of the Hijaz in 1926, ruled from Makkah. He helped unshackle local leaders from their status as vassals of the Ottoman Empire, following a pattern established by his father after the latter had taken the city from 'Ali bin Hussayn. Faysal displayed patience for almost a full year and eventually secured a surrender of the rebel forces. There were very limited casualties, and for obvious reasons that made it a major victory.[47] It was unclear whether 'Iffat was privy to some of the developments and battles that allowed 'Abdul 'Aziz to conquer most of Arabia, all of which preceded her arrival, though her curiosity was such that she most likely learned as much as she could before she and her aunt set sail for Jiddah.

---

[47] Antonius, *op. cit.*, p. 335–337.

When she arrived in Makkah, 'Iffat could not have imagined its eventual expansion both in size and infrastructure, but she probably admired many of its old buildings and archaeological sites. From her history schoolbooks she knew a bit of the city's history, including how in 1803 the Imam Sa'ud bin 'Abdul 'Aziz bin Muhammad bin Sa'ud had captured it, holding it for a decade until 1813. Imam Sa'ud was the grandson of Muhammad bin Sa'ud, who had forged the 1744 alliance with Muhammad bin 'Abdul Wahhab that sealed the fate of the Al Sa'ud as rulers over most of Arabia. 'Iffat may even have known how Ottoman officials, whose control over the Holy City dated to 1517, were infuriated by this loss. Her Turkish history books almost certainly included copious discussions as to how Sultan Mahmud II (r. 28 July 1808–1 July 1839)—who was known as both the *inkilapçi* (reformer) and the *ghazi* (warrior)—assigned the task of resubjugating Makkah under Ottoman rule to his powerful Khedive (Viceroy) of Egypt, Muhammad 'Ali Pasha.[48] She was probably also aware of her family background, courtesy of her uncle, Prince Ahmad Al Thunayan, but she surely never imagined that she herself would one day marry the Viceroy of the Hijaz and live in the Holy City. In any case, whatever thoughts she had had before she arrived could not have prepared her for conditions on the ground.

From a strictly religious point of view, living in Makkah was highly desirable (*mustahab*) since a believer would receive multiple rewards for good deeds and acts of worship made in the Holy City. After all, this was the city where the Prophet wished to live and, according to Abul Qasim Mahmud Ibn 'Umar al-Zamakhshari (1075–1144)—the medieval

[48] The number of books and newspapers published before 1840 in Constantinople was limited to eleven books annually—on the average—increasing to 285 by 1908, and to 87 newspapers/journals in 1875. In his *Ottoman Empire,* Donald Quartaert reports how book production grew between 1729 and 1829, when "180 titles appeared in print while during the mere sixteen years between 1876 and 1892, the number increased to 6,357." As a sign of added literacy and a burgeoning intellectual environment, "10,601 titles appeared between 1893 and 1907," which illustrated significant progress under the rule of Sultan 'Abdul Hamid II. See Donald Quataert, *The Ottoman Empire*, *op. cit.*, pp. 171–172. For a good discussion of learning to which 'Iffat Al Thunayan was exposed, see Benjamin C. Fortna, *Learning to Read in the Late Ottoman Empire and the Early Turkish Republic*, New York and London: Palgrave Macmillan, 2011; and idem, *Imperial Classroom: Islam, the State, and Education in the Late Ottoman Empire*, New York: Oxford University Press, 2002. For a sample of Turkish history books recently reprinted that were available to students nearly 100 years ago, see Hüner Tuncer, *Yüzylda Osmanlı-Avrupa Ilişkileri, 1814–1914* [Ottoman–European relations between 1814 and 1914], Ankara: Umit Yayincılık, 2000; and Sinan Maruoğlu, *Osmanlı Döneminde Kuzey Irak, 1831–1914* [Northern Iraq during the Ottoman period, 1831–1914], Istanbul: Eren, 1998.

Muslim scholar of Persian origin who subscribed to the Mu'tazilite theological doctrine, and was the author of a seminal Qur'anic *tafsir* (commentary) known as *Al-Kashshaf 'an Haqa'iq al-Tanzil*, popularly known as *Al-Kashshaf* (Revealer)—emigration to Makkah was highly recommended. In al-Zamakhshari's own words:

> We have tried and people before us have tried, and we have not found any place that is more conducive to subduing the self, resisting desires, focusing the mind, concentrating one's resolve, making one content with one's lot, repelling the *Shaytan* (Satan), keeping away from temptation and better for one's religious commitment in general, than living in the sanctuary of Allah, close to the House of Allah. To Allah is the praise for having made that easy, blessing us with patience and inspiring us with gratitude.[49]

Though profoundly religious and fully committed to her pilgrimage duties, it is impossible to determine whether such thoughts crossed young 'Iffat's mind when she arrived in Makkah. What she witnessed there was far less positive, since between 1910 and 1932 the city was regularly afflicted with epidemics of various kinds. In fact, records of epidemics from 1831 to 1930, for example, confirm that many died.[50] In 1907–1908 alone, more than 20,000 pilgrims died of cholera, and as late as 1930, two years before 'Iffat's arrival, a number of pilgrims perished in a similar pandemic. Naturally, both Prince Faysal and other members of the Al Sa'ud family knew of these threats to personal health and presumably took necessary precautions, especially since a potentially vulnerable disabled individual was also performing her pilgrimage rites. Still, even if the overall number of pilgrims in 1932 was far less than the astronomical figures of the 21st century, the sight of so many men and women performing Hajj rituals must have been daunting for 'Iffat. But she must

---

49 Al-Zamakhshari, *Al-Kashshaf*, Volume 3, page 464, as cited in Safiur Rahman Mubarakpuri [translated by Nasiruddin al-Khattab], *History of Makkah*, Riyadh: Maktaba Dar-us-Salam, 2000, p. 28.

50 According to an epidemiological study of the period, pilgrims from Mesopotamia (modern Iraq) and the Arabian Peninsula brought cholera to Makkah in the Spring of 1831. Within three weeks, nearly 3,000 pilgrims returning from the Holy City had died of the disease, and Makkah was thereafter regularly invaded by cholera epidemics until about 1912. See "Asiatic Cholera Pandemic of 1826–37," University of California, Los Angeles, at http://www.ph.ucla.edu/epi/snow/pancholera2.html. See also "Cholera: The First Six Pandemics," in *Encyclopædia Britannica Online*, 2012, at http://www.britannica.com/EBchecked/topic/114078/cholera/253250/The-first-six-pandemics.

have been relieved to notice that no women wore the *niqab*, the cloth that covers the face as a part of sartorial *hijab*, a custom of which she disapproved. Indeed, she must have known that the only thing forbidden for women in the Holy City was to wear a *niqab*, ostensibly because a woman was not "to wear over her face something that is sewn."[51]

Her pilgrimage rites completed, 'Iffat and her aunt settled in Prince Faysal's house, which was certainly far from being a palace. No precise date has been recorded for the marriage that followed, though Princesses Sarah and Latifah, the Queen's eldest daughters, recalled their mother telling them that it occurred about three weeks to a month after she and her aunt arrived in the Hijaz.[52] What they recollected with more precision was their mother's description of the Viceroy's house, which lacked basic services and stood in sharp contrast to 'Iffat's dwellings in Constantinople. To be sure, 'Iffat was disappointed by what she saw while at the same time delighted to be amongst her own. She certainly knew that she was marrying a prince and, beyond her own newly found status as a princess, looked forward to a life that empowered her to perform specific duties. But the decision to marry Faysal was certainly not calculated on her part, and even less so on his [as such a union may well have upset plans that the ruler, his father, had envisaged for himself]. However, neither was 'Iffat a total novice: both her aunt and her mother knew through Prince Ahmad Al Thunayan of 'Abdul 'Aziz bin 'Abdul Rahman's exploits and, of course, of the young Faysal who had represented his father in Europe in 1919 when he was no more than a precocious teen, so the future princess would have been amply briefed before setting out for Makkah. In fact, while her journey from Istanbul would prove arduous, she understood that she was about to embark on a unique adventure. She was young and full of life but was finally going home. Few comprehended her desire to belong, to reconnect with her roots. Even fewer were aware that an undeniable consciousness was developing within her that nothing would be the same ever again.

To be sure, 'Iffat Al Thunayan expected to meet Faysal bin 'Abdul 'Aziz, since the invitation letter that authorized their travel clearly indicated that the Viceroy would greet them in Jiddah. She was also aware of the potential for marriage with the founder/ruler and may have psyched herself up for that eventuality. Indeed, because her expectations were relatively low as regards her escort, it is fair to assume that 'Iffat was at ease with Faysal when they first met, psychologically preparing for a visit to Najd and a meeting with the ruler. In other words, even if

---

51 Safiur Rahman Mubarakpuri, *op. cit.*, pp. 134–135.

52 Interviews with HRH Princesses Sarah al-Faysal, Riyadh, 13 October 2010, and Latifah al-Faysal, Jiddah, 12 October 2010.

language barriers prevented her from expressing her feelings, in Faysal 'Iffat found first a friend and a welcoming relative before discovering her lifelong companion.[53] Though austere Arabian traditions seldom allowed for any display of affection, Faysal was love-struck from the moment he met 'Iffat, immediately recognizing that she was truly different from the girls he had met before her. She was urbane and carried herself with poise, wore her long blonde hair with grace over an angelic face with almond-shaped eyes that exuded beauty; there are good reasons to assume he was attracted to her. Of course, as a handsome young prince, Faysal embodied a dignified composure, but overriding this must have been sheer delight that in 'Iffat he had found not only a perfect match but a young woman whose sophistication utterly charmed him. Equally important, of course, were her Sa'udi credentials, since members of the Al Sa'ud family only married spouses from known tribes—which the Al Thunayan certainly were—or carefully chosen sub-tribes, as military conquests created new opportunities. Faysal certainly knew that 'Iffat was his destiny to the extent that, in the words of their son Sa'ud, their marriage was that "rarest gift from the heavens." When asked what would have happened had his mother never taken that initial step to return to Sa'udi Arabia, Prince Sa'ud al-Faysal declared: "Not only would we not be here, but I think that Sa'udi Arabia would have evolved into a very different country."[54]

Faysal bin 'Abdul 'Aziz informed his father in a telegram sent from Makkah to Riyadh that he had married his distant cousin, 'Iffat Al Thunayan. He promised to formally introduce her to the ruler at the first opportunity; perhaps surprisingly, 'Abdul 'Aziz bin 'Abdul Rahman approved. In fact, he had little choice in the matter since the marriage was legal, but at the very least it seems he wished the best for his son. When the ruler finally did meet 'Iffat in person, he knew why Faysal was taken by her charms, and blessed the union with even greater enthusiasm. Indeed, she was a good omen for the family as the third Al Sa'ud Kingdom emerged in the year of her arrival. Naturally, the founder was the architect who sealed the future of the nascent monarchy, although his own brothers and sons, along with many others, also worked tirelessly to create a viable political entity. 'Iffat Al Thunayan was certainly one of those others, determined to advance the prosperity of her nation,

---

[53] This was also Prince Faysal's approach as he befriended his cultured distant cousin and connected with her at a different level. Universally recognized by family members and friends who knew them well, 'Iffat and Faysal were true friends, as well as a couple.

[54] Interview with HRH Prince Sa'ud al-Faysal, Minister of Foreign Affairs, Riyadh, 26 October 2010.

against what at the time seemed significant odds. Under normal circumstances, her journey from her native Constantinople—whose legacy she would never forget—to her adopted Makkah would have been extraordinary, even had she simply married into royalty and raised a family. Instead, it became an astonishing adventure, as she assumed the burdens of duty in a country bound by strict traditions. Of course, she did raise a family, though 'Iffat and Faysal saw to it that each and every one of its members would follow their example of service to the nation. Hers was a difficult history, burdened with the early death of a father on the battlefield in a collapsing empire, the remarriage of a mother, and the addition of siblings in a harsh financial environment, as well as the responsibility she had assumed for her disabled aunt. Barely 16 years old when she arrived in Jiddah, 'Iffat Al Thunayan was already a mature young lady with a strong sense that fate had brought her to the Holy City. But she never forgot the years in Constantinople, which had shaped her outlook on life and made her all the more determined to bring positive change to the place she now called home.

2

A Pillar of the Al Sa'ud

According to Robert Lacey, Prince Faysal bin 'Abdul 'Aziz made a stop in Istanbul after his 1932 visits to Warsaw and Moscow, and brought "back with him a new wife, a woman whose impact on Sa'udi Arabia was to prove, in its way, more revolutionary than anything that a Soviet friendship treaty was likely to have achieved."[1] The colorful reportage notwithstanding, while 'Iffat Al Thunayan was certainly an "intelligent, articulate and forceful" young woman—the only Al Sa'ud princess who became popularly known as a "queen"—the Viceroy of the Hijaz did not find his future wife in Turkey.[2] Lacey further reports that 'Iffat and her mother, Asia, asked Faysal during this Istanbul sojourn to help settle a land dispute in Ta'if between her late father, Muhammad Sa'ud, and uncle Ahmad, though there is no evidence of such a property nor of a quarrel over it. Muhammad Sa'ud Al Thunayan may well have inherited some land in Ta'if, or elsewhere in Sa'udi Arabia, although he himself never set foot in the Kingdom and, presumably, was far too immersed in his military duties to stimulate such a clash. Moreover, Ahmad Al Thunayan acted as an advisor to both the founder and Prince Faysal though, once again, it was not known whether he actually owned any properties—alone or together with family members—in Ta'if or anywhere else.

Lacey's reportage is not limited to land deals or alleged disputes, which, at least in the early 1900s, required princely interventions to

---

[1] Robert Lacey, *The Kingdom: Arabia and the House of Saud*, London: Hutchinson, 1981, p. 241.

[2] According to a Turkish source, Faysal's first visit to Istanbul and Ankara occurred between 8 and 14 June 1932, whereas 'Iffat and her aunt Jawharan arrived in Makkah during mid-January 1932. For details on Faysal's first visit to Istanbul, see Mustafa Öztürk, "Al-'Ilaqat al-Turkiyyah-al-Sa'udiyyah fi Itar 'Ahd al-Malik Faysal bin 'Abdul 'Aziz" [Turkish–Saudi Relations under King Faysal bin 'Abdul 'Aziz's Rule], in *Proceedings of the King Faisal bin Abdulaziz Al Saud Studies and Research Conference*, Riyadh, Saudi Arabia: King Abdulaziz Foundation for Research and Archives (Al-Darah), 2009, Volume 3, pp. 406–436.

resolve and which presumably Prince Ahmad could have arranged given his proximity to the founder.[3] He claims, for example, that Faysal "had an eye for attractive young ladies," so that, when prompted by ʻIffat to look into this land issue, he suggested that mother and daughter should come to Jiddah where he could arrange everything to their "advantage." The Prince, who apparently "led a wild youth," and disappointed "foreign diplomats in the 1920s and early 1930s [who] never thought he would amount to much [because] he was so tied up by his women," must have thwarted such facile and gratuitous prognostications. Yet, the assertion that ʻIffat "changed all that" is accurate if for the wrong reasons. To be sure, Faysal "settled down with her to a marriage remarkable, in its time, for the comparative equality between the partners—and also for the strictness with which their children were brought up."[4] Above all else, the future monarch could not have failed to notice ʻIffat's presence in the house, as the Princess made creative changes without upsetting existing traditions. Naturally, any husband, and more importantly any leader, would be impressed by the grace with which his spouse conducted herself. Yet to assert that ʻIffat was a political partner who literally tamed Faysal would be a gross exaggeration, for neither was she so aggressive as to impose her will—especially in the 1930s and 1940s when she was busy raising her children—nor was he so lame as to forgo local traditions that did not allow for women to voice their views on socio-political changes. Such transformations occurred, of course, though much later than many assumed, probably in the late 1960s or early 1970s and always if, and only if, whatever recommendations the Queen made served the intrinsic interests of the Kingdom of Saʻudi Arabia and carried Faysal's full consent. In more ways than one, ʻIffat Al Thunayan became a pillar of the Al Saʻud family not because she imposed herself but because she knew how to increase the social capital of the nation.

This chapter focuses on the personality of the late Queen, starting with her known biography, before dwelling on the vision she shared with Faysal. Her 1932 marriage to the Viceroy of the Hijaz certainly opened many doors, though she still found it difficult to adapt to conditions on the ground. Nevertheless, ʻIffat slowly tackled the problems that confronted her, and invested time, money, and effort in empowering family

---

[3] Moreover, there is no evidence that Prince Ahmad Al Thunayan ingratiated himself with his ruler for financial reasons, claims to the contrary notwithstanding. Had he wished to embark on such a scheme, chances were excellent that he would not have left Riyadh to return to Constantinople, where he died within a year of his return.

[4] Lacey, *op. cit.*, p. 242.

members, friends, and even acquaintances. She consulted often with the Viceroy but not only him; over the years, she developed a network of contacts within both the Al Sa'ud and society at large, communicated frequently with other princesses, welcomed them in her *majlis*, and reciprocated visits as needed; she also learned local traditions, adopting them as her own even when these were dramatically different from what she knew or had been taught by her parents and aunt: all of these strategies strengthened her presence in the Kingdom. Most family members visited Faysal and 'Iffat, shared meals with them, and participated in conversations on a slew of issues that concerned the Al Sa'ud. Without exception, each and every male member of the ruling family held 'Iffat in the highest esteem, even if their positive sentiments were not universally shared among some female members. Above all, it was the strength of her character that shaped the way in which just about everyone regarded her. It was her presence—veiled, never flaunted—that earned her the genuine support and respect of most of those who knew her.

A GLIMPSE INTO 'IFFAT'S CHARACTER

In the absence of written documents, what follows is a glimpse of 'Iffat Al Thunayan's personality as perceived by family members, friends, and acquaintances. How she transformed adversities into challenges and how she overcame discrimination by investing in the Al Sa'ud merits discussion. By focusing on her offspring and grandchildren, by assessing how the latter recalled their mother and grandmother, it becomes easier to decipher the eclectic character of the individual. In the words of Princess Hayfah bint Sa'ud al-Faysal, a professor of English literature at King Sa'ud University, Queen 'Iffat "was much more than a mere survivor." "My memory of her," declared this gifted scholar, "is that of a strong woman who did not know what the word *no* meant. When she set her mind on doing something, no matter how important or trivial," insisted Hayfah bint Sa'ud,

> she saw it through. It was strange but we could all tell that our grandmother was a rock, afraid of nothing and no one, and I think that she drew her strengths from her devotion to God. Of course, her confidence also came from King Faysal, but I think that she would have succeeded no matter what. Simply stated, she defined depth for us, though her power was always articulated in the gentlest voice you could imagine. She was fierce in her determination to right a wrong and get things done. How could you not admire such a

woman? Still, let me tell you, she persevered against some pretty tough odds and it was truly providence that allowed her to overcome many, many difficulties.[5]

'Abdul Rahman al-Faysal, an officer who served in the Kingdom's Land Forces, appreciated his mother's "magnetic" pull, someone whose very existence drew one to get as close to her as possible. "She used to tell us all that we were the nation's eyes, which meant that much more was expected of us, and that every other eye throughout the country was focused on us, which meant that we had to perform above the call of duty. Such was the late Queen's influence on us," the Francophone son opined in appreciation of her diligence.[6] Others spoke with equal reverence, all recalling Queen 'Iffat's temperament as measured but firm, her motherly love total but strict, a doting grandmother who, over the years, witnessed the birth of dozens of grandchildren and valued each one equally. Without exception, everyone who kindly shared their personal reminiscences revealed a warm and caring personality. All were persuaded that 'Iffat was a true believer, someone who performed her prayers without fail and complemented her devotion with sustained work. "She believed in fulfilling God's commendations and refused to settle into a life of plenty just because she was a princess or the wife of a monarch," said Nurah bint Turki al-Faysal, an astute granddaughter who assumed many of her grandmother's education responsibilities at Dar al-Hanan and Effat University.[7] Ahmad 'Abdul Wahhab, a long-time family associate who became the monarch's Chief of Protocol and who was close to the royal couple, declared that "both Faysal and 'Iffat were pious people. There was no pretending with them. They were simply devoted to God, whose entire outlooks in life centered on profound faith, something that cannot be made up. How can one fake such devotion," he wondered, affirming his persuasion that if they were both successful, it was because of their devotion to God, country, and each other.[8]

Equally important, the Queen's sons and daughters were unanimous in their appraisals of their parents' love towards each other, even if most recognized that it was not easy being Faysal's spouse. As Viceroy and Foreign Minister before he became heir apparent and then King, Faysal was immersed in work and kept a full schedule. It was up to 'Iffat to carve

---

[5] Interview with HRH Princess Hayfah bint Sa'ud al-Faysal, Riyadh, 16 October 2010.

[6] Interview with HRH Prince 'Abdul Rahman al-Faysal, Riyadh, 13 October 2010.

[7] Interview with HRH Princess Nurah bint Turki al-Faysal, Jiddah, 17 October 2010. Details of the young princess's activities are discussed in Chapter 3.

[8] Interview with HE Ahmad 'Abdul Wahhab, Jiddah, 20 October 2010.

time in this busy schedule for herself and the family, masterfully shaping her interests to coincide with his—especially if they assisted the country and its inhabitants—while ensuring that Faysal was kept updated on every single development at home. In turn, he trusted her completely, welcoming her skillful leadership not only in running his household but in clearly identifying how the family could best serve the nation. Whether the eventual synchronization that emerged between husband and wife was a natural evolution or the result of hard work is something that cannot be definitively ascertained, though it was probably more a case of the latter. Suffice it to say that 'Iffat was not shy and knew exactly what she wanted, something that came across in dozens of conversations held with her offspring.

Given a fair wind, children ordinarily have a natural tendency to regard their parents and grandparents in a positive light, but even so it was interesting to notice how genuine the affection was which every one of Queen 'Iffat's children and grandchildren bore for their mother and grandmother. While Hayfah bint Sa'ud al-Faysal perceived her grandmother in true Shakespearean terms that perceived the elder in terms of awe, which also reflected the young scholar's work in English literature, the feeling was widespread among others too. Several family members as well as friends confirmed the Queen's mischievous style, which was orchestrated to push interlocutors to do a lot more than they might have originally cared to do. Princess Hayfah al-Faysal's daughter, Rimah bint Bandar bin Sultan, an energetic young mother in her own right, recalled how the Queen persuaded her not to wear jeans, which she did not find particularly attractive, "for you never know who might come in through the door." "She did not tell me not to wear a pair," declared Princess Rimah, "she just reminded me that I ought to factor in other considerations especially in this environment."[9] Al-Bandari bint 'Abdul Rahman al-Faysal, the erudite Director-General of the King Khalid Foundation, recalled her grandmother's admonition to always speak like a lion, often expressed in Turkish ["Aslan Gibi Konush"], which was her way to instill confidence in the youngster. "When she was mad, she addressed her concerns without bitterness or vindictiveness, and she wanted us to channel our anger into productive outlets. If I complained about something, for example, she would counsel me to calm down first and not to seek revenge at a later stage. When I think of her counsel, I cannot but smile deep inside, conscious that my grandmother affected me in more ways than I can ever express."[10]

---

[9] Interview with HRH Princess Rimah bint Bandar bin Sultan, Riyadh, 26 October 2010.

[10] Interview with HRH Princess Al-Bandari bint 'Abdul Rahman al-Faysal, Riyadh, 15 October 2010.

'Iffat's firstborn, Sarah, a remarkable woman who has confronted her share of adversities and who entered her country's history books after she was appointed a member of the Majlis al-Shurah (Consultative Council) in early 2013, was mesmerized by the future Queen.[11] "She was a real queen, in every sense of the word," Princess Sarah al-Faysal emphasized, adding, "And though you might think that I am just saying this because she was my mother, believe me when I tell you that everyone felt her aura. I, for one, would not have endured what she went through, but she never lost her bearings."[12] The youngest daughter, Princess Hayfah al-Faysal, clarified:

> "While everybody called her beautiful, I think her inner beauty came out more than her outer beauty. She was a dark blonde, with very bright, honey-colored eyes. She had great character and was very strong. She had to be strong to live the life she lived. She was just a giant of a woman, really. She was also wise, beyond anything you can think of. You had to run to keep up with her," Princess Hayfah reminisced, "She had so much energy. When she was going somewhere, she went somewhere. And when she was doing something, she did it. It was difficult to keep up with her but I can honestly say that it was not boring. My brothers and sisters, along with members of our ever growing family of friends and acquaintances, we were her army and she simply wanted all of us to excel."[13]

Princess Lulwah al-Faysal focused on her mother's laughter, which apparently was contagious. "She was vivacious and alive, vibrant and quick in her laughter. When she laughed, she laughed from the heart. If she got angry, she really got angry and showed it, and then it was over. You knew you could not go beyond a certain point. One look was enough."[14] Others confirmed Queen 'Iffat's jovial temperament, someone who appreciated a joke and who seldom frowned on what were taboo comments on peculiar characters, even if she was also discreet and vigilant. A tape recording of a family conversation held in the late Queen's Paris apartment in the early 1990s reveals what a happy go-getter she was. With several of her granddaughters asking all kinds of questions, the Queen seldom misses a beat, jumping from one to the other, providing examples from her own life, and commenting on everyday occurrences. She laughs out loud when one girl wonders what

[11] See below for additional details on the Majlis al-Shurah appointment.
[12] Interview with HRH Princess Sarah al-Faysal, Riyadh, 13 October 2010.
[13] Interview with HRH Princess Hayfah al-Faysal, Jiddah, 25 October 2010.
[14] Interview with HRH Princess Lulwah al-Faysal, Jiddah, 17 October 2010.

it meant to be Faysal's spouse and whether she would do it again. It is a happy laughter, emerging from her guts, affirming that she is lucky to have had a husband like hers, "although I was shunned at first." "My life was difficult at the beginning," she said, "because the closed society in Makkah saw me as an outsider. I was the *Turkiyyah*, someone who did not fit. Yet I was lucky that your grandfather stood by me and, gradually, I won over my many critics. You will not have that problem, but you should nonetheless settle on someone who loves you and who laughs with you. King Faysal had a good sense of humor and his smiles were golden."[15] When several asked her for advice on what to do with their lives, she unhesitatingly told them to educate themselves and not to settle for sedentary lives. "My mother would probably give the same advice to today's Sa'udi women that she gave to her own generation," declared Princess Lulwah al-Faysal: "Educate yourself. Be good mothers. Bring up perfect Sa'udis. Build your country."[16]

A weak individual could not possibly have made such recommendations then or now, and it was to 'Iffat Al Thunayan's credit that her inner strength was immense though always enveloped in kindness. Of course, she was not unique in these qualities: many others in the Kingdom and elsewhere have displayed such strength, such benevolence. In Queen 'Iffat's case, however, there was a third key ingredient that gelled her character: endurance. For in addition to fortitude and compassion, both of which allowed her to overcome serious hardships, it was her sheer perseverance that allowed her to achieve much of what she will always be remembered for. Whenever she faced a hurdle, 'Iffat tried to jump it, and whenever she confronted a hardship, she attempted to overcome it. There simply was no thought of stumbling and not getting up, something she taught her offspring rather well, and as some of the stories recalled in this book testify, she seldom encountered a challenge she refused to address. The Queen set out specific goals and displayed patience. It was this inner capacity, an innate stamina, which allowed her to channel so much energy into her work in the fields of education and health, in particular, both of which are habitually slow-moving subjects requiring teamwork and time. Through this ability to endure, backed by faith, intellect, charm, and elegance, 'Iffat persuaded.

---

[15] I thank HRH Princess Al-Bandari bint 'Abdul Rahman al-Faysal for sharing this taped conversation. Although the audio quality on the cassette was rather poor, it was clear enough, featuring the queen's legendary laughter. The Princess was also kind enough to show me several photographs of the late queen at various periods of her life that allowed me to become familiar with the subject of this biography.

[16] Interview with HRH Princess Lulwah al-Faysal, Jiddah, 25 October 2010.

Perhaps the best evidence of her character was the all-too-visible association of the veil and the *niqab*, the first worn by a majority of Muslim women and many non-Muslims in the developing world, and the second donned by ultraconservative women in the Kingdom and a few other Muslim countries. Although this topic is addressed in Chapter 5 in more detail, it is important to introduce it here, as her views on the issue reveal an essential aspect of the Queen's character.

Queen 'Iffat Al Thunayan wore the *hijab* in public but never put on a full *niqab* to cover her face. She respected local traditions and was a modest woman whose station in society required that she display conviction, tact, and respect for national norms. She had a very good idea of who she was, whose spouse she had become, and what kind of a model she ought to be to her children and extended family members, all of which added to the burden that she carried throughout her life. Moreover, it would be a mistake to assume that she refused to don her *hijab* whenever she stepped out; but it is true that she seldom wore it when abroad, precisely because she understood the power that the image of the veil represented in the eyes of the rest of humanity. Most remarkably, she wore attractive Western-style dresses at official functions whenever she traveled with her husband in Western countries and, like most women, enjoyed the latest hairstyles. It may be useful to note that Prince Faysal also wore Western clothes as appropriate and necessary although the tradition died after he became a monarch. In the event, he always let his spouse shine and as remembered by Shaykh Jamil al-Hujaylan, who served as Sa'udi Ambassador to France between 1968 and 1996, the Queen wore an elegant chignon—when hair is pinned into a knot at the back of the head—at the table of President Georges Pompidou at the Élysée Palace in Paris during an official function in 1972. "She was so elegant," said the future Secretary-General of the Gulf Cooperation Council (1996–2002), "and really she lit the official residence of the President of the French Republic with her presence that day."[17]

Impeccably dressed at all times, the Princess and future Queen never objected to Sa'udi girls and women wearing *hijabs* in public, but she also wanted those who could afford it to be presentable and elegant. For her, one could be conservative in beliefs and outlook without neglecting oneself. Towards that end, she ensured that her daughters and relatives were all similarly attired, and she also made sure that students attending the *Madrasah al-Numuzajiyyah lil-Banat* [Model School for Girls] in Ta'if, or *Dar al-Hanan* in Jiddah, were properly dressed. She even personally tailored some of the first uniforms that her daughters and the handful

---

[17] Interview with Shaykh Jamil al-Hujaylan, former Ambassador to France and former Secretary-General of the Gulf Cooperation Council, Riyadh, 19 March 2012.

of girls that attended the Ta'if School in the mid-1940s wore. Over the years, 'Iffat Al Thunayan distinguished herself by always being as elegant as possible, even if she followed the Holy Scriptures, which required women to be modest. She did not believe that girls who had not reached puberty were required to veil and, since children were not asked to fast during Ramadan, so the contemporary proscription to habituate underage girls to donning the *hijab* was probably an invalid requirement in her eyes. To be sure, this was an extremely controversial subject, with various interpretations or understandings of the Holy Qur'an competing for audiences, though the late Queen was not hesitant in expressing her own view to family members and trusted friends. The chances are excellent that she would have applauded the July 2012 "Moroccan rights organization [the Center for Women's Equality], which launched an awareness campaign against the veiling of young girls, describing it as a major form of child abuse." While its authors conceded the rights of adults to choose for themselves, they strongly objected to forcing girls between the ages of three and ten to wear the headscarf. Their slogan—*So that girls won't live in eternal darkness*—called on Arab human rights organizations as well as legislative bodies to join this campaign against what they concluded was "a flagrant violation of innocence and childhood."[18] Queen 'Iffat would have certainly concurred, a point it is important to emphasize, since she supported the wearing of the veil in public but seldom in private. She certainly believed that children ought first to learn about religion—what is prohibited and what is not—before choosing for themselves how to live in piety. She wanted students at *Dar al-Hanan* and Effat University, as elsewhere, first to strengthen themselves psychologically before making the choices that would stay with them throughout their lives. In the event, the late Queen would certainly have agreed that forcing young girls to wear the veil was not part of Islam. Frightening children into wearing the headscarf, ostensibly to protect them from harassment, or because it was a religious obligation, or even because those who did not wear it "would go to hell," was not in her repertoire of choices. On the contrary, the Queen wanted young girls to develop and blossom, both physically and mentally without being ashamed of themselves or their bodies. She certainly discouraged her girls from confusing traditionalism with fanaticism and liberalism with immorality. Consequently, it is logical to assume that what she wanted for her own daughters she desired equally for all Sa'udi girls and, for that matter, all Muslim women. Above all else, 'Iffat Al Thunayan did not

---

[18] Manal Wahbi, "Campaign against veiling young girls launched in Morocco," *Al Arabiya*, 1 July 2012, at http://english.alarabiya.net/articles/2012/07/01/223803.html.

want impressionable Sa'udi girls to be confused and, especially, to isolate themselves from the outside world.[19]

It is important also to address the sensitive question of sexual harassment and how the late Queen proposed to deal with this most serious threat to women in general. Although the trend toward wearing the *hijab* has been on the rise throughout the Arab world in recent decades—ostensibly to prevent such pestering—tellingly, many women still complain about being sexually harassed. Regrettably, such behavior is a universal nuisance in every society on Earth, though awareness of how to prevent it is more absent in paternalistic communities than those in which the rule of law prevails. Indeed, among the saddest incidental features of the 25 January 2011 Egyptian Revolution, for example, were the reported assaults on several women, including those wearing veils, gathered at Tahrir [Liberation] Square. At the time, confused military officials ordered forced "virginity tests" on those women arrested and held in military prisons. Though a judge eventually ruled that such tests were illegal, the damage was done, with the image of the Muslim woman being further tarnished through no fault of her own.[20] Still, while such developments did not occur in Sa'udi Arabia, where full public segregation prevented such *ikhtilat* [mixing], the image of Muslim women around the world has been closely associated with that of Sa'udis precisely because of the policy of segregation. This was as true in 2014 as it was in 1932 and throughout most of the history of Islam, although the degree to which ultraconservative sentiments translated into actual policy and, more importantly, the implementation of such gender segregation increased after the 1979 Makkah Mosque takeover. By all accounts, while Sa'udi Arabia practiced segregation, few recalled seeing women wearing a full *niqab* before the tragic assault on the Holy Haram and Riyadh's strict countermeasures. On the contrary, most Sa'udi women wore their black *abayas* over their dresses in a particularly interesting way, covering their upper bodies only, while folding the bottom parts of the garment over their hands.[21] It was in the aftermath of the 1979 tragedy, under the rule of King Khalid bin 'Abdul 'Aziz, that a stricter

---

[19] This analysis is based on dozens of conversations with Sa'udi women who kindly answered my many questions, including members of the ruling family but also university professors and students.

[20] Riazat Butt and Abdel-Rahman Hussein, "'Virginity Tests' on Egypt Protesters are Illegal, says Judge: Decision may open door to financial compensation for women subjected to tests during anti-government protests," *The Guardian*, 27 December 2011, at http://www.guardian.co.uk/world/2011/dec/27/virginity-tests-egypt-protesters-illegal.

[21] This was confirmed by Princesses Sarah, Latifah, and Lulwah, as well as by Mona al-Fadli, who worked with Queen 'Iffat in the *Jam'iyyah al-Khayriyyah fi Jiddah*

segregation was introduced as the clergy gained greater leeway to offer narrower interpretations of public modesty, and women were made to wear *hijabs* as well as the *niqab*, even if the latter was frowned upon in the Hijaz.

Ironically, some of the more conservative initiatives that further separated men from women did not originate in the Kingdom, but came from Asia, especially Pakistan. On 4 September 2002, a "World Hijab Day" was launched by the Jama'at-i-Islami, Pakistan's largest Islamist group, essentially to "counter the infidels' conspiracies against the Islamic tenets," according to Batool Zehra writing in the Karachi *Express Tribune*.[22] Of course, the holiday was not celebrated in the Kingdom, though whether such a holiday was authentic or even necessary was subject to energetic debates.[23] What were not debatable were the actions and reactions that the wearing of veils solicited, both in the Muslim and Western worlds, something that Queen 'Iffat was especially aware of after the years she had spent living in Paris. While it is impossible to know what her reaction would have been to the French Government's decision to ban the wearing of the headscarf in schools, 'Iffat Al Thunayan would surely have drawn a pragmatic distinction between public modesty and the imposition of one's values in a non-Muslim environment, something that several members of the family confirmed. Admittedly, this was not a topic that many of the male members of the family interviewed for this book felt at ease with, although the subject posed few dilemmas for most of the granddaughters, who readily clarified their grandmother's perceptions. Of course, many Muslims in France—on both sides of the controversy—were seriously upset by the proposed ban, and the issue has not gone away with the subsequent prohibition. Yet, Queen 'Iffat was adamant in her refusal to kowtow to narrow-minded interpretations that confused

[Benevolent Society of Jiddah], and who looked after some of the neediest women in town. Interview with Mona al-Fadli, Jiddah, 22 March 2011.

22 "September 4: JI Calls for Hijab Day," *The Express Tribune* (Karachi, Pakistan), 1 September 2012, at http://tribune.com.pk/story/429457/september-4-ji-calls-for-hijab-day/. For photos and colorful banners, see "World Hijab Day: 'My Right, My Pride'," *The Express Tribune* (Karachi, Pakistan), 4 September 2012, at http://tribune.com.pk/multimedia/slideshows/431247/; Ilene Prusher, "World Hijab Day: Muslims Debate where the Headscarf Belongs: The Holiday Comes Just After a Woman Anchor Appeared on Egyptian State TV Wearing the Hijab for the First Time," *The Christian Science Monitor*, 4 September 2012, at http://www.csmonitor.com/World/Middle-East/2012/0904/World-Hijab-Day-Muslims-debate-where-the-headscarf-belongs.

23 In fact, the holiday was not known in the Arab world in 2014, and few media outlets discussed it.

rather than clarified, holding to the view that a believer did not hide her faith behind a veil, even if she practiced modesty.

In the aftermath of the Arab uprisings in the relatively open societies of Tunisia and Egypt, disturbing new trends emerged that limited existing freedoms, with conservative elements extolling the virtues of the veil "while more liberal voices insisted that a woman should not be forced to don the garment essentially for social reasons. More extreme opponents perceived the veil as a vivid display of oppression."[24] Amazingly, several months after the Egyptian Revolution of January 2011, the state-run television network put up Fatmah Nabil, a woman wearing a simple white veil covering her hair and neck, to read the midday news. The event made the headlines because Egyptian television seldom allowed a woman wearing the head covering to anchor a news program even if veiled women newscasters were on the air in Sa'udi Arabia and elsewhere throughout the Gulf region. Nabil, who represented the anti-secular trend, expressed her joy after so many years of "bitter injustice" in which she had been forced to work essentially behind the camera. In a traditional society like Egypt, where the vast majority of women wore the veil, the move was a commonplace development and it fell to excitable officials to point out that veiled broadcasters were visible on the region's premier network, Al-Jazeera. What was far more remarkable, however, was the fact that Fatmah Nabil broke this reverse glass ceiling in Egypt. No doubt Queen 'Iffat would have been pleased to see Fatmah Nabil on the air, not because she was wearing a veil but because her fellow newscasters deemed her competent enough to present bulletins. Likewise, she would have wholeheartedly supported Sa'udi women news anchors and program presenters, several of whom wore attractive and colorful *abayas* and veils, instead of the black *abaya* that the vast majority of Sa'udi women slipped on in public.

If Egyptian television was no longer an anti-*hijab* institution, the Egyptian Ministry of Foreign Affairs was still staunchly opposed to the garment and seldom seconded veiled diplomats to non-Muslim countries. Officials wished to portray the image of the emancipated Egyptian woman—even if the trend was in the opposite direction—and appointed female ambassadors, consuls, and other representatives throughout their Western missions. Inasmuch as dozens of Arab women from Egypt, Jordan, Lebanon, Syria, Kuwait, Oman, and several North African coun-

---

[24] Sara Malm, "Female Egyptian News Presenter Becomes First to Wear Islamic Headscarf on State TV after Hardline Regime Reverses Ban on Hair Covering, *The Daily Mail*, 3 September 2012, at http://www.dailymail.co.uk/news/article-2197790/Fatima-Nabil-Female-Egyptian-news-presenter-wear-Islamic-headscarf-state-TV-Muslim-Brotherhood-regime-lifts-ban.html#ixzz3558BrYbF.

tries were entrusted with sensitive diplomatic portfolios, this was a real sign of progress. Queen 'Iffat would have been truly proud to hear that her own country's Ministry of Foreign Affairs started recruiting qualified female applicants for attaché positions in its embassies abroad, and while most would probably wear a veil in public, the more important aspect of this innovation was the fact that women were becoming active members of society making a useful contribution to their country.[25] That, ultimately, was her victory, as she never allowed a mere veil to prevent her from accomplishing significant things. It is also a good illustration of her character: unassuming but iron-willed, someone that fought for change without undermining indigenous traditions.

Marriage to Faysal

A further, revealing part of her character was the Queen's views on marriage, including her own, and relationships in general between men and women. During one of her rare interviews, the late Queen described her marriage in the following terms: "I met King Faysal on account of family ties and we both felt complete with each other. His personality impressed me—and for a while we would speak through a translator because I did not speak Arabic as I was born in Turkey . . . though gradually, I learned the language."[26] Although the late Queen's daughters answered numerous questions in interviews for this book, none could remember any stories about the actual marriage ceremony that sealed her union with the Viceroy of the Hijaz. Princess Sarah believed that it was a regular ceremony where her mother, accompanied by several Al Thunayan family members, including her aunt Jawharan, attended to the

---

[25] The decision to recruit female applicants was made by Queen 'Iffat's son, Foreign Minister Sa'ud al-Faysal several years ago, although the institution said that the positions were open to "women of Sa'udi origin" who have obtained university degrees graded as at least "good" in political science, law, economics, media studies, and English, French, or Spanish. The fact that the ministry sought applicants who were already relatively qualified and were competent in any of three 'world languages' prior to applying indicated that successful candidates would be entrusted with positions of responsibility after a short eight-month training program. Prince Sa'ud al-Faysal, as well as the entire government, were certainly aware of the need to present a different image of the Sa'udi women to the rest of the world. See "MOFA Seeks Female Attachés," *The Saudi Gazette*, 1 June 2011, at http://www.saudigazette.com.sa/index.cfm?method=home.regcon&contentID=20110601102055; see also Mira al-Kaabi, "Saudi Women and Political Science, *Arab News*, 20 July 2012, at http://www.arabnews.com/saudi-women-and-political-science.

[26] *Al-Majalis*, Number 673, 19 May 1984, as cited in Rania Sulayman Yunis Salamah, *Dar al-Hanan*, Jiddah: Madaris Dar al-Hanan, 1429H [2008], p. 25.

traditional practices that relate to wedding ceremonies and marriage rituals. Prince Faysal probably gave his bride-to-be several pieces of clothing, since one of the Qur'anic premises for marriage is for both husband and wife to act as each other's protectors and comforters, just as real garments "show and conceal" the body of human beings. There are no records as to whether 'Iffat Al Thunayan exchanged any gifts with her husband-to-be, though her family's financial situation probably did not allow for such largesse. Nevertheless, it must be assumed that preparations for the bride and groom were arranged by members of Prince Faysal's household, revolving around various applications of oils and perfumes to the bride's hair, washing her hair with amber and jasmine extracts, use of the *Kuhl* or Arabian eyeliner, and decorating the hands and feet with *hinnah* (a ritual known as the *Laylat al-Hinnah* that needs to be performed a few days before the actual wedding). Because such rituals were and still are usually performed in the presence of family members and guests, one must assume that several were present, invited to partake in special meals, and to celebrate with the couple. More important, because Prince Faysal's mother, Tarfah bint Al Shaykh, had passed away in 1912 when the young boy was barely five months old, many of the family duties fell on his maternal grandmother, who reared him, and his maternal grandfather, 'Abdallah bin 'Abdul Latif Al Shaykh, who taught him early on about essential duties.

Moreover, because traditions required that the bride stay at her dwelling for about forty days until the marriage night, it was logical to assume that 'Iffat spent much of this time with her mother and aunt in the Makkah home they rented. Faysal and his family members offered 'Iffat all of the items that she needed to create her trousseau, a dowry composed of her wedding dress, jewelry, perfumes, and silk clothing, among other items. Lest one conclude that these were substantial, limited financial conditions meant that most of the items she received as gifts were hand-sewn by family members, although Faysal gave his bride several pieces of jewelry.

It was important to compare the type of traditional *badu* (Bedouin) wedding dresses worn in ceremonial gatherings nearly a century ago with the current fare that is closer to Western tastes, though Princess Sarah encouraged Riyadh ladies to keep the traditions alive at the al-Nahdah Philanthropic Society for Women by producing authentic clothes.[27] These carefully tailored outfits reflected local tribal traditions that preserved indigenous norms and allowed Sa'udi women to perpetuate Oriental tastes.

[27] The work of the al-Nahdah Philanthropic Society for Women is discussed in Chapter 4.

The Faysal–'Iffat union was not simply a marital agreement for it also focused on the coming together of two branches of the family. 'Iffat's *khutbah*, the pre-marriage ceremony that was held a week before her actual *nikah* (wedding), was somewhat unusual because neither the groom's father nor the bride's father were present. According to custom, it was the duty of the groom's father to formally ask the bride's father for the hand of the bride in marriage. Still, the presence of a *wali* (marriage guardian for the bride) was not a requirement in Islam because scholars could not agree whether a *wali* was indispensable in Muslim *fiqh* (jurisprudence). Normally, however, the formality was observed so that family members present could share a light snack and drink mint tea before proceeding to draft a sort of Islamic prenuptial agreement or marriage contract agreement known as the *kitab*. It is not known whether Faysal participated in the ceremonial procession that involved several family members going towards the bride's "home," perhaps in a reenactment of the war dance known as the *'Ardhah*, meant to display the participants' joy. It is likely that such a ceremony occurred given the importance of the event—the wedding of a prince—though few remembered whether 'Iffat performed *tarwa'ah*, which completed the bride's departure for the groom's house, perched as she would have been atop a camel fitted with a *houdah*—a special, comfortable saddle. What was known was that Faysal welcomed 'Iffat into what passed for his "palace" at the time, which was neither a palace nor offered the kind of comfort that she had been used to in her modest Constantinople dwelling. Still, she gradually transformed the place into a home, as she embarked on her lifelong journey with Faysal.

Thus, it may be safe to observe that 'Iffat Al Thunayan was a devoted spouse and perceived her companion as a lifelong partner, someone she loved, respected, and honored. For her, marriage was not only a responsibility to raise a family and provide the comforts of life to all those within its embrace, but also an opportunity to instill values in each other as well as the offspring created as a result of the union. Consequently, it would be a grave error to assume that she understood her role as that of a submissive woman, for as a true believer she submitted only to God. Rather, 'Iffat and Faysal understood the equality of the partnership between spouses, as both entered into their matrimonial relationship with such a vision. Men and women needed to be authentic with each other, she thought, and though Faysal took another wife for political reasons, it was fair to state that King Faysal and Queen 'Iffat remained in complete harmony as a couple. Faysal's children from women other than 'Iffat were legitimate and integral parts of his household, though it would also be fair to assert that his relationship with 'Iffat was substantively different, an equal partnership that stood out not only in his own immediate environment but throughout the vast Al Sa'ud familial enterprise, where multiple marriages produced thousands of offspring with names that resembled each other.[28]

SONS AND DAUGHTERS

The chemistry that united 'Iffat Al Thunayan and Faysal bin 'Abdul 'Aziz was rare. It would not be an exaggeration to suggest that among various Al Sa'ud princely marriages, then as now, this one stands out for its unparalleled success in producing a closely knit family unit of highly educated princes and princesses instilled with that rarest of concepts: service to faith and nation.[29] Inasmuch as Faysal was a devoted father to all of his children, the mere fact that 'Iffat's nine surviving offspring somehow managed to embody these two attributes, serving their faith and assuming genuine nation-building burdens as they devoted themselves to the Kingdom, was most likely 'Iffat's doing. Moreover, to say that the Faysal–'Iffat couple conspired to succeed would come close to describing it properly, although Princess Latifah al-Faysal offered a far better assessment, from the perspective of a daughter who carefully observed her parents and how they behaved with each other:

> My mother was truly a friend to my father, as well as being a wife and a mum. She knew what her husband wanted and I think that my father also knew what she wanted, at least most of the time. One could feel the osmosis between them, and both shared an uncanny characteristic: they would never propose anything without first studying it thoroughly. Before they embarked on a grand scheme,

[28] Faysal bin 'Abdul 'Aziz married Hayah bint Turki bin 'Abdallah al-Juluwi in 1926 at a time of serious tensions before the emergence of the Third Kingdom. In turn, Princess Hayah gave Faysal two sons—Prince Khalid (1940–), the former Governor of Makkah and current Minister of Education as well as the head of the King Faysal Foundation for several years; and Prince Sa'ad (1942–), a leading businessman—as well as a daughter, Princess Nurah. King Faysal, whose first marriage to Princess Sultanah bint Ahmad al-Sudayri took place in 1920 when he was barely 15 years old, had a son from that relationship: 'Abdallah (1921–2007). There were two other marriages, one before 'Iffat, with Hussah bint al-Mahanah and a second after 'Iffat, with Jawharah bint Sa'ud al-Kabir, which between them produced three children: 'Anud, Jawharah, and Masha'il.

[29] Although direct quotations in this section are all attributed, it is important to repeat that the late Queen's offspring were especially forthcoming in repeated conversations, answering multiple questions.

> whether it related to education or health concerns or any other subject, one could be sure that both had either thought about the scheme themselves, or delegated others to look into the matter first. I cannot recall of a single instance when major initiatives were taken haphazardly and even the botched Ta'if Model School for Girls initiative was carefully planned, even if my mother's enthusiasm may have been premature.[30]

For Queen 'Iffat, the family was the center of her earthly universe, and her children represented her aspirations. Although several miscarriages left her distraught, those tragedies awakened her to the fate that befell women in the Kingdom at a time when prenatal health care was minimal, stiffening her resolve to introduce properly staffed clinics as soon as possible. In the event, 'Iffat gave Faysal nine children—four daughters and five sons—all of whom reached the pinnacle of authority in serving the nation. Naturally, the couple had high expectations, and if the boys enrolled in the military or accepted various civilian posts, the four girls saw their duties increase over time, too. 'Iffat loathed idle hands and insisted that each one of her sons and daughters would prepare himself or herself for a fully participatory life. Of course, this was not unusual, but in reality it stood out among royalty for whom the very definition of work had always been very different from their subjects. In the event, 'Iffat and Faysal were amply satisfied with what their offspring accomplished, and while much of the credit must be given to the individuals in question, it would be an error not to underline the efforts expended by the parents in pushing all nine towards excellence. While much is known of Foreign Minister Sa'ud al-Faysal on account of his diplomatic prowess, less is known about his brothers and sisters, which it is hoped the following descriptions will do something to remedy.

Sarah al-Faysal

Princess Sarah al-Faysal was born in 1935, and married Prince Muhammad bin Sa'ud, a son of King Sa'ud bin 'Abdul 'Aziz who became the Minister of Defense between 1960 and 1962. She never had children of her own, and while Muhammad married several other women, but Sarah's relationship with her husband was still highly politicized on account of undeniable family disputes between her father and her father-in-law.[31] Prince Muhammad, who passed away on 9 July 2012 at the age

---

[30] Interview with HRH Princess Latifah al-Faysal, Jiddah, 12 October 2010.

[31] For a discussion of the Sa'ud–Faysal relationships, see Joseph A. Kéchichian, *Faysal: Saudi Arabia's King for All Seasons*, Gainesville: University Press of Florida, 2008, pp. 57–88.

of 78, wielded significant influence in his capacity as a member of the Allegiance Council, which was technically empowered to select heirs to rule the Kingdom. Moreover, as Defense Minister in his father's controversial government, Prince Muhammad sided with King Sa'ud against the then heir apparent, Faysal, with everything that step entailed.[32] Sarah was caught in the storm though she seldom allowed family disputes to affect her life. Muhammad did not follow his father into exile, which meant that Sarah could frequently visit her parents and siblings or meet them in Europe during their vacations. Remarkably, family reconciliations followed the long separation as Muhammad and his brothers and sisters were rehabilitated, many of them choosing to return to Sa'udi Arabia.[33] In fact, King Fahd bin 'Abdul 'Aziz appointed Muhammad bin Sa'ud as governor of Al Bahah province in southwestern Sa'udi Arabia, where the Prince served from 1986 to 2010.[34]

A remarkable woman in her own right, Princess Sarah was eminently discreet when queried about her complicated family relationships, as she focused on her mother's—and her own—work with various charities. An elegant woman with impeccable manners, Princess Sarah proudly recounted how she involved herself in charity work, given the immense needs in the Hijaz and, after the family moved to Riyadh, in Najd. As the eldest, she recalled conversations with her mother and the latter's facial expressions that apparently registered joy and sadness, as she remembered her mother's frustrations when she first arrived in the Kingdom. Not only did the future Queen face a language barrier, the princess emphasized, but she also could not avoid the feeling that many perceived her as an intruder, even if she hailed from a Muslim country and carried herself with the dignity of an Al Thunayan. "My mother's first few years in the country were difficult ones," Princess Sarah said, "though her life changed when I was born, as she then realized what she could accomplish with her own family." A bilingual (Turkish–Arabic) assistant, upon whom 'Iffat came to depend, was brought from Cairo to help the young

[32] Few wished to elaborate on this sensitive issue though the wounds lingered.

[33] Stig Stenslie, "Power Behind the Veil: Princesses of the House of Saud," *Journal of Arabian Studies: Arabia, the Gulf, and the Red Sea* 1:1, 2011, pp. 69–79.

[34] Associated Press, "Funeral prayers for Saudi Prince Mohammad," 9 July 2012, at http://gulfnews.com/news/gulf/saudi-arabia/funeral-prayers-for-saudi-prince-mohammad-1.1046486. It might be useful to point out that various sources report that Prince Muhammad and Princess Sarah had several children together, but this was not accurate. See, for example, DataArabia, "Family Tree of Muhammad bin Saud bin Abd al-Aziz Al Saud," at http://www.datarabia.com/royals/famtree.do?id=175975; and Sabri Sharaf, *The House of Saud in Commerce: A Study of Riyal Entrepreneurship in Saudi Arabia*, New Delhi: I.S. Publications, 2001, p. 72, which also lists some of her alleged investments.

princess with her needs. At a later date, Sevgi Khanum joined the household as a native Turkish companion, remaining with the late Queen for most of her life. Her presence was truly appreciated by Sarah, who learned to speak fluent Turkish from her mother and learned tolerance from both.

Except for Faysal, who cheerfully helped his wife—bringing loads of clothes (always the latest fashions) from his many trips, and otherwise being head over heels for her—few family members received 'Iffat with open arms. As an attractive young woman who loved to dress up in pastel colors, 'Iffat enjoyed putting on nice clothes even if she always wore a veil in public. She enjoyed long trainers and preferred colorful dresses although she settled for more sophisticated wear as she aged. Indeed, in her maturity she increasingly settled on autumn colors, even if, as Princess Sarah vividly recalled, "she never wore a *niqab*." 'Iffat Al Thunayan respected traditions and wore the black *abaya* whenever she stepped out of the house, but she never masked her face. None of her four daughters and countless granddaughters, friends and acquaintances, all of whom graciously answered a myriad of questions over the course of two years, covered their faces either. This at the very least was a concrete legacy of the Queen, something that stood out as a vivid expression of her likes and dislikes.

An equally critical bequest of the late Queen, which she never stopped hammering home, was that her offspring should serve the nation. Though Princess Sarah concentrated her own contributions in various charities she helped establish, King 'Abdallah bin 'Abdul 'Aziz entrusted her with new responsibilities when he appointed her one of thirty women members of the Majlis al-Shurah (Consultative Council) on 10 January 2013.[35] The Princess joined her sister-in-law, Princess Mudhi bint Khalid, a daughter of the late King Khalid bin 'Abdul 'Aziz (r. 1975–1982), as one of two members of the ruling family to be so chosen in this inaugural female group. Even if the *majlis* was an advisory assembly, the presence of thirty women, including Princess Sarah, is bound to lead to significant changes over the coming years. Inasmuch as her presence in the assembly is a historical development, one can only surmise how proud the late

35 "Saudi Arabia: Sara Al-Faisal and Mudhi Bint Khalid join Shura council," *Gulf States Newsletter*, Issue Number 939, 24 January 2013, at http://archive.crossborderinformation.com/Article/Saudi+Arabia+Sara+Al-Faisal+and+Mudhi+Bint+Khalid+join+Shura+council.aspx?date=20130124. See also Joseph A. Kéchichian, "Saudi Women Appointed to Shura: Critics Wonder Whether the Latest Measure of Abdullah is a Symbolic Gesture Aiming to Boost Morale of Women," *Gulf News*, 11 January 2013, at http://gulfnews.com/news/gulf/saudi-arabia/saudi-women-appointed-to-shura-1.1130991.

Queen would have been had she lived to see the day when women joined the institution to better serve the Kingdom. That, in the end, was how she measured her own children's contributions to their country.

Princess Sarah recalled her mother's honey-colored eyes and chestnut-colored hair, which others described as dark blonde, and reminisced over how Queen 'Iffat was always well groomed and faultlessly dressed. She brought up her daughters in a similar manner, teaching them that their stations in this life imposed certain conditions, and that being presentable was one such duty. Even when arrangements were made for Princess Sarah to marry Prince Muhammad bin Sa'ud, at a time when the cousins barely knew each other, 'Iffat advised her daughter to be the ideal wife. "You might not know him yet," 'Iffat told her daughter, "but you will get to know him and learn how to surmount difficulties." "Above all else," she told the anxious young bride, "never bring up political difficulties into your family life. You just be the best wife you know how to be."[36] Such advice notwithstanding, 'Iffat was vigilant and though Sarah moved to Riyadh while the bulk of the family was still in Jiddah, the future Queen visited often. She also expected her daughter to remain attached to her siblings, which was vintage 'Iffat. Princess Sarah's warmest recollections of her mother were her many mannerisms, and how she used to share the many inconveniences she endured by mimicking certain people that her memory allowed her to remember. Often, Queen 'Iffat fell back on humor—which everyone acknowledged was contagious—in facing adversity. She taught Sarah and her sisters to be ladies and her sons to be gentlemen, worthy of Faysal, though she probably enjoyed it immensely to see them succeed in their own right.

Muhammad al-Faysal

Born in 1937, Prince Muhammad was the first al-Faysal son to study overseas, both at the coeducational preparatory boarding Lawrenceville School located in the Lawrence Township in New Jersey, and at the nearby Hun School of Princeton. He then enrolled at Swarthmore College in Pennsylvania but transferred to Menlo College in Atherton, California, in the heart of Silicon Valley 20 miles northwest of San Jose, from where he earned a Bachelor of Science degree in business administration.[37] Upon his return to the Kingdom, Prince Muhammad worked at the Sa'udi Arabian Monetary Agency (SAMA) and was named Deputy Minister of Water at the Ministry of Agriculture, accepting the position

---

[36] Interview with HRH Princess Sarah al-Faysal, Riyadh, 13 October 2010

[37] Katrina Thomas, "America as Alma Mater," *Saudi Aramco World*, Volume 30, Number 3, May/June 1979, pp. 2–11.

of Governor at the Saline Water Conversion Corporation in 1974. Then, in July 1977, Prince Muhammad resigned from his post and opted for private business.[38]

Seeing a unique opportunity with the emergence of a brand-new investment sector, Prince Muhammad founded the Faysal Islamic Bank of Egypt, then a groundbreaking institution that became the first modern bank run in accordance with *Shari'ah* Law. At the time, the bank was set up in Cairo because Sa'udi Arabia refused to authorize the idea that interest could be collected from or paid to account holders, in compliance with a total legal ban on usury. It took a while, but in time the regulatory authorities were won over and religious leaders convinced that Islamic banking was founded on the premise of lending without interest, which meant that the Faysal Islamic Bank was in full compliance. Remarkably, Prince Muhammad retained the chairmanship of the bank, not so as to accumulate wealth but in order to invest in developing countries, especially in the Muslim world; hence the Faysal Islamic Bank opened its first branch in the Sudan in 1977, with additional offices in Bahrain, Niger, and Pakistan. In 1981, he founded the Dar al-Maal Al Islami Trust in Switzerland, which encouraged global Islamic finances specializing in Islamic banking, Islamic investment, and Islamic insurance.[39] The Trust became a Bahamas-incorporated holding company with portfolios of Islamic banks in several countries. Encouraged by this success, in 1990 Prince Muhammad founded the Faysal Private Bank, the first Swiss bank—fully chartered in 2006 by the Swiss Financial Markets Authority—to be exclusively dedicated to innovative wealth and asset management in accordance with the principles of Islamic finance. The bank stood as a pioneer banking institution in the industry with Prince Muhammad serving as the Chairman of the Board of Directors.[40] In addition to these responsibilities, Prince Muhammad was also a shareholder of *Saudi and Gulf Enterprise Ltd*, a Jiddah-based conglomerate.

Dedicated to principles cherished by his parents, Prince Muhammad also served as the Chairman of the Board of Trustees of the King Faysal Foundation, looking after several charities throughout the Kingdom and in several Muslim countries. He married Munah bint 'Abdul Rahman bin Azzam Pasha, with whom he had three children: 'Amr, Mahah, and Rimah. As discussed below, Prince Muhammad's well-judged investment

---

[38] This was confirmed by Prince Turki al-Faysal as it was not possible to interview the ailing Prince Muhammad al-Faysal.

[39] For additional details, see the Dar al-Maal Al Islami Trust worldwide webpage at http://www.dmitrust.com/.

[40] For further details on the bank, see the dedicated worldwide webpage at http://www.faisalfinance.com/index_en.aspx.

propositions certainly helped propel the King Faysal Foundation to its current preeminent position as a philanthropic organization, something of which Queen 'Iffat would have heartily approved. She used to remind all of her children to spend wisely for she knew that while money was important, earning it was an acquired skill and spending it required even greater dexterity.

Latifah al-Faysal

By all accounts, Princess Latifah, born in 1939, was the al-Faysal family's living memory, exuding her mother's self-confidence and her father's serenity. In being interviewed, she recollected major aspects of her parents' lives and provided intimate details that gave insights into the characters of those concerned. Many of the dates that appear in this book referring to specific members of the family were double-checked with this astounding woman, who was both generous with her time and always ready to verify obscure points. She demonstrated innate skills that allowed her to jump from one culture to the next, fluent as she was in Arabic, English, French, and Turkish [the last only true for the Queen's first four children]. Importantly, Princess Latifah confirmed how her mother made arrangements to bring her own mother, Asia, and her half-brother, Kamal Adham, from Istanbul so that they could also settle in Sa'udi Arabia at a time when such resettlements required royal decrees. This was no mean accomplishment, for the deeds for the entourage, which included an uncle by the name of Sulayman 'Abdallah Al Thunayan, all required the approval of the founder-monarch, King 'Abdul 'Aziz. Princess Latifah recognized that while her mother maintained cordial ties with other ladies at the court, there were no friendly visits, at least not during the 1930s and perhaps not until World War II. Whether others in the family realized how hurtful some of their actions were cannot be determined at this distance, although 'Iffat was loath to complain and seldom did to any of her children. On the contrary, she understood her role as the spouse of the Viceroy in the Hijaz and let time gradually strengthen several ties she had nurtured in Makkah and Ta'if, where leading non-royal families supported her. If 'Iffat had welcomed some of the Makkah women into her *majlis*, her relationships with the women of the Al Sa'ud warmed and gradually evolved during the war, because by then she could communicate in Arabic with relative ease. Equally important, World War II proved to be something of a minor breakthrough, because she knew something of the outside world and could share her insights with the curious. At the time, she certainly knew much more than most members of the Al Sa'ud family, with the exception of her globetrotting husband, though the vast majority learned quickly as travel opportunities improved after the war. For Princess Latifah, the post-war years were critical for the partnership of Faysal and 'Iffat, as their children's education preoccupied them and the Queen embarked on all sorts of education, health, and charity work.

Princess Latifah married 'Abdul 'Aziz bin Sulayman Al Thunayan—she bore him a son, Turki—and was one of her mother's permanent assistants. She was privy to the Queen's various ideas, thoughts, and projects, and helped to implement most of them. Often, she acted as a go-between among various parties, cajoling some into action on behalf of her mother, and insisting that particular steps be taken to remedy whatever shortcomings were detected. In short, Princess Latifah became her mother's shadow minister, a position that the young woman assumed with considerable poise.

Sa'ud al-Faysal

Sa'ud al-Saysal was born in 1941 and first attended school in his native Ta'if, including a spell at the experimental Model School, an institution that was well regarded by both students and parents alike. In time, however, his parents decided that along with his older brother Muhammad, Sa'ud would be enrolled at the private Hun School of Princeton, New Jersey. While the other Faysal boys would follow the two elders, starting off their academic careers at the same celebrated preparatory boarding institution, the decision to enroll Muhammad and Sa'ud at the boarding facility was neither easy nor uneventful. Because the founder-monarch preferred to keep his children and grandchildren close to him, the two Faysal boys were whisked away when the ruler was otherwise preoccupied with stately affairs. Hun was not yet the home for international royalty that it eventually became, though an increasing number of world leaders saw merit in matriculating their offspring in Western, especially American, boarding institutions whose reputation for providing first-rate education was unparalleled.

From Hun, the future foreign minister enrolled at Princeton University, where he earned a Bachelor's degree in Economics. Upon his return home, the young prince became an economic consultant for the Ministry of Petroleum and, in 1966, accepted a position with the General Organization for Petroleum and Mineral Resources (Petromin). Five years later, in February 1970, Prince Sa'ud became the Deputy Governor of Petromin for Planning Affairs, by all accounts a critical new post within the growing state bureaucracy. In 1971, he became Deputy Minister of Petroleum, allowing him to gain intrinsic knowledge of oil affairs at a time when tensions were running high in the aftermath of the 1973–1974 Organization of Arab Petroleum Exporting Countries embargos against the United States and The Netherlands.

King Khalid bin 'Abdul 'Aziz entrusted the foreign ministry portfolio to Prince Sa'ud after King Faysal died in 1975. Faysal had been the Kingdom's first Foreign Minister, serving between 1929 and 1975, a period of more than 45 years; and Sa'udi Arabia was still a divided land. Faysal represented his father before the country formally declared political independence in 1932, and not only served for decades in that capacity but in his person embodied the very definition of Sa'udi foreign policy. To his credit, the monarch had trained his son well, a view confirmed by the universal acknowledgment that his son, the Foreign Minister, matched the best and the brightest.[41] Much like his father, Sa'ud has served his country, starting with his first consultancy, and has been in office as the head of the Kingdom's diplomatic service for nearly four decades. By virtue of this service, Sa'ud al-Faysal is the world's longest-serving current Foreign Minister, and though at least one commentator has opined that he is "not a decision maker," just someone who "executes policies," such remarks reflect unfamiliarity with both the Kingdom and the incumbent.[42] A particularly bright individual, Sa'ud's 1975 appointment was meant "to co-opt the best-known member of the next generation as a reinforcement against any attempt to change the order of succession," which is telling to say the least.[43] Still, it would be a mistake to conclude that Prince Sa'ud was nothing more than a messenger of the four monarchs he served so loyally, someone who enjoyed spending half of his life in airplanes. In fact, he was in the past and is at present the single-most critical architect of the Kingdom's

---

[41] It is important to point out that while Prince Faysal was indeed the first foreign minister of the Kingdom, the founder-monarch relied on Shaykh Yusuf Yassin, a remarkable man who hailed from Latakiyyah in Syria and was naturalized by 'Abdul 'Aziz, to assist Faysal. In fact, Yassin played such a critical role in the Kingdom's contemporary history that King Sa'ud bin 'Abdul 'Aziz kept him in his post, while Foreign Minister Faysal bin 'Abdul 'Aziz considered him his most important advisor. For additional details on Yassin, see Sabri Falih al-Hamdi, *Al-Mustasharun al-'Arab wal-Siyasah al-Kharijiyyah al-Sa'udiyyah Khilal Hikm al-Malik 'Abdul 'Aziz bin Sa'ud (1915–1953)* [The Arab Advisors and the Foreign Policy of Sa'udi Arabia under the Rule of 'Abdul 'Aziz bin Sa'ud (1915–1953)], London: Dar al-Hikmah, 2011, pp. 125–166.

[42] The remarks were attributed to Emad Gad, an international affairs expert at the Al-Ahram Center for Political and Strategic Studies in Cairo. See Michael Slackman, "A Legacy of Regret for a Saudi Diplomat," *The New York Times*, 16 December 2009, p. A18, also available at http://www.nytimes.com/2009/12/17/world/middleeast/17faisal.html?_r=2.

[43] Alexander Bligh, *From Prince to King: Royal Succession in the House of Saud in the Twentieth Century*, New York and London: New York University Press, 1984, p. 90.

foreign policy, though he is also astute enough to know that a monarchy can only have one ruler. Better than most, precisely because he is the son of a former king, Prince Sa'ud knows full well that while he may offer his best advice to the sovereign, the final decision always falls on the ruler, and his own responsibility is therefore loyally to carry out foreign policy resolutions.[44]

Over the years, Prince Sa'ud has articulated the Kingdom's foreign policies with great intelligence—especially in the volatile Arab rejectionist arena—without compromising its independent direction. He was close to Kings Khalid and Fahd, and is probably one of King 'Abdallah bin 'Abdul 'Aziz's most respected advisors, which allows him to engage in the necessary winnowing that decision-making necessitates. With impeccable credentials, and by virtue of the many responsibilities assigned to this senior member of the ruling family, Sa'ud al-Faysal remains one of the critical members of the Al Sa'ud even if he has been dogged by poor health in recent years. Moreover, as a highly regarded official throughout the global diplomatic community, Prince Sa'ud has enjoyed the support of his monarch in being granted the leeway to shape policy. As a sign of confidence in his nephew, on 20 November 2009 King 'Abdallah appointed Prince Sa'ud to the chairmanship of the Supreme Economic Council of Sa'udi Arabia, the body that develops the country's long-range economic agenda and puts in place fundamental policies. This position alone, among so many others, illustrates the immense burden that has been placed on his shoulders over time, which he carries with aplomb. To conclude that he is "not a decision maker," just someone who "executes policies," is just plain wrong.

Of course, while it is beyond the scope of this study to provide a full assessment of what Prince Sa'ud has accomplished for his country, it may be useful to highlight a few key achievements to further demonstrate what this particular al-Faysal has contributed to his nation. Much like his late father, the imposing Sa'ud commands respect, enjoys the reputation of being a good listener, projects an open mind, and seldom rejects advice even when it might not necessarily please him. Like his parents, he cherishes a good debate before coming to a conclusion. Inasmuch as his position requires from him the kind of intellectual rigor that a foreign minister must display, Prince Sa'ud is well served by a relatively efficient ministry and a small circle of advisors who act as his eyes and ears and prepare up-to-date reports that cover the gamut of international concerns. Those who know him can testify that he is an avid reader and takes full advantage of his long plane rides to catch up on a myriad of

---

[44] This point is often overlooked by critics though few appreciate monarchical constraints and, just as important, strict protocol.

subjects. Naturally, there are several issues that are dear to him, as they were to King Faysal and Queen 'Iffat. Among these was the question of Palestine, the fate of Muslim countries, and the Kingdom's vital relationship with the United States.

No issue has dogged Prince Sa'ud more than Palestine, as he himself has acknowledged in one of his many interviews. "We have not yet seen moments of joy in all that time," the Prince told *The New York Times* in 2009, "only moments of crisis; we have seen only moments of conflict, and how can you have any pleasure in anything that happens when you have people like the Palestinians living as they are?"[45] Though a critic from the Al-Ahram Center for Political and Strategic Studies, Emad Gad, concluded in 2009 that he had accomplished nothing for the Palestinian cause, Prince Sa'ud did not simply brush away such a harsh assessment, arguing that, "Peace until now has been like holding water or sand in your hand. You see the amount of water, you think you can hold something in your hand, but it falls away. Sand is the same thing. So unless there is something to hold in your hand and to point to as a success and as an achievement, then you have done nothing."[46] This was a rare acknowledgment reflecting what is a grave political concern, one that has dogged Arab rulers for decades, and which begs for a long-lasting solution that recognizes the rights of the Palestinian nation. What the Foreign Minister was too diplomatic to say was revealed in his overall appraisal as to why so little progress has been made on this core issue. In a frank assessment, Prince Sa'ud declared: "The absolute backing of the United States to Israel has had the effect that rather than making Israel safe for making peace, it has made Israel see the option of living in the area without the acceptance of the people of the area and this has led to many years of conflict between Israel and the Palestinians."[47] Whether this evaluation is correct is a matter for debate, of course, although it certainly does include an element of truth. Suffice it to say that Prince Sa'ud, like the overwhelming majority of Arabs, especially Palestinians, never accepted the double standard that always granted Israel the benefit of the

---

[45] Slackman, *op. cit.*

[46] Slackman, *op. cit.* Of course, the frustration over the Palestine Question was shared by King Faysal as with King 'Abdallah and several other Sa'udi and Arab leaders. See Kéchichian, *op. cit.*, pp. 181–183. See also Ghassan Salameh, *Al-Siyasah al-Kharijiyyah al-Sa'udiyyah Munzu 'Am 1945* [Sa'udi Foreign Policy Since 1945], Beirut: Ma'had al-Anma' al-'Arabi, 1980, pp. 192–96 and 539–34; Rosemarie Said Zahlan, *Palestine and the Gulf States: The Presence at the Table*, London: Routledge, 2009; and Andrew Scott Cooper, *The Oil Kings: How the U.S., Iran, and Saudi Arabia Changed the Balance of Power in the Middle East*, New York: Simon & Schuster, 2011, pp. 17–50.

[47] Slackman, *op. cit.*

doubt even when actions committed by the Jewish State seldom mimicked the deeds of a democratic political entity.

Beyond the question of Palestine, Prince Sa'ud and all senior Al Sa'ud ruling family members without exception have long been seriously preoccupied with the fate of Muslim countries in which poverty is prevalent. Given economic discrepancies among Muslim societies, King Faysal embarked on what was—and remains—the single largest transfer of wealth from one Muslim society to the Ummah at large. Indeed, the total amount of financial assistance granted by Sa'udi Arabia to fellow Muslim countries reached the hundreds of billions and, more importantly, became a model by which other well-off countries could emulate Riyadh.[48] Details for total aid disbursed between 1988 and 2011 was not readily available, though Riyadh has continued in recent years to allocate over a billion dollars in annual aid, which means that the figures probably topped US$ 35 billion. More importantly, on a per-capita basis the country may be said to be the largest worldwide donor, especially since loans are without conditions, funds are generally made available quickly and easily, repayment terms are generous (up to 50 years with a 10-year grace period), and the cost of loans is generally one percent. As Foreign Minister, and with the full consent of his ruler, Prince Sa'ud has thus carried a generous portfolio as he has traveled the world and pleaded the cause of Muslim societies. Like his parents, he accepted the responsibility of sharing wealth and, whenever appropriate, of providing the means to empower individuals to excel. Inasmuch as such behavior stood out within the international

---

[48] In 1974, the Kingdom created the *Saudi Fund For Development* with a 10 billion Riyals capital, to stimulate economic growth in developing countries. In the next four years its soft loan disbursements reached $3.1 billion in 51 countries, many of them with the lowest per-capita income brackets in the world, focusing on sorely needed transport, power and water projects. Between 1975 and 1987, total assistance amounted to US$ 48 billion, second only to the United States of America. The Official Development Assistance (ODA) ratio to Gross National Product (GNP) for Sa'udi Arabia averaged 4.2% over this period, well above the highest among the Organization for Economic Cooperation and Development (OECD) countries Development Assistance Committee (DAC), which averaged 0.35%. Although commitments and especially disbursements declined in the 1980s and 1990s due to the collapse of oil prices, the Kingdom's net development assistance stood at US$ 2.1 billion in 2006, double the US$ 1 billion given in 2005. It was important to add that the various Saudi Funds earmarked for development projects were attached to the Ministry of Finance. Naturally, there were private associations that disbursed aid to fellow Muslim countries as well, though a complete measurement was nearly impossible. For SFD data, see "Saudi Fund For Development (SFD)", 30 April 2008, at http://www.hipc-cbp.org/files/en/open/Guide_to_Donors/Saudi%20Fund_30_04_08.pdf.

community, especially in the United States, which was well known for its global generosity in assisting the less privileged, many noticed the Sa'udi pattern, too.

With respect to Sa'udi–American ties, Prince Sa'ud has long appreciated the vital importance of the relationship, even if the Sa'udi Foreign Minister has not been shy at times in expressing his diplomatic frustrations. In 2004, he declared a wish to see a steady reduction of the Sa'udi dependence on US-dominated security arrangements, although Riyadh also never wavered from its strong pro-American stance. In the aftermath of 9/11, and both the Islamophobia that gripped several Western countries and the rabid anti-Sa'udi views spreading in the United States, especially within extremist groups, relations cooled a bit, but it would be an error to conclude that Riyadh abandoned its vital ties with Washington. Prince Sa'ud, much like his father and King 'Abdallah bin 'Abdul 'Aziz, perceived Washington in positive terms and foresaw close ties.[49] As a frequent representative of the Kingdom in international forums, Prince Sa'ud al-Faysal led his country's delegation to the November 2009 G-20 Summit in London, among other such representations. In the aftermath of the Arab uprisings starting in late 2010, he worked with Gulf Cooperation Council member-states to place a GCC peacekeeping operation in Bahrain and, starting in mid-2011, encouraged Damascus to address intrinsic challenges to avoid a catastrophic conflict erupting in Syria. Against the backdrop of remorseless violence that then overwhelmed that country, in March 2012 Prince Sa'ud declared that it was a "duty" to arm the Syrian opposition, and to help the opposition defend itself against the bloody crackdown by forces loyal to President Bashar Al Assad.

In one of his more passionate moments, and during a joint news conference with US Secretary of State Hillary Clinton, he maintained that "the arming of the opposition is a duty . . . because [the Syrian Revolution] cannot defend itself except with weapons."[50] Over time, fundamental differences have emerged between Riyadh and Washington over what to do about the Syrian killing fields, and while

[49] For Faysal's views of the United States, see Kéchichian, *Faysal*, *op. cit.*, pp. 78–80. For King 'Abdallah's views, see Christopher M. Blanchard, "Saudi Arabia: Background and U.S. Relations," Washington, D.C.: Congressional Research Service, RL33533, 19 June 2012. For a gratuitous evaluation, see Bruce Riedel, "Brezhnev in the Hejaz," *The National Interest*, Number 115, September/October 2011, pp. 27–32.

[50] Al Arabiya Television Network, "Saudi FM says Supporting Syrian Opposition is a 'Duty'," 31 March 2012, at http://mar15.info/2012/03/saudi-foreign-minister-says-supporting-syrian-opposition-is-a-duty/.

it was customary for both parties to blame Russia, China, Iran, and Hizballah for the assistance they provided the Ba'ath regime in Damascus to do as it pleased, Sa'udi Arabia did not accept that the uprising, initially peaceful and non-sectarian, would be allowed to descend into an inferno while the world watched. The Sa'udis have refused just to observe as civilians were subjected to brutal attacks on a daily basis simply because past engagements in Iraq and Afghanistan have proved too costly, politically and militarily. Strongly motivated by that moral imperative, the Kingdom has provided financial aid, along with limited military assistance, to the Free Syrian Army.[51] Of course, frequent accusations that Riyadh is a main supplier of advanced weapons have soiled the discussion, though this was not the case; the affable Sa'udi Foreign Minister may be a diehard Arab nationalist and a lifelong champion of Arab and Muslim rights, but he is also a highly pragmatic leader.

Decidedly articulate, and capable of conversing in seven languages, Prince Sa'ud has often been courted by international media outlets on account of his near-native command of the English language. A recent struggle with Parkinson's disease and back pain may have slowed him down, but his commitment to his parents' philanthropic institutions has not diminished. As a founding member of the King Faysal Foundation, and as Chairman of the Board of Directors for the King Faysal School, one may wonder how he assumes all of these burdens with such flair. Simply stated, Prince Sa'ud considers it a duty to fulfill these goals, recalling that his mother was the first to set the example. "She considered her many sacrifices for us and the country as a duty," he divulged in a poignant moment that revealed why he willingly assumed these tasks.[52] His teary eyes lit up when he recounted how Queen 'Iffat had counseled him, reminding him of his intrinsic responsibility to fulfill King Faysal's work and to build on his legacy. It was a rare moment for someone heavily burdened with important tasks but who was not afraid to shed a tear as he relived a particularly personal recollection. The father of three sons—Muhammad, Khalid, and Fahd—and three daughters—Hayfah, Lanah, and Rim—Prince Sa'ud has still found the time to be a member of the Society for Disabled Children and the Madinah Society for Welfare and Social Services, two institutions that were dear to Queen 'Iffat Al Thunayan.

---

[51] Joseph A. Kéchichian, "Clearing the air on US–Saudi ties crucial: Beyond 'fence-mending', Obama's mid-March trip ought to be courageous to prevent Riyadh from going its 'own way' since that will serve neither's interests," *Gulf News*, 12 February 2014, p. A2.

[52] Interview with HRH Prince Sa'ud al-Faysal, Riyadh, 26 October 2010.

'Abdul Rahman al-Faysal

Prince 'Abdul Rahman al-Faysal was born in Ta'if in 1942 and like his brothers first went to the United States for his secondary education where Jamil Murad Baroody, the Christian Lebanese-born diplomat who represented the Kingdom from 1947 until his death in 1979, used to visit and take the boys out for pizza.[53] Baroody was not the only visitor, as Faysal's sons sat through weekly tutorials offered by Professor Philip Hitti, who focused on Arab and Muslim affairs.[54] At the time, neither 'Abdul Rahman nor any of his brothers had a car and each received a $15 monthly allowance. Both Faysal and 'Iffat insisted that their sons should concentrate on their studies, and though their language skills were limited when they arrived, all graduated with distinction, something that was neither easy nor routine. "My mother in particular," recalled 'Abdul Rahman, "was quite strict with us. When King Faysal recommended that I enroll at Sandhurst in the UK and consider a career in the military, I inquired what was expected from me after I graduated. It was my mother who responded, declaring: graduate first."[55] In the event, the young man attended and graduated from Sandhurst, returned to Riyadh as a second lieutenant, and embarked on a distinguished career in the Royal Sa'udi Land Forces.

Before long, Prince 'Abdul Rahman was given the responsibility of putting together several tank units, which were then introduced into the army. He recruited loyal *badu* tribesmen and first invested in his men, creating a fit fighting force able to withstand the pressures of tank warfare in the desert environment. This entailed feeding his men with the kind of balanced meals that few were accustomed to, building up their

---

[53] Jamil Murad Baroody (1905–1979) was the longest serving national representative to the world body at the time of his death. Before King 'Abdul 'Aziz appointed him as the permanent representative in New York, Baroody was commissioner general for Lebanon at the New York World's Fair (1939) and a faculty member at Princeton during World War II. Faysal knew the Catholic Lebanese well and invited him to attend the UN Charter Conference in San Francisco in 1945. Born in the Shuf District in the small village of Suk al-Gharb, Baroody was a staunch defender of Arab causes, which ingratiated him to both the ruler and his foreign minister. See Abdullahi A. An-Na'im, "The Position of Islamic States Regarding the Universal Declaration of Human Rights," in Peter Baehr, Cees Flinterman and Mignon Senders, eds., *Innovation and Inspiration: Fifty Years of the Universal Declaration of Human Rights*, Amsterdam: Koninklijke Nederlandse Akademie van Wetenschappen, 1999, pp. 177–192, especially pp. 185–186.

[54] Philip Khuri Hitti (1886–1978), who was born in Shamlan, Lebanon, was a leading professor of contemporary Arab and Islamic studies in the United States. Like Baroody, the Catholic Lebanese-American was a diehard Arab nationalist.

[55] Interview with HRH Prince 'Abdul Rahman al-Faysal, Riyadh, 13 October 2010.

stamina before starting to train them for mechanized warfare, and earning their loyalty by creating an *esprit de corps* that only some enjoyed in their respective tribal settings. The enterprise was far more difficult than many assumed, but gradually a new generation of fighters emerged, capable of doing a lot more than simply getting behind the turret and aiming randomly. Most earned their stripes as they pledged allegiance to the Kingdom of Sa'udi Arabia. This world-class fighting unit was the result of hard work and unprecedented discipline, both ideas that the Prince's parents had instilled in him since childhood.

When Riyadh opted to upgrade its tank brigades, Prince 'Abdul Rahman was put in charge of the program as the first Sa'udi armored unit, designated the Fourth Armored Brigade, was structured and trained along French lines. It was equipped with 300 AMX-30 main battle tanks and 500 AMX-10P armored infantry fighting vehicles. In time, between the late 1970s and the mid-1980s, four mechanized brigades were created by converting infantry brigades and equipping them with a variety of American and French armored fighting vehicles. Gradually, newer anti-tank weapons were introduced, such as the American TOW, the British Dragon, and the French HOT, many of them mounted on armored vehicles. Moreover, 'Abdul Rahman oversaw the introduction of the Kingdom's tactical air defense systems, based around the French Crotale surface-to-air missile (SAM), now supplemented with Stinger and Redeye shoulder-fired missiles. The SAMs were known as the Shahine, and were built especially for Sa'udi Arabia. Thomson-CSF assumed the development of radar and electronic systems, while Matra constructed the missiles. The project began in 1975 under Prince 'Abdul Rahman's diligent supervision, and was tested in 1979, with deliveries in 1982 and 1983. Thirty-six complete systems were sold, since raised to fifty-three during replenishment phases, mounted on the AMX-30 MBT chassis modified with armor that offered good protection to personnel and equipment. Credit for the gradual absorption of radar and computer expertise to process the threat assessments is also due to the team that Prince 'Abdul Rahman led.[56]

Prince 'Abdul Rahman married Mudhi bint Khalid bin 'Abdul 'Aziz, a daughter of the late King Khalid and his spouse Sitah bint Fahad Al Damir.[57] Princess Mudhi, who joined her sister-in-law, Princess Sarah al-Faysal, as one of thirty female members of the Majlis al-Shurah in

---

56 For details on the missile system, see "Shahine Missile sur Véhicule Blindé," at http://www.armyrecognition.com/europe/France/vehicules_missiles/Shahine/Shahine_France_description.htm.

57 King Khalid bin 'Abdul 'Aziz and Sitah bint Fahad Al Damir had seven children: Jawharah, Nuf, Mudih, Hussah (d. 2011), al-Bandari, Misha'al, and Faysal. Bandar

January 2013, gave Prince ʻAbdul Rahman three children—Sarah, Saʻud, and al-Bandari—with, in a rather rare phenomenon, two monarchs for grandfathers (Faysal and Khalid). Prince ʻAbdul Rahman passed away on 5 March 2014 at the age of 72 after a long illness.

Bandar al-Faysal

Prince Bandar al-Faysal was born in Ta'if in 1943. After leaving Hun, he attended Pomona and Whittier Colleges in California and later, once completing his Royal Air Force pilot training at Cranwell, England, went on to the University of Washington to study for an advanced degree. A commander in the Royal Saʻudi Air Force for 42 years, Prince Bandar piloted Lightnings, F5s, Hawker Hunters, Mirages, and Jaguars. He retired from active duty in 2006, to a life of intellectual curiosity while tending to his large farm outside Riyadh. An avid reader, Prince Bandar welcomed in his *majlis* some of the capital city's many intellectual voices, exchanging ideas and, equally important, gaining valuable insights into trends in the public discourse.

Prince Bandar's most vivid recollection of his mother was the constant reminder that Faysal's offspring "serve the nation," and that it was an obligation to do whatever one could to advance the interests of the Al Saʻud and the Kingdom.[58] He believed that the Atatürk legacy had made an impact on her life, and because she had been marginalized in the nascent Turkish Republic on account of her Saʻudi background, ʻIffat Al Thunayan had known what needed to be avoided. Simply stated, one was obligated to serve his/her nation, to one's best abilities. Of course, what she witnessed in the Kingdom was equally devastating, especially the sheer poverty which was then a fact of life and which she was determined to change through the power of education. Few members of the family made the future Queen feel at home, but the founder at least had made her feel like a Saʻudi, which was why, Prince Bandar explained, ʻIffat Al Thunayan had set out to prove herself. Importantly, to assuage any anxiety his young bride might be feeling, Prince Faysal welcomed ʻIffat's family into the Kingdom and treated them as if they were his own. More importantly, and though this point was reiterated by others, too, Prince Bandar was adamant that his father implicitly trusted his mother's judgment. "She was never afraid," the son elaborated, "and this was something that she shared with my father." Yet she also insisted that the fundamental reason why every Al Saʻud should

bin Khalid and ʻAbdallah bin Khalid are from a separate mother, Nurah bint Turki bin ʻAbdul ʻAziz bin ʻAbdallah bin Turki Al Saʻud. Two other marriages produced no offspring.

[58] Interview with HRH Prince Bandar al-Faysal, Riyadh, 15 October 2010.

serve his country was because if "we do not serve, our power will be taken away from us." It was a "use it or lose it" equation that 'Iffat Al Thunayan "understood to perfection, and which is why she became a Queen in this country."

Like all parents, Faysal and 'Iffat doted on their nine children. Prince Bandar provided exceptional insights into his parents' evaluations of their offspring, with both of them recognizing each child's hidden talents. According to Prince Bandar, "King Faysal thought that Turki [al-Faysal] had the eyes of a wolf, and that he was extremely smart," which was why the latter was trained to assume one of the most challenging duties in the country: Head of Intelligence. "My mother encouraged father not to always reward us in whatever one of us was involved in. She was not moved as she insisted that we were doing our duty. She could talk to him frankly and he would accept her advice because he knew that she was right." Inasmuch as similar encounters occurred with other monarchs, Queen 'Iffat must be considered one of the pillars of the Third Monarchy, for she gently reminded her half-brothers that to rule is to serve. "Once, King Khalid visited Queen 'Iffat with the news that he had just dismissed Musa'id bin 'Abdul 'Aziz from the position of Minister of Finance, which upset my mother. The ruler was shocked by her admonition because he had, apparently, breached the close family circle that was the heart of power. She just did not believe that the Al Sa'ud could afford to make such errors and had the audacity to speak the truth," Prince Bandar recounted.[59] It needs to be acknowledged that senior Al Sa'ud family members held Queen 'Iffat in such high esteem that her criticisms were never rejected. They all knew that she was counseling unity and was protective of the ruling family. In this regard, Prince Bandar mentioned a poignant scene in Jiddah sometime in 1997 or 1998 to illustrate the respect and loyalty that senior Al Sa'ud members displayed towards the Queen. Though in a wheelchair, King Fahd visited 'Iffat Al Thunayan, sitting next to Prince 'Abdallah al-Faysal (1922–2007), King Faysal's eldest son. Remarkably, and despite their incapacitation, both men wanted to pay their respects to her, something that many noted with emotion.

A steely-eyed and gregarious man who exudes authority, Prince Bandar was emotional as well as intellectually engaged when discussing his mother. He was genuinely impressed by what 'Iffat Al Thunayan had been able to achieve, a legacy that he wished to hand on to his own son, Sultan, and his daughter, Hanah, which could only be accomplished through their own respective services to the nation.

---

59 *Ibid.*

Turki al-Faysal

Prince Turki was born in Makkah in 1945 and first attended the Ta'if Model Elementary and Intermediate Schools before making the pilgrimage to the Hun School of Princeton, although he finally graduated in 1963 from the Lawrenceville School in New Jersey. The youngest of the seven who attended boarding school, Prince Turki readily acknowledges that he could not wait to join the others and repeatedly pleaded with his father to let him go. Faysal eventually agreed, aware that Turki's older brothers would look after the youngster, who was barely fourteen, when he first arrived in the United States. It would be safe to assume that the father knew that this education would allow his children to acquire what was not available elsewhere and, more importantly, to learn about the rising power that was America, a country that literally held the fate of the free world in its hands. Inasmuch as Faysal's intuition proved to be correct long before the Cold War pitted Washington against Moscow, the al-Faysal boys learned about America—and Americans—especially when the country was politically straightforward and remarkably at ease with itself throughout the 1950s even if the country exploded towards the mid-1960s when the Civil Rights Movement and anti-Vietnam War protests gathered momentum. That exposure served them and the Kingdom well.

Prince Turki enrolled at Princeton University though he quickly transferred to Georgetown in Washington, D.C., which proved to be an entirely new experience compared with the sheltered life he had lived at Princeton. The de facto capital of the so-called free world impressed him and it was not long before the young prince had adapted to life at the Jesuit institution. By his own evaluation, Georgetown allowed him to discover that he and the Jesuits "shared a motive in life: to serve God and, through work, to worship God." In one of his more revelatory declarations, Prince Turki has added: "For me, [worshipping God] means living the life of a true Muslim; learning to use modern methods and technology in order to better worship God in a modern age. Some people are anxious lest, as we adapt the technology of those who hold views different from ours, our values be eroded because they won't be portrayed as 'progressive.' But the majority in Saudi Arabia believe that our faith in God is such that it can endure the enticements of materialism."[60]

Back in the Kingdom, in 1973 the young prince was appointed an advisor in the Royal Diwan [court], acting as a deputy to his uncle, Kamal Adham.[61] Starting in 1977, he succeeded Adham as the Director General

---

[60] Thomas, *op. cit.*, p. 6.

[61] Because decision makers required critical information, Riyadh set up an intelligence service in 1955, under the name of "Al-Mabahith Al-'Amah" or General

of the *Istikhbarat al-'Amah* [General Intelligence Directorate (GID)], the Kingdom's main foreign intelligence service, a post he kept for 24 years.[62] Both Kings Khalid and Fahd, as well as then heir apparent 'Abdallah and other senior members of the ruling family, relied on his expertise until 2001 in what was one of the most sensitive posts in the country. The position allowed Prince Turki to oversee all intelligence matters affecting Sa'udi Arabia, which meant that the Al Sa'ud depended on him to protect the country and its citizens from internal as well as external foes. At the GID, and over time, critical portfolios required the kind of expertise that could only be gathered by both intelligence work and intuition based on historical knowledge. Yemen and Afghanistan became priorities for Riyadh, and both portfolios fell on Prince Turki's lap, though he was ably seconded by Sa'ud bin Fahd, an equally hardworking deputy. Together, the two men developed close working relationships with several foreign intelligence institutions, including the Central Intelligence Agency (CIA), the British Secret Intelligence Service (SIS) better known as MI6 [Military Intelligence—Section 6], and the Direction Générale de la Sécurité Extérieure [DGSE], as the French service is known. Inasmuch as intelligence duties tended to be clandestine, Prince Turki's time-tested capabilities, and his unique role within the ruling family, guaranteed him a rare privileged position notwithstanding that he fully understood the parameters of his duty towards his nation.

If Yemen was a relatively loaded topic that could be made manageable through a combination of riyal diplomacy (financial incentives) and invoking longstanding tribal affinities, Afghanistan proved to be truly problematic. His furtive efforts to meet and negotiate with Taliban officials as well as authorized personnel in the Directorate for Inter-Services Intelligence [ISI]—the Pakistani body that developed close associations with Afghani leaders over the fate of his renegade countryman 'Usamah bin Ladin—fatally undermined Prince Turki's mandate.[63] Without a

---

Investigations (GI). King Sa'ud bin 'Abdul 'Aziz split the GI—a separate intelligence service saw the light of day in 1956 with Royal decree number 11, which ordered the creation of a special department under the title of *Maslahat Al-Istikhbarat Al-'Amah* or the *Iskhbarat al-'Amah* [General Intelligence Department—GID]. The Mabahith were entrusted to 'Abdul 'Aziz bin Mas'ud, who served as head of GI between 1970 and 1986, while King Faysal relied on his brother-in-law, Kamal Adham, to look after the GID.

[62] Prince Turki's resignation, effective 31 August 2001, was unexpected because King Fahd had extended his term in office on 26 May 2001, to serve for another four years. See "Full text of royal decrees on official appointments," 24 May 2001, at http://www.saudiembassy.net/archive/2001/statements/page9.aspx.

[63] Arnaud de Borchgrave, "Saudis' James Bond and George Smiley," in *The*

doubt, the dismissal was rough—after 24 years on the job—but, true to his discreet character, the prince has seldom spoken about the way his tenure as Head of the GID ended. Ironically, he would be handed even more demanding responsibilities when the late King Fahd bin 'Abdul 'Aziz appointed him to the Court of St. James, as Ambassador to London (while he simultaneously held the non-resident ambassadorship to the Republic of Ireland). Then, in July 2005, he was assigned an even greater challenge when he became Ambassador to the United States. Prince Turki chose to interact with Americans to help alter some of the negative perceptions of Muslims that pervaded the country after 9/11 and, towards that end, he visited 37 different states during his relatively short tenure, delivering countless speeches to a variety of audiences. While he cautioned interlocutors about Afghanistan, Iraq, and Iran, three countries that were caught in the vortex of the American war against terrorism, he almost always argued that the Palestinian question was the key concern that needed attention, and he never wavered from this core issue.[64]

Still, the consequences of 9/11 put a strain on Sa'udi–American ties, something that Prince Turki knew all too well and led him to tackle the challenges head on. Long before he assumed sensitive ambassadorial positions, the Prince directly challenged leading *'Ulamah* in the Kingdom, especially those who gave the appearance of nonchalance. According to one of his advisors, the journalist Jamal Khashoggi, Prince Turki chastised Shaykh 'Abdallah al-Turki, then the Secretary-General of the World Muslim League and a member of the Council of Senior *'Ulamah*, arguing that religious authorities were advised to focus on religious matters. "Those responsible for affairs of state are the rulers," the Prince reportedly declared, with religious scholars called upon "only [to] act in an advisory capacity."[65] This was, by all accounts, a clear admonition that religious authorities had surpassed their writ, but also a stark reminder of the challenges faced by King Faysal—and Queen 'Iffat—in the early 1960s after the decision was made to introduce public schooling for girls in Qasim Province.

Washington Times, 29 July 2005 at http://www.washtimes.com/functions/print.php?StoryID=20050728-081358-7342r. See also "Profile: Prince Turki al-Faisal," *BBC NEWS*, 20 July 2005, at
http://news.bbc.co.uk/go/pr/fr/-/2/hi/middle_east/4700589.stm.

64 Interview with HRH Prince Turki al-Faysal, Riyadh, 16 October 2010.

65 Jamal Khashoggi, "Saudi Religious Establishment Has Its Wings Clipped," *The Daily Star* [Beirut, Lebanon], 1 July 2002, quoted in Rachel Bronson, "Rethinking Religion: The Legacy of the U.S.–Saudi Relationship," *The Washington Quarterly* 28:4, Autumn 2005, pp. 119–137, the quote is on page 124.

Prince Turki relied on the power of his pen on 13 October 2001, when he went on record with an even stronger warning: "God help us from Satan," he wrote in a widely read column referring to 'Usamah bin Ladin, calling him "a rotten seed like the son of Noah, . . . [which] the flood will engulf . . . like it engulfed him."[66] On 5 November 2011, Prince Turki spoke on Sa'udi television debunking incredulous religious men who asked for evidence to link bin Ladin with some of the deeds he was alleged to have committed. Like a skilled exegetist who has mastered every word he utters, in a carefully weighed interpretation Prince Turki insisted that the religious edicts issued by bin Ladin were the main evidence for his guilt because they called for attacking American soldiers and civilians. "Only those people devoid of feelings will still ask for evidence," because "those who still call for evidence are closing their eyes to the facts and are searching for justification of [bin Ladin's] acts," concluded the Prince.[67]

The preoccupation with 9/11 notwithstanding, Prince Turki's primary concern was the Israeli occupation and the fate that befell Palestinians following the events of 1948 [though it is also true that he supported King 'Abdallah's 2001 League of Arab States peace initiative, which contemplated normalization of ties with Israel in exchange for a full withdrawal to the 1967 borders]. Like most Arabs, he lamented the policy of successive American administrations toward the Middle East, in particular their concerned support for Israel and apparent callousness towards Palestinians, insisting that that country's nuclear weapons posed genuine security threats to the entire region. Consequently, Prince Turki called on President Barack Obama not just to talk the talk but also to "walk the walk" on the two-state solution for Palestine and Israel, even if Washington displayed little interest in the decaying dispute.[68] As an aside, but one indicative of the man's character, Prince Turki made a point of shaking hands with the Israeli Deputy Foreign Minister Danny Ayalon at the February 2010 Munich Security Conference after Ayalon declaimed that "the person from a certain country with a lot of oil refused to sit on the same panel with me," a

---

[66] Turki al-Faysal, "Hazihi Hasilat Fasadak" [This is the Harvest of your Corruption], *Al-Sharq Al-Awsat*, Number 8355, 13 October 2001, at http://www.aawsat.com/leader.asp?section=3&issueno=8355&article=61383&search=%CA%D1%DF%ED%20%C7%E1%DD%ED%D5%E1&state=true.

[67] Quoted in Jamal Khashoggi, "Kingdom has Big Role to Play in Afghanistan," *Arab News*, 4 November 2001, at http://www.arabnews.com/node/215982.

[68] Abeer Alam, "Saudi Prince Criticises US Mideast Policy, *The Financial Times*, 17 May 2010, at http://www.ft.com/intl/cms/s/0/127c5c0c-60fe-11df-9bf0-00144feab49a.html.

remark which clearly touched a nerve. Prince Turki did not take kindly to the erroneous assertion that “the Kingdom of Saudi Arabia, with all its wealth, has not given a penny to the Palestinian Authority,” and responded by stating that he did not object to sitting on the same panel with Ayalon because the latter was an Israeli diplomat but because of Ayalon’s “boorish conduct with the Turkish ambassador to Israel, Ahmet Oğuz Çelikkol.” When Ayalon asked the Prince to come up to the podium to shake hands and show that there were no hard feelings, Prince Turki retorted that the Israeli “should step down from the podium and come” towards him, which duly occurred; when the two men were standing “face-to-face . . . [Ayalon] apologized for what he had said and [Turki] replied that [he] accepted his apology not only to [him] but also to the Turkish ambassador.”[69]

On 26 May 2014, the German Marshall Fund of the United States (GMF) hosted a public panel discussion in Brussels between Prince Turki and General Amos Yadlin, a former Israeli head of military intelligence who became the Director of the Institute for National Security Studies in Tel Aviv. The conversation addressed the most pressing foreign and security policy issues that faced leading countries in the Middle East, including the future of the Middle East Peace Process, the impact of a potentially nuclear Iran on the region, and the conflict in Syria, all of which illustrated the lengths to which Sa‘udi officials were willing to go to reach a permanent peace.[70]

Faithful to his late father’s legacy, this powerbroker assumed additional duties at the King Faysal Foundation, where he served as the Chairman of the King Faysal Center for Research and Islamic Studies, a top-notch institution in the Sa‘udi capital.[71] Prince Turki married Nuf bint Fahd bin Khalid Al Sa‘ud, who gave him six children: Masha‘il, Nurah, Faysal, Mudhi, ‘Abdul ‘Aziz, and Sa‘ud. A soft-spoken and deliberate individual who values discretion and loyalty, Prince Turki applied

[69] In January 2010, Ayalon made a show of publicly humiliating Çelikkol, to demonstrate displeasure with a Turkish television show critical of Israel, by sitting the Turk on a lower chair while his own was so highly placed that it suggested a form of false superiority. In the event, Prince Turki further refuted Ayalon’s mistaken claim that Sa‘udi Arabia was miserly in supporting the Palestinian Authority (PA). See “Handshake Israeli Apology to Saudi: Prince Turki,” *Al Arabiya*, 7 February 2010, at http://www.alarabiya.net/articles/2010/02/07/99646.html.

[70] For the full video features, see The German Marshall Fund of the United States, “Former Intelligence Heads of Israel/Saudi Arabia Debate—Brussels,” 26 May 2014, at http://www.gmfus.org/israel-and-the-middle-east-seeking-common-ground/.

[71] As stated in the Introduction, and as a full disclosure, the author joined the King Faysal Center for Research and Islamic Studies as a Senior Fellow in October 2013, after this book was already completed.

the teachings he received at home and from the Jesuits at Georgetown. In his own words: "I am lucky to have received the most formidable arsenal any person can dream of having with two of the best educations available, the Islamic and the Catholic," which, collectively, have confirmed his deep faith in God.[72] As a devout believer, he certainly lived up to his parents' teachings, even if his duty towards his nation extracted the kind of sacrifices that Riyadh demanded from few of its sons or daughters.

Lulwah al-Faysal

One of the most publicly visible female members of the Al Sa'ud ruling family, Princess Lulwah al-Faysal was privately tutored during the first few years of her life in Ta'if, though her mother felt no imperative to enroll her in the Model School for Girls.[73] As will be discussed in Chapter 3, the Model School for Girls experiment led to the creation of permanent institutions that looked after female education, though the Princess was eventually enrolled in a high school in Lausanne, Switzerland. That is where she learned French and English, two languages she has mastered, in addition to her native Arabic and near-native Turkish. What she learned in Switzerland seldom compared with what she learned from her parents, however, including the ability to hold a conversation without fear and to entertain critical opinions. Unlike princesses who enrolled in boarding schools with their nannies, Princess Lulwah learned how to make reservations to take her showers, and though the first few months were not pleasant for the eleven year-old, she soon learned to cope.

In a candid conversation, the Princess recalled how the first thing her mother would insist upon when she returned home during school breaks was that she take a Turkish bath. "My mother was a stickler for hygiene and she wanted us to be well groomed, well dressed, and well behaved. She wanted us to emulate her in every way possible," the Princess contended.[74] Inasmuch as her mother would try to use her persuasive skills to get the youngsters to do certain things, Princess Lulwah al-Faysal was sure that her failures would be temporary, as the Queen knew that none of the children could turn down their father and they would always try to excel. Faysal was, in certain ways, the future Queen's indispensable promoter-in-chief, and all of the children learned

---

72 Interview with HRH Prince Turki al-Faysal, Riyadh, 30 March 2011.

73 There are several spellings in print for the name of the Princess, including Lolowah bint Faisal and Loulwa Al-Faisal, although the academic transliteration followed in this volume renders it as Lulwah al-Faysal.

74 Interview with HRH Princess Lulwah al-Faysal, Jiddah, 17 October 2010.

that early on. Princess Lulwah married one of her cousins, Sa'ud bin 'Abdul Muhsin bin 'Abdul 'Aziz, but the relationship lasted no more than a decade.[75] She had three children from that marriage—Nuhah, Nurah, and Faysal—which prompted her to become a prominent activist for women's education and other social issues as she dedicated her life to improving existing conditions. Starting in 1970, for example, she played a leading role in the al-Nahdah Philanthropic Society for Women (discussed in detail in Chapter 4).

A year after King Faysal passed away, Princess Lulwah and her siblings established the King Faysal Foundation, to invest in concrete projects that improved lives in the Kingdom and in as many Muslim countries as possible. Though Princess Lulwah assumed the presidency and chairmanship of the Board of Trustees of the al-Maharat Cognitive and Skill Development Center in Jiddah starting in 1994, most of her attention was devoted to education, which was also her mother's favorite area of engagement. Encouraged by Queen 'Iffat, Princess Lulwah was elevated to Vice-Chair of the *Dar Al-Hanan* school. Simultaneously, she held the position of General Supervisor. After 1999, she started her service on the Board of Trustees of Effat College, where she still serves as Vice Chair of the Board of Founders as well as the Board of Trustees, and fulfills the demanding role of General Supervisor. For a full decade before Effat College was formally inaugurated, the Princess was the late Queen's assistant as they both supervised *Dar Al-Hanan* and prepared the college for its soon-to-be-changed role. As the Queen's health deteriorated, it fell on the Princess to carry the heavy burden, especially between 1997 and 1999, when she headed the planning committee for the Effat College Project.

Princess Lulwah was the Head of the Higher Women Committee set up to support Kuwaiti families in the aftermath of the 1990 Iraqi invasion and occupation of the Shaykhdom, which further awakened her to additional regional and global responsibilities. She allowed herself to be photographed for the first time in 2005, which projected the image of a genuine decision maker at once traditional and modernizing, someone who was at ease in the East just as much as the West. In fact, in her capacity as a super-ambassador as well as a frequent participant in global conferences, Princess Lulwah has seldom shied away from given presentations on Sa'udi Arabia and, in a style that emulated her late father, of answering impromptu questions from her audiences. With the backing of her brothers, especially Foreign Minister Sa'ud al-Faysal and Ambassador Turki al-Faysal, Princess Lulwah has represented her

[75] HRH Prince Sa'ud bin 'Abdul Muhsin bin 'Abdul 'Aziz was appointed Governor of Ha'il Province in 1999 and continues to serve in that post.

country at various international forums. For example, she has served as a member of the Committee of International Trade of the Sa'udi Chambers of Commerce and Industries and, in 2006, led a delegation of Sa'udi businesswomen to Hong Kong at a time when King 'Abdallah bin 'Abdul 'Aziz was forging a new policy towards China. On several occasions, she has participated in Sa'udi trade missions abroad, and accompanied senior members of the ruling family—meaning the ruler or the heir apparent—on sensitive diplomatic travels as was the case in 2005 when the then heir apparent, 'Abdallah, went to Crawford, Texas to meet with President George W. Bush.[76] These were demanding trips that necessitated preparation and coordination with both the Palace and the Ministry of Foreign Affairs. In fact, she was briefed on sensitive dossiers before embarking on these trips, precisely so that she could address whatever questions arose from a position of knowledge.[77] Towards that end, while the courtesy was extended to other members of the ruling family who were similarly tasked, the tradition bodes well for the Al Sa'ud.

Princess Lulwah delivered several addresses on the advancement of Muslim women and lamented conditions in her country that limited their potential. During a public session at the 2007 World Economic Forum in Davos, Switzerland, for example, she spoke out against the ban on driving for women in the Kingdom, expressing the hope that women would one day drive in Sa'udi Arabia, which some interpreted as "a rare and direct challenge to the driving ban imposed by the Kingdom's ruling male elite."[78] To be sure, her comments were frank and on the record, but she was pragmatic in insisting that the alternative was to create an effective transportation system that the vast country did not currently possess. In other words, though her comments reflected the frustration that millions of Sa'udi women feel, and while most of the media was interested in her views on women driving because it was—and is—rare that members of the ruling family speak in public or in front of the media on this subject, she did not call for a decision by fiat. Rather, though she had never before publicly pushed for an end to the driving ban, she nevertheless insisted that it be done legally, not haphazardly in an attempt to defy the state.

---

[76] Saudi–US Relations Information Service (SUSRIS), "Building Bridges: A Conversation with Princess Loulwa Al-Faisal," 2 June 2005, at http://www.susris.com/2005/06/02/building-bridges-a-conversation-with-princess-loulwa-al-faisal-2/.

[77] This information was confirmed by HRH Khalid bin Sa'ud bin Khalid Al Sa'ud, the Deputy Minister of Foreign Affairs, Riyadh, 27 October 2010.

[78] Sally Buzbeen, "Saudi Princess Would Let Women Drive," *The Washington Post*, 25 January 2007, at http://www.washingtonpost.com/wp-dyn/content/ article/2007/ 01/25/ AR2007012500929_pf.html.

Princess Lulwah's 2007 appearance at Davos was remarkable for another reason, and it is important in this context to emphasize her contributions to critical global conversations. During a session discussing the promotion of religious tolerance, she shared the podium with the former Iranian President, Mohammad Khatami; the Prime Minister of Malaysia, 'Abdallah Ahmad Badawi; the Head of the International Jewish Committee for Inter-Religious Relations, Orthodox Rabbi David Rose; the President of Georgetown University, John J. DeGioia; an American cleric who was the editor of *Sojourners*, Jim Wallis; and the then French Minister of the Budget and State Reform, Jean-François Copé.[79] The fact that she offered useful recommendations and carried herself with poise among such a distinguished list of interlocutors highlighted her intrinsic capabilities. Naturally, as a speaker who had mastered her subject rather well, her advocacy was to be expected but only insofar as it helped underprivileged individuals. During the 2008 World Economic Forum Annual Meeting, she chaired the working session, "What Kind of Education for What Kind of World?," delivering a presentation that focused on the philosophy of education. Year after year, she concentrated on critical topics that sought gently to persuade her audiences to entertain different opinions, without neglecting her core advocacies advancing the rights of Sa'udi women. Much like her mother, Princess Lulwah lamented the misconceptions about Sa'udi women in the West, while insisting that Muslim women were accorded equal rights even if these were not necessarily the same rights as men enjoyed.

In 2003, Princess Lulwah was the keynote speaker at the London Middle East Institute Conference held at the London School of Oriental and African Studies (SOAS), where she spoke on redefining roles for women in the Gulf region. She revisited the topic at the Jiddah Economic Forum in 2003, and touched upon the theme at various other venues, almost always emphasizing the role of education in improving basic conditions. Importantly, she underscored the necessity to educate both men and women, since it was essential, she concluded, to include men in any scheme intended to improve women's welfare. As part of her work for Effat University, Princess Lulwah received an honorary degree from Mount Holyoke College in 2009, further illustrating the esteem in which she is held.

What troubled her were repeated questions on the lack of opportunities for women in the Kingdom: "Well, if [critics] were to listen only to the media they would think that the women in Saudi Arabia are

[79] See the Princess's intervention at the Davos Annual Meeting 2007, panel on "Rules for a Global Neighbourhood," available on *YouTube* at http://www.youtube.com/watch?v=hMkGBPy8sQk.

completely suppressed, not educated, and don't have any jobs. The reality is that while education started for men in 1960, it started for women just two years later in 1962. Actually, prior to the start of the Ministry of Education there already were schools for women, private schools, including *Dar-Al-Hanan* which my mother [Queen Effat] opened in 1955." She continued: "You should also know that at that point in our history we were a country of 5% literacy and at the moment we're a country of 5% illiteracy. That shows how far we have come in just seventy years—even less if you consider that formal education started 50 years ago." The Princess was bewildered to receive questions that literally wondered whether women had any rights in Sa'udi Arabia, though she cheerfully answered them since she firmly believed that it was her duty to elucidate: "It's not just Americans who are not familiar with these facts. We're asked about the same things in other places too. I don't know why. Now I'm not saying that we're angels or perfect—there are some families that are stricter with women. However, education for women has never been taboo since it was accepted in 1962. From the moment the public schools opened for women they have never closed down." That was a unique testament, in a way, to her mother's achievements, but also to her own.

Hayfah al-Faysal

Princess Hayfah al-Faysal was born in Paris, France, and as the youngest member of the al-Faysal family may be said to represent the link between 'Iffat's children and several of her grandchildren. Although Princess Hayfah and her husband, Prince Bandar bin Sultan bin 'Abdul 'Aziz, have eight children of their own—Lulwah, Rimah, Khalid, Faysal, Nurah, Fahd, Hussah, and 'Abdul 'Aziz—she stands out in the hierarchy on account of her different upbringing and, more importantly, because she lived a significant portion of her life in the United States where her husband earned advanced degrees and served as Ambassador between 1983 and 2005. In a 2003 interview with Elsa Walsh, the Princess recounted how she first met her husband and the feeling she had before they were married, especially since 'Iffat Al Thunayan and Hassah bint Ahmad Al Sudayri, Bandar's grandmother and protégée, probably discussed compatibilities. The two women liked each other but also ensured that appropriate introductions were made between their offspring.[80] In the event, Hayfah married Bandar in 1972, and followed him to the US where the Prince was enrolled at the Johns Hopkins School of Advanced International Studies. To his credit, Prince Bandar used his

---

[80] Elsa Walsh, "The Prince: How the Saudi Ambassador Became Washington's Indispensable Operator," *The New Yorker*, 24 March 2003, pp. 48–63.

technical knowledge to assist his brother-in-law Prince Turki al-Faysal, the then Chief of Intelligence who was dispatched by the ruler to Washington to lobby for the sale of F-15s to the Kingdom. His performance was duly noted by Prince Turki as well as both King Khalid and heir apparent Fahd. Shortly thereafter, Bandar was appointed Ambassador to the United States, earning the support of political elites across the board.[81]

While Bandar was busy serving his country in the US, which required frequent travels back and forth to the Kingdom, Hayfah raised the children. According to their fourth son, Faysal bin Bandar, the children can be divided into three distinct groups, the four "originals" who grew up together when their father was an active-duty air force pilot in the Kingdom, the next four who became known as the "substitutes" or the "replacements" because they were raised in Washington, D.C., and two adopted children who played important roles in the couple's lives.[82] In many ways, this was a truly Sa'udi-American family, with roots in both cultures that explained not only Prince Bandar's political knowhow but also reinforced Princess Hayfah's credentials. That she could raise her children in two cultures which differed from each other in so many ways, and that she could do it with some success, is credit to her immense skills, especially when she was often left to look after them when her husband was otherwise occupied with his political duties. An attractive individual at ease in Sa'udi Arabia just as much as in the West, Princess Hayfah has drawn succor from her own mother, whose courage was contagious to all those who interacted with her. Much like Queen 'Iffat, Princess Hayfah's priorities have centered around her family, though she has also learned to serve the community at large through various charities. As the Chairperson of the Zahra Breast Cancer Association in Sa'udi Arabia, the Princess wanted to increase awareness of this devastating disease. In

---

[81] For two worthwhile discussions on Prince Bandar bin Sultan, see William Simpson, *The Prince: The Secret Story of the World's Most Intriguing Royal—Prince Bandar bin Sultan*, New York: Harper, 2006; and David B. Ottaway, *The King's Messenger: Prince Bandar bin Sultan and America's Tangled Relationship with Saudi Arabia*, New York: Walker & Company, 2008.

[82] William Simpson, a friend of the family who interviewed several of the couple's children, attributed this description to Faysal bin Bandar. The ten included the following eight natural-born offspring: Lulwah (b. 9/1973), Rimah (b. 6/1975), Khalid (b. 7/1977), Faysal (b. 10/1980), Nurah (b. 9/1984), Fahd (b. 7/1987), Hussah (b. 4/1993), and 'Abdul 'Aziz (b. 8/1994). In addition, Hayfah and Bandar adopted Salmah, the daughter of a couple working for them, both of whom passed away while Salmah was still young. Jan Garcia was also adopted by Bandar although that adoption was arranged so that the young woman could marry Bob Lilac, who was then working for the Prince in the Kingdom. See Simpson, *op. cit.*, pp. 373–381.

addition to sponsoring regular conferences, members of the association embarked on widespread campaigns in schools, universities, shopping malls, and mosques, where volunteers spoke regularly with women about the importance of early detection and getting regular mammograms to detect breast cancer tumors. By tackling this taboo subject, Princess Hayfah demonstrates how she has been able to apply the legacy of the late Queen 'Iffat, who wanted Sa'udi women to educate themselves in every possible way.

Naturally, supporting a worthy charity or generously giving assistance when individuals have asked for it can also complicate life. In the aftermath of the 9/11 attacks in the United States in 2001, when the ambassadorial couple were serving in Washington, D.C., allegations emerged that Princess Hayfah provided financial assistance to a Sa'udi national by the name of 'Umar al-Bayumi who, in turn, helped two of the hijackers upon their arrival in the San Diego area in California. Despite later investigations revealing that al-Bayumi was a Sa'udi intelligence asset, there was no evidence that Princess Hayfah al-Faysal provided financial assistance to 'Umar al-Bayumi. Thorough investigations confirmed that some payments were in fact made in April 1998 to 'Usamah Basnan, a Sa'udi national living in Southern California who apparently wrote to the Ambassador's wife requesting aid for his wife's surgery. The Princess sent Basnan several checks—the disputed totals ranged between $51,000 and $73,000—although his wife, Majidah Dwiqat, was not actually treated for the thyroid operation for another two years. Incredibly, Majidah Dwiqat signed some of these checks over to her friend Manal Bajadr, the wife of 'Umar al-Bayumi. This convoluted relationship was obviously critical and in the frenzied search for culprits, federal investigators in the United States conducted intrusive banking searches to link dots and show, if possible, alleged Al Sa'ud family support to the 9/11 hijackers. The *Final Report of the National Commission on Terrorist Attacks Upon the United States*, more commonly known as the 9/11 Commission Report, concluded that while Sa'udi Arabia was long "considered the primary source of al Qaeda funding, . . . no evidence [was found] that the Saudi government as an institution or senior Saudi officials individually funded the organization."[83] What was more interesting was the footnote that followed this sentence, which read: "David Aufhauser interview (Feb. 12, 2004). *We have found no evidence that Saudi Princess Haifa al Faisal provided any funds to the conspiracy, either directly or indirectly*. See Adam Drucker

[83] *The 9/11 Commission Report: Final Report of the National Commission on Terrorist Attacks Upon the United States*, New York: W.W. Norton & Company, [2004], p. 171.

interview (May 19, 2004)."[84] Notwithstanding this exoneration, the Princess was perturbed and, according to a Sa'udi daily, "became 'so terrified' that she asked that all checks drawn against her bank account with the Riggs Bank in Washington DC since 1994 be examined."[85] Of course, declarations that Princess Hayfah's gifts were simply an act of Muslim charity, better known as *zakat* and which is an obligation especially when one is able to extend a hand, fell on deaf ears. Many other Sa'udi nationals living outside the Kingdom who required and requested aid were routinely assisted. In fact, there was nothing particularly unusual in the help extended to a husband seeking financial aid for his wife's operation, a tradition that was well established in the Faysal household, indeed throughout the vast Al Sa'ud realm. Simply stated, what Princess Hayfah did—to the extent that she was aware of any transfers that were made in her name—was to extend a financial hand, as she and members of her family did to countless others over the years. In that sense she carried on the legacy of her parents, especially her mother whose generosity was universally acclaimed while she was alive, as amply documented in the countless charities she sponsored and that continue to flourish well after her passing away.

FAMILY, FRIENDS, AND ACQUAINTANCES

Even if Queen 'Iffat found herself relatively isolated when she first arrived in Makkah, her innate skill at making friends clearly carried her through many difficulties, with several individuals recalling how she managed socially. Of course, among all of King 'Abdul 'Aziz's wives, Hassah bint Ahmad al-Sudayri stood out as her closest friend, a congenial individual and someone who valued the "*Turkiyyah*'s" intrinsic class. Princess Hassah, whose sons Fahd, Sultan, 'Abdul Rahman, Turki, Nayif, Salman, and Ahmad dominated Al Sa'ud family politics like few subgroups have, had known that 'Iffat would live up to her Al Sa'ud credentials. Her Al Thunayan pedigree was as authentic as that of any other Al Sa'ud member, supplemented by the broad-based experience she

[84] The 9/11 Commission Report, *ibid.*, p. 498, footnote 122. It was unclear whether David D. Aufhauser (U.S. Treasury Department), or Adam B. Drucker (FBI), originated the quote but the direct reference to Princess Hayfah was printed in black and white.

[85] Nimrod Raphaeli, "Financing of Terrorism: Sources, Methods, and Channels," *Terrorism and Political Violence* 15:4, Winter 2003, pp. 59–82, the quotes, attributed to *Al-Riyadh* daily newspaper, are on pages 72–73.

had gained as a teenager in Constantinople, then still the center of the Muslim universe. Furthermore, Princess Hassah appreciated what the young 'Iffat represented to the growing family and, rather than shun her, welcomed her openly.[86] Inasmuch as both Fahd and Sultan were Faysal's allies, as well as loyal lieutenants at the Ministries of the Interior and Defense, the rapprochement was even closer than many assumed. In fact, Fahd and Sultan were regular visitors to Faysal's home, and shared family meals, which meant sitting down at the same table with 'Iffat since the Princess made it a habit to open her table to family members and, rather than feed the men separately, ensured that in her house both men and women sat together to break bread. Not surprisingly, both Fahd and Sultan, among others, were regular visitors to 'Iffat's home after Faysal was assassinated in 1975. They consulted the Queen on a variety of subjects and valued her advice and friendship. Like their mother, Princess Hassah, both Princes Fahd and Sultan made it a point to ensure that Queen 'Iffat was shown the respect she had earned within the family after her husband was gunned down instead of simply being looked after like the vast majority of Sa'udi princesses. They were fully conscious of her unique role and demonstrated time and again that 'Iffat Al Thunayan had earned her credentials.

Back in the 1930s, several other princesses had also welcomed 'Iffat, though not at the beginning. It would be an understatement to say that the young Princess was somewhat lonely and this encouraged Faysal to favor her request that the rest of her family in Turkey should quickly return home, too. Among the individuals who made the voyage home and who left an impact both on her life as well as that of the Kingdom was the future Queen's brother, Kamal Adham.

Kamal Adham: The Cherished Brother

Queen 'Iffat's Turkish-born half-brother was raised into manhood by King Faysal. Kamal Adham was born in 1929 in Istanbul to a Turkish mother and an Albanian father who took him to Jiddah when the toddler was one year old. He attended Victoria College in Cairo at about the same time as King Hussayn of Jordan, future Jordanian Prime Minister Zaid al-Rifai, Sa'udi businessman Adnan Khashoggi, and the actor Omar Sharif. The young Kamal excelled in school and attended Cambridge University in Britain. An early companion of the future ruler, Adham achieved more than was expected of a family member, even if his upbringing had endowed him with undeniable attributes. He entered into the Al Sa'ud inner circles, but relied on his innate intelligence to advance, aware that utmost loyalty was his destiny. An astute businessman,

---

[86] Lacey, *op. cit.*, p. 345.

Adham became a multimillionaire in 1957, when he brokered an offshore oil concession between the Kingdom and Japan's Arabian Oil Company.

A handsome man—the product of his father's Albanian origins—Adham was a debonair individual who shared with his sister the love of country and service to the crown. His primary interest in life was the promotion and protection of Sa'udi Arabia, especially King Faysal, as he worked diligently to execute every task entrusted to him. Devoted to both his sister and brother-in-law, the young Adham, who was fluent in four languages—Arabic, Turkish, English, and French—proved to be an ideal asset and, while he went straight into business after Victoria College with several Lebanese and Egyptian friends, his value to the monarchy increased over time. His business empire started small, as he built the first bottling plant for 7-Up in Sa'udi Arabia, but he quickly moved on to other businesses that, eventually, became a conglomerate.

Kamal Adham was very close to King Faysal, and advised the ruler on the Kingdom's foreign policy interests, and thus he was the obvious choice when the ruler decided at the height of the Arab Cold War that the country needed a foreign intelligence service. At a time when severe internal disputes polarized the Al Sa'ud, the loyal Adham could be trusted to perform this responsibility, mixing his role as businessman with these official duties. By all accounts, this intelligent man almost single-handedly created the Foreign Liaison Bureau and acted as a contact between the King and key Western intelligence services. More importantly, he was one of the few men Faysal trusted completely, as the two of them went about shaping the history of the Middle East in ways that were not well understood at the time, though many commentators now acknowledge the impact Adham had on critical events. Indeed, he fostered and maintained nascent ties with several Arab intelligence services, most successfully with his Egyptian counterparts, allowing him to engineer the 1967 Faysal–Nasir reconciliation. His prowess was such that, according to William Powell, "in the 1970s, not without some boastful exaggeration, . . . little happened in [the Israeli intelligence] Mossad, without Kamal Adham's knowing about it within twenty-four hours."[87]

It is nearly impossible to recount the full range of Kamal Adham's numerous intelligence exploits, but several episodes do deserve attention for the way they illustrate the trust King Faysal placed in his brother-in-law. Faysal encouraged Adham to maintain close associations with Egyptian President Anwar al-Sadat and other senior Cairenese officials. These proved to be exceptionally valuable in ways that are made clear in

---

[87] William Powell, *Saudi Arabia and Its Royal Family*, Secaucus, New Jersey: Lyle Stuart, Inc., 1982, pp. 268–269.

the succeeding paragraph, and are a major reason why he enjoyed such a high reputation with the ruler [even if his involvement in the multifaceted and complicated 1977–1978 Bank of Credit and Commerce International scandal, which involved several Western figures as well as established officials in Abu Dhabi and other United Arab Emirates Shaykhdoms, subsequently tarnished that reputation].[88]

Like most young men who grew up in the Arab World in the 1950s, Kamal Adham was a great admirer of Jamal [Gamal] 'Abdul Nasir of Egypt. But after Nasir pretty much telegraphed his desire to overthrow the Sa'udi monarchy, Adham became disillusioned with the Egyptian leader.[89] Throughout the 1960s and early 1970s, when Sa'udi Arabia was faced with the Nasir challenge, Riyadh responded to the rising wave of Arab nationalism by emphasizing core Islamic values, which were the basic foundations of its foreign policy. Rejecting both secularism and socialism, for example, King Faysal supported Yemeni tribes who favored the monarchy and, in the aftermath of the 1967 Arab–Israeli War, sought a rapprochement with Egypt to end the Arab Cold War (1957–1967). The man entrusted with this strategy was Adham, who by then had established a valuable friendship with Vice President Sadat. Adham further encouraged Sadat after the latter became President in 1970, especially in the aftermath of the 1973 war, the response to which called for bold political initiatives. Adham's personal investments with Sadat paid off handsomely as he became an unofficial advisor to the new Egyptian President, and in turn the two men—with King Faysal's full knowledge and support—worked closely with Washington to oust the Russians from Egypt.

---

[88] It is important to note in this context that while senior American officials, including influential Bush family members, have always downplayed their intimate ties to the Al Sa'ud, well-informed observers have been incredulous. According to two well-placed writers, when George H.W. Bush was questioned by Congress on the issue and denied any knowledge of Adham, few believed him: "Adham had been the director of Saudi Arabia's equivalent of the CIA in 1976, when George [H.W.] Bush headed the CIA. The American agency had been helping to modernize Saudi intelligence during Bush's tenure, and Kamal had been Saudi Arabia's main liaison with the CIA. Even without that connection, the chances were slim to none that George Bush, who was known throughout the Middle East as 'the Saudi Vice President,' and had more first-hand knowledge of the Middle East than any previous US president, didn't know the Sheikh. 'Flat impossible,' State Department and intelligence sources told Beaty. Kamal Adham had been a main man in Saudi Arabia for the past two decades, whether you were making business deals or policy." See Jonathan Beaty and S.C. Gwynne, *The Outlaw Bank: A Wild Ride Into the Secret Heart of BCCI*, New York: Random House, 1993, p. 275.

[89] Kéchichian, *op. cit.*, pp. 57–74.

Sadat needed peace to relieve the pressure that military spending placed on the Egyptian economy, though he also desperately needed assurances that whatever steps he took with the United States and Israel would not isolate him. It was likewise important that his bold initiatives should not increase Egypt's economic vulnerability in the Arab world. When Jimmy Carter made Sadat specific promises, the contemporary Pharaoh knew that Washington would almost automatically side with Israel, which was why Cairo sought meaningful assurances from its Arab allies. Less well known were the Sa'udi intelligence chief's subsequent resourceful negotiations with hesitant Arab leaders who perceived Sadat's actions with reservation.

His Egyptian accomplishments notwithstanding, at about the same time Adham was mired in the Bank of Credit and Commerce International (BCCI) scandal, accused of playing a key role in the secret and illegal takeover of the "First American" bank. In 1992, with prosecutors identifying his complicity as a BCCI front man in the United States, Adham pleaded guilty under a plea bargain. He cooperated with U.S. law enforcement investigations, was fined $105m, but received a suspended sentence.[90] Over the years, Adham had befriended several of Washington's most powerful men, including Clark Clifford, the former Defense Secretary under Lyndon Johnson and a prominent attorney for BCCI, as well as Robert Altman, a lawyer representing President Carter's

---

90 Although there may have been a link between the two, few acknowledged a linkage, and fewer commented on the Sa'udi's motivations. In the event, the John Kerry Senate Committee Report that delved into BCCI concluded that "Adham was at the same time in business with a retired CIA station chief [Raymond H. Close] whose activities caused people in the U.S. and Saudi governments to question whether he was truly 'retired,' acting as an intermediary for the U.S. in negotiations regarding Camp David, and acting as a phony 'lead shareholder' in a take-over of the largest bank in the nation's capital on behalf of BCCI." The bank in question was First American, and Close, who was the CIA's station chief in Sa'udi Arabia for years, chose immediately to work for Adham upon leaving the CIA in 1977. What their relationships were and how much coordination existed between Adham and Close are impossible to determine. Suffice it to say, as Jeff Gerth reported in *The New York Times*, that former US Government officials confirmed that Raymond H. Close, while serving in the CIA and since retirement, was often clouded in mystery. Gerth believed that Close was still working for the CIA in some capacity, although he officially retired in 1977, which added to the confusion since some Sa'udis privately shared the same perception. See John Kerry and Hank Brown, *The BCCI Affair: A Report to the Committee on Foreign Relations*, Washington, D.C.: United States Senate, 102d Congress 2d Session, Senate Print 102–140, December 1992, p. 292; see also Jeff Gerth, "C.I.A. Reported to Have Used Bank That Regulators Seized," *The New York Times*, 13 July 1991, at http://www.nytimes.com/1991/07/13/business/cia-reported-to-have-used-bank-that-regulators-seized.html.

Director of the Office of Management and Budget, Bert Lance. Regrettably, these men were also implicated in the BCCI scandal, among others. Adham was on intimate speaking terms with President Carter and his Director of Central Intelligence, Admiral Stansfield Turner, but he protected them throughout the investigation. No matter how convoluted some of Washington's policy initiatives were, including supporting the Mujahhidin in Afghanistan after the 1979 Soviet invasion and occupation of that troubled state, first and foremost Adham remained loyal to crown and country and always kept senior family members fully appraised of what he was doing on their behalf.[91] Of course, he only acted whenever called upon to do so, with Riyadh's complete approval.

Though few pictures exist of Kamal Adham, press accounts from the late 1970s refer to him as the "godfather of Middle East intelligence," which misleadingly carries a negative connotation. In fact, while he maintained close ties with several Western and Arab intelligence agencies, Adham was far more than a liaison. He served the Kingdom of Sa'udi Arabia and its rulers with distinction, often carrying out delicate missions that may well have involved questionable financial deals, but always with the aim of advancing intrinsic Sa'udi and, indirectly, Arab interests. As *Washington Post* journalist Bob Woodward once described it, "relations between the CIA and the Saudi intelligence service were generally good, going back to the days when the legendary and enormously wealthy Kamal Adham had been its head."[92] Woodward further opined that "in 1970, the Saudis had provided then Egyptian Vice President Sadat with a regular income," and while "it was impossible to determine where Saudi interests in these arrangements ended and American CIA interests began," he concluded that Adham played a critical role in bringing the two sides closer to each other. Like the roles given to other intelligence officers, Kamal Adham's responsibilities in Sa'udi and Arab history were discreet, not only because he practiced the quintessence of behind-the-scenes politics but also because he actually believed that genuine leaders needed to rely on trusted aides who might sometimes be called upon to take the fall for their leaders' policy choices. It was in this tradition that

---

[91] Ironically, though George H.W. Bush—who was CIA Director before he became the 41st President of the United States—once denied even knowing Kamal Adham, the Sa'udi never turned his back on his allies. He acknowledged that Washington had helped to modernize Sa'udi intelligence during Bush's tenure and, in exchange, Adham facilitated American–Pakistani contacts at the height of the Cold War. Suffice it to say that Adham played a key role that further explained what a valuable person he was for the Al Sa'ud. See Beaty and Gwynne, *op. cit.*, p. 275.

[92] Bob Woodward, *Veil: The Secret Wars of the CIA, 1981–1987*, New York: Simon & Schuster 1987, p. 347.

Adham sacrificed his standing as he attended to his nation's core interests. Perhaps the greatest compliment that Kamal Adham could have received was to be replaced by Prince Turki al-Faysal, the son of the monarch and a close ally.

Over the years, much has been written about Kamal Adham and the alleged business deals that allowed him to acquire a respectable fortune. Inevitably, rumors reached King Faysal, who protected his brother-in-law not only because he was family but also because he knew how valuable his work was. When in 1961, for example, 'Abdallah Tariki, the Kingdom's Oil Minister, heard that Adham had guaranteed a concession to Taro Yamashita, Chairman of the Japanese Petroleum Trading Company, who was ready to sign a major contract with Sa'udi Arabia, he was beside himself. During a subsequent cabinet meeting, Tariki launched an attack on Adham, which did not sit well with Faysal. According to available reports, Adham wished to secure a 2 percent commission from the Japanese that did not conform to the Oil Minister's business plans, though it is true to say that Tariki and his supporters did not understand the various standard maneuvers needed to secure such a contract. Faysal confronted his minister by asking him whether he had any proof for his allegations before moving on to other items on the cabinet's agenda. In the event, Faysal did not reveal his motives, though his style was such that he seldom betrayed his thinking. What is clear, however, is that beyond the Prime Minister's mistrust of Tariki—especially the latter's flamboyant presence on the international scene—lay what Faysal feared most: that "someone outside of the clan should be speaking so loudly on behalf of Saudi Arabia."[93] It is also clear that he protected Adham, whose business accords were tolerated because he, at least in Faysal's perception, acted as a valuable asset in so many areas for which he justifiably rewarded himself.

A well-known philanthropist, Adham made a significant donation to the Carter Center at Emory University and to the American University of Cairo (AUC). As a member of the AUC Board of Trustees, as well as the principal benefactor of the AUC "Adham Center for Television Journalism," the only institution that bears his name, Adham was also supportive of this body's media efforts. He encouraged young Arabs to acquire sophisticated television skills and argued that Arabs were responsible for writing their own history, even if circumstances required them to cooperate with competitors.[94] He also often reminded his own children

[93] Lacey, *op. cit.*, p. 340.

[94] In a moving eulogy delivered on 15 December 1999 by the Adham Center Director, 'Abdallah Schleifer, Shaykh Kamal Adham was remembered for his foresight and generosity. "His role in history was discreet," declared Schleifer, "not

that Sa'udi Arabia was their home and that it was the duty of every member to serve the Kingdom and its rulers. His motto was "Loyalty to the Al Sa'ud," and he was grateful to King Faysal as well as his sister for all that both had done for him and his family.[95] His son recalled the father's attachment to the Queen as someone who was "unbelievably protective of her" and who ensured that all of her private expenses, including her extensive travels after Faysal had passed away, were all handled by his private office. Kamal Adham himself passed away in Cairo on 29 October 1999, just a few months before his sister 'Iffat died in Riyadh, on 17 February 2000—" to prepare heaven for her and to look after her there too."[96]

Muzaffar Adham Rif'at: A Beloved Sister

A beloved sister of 'Iffat Al Thunayan, Mawarah Muzaffar Adham was an indispensable companion who, over the years, stood by the Queen through thick and thin. Practically raised by 'Iffat, Muzaffar grew up in Makkah and Jiddah and eventually married Dr. Sayyid 'Ali Rif'at, King Faysal's personal physician since 1959, who was part of the Egyptian community in the Hijaz. Their daughter, Halah Rif'at, recalled how her aunt doted on Muzaffar and her offspring. In fact, the Queen's sister was part of her permanent entourage and accompanied her on most of her travels. "We almost always traveled in large groups," reminisced Halah Rif'at, "which averaged about 25 to 30 persons. Khalti [My Aunt] was an inclusive individual and wanted her extended family to be part of her adventures. Though logistically cumbersome, we somehow made it to various restaurants, museums, plays or movies in Paris or London or wherever we went. In winter months, we all went to Megève [a ski-resort near Mont Blanc in the French Alps]; we were always on the go, discovering new places, which was exactly what the Queen enjoyed doing."[97]

'Iffat and Muzaffar were typical young women who enjoyed life to the fullest. A gramophone that played music, something that was truly rare in Makkah, was carefully hidden in a closet though both spent

---

simply because he practiced the quintessence of behind-the-scenes politics reflected by the rare number of photos of the Shaykh that exist in [the] public domain, but also because he was above all else an intrinsically modest man." The Director spoke of how Adham made possible various overtures, including his annual donations to the Center, as well as emergency subsidies to fund a variety of programs. See 'Abdallah Schleifer, "Adham Center Founder Sheikh Kamal Adham Remembered," Cairo, Egypt: American University of Cairo, 15 December 1999, at http://www.kpd-online.info/news/oldnews/sheikh.htm.

95 Interview with HE Shaykh Faysal Kamal Adham, Jiddah, 9 December 2010.

96 Interview with HE Shaykh Faysal Kamal Adham, Jiddah, 9 December 2010.

97 Interview with Halah Rif'at, Jiddah, 24 October 2010.

countless hours listening to it, dancing, and otherwise being teenagers. A relative confirmed that Muzaffar was an excellent dancer and actually enjoyed expressing her artistic talents, which the Queen appreciated and which allowed her own daughters to join in the festivities.[98] By her sheer presence next to the Queen, Muzaffar was the breath of fresh air that 'Iffat needed, especially during the first few years in Makkah. She died in Paris after a brief illness on 15 December 1984.

Ahmad 'Abdul Wahhab: The Embraced "Son"

Among the more prominent friends who truly made a difference to the lives of Faysal and 'Iffat stood Ahmad 'Abdul Wahhab, who hailed from a prominent Makkah family and whose ancestors were entrusted with the upkeep of the *Masjid Al-Haram* mosque. The role was a largely ceremonial position that imbued traditions, but the acknowledgment gave the 'Abdul Wahhabs a unique standing. Ahmad's father passed away when he was still young, so the young boy was literally adopted by Prince Faysal and Princess 'Iffat, who raised him as one of their own. A gregarious spirit who was immensely beholden to the royal couple, Ahmad often repeated the anecdote that professed to explain the origins of 'Iffat's title—how she came to be known as a "Queen." When her passport was apparently changed after King Faysal acceded to the throne, 'Umar al-Sakkaf, then Deputy Foreign Minister responsible for ruling family diplomatic paperwork, apparently asked Rashad Pharaon—then a retired minister who was still close to the late ruler—what to write and, according to Ahmad 'Abdul Wahhab, was told to write *malikah* (queen).[99] Several pages from her expired passports, reproduced in Appendix II, confirm that 'Iffat Al Thunayan was officially a "Queen."[100]

---

98 Interviews with HH Mansour Al Thunayan, Jiddah, 22 October 2010.

99 Interview with Ahmad 'Abdul Wahhab, Jiddah, 20 October 2010. Rashad Pharaon, born and trained in Syria, was the founder monarch's private physician starting in 1936. He enjoyed the confidence of Al Sa'ud family members and was eventually appointed Ambassador to France in 1947. In 1954, Dr. Pharaon became the Kingdom's first minister of health, was a senior delegate to the United States between 1963 and 1964 and, because of his widespread contacts, became a close advisor to Prince Faysal.

100 An examination of three separate passports confirmed that the Queen abided by local traditions not to have her photograph reproduced; that was also the case for the vast majority of Sa'udi women. In 2012, the Majlis al-Shurah accepted an official Ministry of the Interior request to change the law and henceforth demand that female citizens carry photos for security reasons, which meant that the need arose for these women to uncover their faces to female officers if they wore the *niqab*, to verify their identities. The Queen's passports revealed extensive travels; her preferred destinations were France, Switzerland, the United Kingdom, and the United States.

Still, while Ahmad 'Abdul Wahhab's anecdote has been repeated often enough, there is no evidence to support its assertion, even if it is interesting to note that King Faysal did not object when he heard that his spouse was referred to as a "Queen." In fact, if the passport story were accurate, few Sa'udis would have been privy to what was inscribed inside the Queen's travel documents, whereas she was widely referred to as Queen 'Iffat on account of both her open *majlises*, where she received any Sa'udi woman who wished to visit, and because she invested in the Jiddah office building that became known as the *'Imarat al-Malikah* [The Queen's Building]. Shaykh Ahmad confirmed that the tradition died with Faysal, and no first ladies were known as queens after 'Iffat—not because none deserved the title, but simply because none wished to assume as many responsibilities as Queen 'Iffat had taken on. Of course, many Sa'udi women are and have been influential, but, truth be told, only 'Iffat implemented a vision that dramatically improved the lives of so many men and women in Sa'udi Arabia. The passport story is entertaining, of course, but what distinguished 'Iffat was in giving the Ahmads of her nation the opportunity to partner with "educated women," precisely to eliminate what she perceived to be the weak link in her society.

Ahmad 'Abdul Wahhab was considered a part of the family, so naturally he traveled to Victoria College in Cairo with Kamal Adham and many others. Rather than pursue higher education, however, Ahmad embarked on a business career that built on his friendships and connections. Long before rollerdexes or electronic databases invaded privacies, Ahmad 'Abdul Wahhab was a genuine living Middle East networker who knew just about everyone—royals and commoners alike. His people skills were legendary and his storytelling capabilities unsurpassed. Trusted by both Prince Faysal and his spouse, Ahmad devoted a great deal of time to family affairs, looking after the girls in Lausanne or volunteering to keep the boys informed of their father's specific requests in New Jersey. In a way, Ahmad invented his own position within the Faysal household, becoming the Prince's Chief of Protocol, both within immediate family circles and, naturally, within his larger circle of contacts. It was but a small leap from that spot to becoming the ruler's official Chief of Protocol when Faysal's turn came to rule, even if no such "position" existed in reality. For nearly three decades, Ahmad 'Abdul Wahhab offered his loyal services to King Faysal and, after his death, to both Kings Khalid and Fahd. In a modest way, and without exaggeration, his presence in Faysal's household allowed this gifted and gregarious individual to excel in ways that even he seldom fathomed.

THE MAST OF THE NATION

At the King Faysal Foundation’s 20th anniversary celebrations, which were held under the patronage of then Second Deputy Prime Minister and Minister of Defense and Aviation, the late Prince Sultan bin ‘Abdul ‘Aziz Al Sa‘ud recounted two personal anecdotes that reflected the high esteem in which King Faysal was held by world leaders. The first, confessed Prince Sultan, occurred during a visit to India in 1960, when Jawaharlal Nehru confided to him “that everything would go well if the Kingdom rallied behind two important things: the *Ka‘abah* [in Makkah], representing Islam; and Faisal, as a sincere leader and reputed statesman known for being fair and gentlemanly.” The second anecdotal recollection, which highlighted the monarch’s legitimacy in the eyes of his subjects, was when, shortly before the King was assassinated, Prince Sultan met a blind camel herder who was planning a visit with his daughter and her husband and who, “since he had no other relatives to whom he could entrust the animals, stated that he was planning to leave his 400 camels in King Faisal’s care.”[101] The anecdotes reflected on half of the Faysal–‘Iffat equation, and though protocol necessitated that the Second Deputy Prime Minister concentrate his remarks on his brother, just about everyone in the Kingdom knew that Faysal was ably seconded by an amazing queen.

Less than two decades after her arrival in Sa‘udi Arabia, ‘Iffat Al Thunayan became a true Al Sa‘ud pillar, someone who worked hard to buttress family credentials. From Constantinople, which became Istanbul a year before she left, ‘Iffat brought culture and sophistication. Her exposure to educational and health services, as well as their lack of availability in Makkah, meant that she quickly realized what was required and how fast she had to move. Without wasting a moment, she embarked on lifelong adventures that distinguished her from others in the tradition-bound and largely entrenched society that greeted her. Rather than isolate herself and endure the *Turkiyyah* label with stony-faced resignation, ‘Iffat took adversity in her stride and focused on doing the impossible. All of her work amply illustrated the character of an exceptional woman, a dreamer who did not see her gender as a handicap, an idealist who chose her goals and worked to realize them.

‘Iffat and Faysal emphasized above all else the education their children received, but not just their own children. The first three girls, Sarah, Latifah, and Lulwah, were among the first Sa‘udi girls to have an English nanny, Mrs. Mellor, whose own legacy was visible in the command of

---

[101] “King Faisal Foundation’s 20th Anniversary,” 16 May 1996, at http://www.saudiembassy.net/archive/1996/news/page163.aspx.

the English language that the princesses displayed.[102] Of course, they were not alone in receiving such attention as the founder's brother, Prince 'Abdallah bin 'Abdul Rahman, had already started a private school next to his Riyadh palace to educate both sons and daughters together. Yet, what distinguished Sarah, Latifah, and Lulwah from their cousins was their mother's background. Even if the three girls did not know it at the time—for 'Iffat shared few details of the hardships she endured in the tumultuous history at the end of the Ottoman Empire—their mother was a credentialed teacher in her own right and had been preparing for an academic career before she returned to Sa'udi Arabia. According to family members, her teaching credentials were one of the documents found in her papers, something that no one in the family knew anything about when she passed away in 2000. What 'Iffat wanted was crystal clear: she yearned for her daughters to learn sciences, geography, and history, and to be exposed to a variety of other subjects, in addition to attending religious courses. 'Iffat was not afraid that her sons and daughters would neglect their faith if they began to understand Copernicus, for example, rather than spew out the belief that the earth was flat. She was not fearful that her children would forgo cherished values if they learned how to draw the human face and form. She was persuaded that learning how to read maps would make them appreciate their country and region, as they would better understand their environments. Indeed, while much was expected from the offspring of the Viceroy, 'Iffat knew that they must first be prepared and that such knowledge did not come by wasting one's life away. Such were the reasons why Sarah, Latifah, and Lulwah were pushed hard. Similarly, Muhammad, Sa'ud, 'Abdul Rahman, Bandar, and Turki, the boys who were then enrolled in the Ta'if school under Spartan conditions, stood out among their many cousins. That was also one of the reasons why the girls as well as the boys were enrolled in European and American private schools before, in several cases, attending university. Like their mother, Sarah, Latifah, Lulwah, and later on Hayfah, could not only read and write—an unusual activity for women of the time—but all four were smitten by 'Iffat's sense of curiosity and dedication. That is not to say that other Sa'udi princesses were not equally endowed with the educational tools to accomplish whatever they wished to; over time, many did, some making exceptional contributions in their own right. Rather, 'Iffat's offspring, especially the four girls, received special attention from their mother, and not just their nannies. Often, 'Iffat would visit the young girls in their Swiss boarding school near Lausanne, not only to inquire about their academic progress but also

---

[102] Princess Hayfah, the youngest, was born in Paris in 1951, and was provided with several private tutors before attending school.

to set the bar even higher than they had cared to consider. It was not unusual for 'Iffat to demand excellence from her offspring simply because she knew that they could deliver and because she knew that their contributions were necessary in order to change Sa'udi society. By doing so, that is, by emphasizing what could be achieved to her husband, children, grandchildren, friends, and acquaintances—even total strangers who sought her assistance—'Iffat Al Thunayan transformed herself into a pillar of the Al Sa'ud.

3

Education for a Re-Born Nation

Because of long-established traditions that have encouraged the practice of segregation within the Kingdom of Sa'udi Arabia, socio-economic and political conditions that affect women have been defined by vehement prohibitions that have inevitably weakened a woman's position in society.[1] For much of the Kingdom's contemporary history, Sa'udi women have been excluded from public life, a subject that is now the source of heated internal debates. By the beginning of the 21st century, while much remained to be done and gender segregation continued to be the state's official policy, conditions had also improved, in some instances dramatically. For one thing, the numbers of female graduates from secondary schools and universities has exploded, even if most women graduates are idle as they have limited options in public life after they have earned their diplomas. The key question for observers of the Kingdom and for concerned Sa'udis is how long this pool of talented individuals can remain inactive outside of traditional family settings? Because female university graduates are exposed to a variety of subjects and can study whatever they wish, many opt for entrepreneurship, which inevitably requires them to mix with men [*ikhtilat*], a practice frowned upon by conservative Sa'udis. Notwithstanding this strict observation over *ikhtilat*, it would be a mistake not to take note of the significant progress of the past few decades that has come about through a gradual relaxation of specific principled norms, allowing most girls to receive basic education and an increasing number to pursue higher degrees at home or overseas. A world away from the dire conditions that pertained when 'Iffat Al Thunayan arrived in Makkah, the changes introduced during the past few decades have permanently altered women's education in the country. In turn, the education of so many women—fulfilling one of the late Queen's most cherished objectives—has altered the country itself, no matter how dysfunctional it is still perceived as being by its critics.

---

[1] Amani Hamdan, "Women and Education in Saudi Arabia: Challenges and Achievements," *International Education Journal* 6:1, March 2005, pp. 42–64.

This chapter first proposes to describe what conditions were like before 1932, when learning was exclusively associated with religious institutions, making education an exercise for the privileged few. It then examines various state-sponsored initiatives introduced by the government of the nascent Kingdom. In fact, whatever achievements the many pioneers may have accomplished, compared with what 'Iffat had been used to in Constantinople, early education institutions in the country of which she would one day be Queen were rudimentary at best. But it is necessary to gain some insight into these conditions to better ascertain the progress that has been made since. Regrettably, limited resources meant that whatever provision was available was meager, and even members of the ruling family, who received private tutoring at what passed for the ruler's "palace," were not particularly well served, with young underprivileged girls faring far worse. Identifying these disadvantages from the outset, 'Iffat Al Thunayan was determined to introduce fundamental transformations for she truly believed that Sa'udi Arabia needed all of her children to grow in healthy, tolerant, and awakened environments.

Towards that end, the discussion focuses on her early efforts at Dar al-Hanan, a vital school that became the standard against which every other primary and secondary institution was measured. It then looks at the first women's college established in the Kingdom, Effat College, which later became a full-fledged university. The chapter then examines the vital role played by the King Faysal Foundation as the country's premier philanthropic organization focusing on education, and closes with an evaluation of the many challenges that education in general, and women's education in particular, faces in the conservative country. By exploring a few of the constraints imposed on educators, as well as the multiple challenges of illiteracy that once weakened the country, it will become clear that Sa'udis who worked to improve literacy rates and granted their daughters the tools to excel were nothing short of miracle workers. 'Iffat Al Thunayan led the way by articulating a vision of women as potential achievers.

FIRST STEPS IN EDUCATION

Outside the traditional religious establishment, few Sa'udis were literate in the modern sense of the word when the Kingdom was reconstituted in 1932, while female literacy rates were very low indeed. To focus simply on one parameter, at a time when living conditions were primitive at best, the uniting of so many diverse tribes under the authority of the founder monarch—again from the single perspective of dramatic improvements in living standards—was nothing short of miraculous.[2] Privileged merchants who crisscrossed the Arabian Peninsula were certainly knowledgeable and, more importantly, were expert accountants as well as navigators with the requisite skills for traveling long distances across the desert. It was safe to state that men and women were certainly educated well for the life they lived, but the kind of knowledge they needed then could not hope to equip them for the challenges of the modern world. Catering to scattered tribes required special forms of education that had been common in Arabia for centuries, even if no formal schooling was encouraged for the masses. Understandably, there is a dearth of reliable statistics for this period, but it has to be acknowledged that when ʿAbdul ʿAziz bin ʿAbdul Rahman Al Saʿud announced the establishment of the Kingdom of Saʿudi Arabia on 23 September 1932, illiteracy rates were high.[3]

Education before 1932

To be sure, there were differences between the normative teachings of Islam and the diverse cultural traditions practiced on the Arabian Peninsula. Whether such differences amounted to inequality was a heated topic, one that was socio-political in nature rather than religious. From its very beginnings in the 7th century to the decline of its three great empires in the 17th century, the Muslim world was not solely about military conquests, or imperial rules, or rotating dynasties, as it is often rendered in historical analyses of Arabs and Muslims. To be sure, violent political developments occurred from time to time, but these events happened in parallel with significant artistic contributions and scientific discoveries that have left their mark on history. Although Islamic arts developed chiefly under the Arab ʿAbbasids, and in various Persian and Ottoman empires, one should not conclude that architecture, calligraphy, painting, and carpet weaving, just to cite these areas, did not exist

---

[2] For two good introductions to these issues, see Ameen Rihani, *Ibn Saʿoud of Arabia*, London: Kegan Paul, 2002 [originally published as *Maker of Modern Arabia or Ibn Saʿoud of Arabia: His People and His Land*, London: Constable and Co. Ltd., 1928]; and Joseph Kostiner, *The Making of Saudi Arabia, 1916–1936: From Chieftaincy to Monarchical State*, New York and Oxford: Oxford University Press, 1993.

[3] Illiteracy here is not meant to imply that people lacked reading or writing skills—which certainly existed, especially for those associated with religious learning, even if the latter was mostly of the memorizing variety—but in the contemporary sense of functional illiteracy, a term that is often used to describe basic skills that are inadequate "to manage daily living and employment tasks that require reading skills beyond a basic level."

on the Arabian Peninsula. However, as in other places, knowledge and learning were also valued there, albeit in more limited fashion than in Cairo, Damascus, Baghdad, or perhaps Isfahan, but the architecture of Old Jiddah—or what is left of this unique heritage—still attests to the ambitious endeavors of earlier Arabian society. Moreover, while significant advances in medicine, astronomy, mathematics, and philosophy occurred predominantly in Persia as well as within the Cairo–Damascus–Baghdad triangle, critical breakthroughs were also recorded in Arabia, especially after the revelation of the Holy Qur'an.[4] Inasmuch as many of these learning processes were the work of Muslim men, little has survived of any female contributions. Still, it would be a mistake to ignore the great respect towards women expressed in Muslim teachings in the Qur'an—on account of their contributions as nurturers entrusted with upbringing children and promoting the welfare of the family—and it was certainly something that the founder monarch could not possibly overlook, even in ultraconservative Arabia. Moreover, because 'Abdul 'Aziz bin 'Abdul Rahman knew perfectly well that women occupied prominent roles in all Muslim societies, tribal pressures aside, it is likely that he had a good grasp of what needed to be done. Realistically, however, in the harsh Arabian environment where poverty was a pervasive fact of life, both men and women were underprivileged, with women slightly more disadvantaged. Under these circumstances, the fact that some Muslim women had reached unprecedented political heights, especially when compared with more economically advanced Western countries, remained a largely theoretical point.[5] Of course, the founder knew that the wives of the Prophet Muhammad were educated—starting with his first spouse, Khadijah bint Khuwaylid, who managed a successful business and was also known as the *tahirah* (virtuous).

Nevertheless, this was a largely historical fact, with few more recent examples for the founder monarch to call upon.[6] That shortcoming aside,

---

[4] Although many studies touch on the importance of education and learning in the Muslim world, three recent additions homing in on the methodologies that were developed ought to be widely read to gain a better appreciation of how difficult a process it was. See Gerhard Endress and Abdou Filali-Ansary, eds., *Organizing Knowledge: Encyclopaedic Activities in the Pre-Eighteenth Century Islamic World*, Leiden, The Netherlands: E.J. Brill, 2006. See also Claude Gilliot, ed., *Education and Learning in the Early Islamic World*, Farnham, Surrey, UK: Ashgate Pub. Co., 2012; and Hunt Janin, *Pursuit of Learning in the Islamic World, 610–2003*, Jefferson, North Carolina: McFarland & Company, 2006.

[5] Noha Ragab, "The Record Set Straight," Online Discussion of *Misconceptions about Women in Islam* (Submission to God alone), at http://submission.org/#/d/idx_misc_women.html.

[6] Nicolas Awde, *Women In Islam: An Anthology From The Qu'ran and Hadiths*,

because the Holy Qur'an was revealed on Sa'udi soil, and given that education was explicitly commended to believers by the Creator, it is logical that learning would be closely associated with religious practices. And while Muslim clergymen are not organized in any sacerdotal sense, they are nevertheless effective.[7] Over the centuries, and in every society, they have organized themselves around groups of learned men and created a certain hierarchy even if the institutions that arose were beholden to civilian rulers. The parallel with Christianity is crystal clear, with education becoming the preserve of monks cloistered in monasteries throughout both Europe and the Arab World. Muslim clerics, likewise, taught the Holy Scriptures to their pupils and often selected the brightest among their flocks to pursue advanced studies.[8] Starting in Makkah and Madinah, and spreading throughout the realm, mosques became both places of worship and centers of learning. Naturally, attention was exclusively devoted to religious texts, but there was also a gradual introduction of other subjects such as psychology and medicine.[9] In the Hijaz, and especially under Ottoman rule, a few schools that taught in Turkish trained pupils to serve the Porte. Most of these schools, which reached even remote corners of what was once known as the Yemen and, of course, every Hijazi hamlet that housed Ottoman troops, catered to the children of soldiers and other officials. Hardly any Arab family patronized them, not only because most teachers hailed from the occupying power and their medium of teaching was the Turkish language, but because "many Arabs apparently feared that matriculation in the Turkish system would increase the possibility of conscription in the Ottoman army."[10] Indeed, the need for able administrators grew over time, so that

---

New York: Hippocrene Books, 2005, p. 10 and *passim*; for an overview of gender questions see Jamal Badawi, *Gender Equity in Islam: Basic Principles*, Plainfield, Indiana: American Trust Publications, 2005.

7 The statement that the "Holy Qur'an was revealed on Sa'udi soil" does not mean that a linkage is being made between Islam and Sa'udi Arabia as a country nearly 1450 years ago. Rather, and simply stated, the founder-monarch appreciated his nascent monarchy's responsibilities towards the Holy Harams. It is worth recalling that the Al Sa'ud were one of the few Arab ruling families that did not trace their roots to the Quraysh tribe into which the Prophet was born.

8 In a largely misogynistic environment, the vast majority of the pupils were male, though exceptions certainly existed and many young girls were taught the Qur'an and the Sunnah of the Prophet.

9 Aminuddin Hassan, Norhasni Zainal Abiddin, and Abdul Razaq Ahmad, "Islamic Philosophy as the Basis to Ensure Academic Excellence," *Asian Social Science* 7:3, March 2011, pp. 37–41. See also Seyyed Hossein Nasr, *Science and Civilization In Islam*, Chicago: Kazi Publications, 2007 [originally published in 1968 by Harvard University Press].

10 Catherine Parssinen, "The Changing Role of Women," in Willard A. Beling, ed.,

towards the end of the 19th century the Hashimite Sharif Hussayn bin 'Ali added Arabic language instruction to the curriculum. Remarkably, several schools were established in Jiddah by the Hashimites, both for boys and girls, even if most did not survive the end of Hashimite rule in Arabia.[11]

One of 'Abdul 'Aziz bin 'Abdul Rahman's first initiatives upon entering Makkah in 1924 was to create a directorate [the Mudiriyyat al-Ma'arif al-'Amah] or a General Education Management Center to coordinate a slew of activities in the Hijaz, including education for boys. 'Abdul 'Aziz understood that he needed to develop both government and private institutions of learning, after he realized there were just four schools in the entire Hijaz: the al-Sawlatiyyah, al-Falah, and al-Fakhriyyah in Makkah, and the al-Falah in Jiddah.[12] His interests grew after he invited Makkah scholars to the first educational conference to convene in the Holy City and contributed a respectable sum during his visit to al-Falah and al-Fakhriyyah. He also encouraged citizens to cooperate in the establishment of private schools by financing them on their own, persuading them that such disbursements brought honor, helped society, and granted the nascent political entity additional legitimizing tools. This led to an increase in the number of private schools for boys. From then on, private schools spread to cover several regions of the Hijaz and beyond, and contributed equally with government schools in the educational awakening that occurred in the Kingdom after 1932.

In 1928, a Majlis al-Ma'arif was created to decide on a new education law, and in 1936 the ruler approved the establishment of a preparatory institute that primed those who wished to travel, or asked to pursue their studies, abroad.[13] Although the founder was eminently aware of what needed to be accomplished in his realm, he was also cognizant of religious

King Faisal and the Modernisation of Saudi Arabia, Boulder, Colorado: Westview Press, 1980, p. 155.

11 Abdul Latief bin Duhaish, "Elementary Schools in Hijaz During the Half Century, AG 1295–1345," in Mohamed Tahir, ed., *Encyclopedic Survey of Islamic Culture*, Volume 3, New Delhi, India: 1986, pp. 35–60. See also Joshua Teitelbaum, *The Rise and Fall of the Hashimite Kingdom of Arabia*, New York: New York University Press, 2001.

12 Among the oldest official schools in Hijaz were *al-Sawlatiyyah* [referred to as As-Sawlatiyyah in the citation that follows] and *al-Falah*. These schools taught the curriculum of *Ahl al-Sunnah wal-Jama'ah*, including the Creed of the *al-Sanusiyyah*. For additional details, as well as rare photographs of the schools, see Darulfatwa of Australia, *Upholding the Methodology of the Master of Messengers*, Bankstown, Sydney, New South Wales: Islamic High Council of Australia, 2012, p. 12.

13 Over time, and as discussed below, the *Majlis al-Ma'arif* was transformed into a full-fledged ministry [*Wizarat al-Ma'arif*], which occurred under King Sa'ud in 1954.

pressures liberally exercised by men habituated to getting their way. He pushed forward and pulled back as necessary, as only he knew how to do.[14] When a few objected to his insistence that girls be educated, for example, he would refer them to the lives of the Prophet's wives, including the young 'Ayshah who was not only educated but could also lead an army of 30,000 soldiers into battle. She allegedly fought with them, helped cook as needed, and nursed the wounded whenever possible. 'Ayshah discussed and negotiated various issues and political matters with the Prophet, 'Abdul 'Aziz would remind skeptics, insisting that the Messenger was wise enough to freely acknowledge her wisdom.[15] Whether the ruler noted that Muslim historical documents, such as the carefully read *Tarikh al-Rusul wal-Muluk* [History of the Prophets and Kings] by Abu Ja'afar Muhammad ibn Jarir al-Tabari (839–923), reported the number of *hadiths* recorded by 'Ayshah, is difficult to ascertain. What he must have realized, however, especially given the future monarch's inherent good judgment, is that many Muslim scholars considered 'Ayshah to be part of the chain of transmission of the sayings and traditions of the Prophet, something he seldom failed to refer to as he buttressed his claims to legitimate rule. Although the Prophet—through his sayings and deeds—recognized that women could indeed play critical roles in Muslim societies, there were limits to how fast 'Abdul 'Aziz could move on this front on account of age-old tribal traditions that still per-

---

In 1960, King Sa'ud decreed that a General Directorate for Girls' Schools be established, which would incorporate all state institutions. Then in 1970, King Faysal issued his famous "Education Policy" directive, the first state-sponsored strategic study of the subject, upon which the Kingdom's subsequent education system has been based. It was a bold step, one that recognized a role for the state in the education of its citizens and that also necessitated the establishment of a formal Ministry of Higher Education—finally authorized in 1975—and coordinated policies across all institutions of higher learning. Carefully tailored steps were initiated over a period of several years, with significant progress recorded in a number of areas, including the education of women. By 2003, the General Directorate for Girls' Schools and the Ministry of Education had been absorbed into the new Ministry of Education and Training, which was in and of itself a major step. Importantly, the Minister was entrusted with two lieutenants, one to supervise the education of boys and the other to concentrate on the education of girls. For background details and statistical details, see Fouad Al-Farsy, *Modernity and Tradition: The Saudi Equation*, Guernsey, Channel Islands: Knight Communications, 1994, pp. 247–261

[14] David Howarth, *The Desert King: The Life of Ibn Saud*, London: Quartet Books, 1965, pp. 55–67.

[15] Ameen Rihani, Ibn Sa'oud of Arabia, *op. cit.*, especially pp. 200–206. See also William Ochsenwald, "The Annexation of the Hijaz," in Mohammed Ayoob and Hasan Kosebalaban, *Religion and Politics in Saudi Arabia: Wahhabism and the State*, Boulder, Colorado and London: Lynne Rienner Publishers, 2009, pp. 75–89.

sisted. His own affinity with women has been amply documented—he enjoyed their company and valued their contributions to society—and hardly any of his contemporaries differed from his view that the nascent monarchy needed educated young people of both genders.[16]

As a further sign of confidence, ʻAbdul ʻAziz appointed Shaykh Hafiz Wahbah as his first Director of Education, before appointing him as Ambassador to the Court of St. James in 1930. Wahbah managed to "introduce the secular school system to the main centers of Arabia itself by providing school buildings and importing competent teachers from various Middle East countries," especially from Egypt and Syria.[17] His successor, Shaykh Tahir al-Dabbagh, continued in Wahbah's footsteps, as did yet another successor, Shaykh Muhammad Ibn Maniʻ, an enlightened cleric who was solidly in tune with ʻAbdul ʻAziz's preferences. All of them agreed with the founder that women's education was to be encouraged, a sentiment the prescient leader shared with Harry St. John Philby, a trusted advisor, when he underlined that it was "permissible for women to read."[18] Philby reported that while the founder ruler regarded reading and writing as being "unsuitable accomplishments for a woman, they [we]re certainly not forbidden."[19] It must be emphasized that a brand-new facility created along the lines of an English public school already operated in Riyadh for the younger princes of the family. It was staffed by competent teachers from Egypt and Syria even if its curriculum was rather limited. Moreover, it is also worth underscoring that Nurah bint ʻAbdul Rahman bin Faysal, the founder-ruler's sister—a woman who played such a critical role in the history of the country—also supported education.[20] According to Philby, the move to create the Riyadh school elicited other members of the family, including the ruler's brother ʻAbdallah, to emulate him with a similar institution

[16] Howarth, *op. cit.*, pp. 30–36. The predisposition for having educated men and women in the monarch's realm was not well understood although it served as a perfect incubator when Prince Faysal and Princess ʻIffat raised various issues with their sovereign to push for new schools and teaching programs.

[17] H. St. John Philby, *Saʻudi Arabia*, London: Ernest Benn Limited, 1955, p. 327.

[18] This quotation is attributed to the founder monarch in Amani Hamdan, *op. cit.*, p. 48 and is buttressed by a reference to Ibrahim Al-Rashid, *Documents on the History of Saudi Arabia*, Salisbury, North Carolina: Documents Publications, 1976. No volume number or specific pages are provided. A thorough check of Al-Rashid revealed no such quotation in any of the US Government dispatches assembled in this vast collection.

[19] H. St. John Philby, *Arabian Jubilee*, London: Robert Hale Limited, 1952, p. 109.

[20] In 2008, the "Princess Nora Bint Abdulrahman University" was formally inaugurated in Riyadh to honor the founder's sister. For additional details, see its dedicated web page at http://www.pnu.edu.sa/en/Pages/Home.aspx.

for his own extensive and growing family. Even the Viceroy of the Hijaz, Faysal bin ʻAbdul ʻAziz, as discussed below, would see to it that a school was build in Ta'if to educate his own sons and daughters.[21] Thus, to say that senior members of the ruling family reached the conclusion that education was a top priority would indeed be an understatement. In fact, parallel to the search for water—which preoccupied the founder long before he became absorbed with petroleum—the King gave specific instructions to focus on education, an area that could no longer be overlooked.

Post-1932 State-Sponsored Initiatives

Such efforts notwithstanding, those who chose to interpret scriptures opted to couch their sociological views within the narrow parameters often ascribed to religious texts, especially with regard to women's education. While Islam strongly encourages the education of both men and women, stressing the need to gain broad knowledge of religion, economics, and political and social affairs, among other subjects, fearful men who loathed a loss of influence almost always fell back on pre-Islamic customs.[22] Some of these customs—practices adopted by Arabian tribes for centuries—denied women equality, even if their relevance to Islam was peripheral.[23] Regrettably, some highly selective and narrow interpretations of Islam espoused by conservative religious scholars in the Kingdom allowed men to decide that women's education was secondary to their larger missions. In the words of one critic, "Islam has been used to first deny then discourage women's education," which was certainly true in some instances.[24] Still, many Saʻudis believed that women's education was necessary not only to allow them to be actively involved in society and make sorely needed contributions to the economy, but also because they appreciated the sociological consequences of idle masses whose energies were wasted. Ironically, however, even among those who

---

21 Whether intra-family rivalries emerged at this time could also be a factor although no evidence existed to imply such competition.

22 Haifaa A. Jawad, *The Rights of Women in Islam: An Authentic Approach*, London: Macmillan Press, 1998, pp. 1–15.

23 Although no references to driving could possibly be found in the Holy Qur'an, for example, in 2014 conservative clerics use the *ikhtilat* [mixing] clause to enforce a rule that prevents Saʻudi women from driving. Inasmuch as modernization ushered in a variety of entirely new phenomena, including driving, one could not possibly find religious arguments to determine whether these practices were *haram* or *halal*; though challenged, clerics continue their adamant insistence that women should not be allowed to get behind the wheel and drive.

24 Jawad, *op. cit.*, pp. 16–29—the quotation is on page 28.

favored advancements in women's education deference to conservative religious scholars continued.[25] Somehow it was deemed appropriate for religious authorities to supervise women's access to knowledge, the majority of reasonable men being persuaded that only gentle nudging would secure Sa'udi women the kind of access that they needed to advance.

In other words, Sa'udi men were called upon to educate themselves about Muslim women's contributions to various fields under the aegis of Islamic studies supervised by the clergy, including political and social affairs. Only by such efforts would women's participation in education be further encouraged, it was thought, since the original intention of the faith was to educate both men and women from the starting point of the study of the religion itself. This line of advance, which historically has not been uncommon in conservative societies, promised to liberate Islamic teachings regarding women even if many objected that liberalism was creeping in in the guise of conservative norms.

Still, the unprecedented accomplishments of the past few decades means credit must be given to the effectiveness of this narrow approach, first adopted by the founder-monarch, despite the more liberal voices who wished to see an accelerated pace of change. In fact, the significant transformations that occurred over the course of nearly a century—in 2009, literacy rates for those over 15 years of age reached 89.96 percent for men and 81.08 percent for women—stood as clear testimony to the success of this method. According to the United Nations Educational, Scientific, and Cultural Organization (UNESCO) Institute for Statistics, which collects data from a variety of sources to compile an index for most countries, the percentages for youth literacy—that is, the percentage of people aged between 15 and 24 who can with understanding read and write a short, simple statement on their everyday life, was even higher. Sa'udi men between 15 and 24 enjoyed a 98.67 percent literacy rate while women in the same age group were at 96.51 percent.[26] The United Nations Development Program (UNDP) provided a combined adult literacy rate for those aged 15 and older of 86.1 percent for the 2005–2010 period, which was relatively high for a developing country.[27] Of

---

[25] Eleanor Abdella Doumata, "Women and Work in Saudi Arabia: How Flexible Are Islamic Margins," *The Middle East Journal* 53:4, Autumn 1999, pp. 568–583.

[26] Index Mundi, "Saudi Arabia—Literacy Rate," at http://www.indexmundi.com/facts/saudi-arabia/literacy-rate.

[27] United Nations Development Program (UNDP), "Selected Facts on Saudi Arabia from HDR 2007/2008 [Updated]," at http://www.undp.org.sa/sa/index.php?option=com_content&view=article&id=22&Itemid=47&lang=en.

course, these percentages were negligible a century earlier, when few Sa'udi men and hardly any women received the kind of education that most youngsters benefit from in 2014. Nevertheless, the education levels in 1932, which were severely restricted, effectively meant that little of the workforce the nascent monarchy required could be indigenous. Consequently, the ruler and his sons relied on a slew of foreign advisors, mostly from Arab countries, to help set up the rudiments of the bureaucracy that has gradually evolved into the world-class institutions that today serve the Kingdom and the millions of pilgrims who gather in Sa'udi Arabia every year. Although no study has been completed to describe the thousands of men and women who flocked to the Kingdom and worked for years on end, the numbers are far larger than have been assumed, with many maintaining unique ties with senior members of the ruling family.[28]

Of course, women still constitute less than 10 percent of the workforce, though efforts are underway to alter this situation. With improved education levels among indigenous populations, and despite sociological problems that limited the number of Sa'udis in vocational sectors and migrant labor forces, the Kingdom was forced to host nearly eight million mostly male foreign workers in 2014 to help build and maintain the country's vast infrastructure. The workforce is bound to change, largely because of improved education levels, but still requires a significant portion of its unemployed youth—estimated at around 30 percent in 2014—to accept less desirable positions currently filled by foreign migrant workers. Inasmuch as socio-religious conditions severely limited the reliance on women for filling such posts, and because women's education has reached highly advanced levels in society, one is obligated to ask how that participation has changed Sa'udi Arabia's labor picture.

It has not always been like that and thus it behooves young Sa'udis, both men and women, to seek insights as to how their country has reached its current position barely half-a century after 'Iffat Al Thunayan began to challenge the unenlightened attitudes which prevented most of the population from fully developing their intrinsic capabilities and contributing to the creation of a new society. How the transformation occurred over such a short period of time deserves particular attention.

[28] In addition to Iraqi, Syrian, Lebanese, Jordanian, and Egyptian advisors who served the ruler, dozens of female assistants, including physicians and nurses from the same countries, joined his entourage to help with the needs of the princesses. Few appreciated their contributions, which were, without a doubt, invaluable.

CREATING INSTITUTIONS

As discussed above, formal public schooling in the Kingdom was rudimentary and, at least before the 1960s, mostly reserved for boys. A few private schools began offering non-religious subjects in some of the larger towns in the 1920s, though it was not until the 1930s that state-sponsored modern education began to take formal shape. By 1951, a network of secondary schools had been created, culminating in the establishment of the Ministry of Education in 1954, then headed by Prince Fahd bin 'Abdul 'Aziz, a future monarch. It was not until 1957 that the first university was opened. The earliest official primary school for girls opened its doors in Riyadh in 1962, but even in this instance the primary goal of education was to learn the Qur'an, the Hadiths, and the Sunnah of the Prophet.[29] Consequently, the first curricula approved by religious authorities for these "public schools" focused on the sacred texts, as pupils were taught how to pray and to follow the rules of behavior of the Muslim community; such studies were deemed not only appropriate but amply sufficient. Of course, most of this education required memorization that was similar to what the *kuttab*, learned men operating out of local mosques, had taught for centuries.[30] Still, the young girls who memorized and could recite the Holy Qur'an by the time they reached puberty were considered to be "educated," following which came segregation and, of course, veiling.[31]

While financial resources were still meager after 1932, King 'Abdul 'Aziz devoted a portion of his income to educational activities, despite the fact that women's education was rudimentary even if theoretically comparable with that of men. In reality, there was no similarity between the two, and as several authors have gone on to analyze, women's education figures were markedly lower than those for men.[32] Because the Kingdom was a patriarchal society, women's education reflected that aspect of daily life which manifested itself in subordination to men. Yet, specific initiatives to improve conditions started as early as the 1940s, when a

---

[29] Al-Jawhara Bubshait, "Saudi Women's Education: History, Reality and Challenges," in *Woman in Saudi Arabia: Cross-Cultural Views*, Riyadh: Ghainaa Publications, 2008, pp. 25–26. See also Mona Almunajjed, *Women in Saudi Arabia Today*, New York: St. Martin's Press, 1997.

[30] Leila Ahmed, *Women and Gender in Islam: Historical Roots of a Modern Debate*, New Haven, Connecticut, Yale University Press, 1992, p. 113.

[31] Soraya Altorki, *Women in Saudi Arabia: Ideology and Behavior Among the Elite*, New York: Columbia University Press, 1988, p. 19.

[32] Doumato, *op. cit.* See also Ghada Karmi, "Women, Islam, and Patriarchalism," in Mai Yamani, ed., *Feminism and Islam: Legal and Literary Perspectives*, New York: New York University Press, 1996, pp. 69–86, especially page 71.

bright young woman by the name of Fatinah Amin Shakir made history. Shakir wanted nothing less than to have the same opportunity granted by the Ministry of Higher Education in financing the education of young Sa'udi men—namely, to be able to study abroad. Her application was promptly rejected on the grounds that it was immoral to allow a young single woman to live and study overseas. Undaunted by this pro-forma denial, Shakir appealed to Prince Faysal bin 'Abdul 'Aziz, whose support of women's education was gradually spreading across the country. In the event, Shakir received her grant, traveled to the United States, earned a doctorate in anthropology from Purdue University, and returned home to contribute to her nation. It was a singular effort that, undeniably, opened the floodgates on opportunities for those who wished to pursue their craving for knowledge.[33] Beyond her own personal success, what Fatinah Shakir's case illustrated was the mindset in the nascent bureaucracy that literally denied women basic education rights, not because those decision makers did not believe that women were capable but because of narrow interpretations of customary social practices.

Hailing from the Hijaz, where a far more heterogeneous population lived, it was easier for Fatinah Shakir to muster the courage to petition the Viceroy and seek solace. It was an entirely different proposition to deal with mass changes, as became evident in September 1963, for example, when Riyadh was called upon to send troops to Buraydah to break up demonstrations objecting to girls' education.[34] In the heart of Najd, Buraydah was where much of this intrinsic opposition occurred, given that the area was entrenched in strict tribal backgrounds that were diametrically opposed to what happened in the Hijaz.[35] Najdi women were less likely to go outdoors and express themselves publicly, a phenomenon reserved for men in most provinces. Indeed, the segregation went beyond customs and, according to a renowned Sa'udi scholar, "whether upper or middle class[,] the role of women in the Kingdom of Saudi Arabia [could] only be seen in the context of their patronymic

---

[33] Fatinah Shakir became one of the very first Sa'udi women to hold a doctorate. Her Purdue University dissertation, which focused on modernization in developing countries, featured an interview with Faysal, the man who had made her dreams come true. See Robert Lacey, *The Kingdom: Arabia and the House of Sa'ud*. New York: Harcourt Brace Jovanovich, 1981, p. 368. See also Saddeka Arebi, *Women and Words in Saudi Arabia: The Politics of Literary Discourse*, New York: Columbia University Press, 1994, pp. 205–215. There is also a useful analysis of Shakir's dissertation on pages 216–222.

[34] Lacey, *The Kingdom*, p. 368.

[35] Much is usually made of tribal differences between the various regions of the Kingdom, something that still pertains in 2014, though far less than in the 20th century.

group and of the national purpose and not as one section of society struggling for its right in isolation from men."[36] In Buraydah, where clashes occurred after the order to send girls to school was given, citizens were forcibly restrained from demonstrating openly their opposition to plans to educate women. Although informal schooling was introduced under King Sa'ud, in 1963 the objection was still acutely sustained. It has taken gargantuan efforts gradually to eliminate misogynist views in this area.

As discussed below, it was 'Iffat Al Thunayan who wholeheartedly pushed for the education of women in Sa'udi Arabia, but it fell on Faysal bin 'Abdul 'Aziz to persuade tribal leaders that formal schooling for girls was important.[37] In Buraydah, elders were shocked at the prospect that their daughters would travel through the public streets every day to attend school, though Faysal's genius for calculated compromises saved the day. Despite sending troops to Buraydah to keep the girls' school open, Faysal did not force parents to matriculate their daughters, and insisted that girls' schooling was not mandatory. Thus it was up to each and every parent to see the consequences of their actions in denying their daughters an education as well as disobeying a royal order. By relying on such an approach, the astute Faysal—who brilliantly understood the traditional thinking of his subjects—achieved both of his goals. As he confided to Fatinah Shakir, his approach was to ask whether there was anything in the Holy Qur'an that forbade the education of women, while working hard to enlighten conservative mentalities that feared women's education. According to one observer, Faysal further stated: "We have no cause for argument, God enjoins learning on every Muslim male or female."[38] What this approach illustrated was the compatibility between traditions and modernization, though the monarch opted to pursue gradual changes rather than impose decisions by fiat, an approach he had perfected after years of contact with his loyal subjects.

For her part, 'Iffat Al Thunayan wanted all Sa'udi women to pursue their learning in the sciences, acquire new languages, and delve into a variety of subjects if those areas of interest were what young women wished to study—not to mention that she genuinely believed the country needed to open up to the outside world. A devout Muslim convinced of the utility of religious education, she was also a firm advocate of secular education, a woman determined to be critical so that everyone

---

36 Mai Yamani, "Some Observations on Women in Saudi Arabia," in Mai Yamani, *Feminism and Islam*, *op. cit.*, pp. 263–282, especially p. 265.

37 Summer Scott Huyette, *Political Adaptation in Saudi Arabia: A Study of the Council of Ministers*, Boulder, Colorado: Westview Press, 1985, p. 74.

38 Lacey, *op. cit.*, p. 368.

might expand their horizons. 'Iffat established the first girls' school in 1954, and enrolled her own daughters to set an example; even if the experiment was not universally acclaimed at first, it was not because she did not foresee problems; rather it was because of the hurdles erected in front of her, which she chose to leap over with her customary enthusiasm.

'Iffat's First Steps in Education

Catherine Parssinen, a former assistant to the Dean of the Graduate School at the University of Petroleum and Minerals in Dhahran, has written that 'Abdul 'Aziz bin 'Abdul Rahman, Prince Faysal bin 'Abdul 'Aziz, and Princess 'Iffat "had numerous lengthy discussions about the educational needs of Saudi Arabia and how they might be realized most effectively." She has further revealed how Queen 'Iffat acknowledged that the consensus among the three conferees "was that the Kingdom confronted the challenge of awakening to the realities of the twentieth century after experiencing a long period of unconsciousness."[39] Parssinen concludes that the shared perceptions of the founder, his son, and daughter-in-law focused on the necessity for reforms, although all three agreed that transformations ought to be introduced with the utmost tact. There were no reasons to impose by fiat cataclysmic decisions that would oblige citizens to change their traditions, but instead courteous, measured, lucid, and above all inclusive mechanisms should be put in place that would obviate any need for state coercion. Education was one of those super-sensitive subjects that would potentially alter the very fabric of such a conservative society, with all three understanding the repercussions of hasty measures that would be rejected by the tradition-bound majority as well as the more change-allergic purists.

Faysal further counseled his spouse that his father's recommendations were in tune with local norms, which 'Iffat understood and shared, as the Viceroy and his Princess adopted a low-key strategy that, above all else, avoided excessive publicity. The couple's priority at this time was to ensure their eldest daughter Sarah and eldest son Muhammad received both religious and secular instruction without provoking religious extremists. Towards that end, and to take the taboo-breaking first step that contemplated the very idea of a secularized education system, 'Iffat set up the Madrasah al-Numuzajiyyah [Model School] in Ta'if in 1944. Rather than make a formal announcement, the school was inaugurated without fanfare "as a private academy" under the able leadership of first

[39] Parssinen, *op. cit.*, p. 156. See also Samirah Ibrahim Islam, *'Iffat Al Thunayan: Tarikh wa Injaz* ['Iffat Al Thunayan: History and Achievements], Jiddah: Al-Multakah al-Thaqafih, 1421 H [2001], p. 22.

Mahmoud Jalaliddin Bayk and then Muhammad Abul 'Ala'.[40] Even if the experiment was kept low-key, it was not long before word spread, and not necessarily in a positive sense. What aroused suspicions was the academy's curriculum, which emphasized sciences and language, and which could not be hidden given that several prominent Jiddahwi families enrolled their sons, too. Since instruction at the school had been carefully designed around a typical English model, both the pupils and perhaps even the remote location of the academy—in the mountainous region of Ta'if, then accessible only with some difficulty—could not but preoccupy the religious authorities. Both Faysal and 'Iffat, partners in this fresh enterprise that promised to alter customs, understood that, in time, the institution's location would change once the number of students increased. In fact, the school moved to Jiddah in 1958, was renamed, and expanded to include an increasing number of young men whose parents wished for them to receive a blend of modern and traditional curricula. This exceptional, groundbreaking boarding school, where women supervised dormitories, welcomed royals and non-royals alike. Many noticed these dramatic transformations and voiced support for the significant improvements they augured in the lives of young Sa'udis.

There were those who feared this exposure and, even worse, perceived with apprehension the prospect of "foreign education," when Riyadh decided that special grants would be available to encourage young men to travel abroad and receive appropriate training.[41] Some frowned on what their sons would learn and, perhaps, bring back in their baggage. Even more were upset that Levantine teachers ushered in alien ideas and fresh perspectives that upset the proverbial apple cart. 'Iffat apparently received several pleas from mothers who did not wish their sons to receive foreign travel grants, ostensibly because "the foreign academies would corrupt their boys and alienate them from their families and roots."[42] Muhammad al-Faysal, Sa'ud al-Faysal, and 'Abdallah Al Thunayan, among a few privileged teenagers, were whisked away without fanfare in 1954 to the Hun School of Princeton, a highly recommended boarding institution in the New Jersey borough. Remarkably, even these relatively high-ranking members of the ruling family were forced to travel surreptitiously so as not to arouse anyone's suspicions, for the Hun School was still alien to local culture.

Such were conditions in the late 1940s and early 1950s, when few members of the family actually trusted the young men who, it is worth

---

40 Lacey, *op. cit.*, p. 364.

41 Parssinen, *op. cit.*, pp. 156–157.

42 Lacey, *op. cit.*, p. 364.

underscoring, would be called upon to lead the country in the future, with all the travel and acquisition of essential knowledge that entailed.[43] Even worse, save for Faysal and 'Iffat, most Sa'udis feared that exposing their sons to alien cultures would cause their own values to wither on the proverbial vine. Of course, most changed their minds as soon as they realized that contemporary education was both beneficial and, more importantly, did not transform believers into unbelievers. After the initial uncertainty and suspicion with which most greeted the first few years of this new experiment, visitors to Faysal's or 'Iffat's *majlis* started to plead with them to help secure prized scholarships. Still, as long as the focus was on young men, dragging Sa'udis into the 20th century was a battle whose outcome was fairly assured. It was an entirely different proposition when attention turned to initiating similar programs for young women. It would take a while for the plans to come together, though 'Iffat stayed determined in her quest to give Sarah the same opportunities that Muhammad received. But beyond the prospects for their own children, what was at stake was nothing less than the future of the country, the outlook for all of its children, and the opportunities they had to excel just as oil money began to change the economic and social landscape.

'Iffat's Second Steps in Education

Raphael Patai—the Hungarian-Jewish Orientalist whose highly controversial book *The Arab Mind* advanced the notion that Arabs advocated little more than a tribal-group-survival thinking—claimed that Islam allegedly considered female education to be not only "merely unnecessary and superfluous, but [also] positively wrong."[44] Of course, this was a wholly incorrect reading of the facts, though not surprising given the ideological loathing of Arabs and their faith displayed in such writings. As discussed earlier, the Prophet Muhammad encouraged education for both men and women, even if narrow cultural attitudes slowed down the process. Because abject poverty had dominated the Arabian Peninsula for centuries, most of its inhabitants considered

[43] It is worth noting that the sole exception to this rule was Faysal himself, who was a frequent traveler beginning at the tender age of 13, though not a regular student in a boarding institution in Europe or the United States. Rather, the world itself gradually became Faysal's classroom, as the young man honed his diplomatic skills by living in it on a day-to-day basis. Was it a coincidence that he searched for the cosmopolitan partner he eventually found in 'Iffat Al Thunayan?

[44] Raphael Patai, *Golden River to Golden Road: Society, Culture, and Change in the Middle East*, 2nd ed., Philadelphia: University of Pennsylvania Press, 1967, p. 462. See also Raphael Patai, *The Arab Mind*, New York: Recovery Resources Press, 2010 [originally published by Scribner in 1967].

education a luxury few could afford—hence illiteracy was so widespread. Still, leading European scholars who visited the Hijaz in the late 19th century observed coeducational instructions offered in Qur'anic education facilities, although girls were withdrawn after puberty and, consequently, could not embark on advanced religious studies. Christiaan Snouck Hurgronje (1857–1936), a renowned Dutch scholar of "Oriental" cultures and languages who traveled throughout the Hijaz and delivered magisterial lectures on Islam, reported that leading Hijazi families who could afford to retain private tutors to educate their children—both boys and girls—did so.[45]

Relying on the same principles she applied at the Ta'if Model School [al-Madrasah al-Numuzajiyyah], the proposed network of girls' schools would have to be in the cosmopolitan cities of the Hijaz and, true to local traditions, it would apply strict segregation to satisfy religious authorities. When the Model School for Girls was created in Ta'if in 1944 there were a handful of pupils, including Princesses Sarah and Latifah, along with Badriyyah bint al-Sulayman, Fatinah Shakir, and Moody 'Abdul Muhsin al-'Anqari. The experiment did not last long as lack of interest in the school meant that 'Iffat reluctantly had to close it down. She hired two private tutors to look after her daughters' education at the palace, including Mrs. Miller, an English teacher, and Mufidah al-Dabbagh, a Palestinian teacher, who between them ensured that the Princesses learned both languages. According to Princess Latifah, her mother "dreamt that the school would become a model institution and that it would welcome a variety of pupils from throughout the area," but in the event few parents agreed to send their daughters to Ta'if. Rather than keep a private school for the exclusive use of her daughters and a handful of children from amongst her closest friends, Princess 'Iffat recognized the need to rethink the project.[46]

"My mother did not just want her daughters to receive a proper education," affirmed Princess Latifah. "Though the Ta'if school was what we would call today a boarding school, which should have encouraged leading families from throughout the Kingdom to send their daughters to it," she explained, what "my mother wanted was for as many girls who wished to receive modern instruction to enroll. The experiment was premature, however, since few parents were ready to be

---

[45] Jamal Alami, "Education in the Hijaz Under Turkish and Sharifian Rule," *The Islamic Quarterly* 19:1–2, January–June 1975, p. 44. See also Christiaan Snouck Hurgronje, "Mohammedanism: Lectures on Its Origin, Its Religious and Political Growth, and Its Present State," 1916, available online as an eBook under the Gutenberg project at http://www.gutenberg.net/1/0/1/6/10163.

[46] Interview with HRH Princess Latifah al-Faysal, Jiddah, 12 October 2010.

separated from their offspring. It was a grand idea, typical of the way my mother thought of things, but way ahead of her time." By the time the school closed, rather than accept failure Princess 'Iffat "was already embarked on her most cherished initiative, while Mrs. Miller or Mrs. Al-Dabbagh were busy with our academic needs. Simply stated, she did not concede an inch to the experiment but thought of ways to improve it. Little did we then know what she had in mind," elaborated Princess Latifah, "but we were all astounded when she came up with the Dar al-Hanan idea."

Dar Al-Hanan

Whether 'Iffat Al Thunayan's next move was discussed with senior religious authorities in the country is impossible to determine—few members of the family were privy to such conversations—but the possibility cannot be ruled out. Simply stated, the determined Princess wanted to revive the moribund Ta'if experiment and, towards that end, contemplated an entirely different scheme. In the event, the decision was made to establish a school for orphans, on the assumption that few would object to such an implementation of Qur'anic precepts calling for the creation of open hospices catering to orphaned children. Naturally, young women would be veiled when traveling to and from the school, despite Queen 'Iffat's strong reservations that the garment was a handicap and therefore one that she seldom encouraged the use of outside the public sphere. Still, she always respected traditions, wore the veil in public throughout her life in Sa'udi Arabia, and encouraged all of her female acquaintances to do likewise. Young women attending the school, therefore, were required to veil in public, though the garment was carefully discarded inside the classroom.

The name selected for the institution, Dar al-Hanan [House of Affection], importantly neither carried any references to orphans nor hinted that the establishment was in fact an orphanage. Indeed, it is revealing that the name was purposefully uplifting, further hinting at what was really on the future Queen's mind. At the time, Princess 'Iffat knew that the challenge was immense, that the experiment would not be a cakewalk, and that she needed to place the running of the revamped school in the hands of someone who could mobilize parents just as much as she could provide quality education to pupils. Against some odds, and lacking a full complement of teachers, the school's principal, Mrs. Mufidah al-Dabbagh, invited several Egyptian, Jordanian, and Palestinian teachers to take up positions in the nascent school. Many were reluctant to accept, given that so little was known about the Kingdom at the time and that the reality of a desert country lacking every imaginable service made it a hard sell. The school opened in 1956 with about thirty pupils nestled in two rooms. There were no orphans amongst them and the going was tough.[47]

'Iffat Al Thunayan funded the school out of her own pocket and "personally helped to sew the costumes for the first young women that enrolled," so she had ample reason to be disappointed when so few registered. "Even the slaves and servants of the royal household were reluctant to let their young female relatives enter the House of Affection," claimed an observer, although the enthusiastic Princess was surely used to such setbacks.[48] Princess 'Iffat was not daunted by the challenge and Dar al-Hanan survived its first year with less than three dozen students, especially after several dropped out in the middle of the academic year. This second failure could be attributed to the fact that the school was marketed as an orphanage—with the undeniable negative repercussions that such an appellation carried despite the religious obligation that existed to support the vulnerable. None of those interviewed for this study could recall what exactly happened that discouraged so many. Nevertheless, the reluctance to accept this institution as a full-fledged center of learning was most likely due to ingrained customs which simply did not see any value in educating girls. The times were changing but so slowly that few understood the phenomenon, albeit 'Iffat was aware of its root causes and persisted as only she knew how.[49] She cajoled women visiting her *majlis* to alter their views, proudly paraded her daughters and the other girls in front of Jiddah's female elites, and solicited from the youngsters details on what they were learning in the classroom. Everyone

---

47 Rania Sulayman Yunis Salamah, *Dar al-Hanan*, Jiddah: Madaris Dar al-Hanan, 1429 H [2008], pp. 46–50.

48 Lacey, *op. cit.*, p. 365.

49 The year 1956 was a particularly bad year because of tensions in the Arab World that preoccupied King Sa'ud, and especially the heir apparent, Prince Faysal. After his initial bombastic 16 January speech that vowed to reconquer Palestine, on 26 July the Egyptian leader Jamal [Gamal] 'Abdul Nasir—who became president on 23 June—nationalized the Suez Canal. The decision sparked international condemnation and led to the 29 October British/French/Israeli invasion of the Sinai Peninsula to push Egyptian troops back towards the canal. On 31 October, Britain and France bombed Egypt and reopened the Canal, landing troops in an offensive that led to a major confrontation. Heightening the tension still further, the Hungarian Revolution began on 23 October, as Budapest attempted to leave the Warsaw Pact. On 26 October the Soviet Army invaded and occupied Hungary, which led to a full-scale revolution starting on 4 November. On 7 November, the UN General Assembly adopted a resolution calling for Britain, France, and Israel to withdraw their troops from Arab lands. This was the context in which *Dar al-Hanan* students trekked to school and, most probably, the reason why most of the burden fell on Princess 'Iffat since Faysal was overwhelmed with urgent foreign policy affairs.

could see and hear how fast the children improved. Indeed, over a very short period of time the first class demonstrated that young girls could learn, develop, and bloom while remaining true to their faith. Gradually, the school transformed itself into a cause, as ‘Iffat gathered allies among Jiddahwi women who, within a single year, were ready and willing to enroll their daughters at Dar al-Hanan. In fact, the experiment worked so well that a formal public presentation followed in 1957, when the school's first press release was issued. Dar al-Hanan was presented as the institution that would educate young Sa‘udi girls to become better mothers and reliable homemakers, while remaining true to their Islamic faith and values. “The mother can be a school in herself,” read the press release; it was important to “prepare her well” for the significant challenges that awaited her as a member of society.[50]

As in every beginning, the experiment survived on enthusiasm and sheer optimism, even if resources were limited.[51] Nevertheless, even if she was reluctant to aggrandize her financial contributions, there was little doubt that the land on which the school was built as well as the seed monies dedicated to the project came from her private purse. In 1964 alone, Princess ‘Iffat contributed one million riyals (about US$ 400,000) for the extensions under construction, a substantial sum at the time.[52] No one in the family actually knew the total sum disbursed to run the school over the years; suffice it say the Queen saw that Dar al-Hanan was fully funded year after year.[53]

In time, Princess ‘Iffat's ideas spread to Riyadh as King Sa‘ud bin ‘Abdul ‘Aziz embraced them too. He inaugurated a school similar to Dar al-Hanan at the Nasiriyyah Palace in the capital to educate his own daughters, and instructed Fahd bin ‘Abdul ‘Aziz, then Minister of Education, to incorporate the *Dar al-Hanan* curriculum into the nascent public school system that was then being prepared. The Jiddah facility thrived and in 1962 King Sa‘ud approved the introduction of female education throughout the country. Aware that the influx of female pupils would necessitate thousands of new female teachers, in what was a true

---

[50] Salamah, *op. cit.*, pp. 53–54.

[51] In the absence of financial records, it has not been possible to determine actual costs even if, as discussed below, the Princess was generous.

[52] Thuraya Qabi, Lead Editorial, “Woman's Page,” *Al-Bilad*, No. 1592, 1 May 1964, as cited in Parssinen, *op. cit.*, p. 159.

[53] According to several daughters of the late Queen who spoke on the matter, proper accounts were kept at the school, though it was not possible to examine actual financial records because of privacy considerations. Still, Princess ‘Iffat saw to it that the school's funding was always in the black. Interview with Cécile Rushdy, *Dar al-Hanan* Principal, Jiddah, 8 November 2010.

stroke of genius Princess 'Iffat embarked on a more farsighted project—to fund a teacher-training school in Riyadh, the *Qulliyat al-Banat* [Girls' College]—anticipating the need for many more instructors than anyone had contemplated up until that time. Although the Kingdom relied on Egyptian, Syrian, Jordanian, Lebanese, and Palestinian teachers, the future Queen was leaps and bounds ahead of everyone else in the hierarchy in anticipating what the next requirement was likely to be. By this point she wanted to push the envelope of innovation and further distinguish her efforts, but to her credit she appreciated the need to coordinate with government officials and to seek state approval for her initiatives.

In spite of everything, 'Iffat was not always successful, in part because she had to contend with the chairman of the religious committee in charge of girls' schools, Shaykh Nasr al-Rashid, an ultraconservative cleric who insisted that the curriculum be substantially revised. He proved a formidable thorn in her side. Rather than have the students devote so many hours per week to sciences, for example, the cleric wanted to replace them with religious instruction, a demand which on account of his position was nearly impossible to ignore. In what must have been one of the most valuable encounters in the cleric's life 'Iffat Al Thunayan asked him to visit her in 1962, so as to press for her cherished curriculum and impart to him the value of having educated women. Little of what transpired during the meeting, which was held in the palace, was ever leaked. There were few outsiders present, though family members recollected how 'Iffat insisted on pushing forward and, more importantly, that she was by no means intimidated by the revered cleric.[54] Of course, 'Iffat was in a strong position because her husband was the heir apparent, but it would certainly be a mistake to assume that she only relied on her family credentials to press the case. Her strength, like Faysal's, lay in her command of the basic doctrines of the faith so that, while she was not a doctor of religious law, she could nevertheless hold an argument rather well. Instead of confronting Shaykh al-Rashid, Princess 'Iffat contended that the value of equipping young women with the knowledge required to make them better people was far greater than fears that such learning would ruin their lives. She did not get everything she wanted from the cleric but neither did he maintain his stance of adamant opposition to instruction in scientific subjects. That, in and of itself, was a victory for Princess 'Iffat, who knew how to persuade and seldom wavered from her objectives. Nevertheless, the encounter raised her awareness yet further, prompting the future Queen to approach the Ministry of Social Welfare to coordinate the school's basic development needs. By mid-1963, and on the recommendation of Anas Yassin, then a rising member of a prominent

[54] Interview with HRH Prince Turki al-Faysal, Riyadh, 16 October 2011.

family that had left its mark on the history of the Kingdom, Princess 'Iffat made arrangements to meet Cécile Rushdy, a young Egyptian expatriate social worker then working at the ministry in Riyadh.[55] She asked her daughter Latifah to sound out Rushdy, a recent graduate from the American University in Cairo who lived with her father in Riyadh and had been hired by the ministry to help set up its social welfare activities. With less than a day's notice, Rushdy flew to Jiddah to visit Dar al-Hanan and to meet the future Queen. Princess Latifah recalled how she and the young sociologist were shocked when they first set foot in the school, realizing that much of the early enthusiasm had been lost, even if the pupils were still there. "As I had not visited the school in several months, I too was surprised by what I saw, even if Dar al-Hanan was operating. This was not what my mother worked so hard to achieve and I could tell that Cécile [Rushdy] was perplexed. Still, it became apparent to me that we had to do something about the school and quickly," affirmed the Princess.[56] "It was a mess," Cécile Rushdy recalled, "and I could not believe that a venerated institution that received so much positive publicity could have reached such levels. Naturally, when the Queen asked for my opinion, I was honest with her and shared my apprehension. Luckily, Princess Latifah was there to back me up in case the thought crossed the Queen's mind that I was exaggerating."[57]

After 'Iffat Al Thunayan had listened to her daughter and Cécile Rushdy, she turned to the future Principal and told her, "I need you to re-open the school. I need you to fix it." Puzzled by 'Iffat's determination, the young woman asked how she could possibly leave her ministry position, or where she would even live in Jiddah since her father was in Riyadh. Myriad questions crossed her mind, though little did she understand that the bureaucratic maze that was the nascent ministry would be handled on their behalf at the highest levels of state. Within a matter of a few days, the Viceroy's office had authorized Cécile Rushdy's transfer from the Ministry of Social Welfare to *Dar al-Hanan*, with a commensurate financial package that was far more than what she was earning in Riyadh. As for housing, 'Iffat simply took in the young Egyptian, assigning her a room at the palace as the young lady befriended the princesses of the household. Shortly after she moved in, Rushdy

---

[55] The son of Shaykh Yusuf Yassin, who was one of the founder-monarch's principal advisors and who helped Faysal bin 'Abdul 'Aziz create the Ministry of Foreign Affairs, Anas Yassin and his brothers were raised in the Faysal household and became part and parcel of the family. In time, Anas joined the Sa'udi Ministry of Foreign Affairs, and was appointed Ambassador to India and Turkey, where he and his mother Bushrah Ahmad Sitti perished in a tragic car accident in 1975.

[56] Interview with HRH Princess Latifah al-Faysal, Jiddah, 12 October 2010.

[57] Interview with Cécile Rushdy, *Dar al-Hanan* Principal, Jiddah, 12 October 2010.

embarked on a complete overhaul of Dar al-Hanan, created a board of supervisors, adopted a budget, designed internal mechanisms, reassigned teachers, settled on school by-laws, even commissioned a school song. She traveled to Beirut to purchase new European-made classroom furniture. She even persuaded the Queen to move the school into a larger facility. By the time the two women were done with their thoroughgoing renovation, Dar al-Hanan was reborn, ready to meet the 1964 school year as a fully updated institution. If it had been eminently clear that drastic measures were required to ensure that primary-school graduates could continue to excel in their education at secondary level, then drastic measures had indeed been taken.[58]

As the photographs reproduced in this book attest, Dar al-Hanan's initial steps were problematic—a case of managing as best they could under the circumstances. Over the years, however, haphazard decision-making was replaced with a carefully organized system that valued accountability and set the bar relatively high. From 1963 to 1964, the number of pupils jumped from 250 to 400, and the kindergarten to 9th grade classes required additional staff members. In 1965, a full science curriculum was introduced, which pleased 'Iffat since she wanted young Sa'udi girls to learn much more than simply how to memorize. Exhibits were organized and the Princess, who enjoyed mingling with students during graduation ceremonies, visited frequently to assess progress for herself. In keeping with his usual style, even the Viceroy, anxious to see what everyone was raving about, made a few visits to the school. Both Faysal and 'Iffat were happy with the transformation. Years later, and gathering in 1988 to celebrate Dar al-Hanan's 25th anniversary, Cécile Rushdy recalled the Queen's words: "Ya bitni, 'amalti shugul kwayis" [My daughter, you did a good job].[59]

Over the span of a few short years, *Dar al-Hanan* introduced a slew of subjects and taught its pupils English and French, in addition to Arabic.[60] Even when Riyadh canceled mandatory French language classes, *Dar al-Hanan* kept teaching the subject, as enthusiastic families

---

[58] In 1965, Shaykh Ibrahim Shakir, Fatinah Amin Shakir's father, donated the new building that accommodated *Dar al-Hanan*'s preparatory, elementary, middle, and secondary classes. Adjoining facilities were secured to cater for those students who opted to live on site in what resembled a boarding facility, while another building accommodated staff members. In 1984, *Dar al-Hanan* moved all levels of education to a purpose-built facility next to the *Khuzamah* Palace, while a more modern facility was erected in the al-Zahra neighborhood, which is where *Dar al-Hanan* is today.

[59] Interview with Cécile Rushdy, *Dar al-Hanan* Principal, Jiddah, 12 October 2010.

[60] For a complete rundown of various subjects taught at *Dar al-Hanan*, with period photographs that illustrate the span of education received by pupils, including sports activities, see Salamah, *op. cit.*, pp. 59–158.

enrolled their daughters in the school. With rare exceptions, everyone was satisfied with the quality of instruction offered, with graduates performing very well in various state examinations and being accepted in foreign universities before such facilities were open to Sa'udi women in the Kingdom. At first, tuition was heavily subsidized, as Princess 'Iffat covered most expenses from her personal purse. Within a few years, emphasized Cécile Rushdy, "we decided to recruit quality teachers. The Queen, who was very generous and seldom nitpicked to save a few riyals, agreed that we ought to pay our employees the salaries they deserved, and these hovered eventually between 15 and 17,000 Riyals per month [about US$ 4,000 to 4,500]."[61] Most received transportation allocations, meaning that the total remuneration package matched their income with the best private sector salaries throughout the 1980s. Gradually, modest fees were introduced and facilities improved—for instance, Dar al-Hanan was the first girls' school in the Kingdom that offered air-conditioned facilities—often as a result of equipment donated by leading merchant families. With philanthropy encouraged, science teachers asked for and received expensive laboratory equipment purchased in Europe; indeed, the Kingdom's first female physicians worked in Dar al-Hanan laboratories during their secondary education, familiarizing themselves with biology, chemistry, and physics in facilities fit for their intended purpose.

Even if many girls wondered about the value of their education, given the dearth of employment opportunities at the time, Princess 'Iffat was fond of saying that Sa'udi girls "were not just being educated to serve men. We want them to become contributing members of society."[62] In part, this explained her pride in seeing several Dar al-Hanan graduates enroll in and complete university studies, the goal the young 'Iffat had dreamed of achieving when she was living in Constantinople. As a credentialed teacher, she yearned for a solid education for herself, her own sons and daughters, and Sa'udis in general. Beyond the acquisition of advanced learning, however, 'Iffat wanted young Sa'udi girls "to learn how to think and how to speak."[63] She wanted them to master the art of good conversation and, above all else, she pleaded for a sense of discipline that she found lacking all around her. It mattered how a woman earned esteem and conducted herself respectfully within her family, larger community, and of course in her country.[64] She was fond of showing her

---

[61] Interview with Cécile Rushdy, *Dar al-Hanan* Principal, Jiddah, 8 November 2010.

[62] Interview with Cécile Rushdy, *Dar al-Hanan* Principal, Jiddah, 12 October 2010.

[63] Interview with HRH Princess Sarah al-Faysal, Riyadh, 13 October 2010.

[64] There is no implication that such attributes did not exist before the late Queen accelerated her various programs, but she strongly believed in preparing an individual

girls off, and whenever foreign diplomats' wives wished to visit Dar al-Hanan, the Queen was the proudest Sa'udi one could imagine, secure in the knowledge that each and every student was a genuine ambassador for the country, creating an impeccable image for outsiders and, more importantly, among themselves. With Dar al-Hanan, Queen 'Iffat achieved her goal of forging a modern institution that catered to young women whatever it cost and however long it took to get there. Above all else, she eliminated from many minds the mistaken notion that it was a bad idea to educate girls, and while she respected traditions—including the wearing of *abayas* and *hijabs* in public—she insisted on developing their minds so that they, in turn, acquired the skills that would enable their sons and daughters to be disciplined and to learn. Whenever she made one of her impromptu visits to Dar al-Hanan, Princess 'Iffat made it a point to meet with teachers, encouraging them and often offering them modest but meaningful gifts. She was fond of calling the teachers "*Umm al-Banat*" [the mothers of their pupils] to further entice them to take their teaching responsibilities as seriously as possible. For years, Queen 'Iffat attended annual graduation ceremonies to impart to seniors the sense of duty as they left their second homes, reminding them to keep in touch and, more importantly, never to forget what they had learned at Dar al-Hanan. Often, she complemented teachers, telling one "*shukran ya bitni, 'amalti al-Khayr*" [thank you, my daughter, you've done well] or "*ya banati, antum al-mustaqbal*" [my daughters, you are the future]—remarks that were genuine rewards in a society that did not emphasize self-esteem.[65]

'Iffat certainly knew how to earn loyalty and seldom lost an opportunity to further strengthen her credentials. When in 1988 the time came to celebrate Cécile Rushdy's 25 years of service and the school's silver jubilee, the Queen coordinated a surprise party with the Assistant Director, Fayzah 'Abdallah Kayyal. People are still talking about the party after all these years, as an occasion on which 'Iffat Al Thunayan summarized their long march together towards the emancipation of young minds, underlying early difficulties and how they had overcome a variety of challenges. "She made her presentation in her unique style," affirmed Fayzah 'Abdallah Kayyal, "offering Cécile Rushdy genuine compliments rather than false praise. She even resorted to a few jokes as she remembered humorous episodes from their long lives together."[66] Of

for life. For her, men and women were made to fulfill their potential, not simply to live and go about their business.

65 Interview with Cécile Rushdy, *Dar al-Hanan* Principal, Jiddah, 8 November 2010.

66 Interview with Fayzah 'Abdallah Kayyal, *Dar al-Hanan* Assistant Principal, Jiddah, 8 December 2010.

course, the Queen's kind words tended to become legendary as 'Iffat Al Thunayan commanded unprecedented loyalty among thousands of her subjects. But at Dar al-Hanan, at least, she proved that beyond the words positive transformations could be introduced that changed an entire nation.

Her initial plans to provide a school for her three eldest daughters—Princesses Sarah, Latifah, and Lulwah—grew into a premier K-12 institution that trained generations of young women [including thousands of expatriates from neighboring Arab countries as well as the children of European diplomats and businessmen who worked in Jiddah and could not easily enroll their daughters in state-sponsored schools] to excel. Over a very short period of time, thousands of young girls matriculated through the private school, which became something of a mini-United Nations given the composition of the student body. More broadly, if only a few dozen girls had received any education in the mid-1950s, by the mid-1970s nearly half of all female children between the ages of six and twelve were attending school, and by 1980 there was a near universal enrollment for the same age group.[67] Literacy levels had reached 60 percent in 1972—a remarkable feat given what it took to get there—though many of the numerous small steps initiated by Princess 'Iffat transformed the educational environment in ways that allowed Sa'udi Arabia to take giant leaps forward.[68]

Effat University

Dar al-Hanan may have started as a cause but was quickly transformed into an establishment that, naturally, cried out for follow-up institutions. As stated above, in 1967 Princess 'Iffat founded the Qulliyat al-Banat (College for Girls) in Riyadh, which channeled many of its graduates into Dar al-Hanan as well as the growing number of public schools. The chief purpose of the Qulliyat was to train indigenous women teachers so that the country could finally embark on the long-cherished goal of attaining self-sufficiency in education. Qulliyat students were provided with housing as well as generous monthly stipends to enable their minds to be wholly focused on learning rather than the pursuit of alternative sources of income. On the Princess's instructions, an "Institute of Management and Administration for Women" was established near Dar al-Hanan, funded by the Ministry of Higher Education. According to one observer, "the primary objective of the managerial

---

67 Parssinen, *op. cit.*, p. 160.

68 "Kingdom Achieves 96% literacy rate from 60% in 1972," *Arab News*, 8 September 2012, at http://www.arabnews.com/Kingdoms-achieves-96-literacy-rate-60-1972.

school [was] to produce qualified female administrators, directors, and managers to assume positions of authority within the system of segregated institutions (including schools, colleges, teacher training institutes, clinics, and hospitals) which served the needs of the Kingdom's women."[69] King 'Abdul 'Aziz University in Jiddah and King Faysal University in Dammam opened their doors to both men and women in 1967 as authorized by the Minister of Education at the time, Shaykh Hassan bin 'Abdallah Al al-Shaykh, especially after major improvements were recorded in higher education throughout the country.

In 1975, Sa'udi women were also allowed to enter the School of Medicine, which was a first, while the Faculty of Dentistry opened its doors to female candidates in 1980.[70] Naturally, King 'Abdul 'Aziz University and other institutions of higher learning offered segregated campuses to those who did not wish to travel abroad, so that they could now enroll at home universities. The one issue that was uniformly accepted and presented no impediments whatsoever was the guardianship question: every campus offered residential accommodations for female students under private or public security guards—mostly under the control of men. This was a local requirement overwhelmingly approved by parents anxious to benefit from learning opportunities without jeopardizing cultural norms. Gradually, most existing institutions welcomed female students, albeit with some restrictions, with the example of the Makkah-based Umm Al-Qurah University standing as a good illustration: women were admitted to all departments at this institution with the exception of physical education, the training of judges, and Islamic economics.

Astonishingly, however, beginning in 1974, the Imam Muhammad Ibn Sa'ud Islamic University in Riyadh, one of the country's premier institutions, authorized women to enroll in four departments within its two specialized faculties: the "Shar'iah College" and the "Fundamentals of Religion College." In 2002, King Khalid University in Abhah admitted women into its computer sciences, biology, and English faculties as well, all of which highlighted the serious progress recorded on all fronts. A single university that did keep its doors closed to women—then as now—was the King Fahd University of Petroleum and Minerals in Dhahran. Whether or not the decision to deny women access to King Fahd University was related to the type of work graduates were expected to do—working in the oilfields as well as coming into contact with "dirty" men—the ban endures. It has become an oddity, especially since many women proved that they could dirty their hands and assume responsibil-

---

[69] Parssinen, *op. cit.*, p. 162.
[70] Jawad, *op. cit.*, p. 28.

ities of this kind elsewhere around the world, ranging from Canada to Russia, and predominantly in Muslim Kazakhstan, Azerbaijan, and even Iraq.

Inasmuch as all of these developments occurred under the supervision of the Ministry of Higher Education, a uniform curriculum emerged that seldom encouraged creativity.[71] In most cases, the language medium used was Arabic, with intrinsic problems of print and electronic resources that were severely limited or that relied on Syrian, Iraqi, or Egyptian sources. While these resources were acceptable, none were on the cutting edge of knowledge, often presenting translations from Western or Soviet books that were significantly dated. It took years for the Ministry of Higher Education to develop the wherewithal to commission the translation of the latest scholarly manuals or to encourage original research by indigenous researchers tasked with producing quality books that would benefit students.

Queen ʻIffat was naturally pleased with the dramatic progress recorded at home, though she wanted to push the proverbial envelope even further, challenging herself as well as her countrymen and women to seek ever greater advancements. The queen welcomed her daughters' wishes to establish a private non-profit college for women in Jiddah, which would carry her name, to begin operating in September 1999.[72] She petitioned King Fahd bin ʻAbdul ʻAziz and heir apparent ʻAbdallah bin ʻAbdul ʻAziz to seek approval for the establishment of the university and encouraged Princess Lulwah and other members of the family to devote all of their energies to bringing her dreams to life. Her letters to her monarch and his heir (originals reproduced in Appendix IV) are studies in devotion to authority, as well as unflinching dedication to her mission. Both letters are worthy of further attention as they illustrate the

---

[71] For the latest official statistical data, see Kingdom of Saʻudi Arabia, *Mu'ashirat al-Taʻlim al-ʻAli fil-Mamlakah al-ʻArabiyyah al-Saʻudiyyah*, Riyadh: Ministry of Higher Education, 2011 [1432 H], http://www.mohe.gov.sa/ar/docs/Doc1/VDMPI022.pdf. See also an important recent ministry publication that provides an official view of how higher education ought to add to the country's development projects. Kingdom of Saʻudi Arabia, *Al-Taʻlim al-ʻAli wa Bina' al-Maʻrifah fil-Mamlakah al-ʻArabiyyah al-Saʻudiyyah: Taqwim Duwali* [Higher Education and the Building of a Knowledge Society in the Kingdom of Saʻudi Arabia: An International Calendar], Riyadh: Ministry of Higher Education, 2010 [1431 H].

[72] Although the formal transliteration of the late Queen's name is ʻIffat, all references to the college, which became a university in 2010, apply the spelling Effat to remain consistent with the institution's preferred wording. See http://www.effatcollege.edu.sa/Pages/Homepage.aspx. It must be added that a second women's university in Jiddah, *Dar Al-Hikmah College* [Wisdom College], began welcoming students at the same time.

care with which the late Queen approached her work and the way she interacted with her brothers-in-law.

Queen 'Iffat's undated letter to King Fahd first acknowledges the progress achieved by women in the Kingdom under the ruler's reign, the better to serve the country so that the Kingdom might distinguish itself throughout the Islamic world, aims that the King shared.[73] 'Iffat Al Thunayan then describes her work with the non-profit institution and explains how she took the initiative to follow up on a 3 June 1997 [18 Safar 1418 H] Council of Ministers decision that authorized the public sector to establish universities and colleges. She informs her monarch that she wishes to inaugurate the first private non-profit college for women just like she had opened the first girls' school a few decades earlier, and encloses the initial blueprints for the contemplated facilities, including a sports arena exclusively to be used by women. She then provides a detailed assessment of the preparations that have gone into putting the school's structure together, estimates Dar al-Hanan's land value at SR 300 million (US$ 80m), and assesses the school's future income in regard to generous donations as well as tuition fees. She closes her letter with a request for a license for the 'Iffat Women's College under the patronage of the King Faysal Foundation which would, in its initial phase, have four faculties: Pharmacy, Computer Sciences, Architecture and Internal Design, and Primary Education.

The letter to heir apparent 'Abdallah carried both a number [2/19/98] as well as a date [29/1/1419 H)] and is slightly more detailed.[74] It first informs the recipient that, in the light of the 3 June 1997 Council of Ministers decision to authorize the creation of public universities, a formal request has been made to King Fahd for an authorization to create the 'Iffat Women's College under the patronage of the King Faysal Foundation. She reminds her reader how much she herself owes the Kingdom and its generous citizens, and that all of her efforts to provide education opportunities to its girls and women are both a duty and a blessing. Her references to religious obligations as well as the immensely valuable contributions made by members of the ruling family are underscored in a unique style that is both deferential and factual. Rather than add colorful language, the tone used in the letter reflects her character, which was that of a woman who knew what she wanted. She

---

[73] Copies of both letters were made available by Dr. Hayfah Jamal al-Layl, the Kingdom's first female university president.

[74] The date [29/1/1419 H] stood for 29 Muharram 1419 H, which was the equivalent of 26 May 1998, although the number 2/19/98 was close. There was the possibility that it represented a different classification though it was not possible to verify this by comparing it with other papers.

then provides a detailed précis on contemplated university facilities and the various agreements signed with the American University in Cairo, Cambridge University in Britain, the French–Sa'udi Center in Jiddah, and King 'Abdul 'Aziz University. She expresses the hope that the initial faculties will be supplemented with necessary additions—including psychology and translation, among other subjects—as demand for them arises. Not wishing to leave any points uncovered, the queen then includes a full list of every step taken to prepare the institution, describing committee work to arrange the organizational structure of the university, reiterating that all finances would be assumed by Sa'udi contributions in the first instance and all tuition at a later stage. She hopes that graduates will contribute to Sa'udi society, and closes her letter asking for the support of the heir apparent in helping her to serve the nation in this way. Both letters are signed by 'Iffat bint Muhammad Al Thunayan, Widow of the Late King Faysal bin 'Abdul 'Aziz, following established protocol.[75]

"Effat" aimed to become a cutting-edge college and by 2005 had reached a total enrollment of 1,500 students at its modern Jiddah campus. Initial academic programs focused on a broad-based core curriculum, though the original goal had been to offer alternatives to what was already available, concentrating on architecture and interior design, computer sciences and special education. All of its courses except for Arabic and Islamic Studies were to be taught in English, and the curriculum itself was based on the American liberal arts college model. The inaugural class offered Bachelor of Arts and Bachelor of Sciences degrees in three undergraduate programs to approximately 200 students. Regrettably, Queen 'Iffat passed away on 17 February 2000 and so did not live to see the end of the first academic year.

Nearly 16 years after its establishment, Effat College has evolved into the leading private non-profit institution of higher learning for women in the Kingdom, operating under the auspices of the King Faysal Foundation and under the leadership of a distinguished administrator, Hayfah Jamal al-Layl. A Dar al-Hanan graduate, Dr. Hayfah—as she is known by one and all—carries on Queen 'Iffat Al Thunayan's unfettered enthusiasm for expanding the horizons of the girls and women in her care, many of whom regard the university as their second home. Like the Queen, Dr. Hayfah toils to prepare women for the job market and increase their chances of finding work opportunities, aware that the 21st century makes unusual demands on everybody. For her "Effat" is the institution in the Kingdom best suited to graduating female citizens

---

[75] Both letters carry her legendary signature, 'Iffat al-Faysal, which is revelatory as it emphasizes her Faysal credentials.

capable of functioning well in a global context and bringing prestige to their nation.[76]

Year upon year, additional faculties have been added—first, Information Systems, Psychology, and English Language and Translation, followed by Business Administration, and, most notably, a department of Engineering for women consisting of two majors: Architecture, and, most strikingly, Electrical and Computer Engineering. Beginning in 2005 as a collaboration with Duke University, where the Dean of Engineering, Kristina Johnson, "took on the project as a way to 'do some good in the world'," [77] the confidence with which these typically male subjects have been embraced represents an educational breakthrough for women in the Kingdom. Neither subject had ever been made available to women in the Kingdom before, but having an established, prestigious institution of higher learning giving the program strong backing encouraged women to excel in these subjects.[78]

A 2008 Ministry of Higher Education decision granted Effat the authority to reorganize itself once again, divided now into the College of Humanities and Social Sciences, the College of Engineering, and the College of Business Administration. In turn, these colleges offered eight programs within which numerous majors could be studied that met national and international standards, and achieved the goals of Effat's strategic plan. A 30 January 2009 [3 Safar 1430 H] royal decree—Number 963/MB—issued by King 'Abdallah bin 'Abdul 'Aziz granted Effat its university status with the following breadth of colleges and departments demonstrating why it now merited that award: the College of Engineering (Electrical and Computer Engineering Department, Computer Science Department, Information Systems Department and Architecture Department); the College of Business (Finance and Accounting Department, Marketing Department, Human Resources Management); the College of Humanities and Social Sciences (Early Childhood Education Department, English and Translation Department,

---

[76] Haifa Reda Jamal Allail, "The Importance of Global Dimension in Citizenship, Family & Education: A Vision for Global Peace—The Case of Effat College," delivered to the World Family Summit held in Sanya (near Hainan), China, 6–9 December 2004 [mimeographed, in author's hands]. See also Isobel Coleman, *Paradise Beneath Her Feet: How Women are Transforming the Middle East*, New York: Random House, 2010, pp. 208–214.

[77] Coleman, *ibid.*, p. 212.

[78] For additional details on the Duke–Effat accord, see Duke University Pratt School of Engineering, "Duke Engineers to Collaborate with Saudi Arabia's Effat College on Computer Engineering Curriculum," 10 February 2005, at http://www.pratt.duke.edu/news/duke-engineers-collaborate-saudi-arabia's-effat-college-computer-engineering-curriculum.

and Psychology Department); a Department of Operations and Information Management; and a Department of Entrepreneurship. The year 2009 was crowned with another breakthrough, when Effat coordinated its efforts with the Executive Master for Islamic Financial Management (XIFM) in collaboration with the Rotterdam School of Management, Erasmus University, and the École Supérieure des Affaires (ESA), based in Beirut, Lebanon.[79] These far-from-minor accomplishments reflect the vision of the late Queen, who wanted nothing short of excellence for her beloved university. The university's core values, based on the Qur'anic injunction to read, clearly identify the future prospects of the nation in its intrinsic ability to graduate students who add to human knowledge and enlightened society. In fact, its international humanistic Islamic values seek to avoid narrow-mindedness, as well as unregulated liberalism, relying on scriptures to help develop well-balanced citizens who, in turn, can thrive on innovation and progress. All of these attributes are eminently consistent with the vision Queen 'Iffat painstakingly worked to achieve, which has clearly come to pass at the institution that is the crowning glory of that vision and the one that bears her name.[80]

A LIFE OF PHILANTRHOPY

Many more individuals benefited from 'Iffat Al Thunayan's largesse than there can be space to mention in a book-length study such as this one. Over the years, hundreds of thousands were assisted through various charities, women's associations, and schools, some of which are discussed elsewhere in this book. Hundreds of close family members and friends benefited from her philanthropy—an aspect of her Al Thunayan and Al Sa'ud heritage—an instinctual generosity which was almost always deployed simply as a tool for improving the future prospects of the nation. Most visitors to her *majlis* left with some form of assistance and, to her credit, this tradition was passed on to her offspring. In fact, her philanthropic spirit was institutionalized after Faysal's death partly through the

[79] These associations allowed for foreign faculty members to teach at Effat and for graduates to spend a semester or more overseas.

[80] The university's code of ethics is based on the divine commandment IQRA' [READ]; this exhortation encompasses lifelong research, social and educational commitment, responsible behavior and creative leadership, and effective communications. See its president's detailed analyses at http://www.effatcollege.edu.sa/About/Pages/IQRAA_Core_Values.aspx.

offices of the King Faysal Foundation, which in turn led to new traditions in the Kingdom, and partly through her own private channels. Moreover, on the evidence of the success of Effat University, several other institutions of learning received assistance from the Foundation, too.

The King Faysal Foundation

Shortly after King Faysal bin 'Abdul 'Aziz Al Sa'ud was assassinated on 25 March 1975, his heirs, including Queen 'Iffat, agreed to establish a foundation to honor the memory of the late King.[81] According to Prince Turki al-Faysal, it was imperative "for us to invest in education as he would have wanted," and though Queen 'Iffat neither directed her children to create the King Faysal Foundation (KFF) nor presided over any of its formal functions, the inevitable reflection that followed Faysal's death on who their father was, what he represented, and what he had achieved, led members of the family to set up one of the most important international philanthropic institutions in the history of the Kingdom.[82] At first, the task seemed daunting, but Faysal's sons and daughters instinctively knew how to proceed, focusing on their late father's concerns for the welfare of peoples everywhere, particularly the disadvantaged. Speaking during the closing ceremonies of the Foundation's 20th anniversary celebrations in 1996, Prince Khalid al-Faysal, then Director-General of the institution and Governor of 'Asir Province (today the Minister of Education), reported that while the starting capital of the Foundation was a mere SR 8 million (US$ 2.2 million), all of which was donated by the heirs, KFF's careful investments and additional contributions made by family members and other donors, had boosted its working capital to SR 1.3 billion (US$ 350 million) at that point. Prince Khalid further revealed that the charitable expenditures of the Foundation reached SR 710 million (US$ 189 million) over the course of its first two decades, which was not negligible, even given that the figures have increased significantly since then.

Over the years, the privately held institution enhanced its vast commercial and industrial holdings, and invested in first-class operations. Its financial strategy rested on a carefully constructed triad: gifts from al-Faysal family members, private donations from senior Al Sa'ud contributors as well as others, and investments in commercial enterprises. This successful model, first adopted in the late 1970s, was to generate as much income as possible to support local projects, no matter in which

---

[81] For additional details on the Foundation, see the dedicated webpage at http://www.kff.com/.

[82] "Transcript of Prince Turki's speech at Princeton," 7 December 2006, at http://www.saudiembassy.net/archive/2006/speeches/page2.aspx.

country these were found. For example, a KFF-funded commercial complex in Mombasa, Kenya, helped secure a steady source of revenues to fund aid projects in several East African countries. A similar KFF-funded commercial complex in Mumbai, India, partially supported programs throughout the Indian Subcontinent. Of course, the largest such revenue-generating facility was the Faysaliyyah Center in Riyadh, which opened in 2000 and now occupies a whole city block. Until The Kingdom Tower was erected in 2002 at 303 meters (994 feet), the Faysaliyyah, at 267 meters (876 feet), stood as the capital's tallest building.[83]

The Al-Faysaliyyah complex stands as the Foundation's most spectacular investment, consisting of five separate operations under a single management—the Office Tower, Five-Stars Hotel, a full retail mall with hundreds of tenants, a series of private hotel suites for the upper-end market, and a banquet and conference center—all of which are landmarks in the heart of the 'Ulayah business district of the capital city. Designed by UK architects Foster & Partners, Al-Faysaliyyah maintains a commercial balance among its diverse entities and ensures successful cross-trading opportunities. Estimated at over US$ 320 million at the beginning of the 21st century, the complex has generated additional profits, all of which have been plowed back into the Foundation's extensive academic, scientific, cultural, and community programs.[84] Other KFF investments have included hotels, shopping centers, apartment buildings, offices, and partnerships in tourism and public relations both inside Sa'udi Arabia and elsewhere.

The late King Faysal thought globally at a time when most decision makers were still mired in national issues, often perceived through the

---

83 A subsequent building frenzy throughout the Kingdom has relegated these towers to the 6th and 8th positions, respectively, on the list of Sa'udi skyscrapers. In 2014, the tallest was the Makkah Royal Clock Tower, a multipurpose steel and concrete facility in the Holy City, measuring 601 meters (1,972 feet), followed by the Jiddah Diamond Tower, a residential complex that will stand at 432m (1,417ft) when completed. In 2014, several new skyscrapers opened, including the Riyadh office tower Capital Market Authority Headquarters, which stands at 385m (1,263ft) tall; the Jiddah Lamar Tower 1 office building, at 350m (1,148ft); the Riyadh residential as well as office building at the King 'Abdallah Financial District World Trade Center at 303m (994ft); and, in 7th place, the Lamar Tower 2 in Jiddah, which is 301m (988ft) tall. See "The Skyscraper Center: The Global Tall Building Data Base," of the Council on Tall Buildings and Urban Habitat, 2014, at http://skyscrapercenter.com/create.php?list_status=COM&status_COM=on&status_UC=on&status_UCT=on&status_DEM=on&list_country=SA&search=yes.

84 http://www.gvpedia.com/Territories/Kingdom-of-Saudi-Arabia/Business-Investment/Education-CSR/King-Faisal-Foundation.aspx.

distorting prism of the Cold War or couched within narrow nationalistic parameters. Faysal's vision was different. He favored long-range economic and social investment programs throughout the developing world—especially though not exclusively in Muslim countries—by allocating financial assistance not only as moral support but precisely to enhance local growth. That was why KFF board members funded an extensive program of activities to care for the needy and to create the necessary wealth that could improve their lives. The KFF represents the best evidence of the motivation that King Faysal and Queen 'Iffat instilled in their offspring, endowing them with a vision that simply needed articulation, their advantages of birth allowing them to implement exceptional projects. In the words of the KFF's trustees: "We were fortunate enough to grow up in the shadow of a man whose greatness was acknowledged not only in the heart of his family but in the eyes of a nation. Our father's love, discipline, and sense of responsibility instilled in us a desire, and perhaps even a need, to ensure that the spirit of King Faisal's altruistic ambitions would live on after his untimely death in 1975."[85] The KFF undoubtedly honored Faysal's legacy, but inevitably it also shared the vision of the Queen, his full partner and someone who had helped him make critical choices in education, health care, and other social concerns.

With regular and unmistakable input from the royal couple's daughters and several grandchildren—Princes 'Abdallah, Muhammad, Khalid, Sa'ud, 'Abdul Rahman, Sa'ad, Bandar, and Turki al-Faysal, along with Prince 'Abdul Rahman bin 'Abdallah al-Faysal—painstakingly applied their parents' and their grand-parents' vision. The Foundation's day-to-day operations were entrusted to Prince Bandar bin Sa'ud bin Khalid Al-Sa'ud, the KFF Deputy Managing Director, whose writ covered a vast mandate: the challenge of taking on a broad range of Islamic, cultural, and charitable endeavors that exemplified King Faysal's humanitarian values while managing a multimillion-dollar enterprise. Naturally, Prince Bandar ran a philanthropic foundation that distinguished itself throughout the Muslim world. Lest one conclude that the KFF was exclusively focused on the Muslim World, it is worth repeating that its activities cover a broad area, including a series of awards comprising what many have come to refer to as the Arab Nobel Prize.[86]

To further enhance the impact of the philanthropic institution, in 1979 the Foundation created an annual prize, the King Faysal

[85] "The Founders' First Board of Trustees of The King Faisal Foundation," at http://www.kff.com/.

[86] Critics implied that the purpose of this prize was to outdo the Nobels, though without offering an iota of evidence to support such a gratuitous assertion. See

International Prize(s) (KFIP), spread across five specific disciplines and awarded to dedicated men and women whose contributions have made a positive difference in those areas. Although the cornerstones of the KFIP are its prizes for service to Islam, Islamic studies, and Arabic literature, the three awards created in 1979, the honors for science, which began in 1982, and especially for medicine after 1984 brought the KFIP to world attention. Following strict selection criteria, recognition of advances that benefited all of humanity, and not just the Muslim world, brought wider attention to the prize. After 1982, and perhaps so as not to duplicate Nobel awards, the KFIP science prize rotated through the disciplines of chemistry, biology, physics, and mathematics in a four-year cycle. The medicine honor was awarded according to diverse, topical themes chosen by an international committee of experts.[87] In 2014, each of the prizes consisted of a certificate handwritten in Diwani calligraphy summarizing the laureate's work; a 24-carat 200 gram gold medal—uniquely cast for each winner; and a cash prize of SR 750,000 (US$ 200,000).[88]

Although the KFF has clearly adopted forward-looking strategies that empowered Sa'udis, Muslims, and others to benefit from recent scientific discoveries, the Foundation has also stressed the late monarch's devotion to Islam and its traditions through the work conducted at the King Faysal

---

Natasha Mozgovaya, "U.S. professor becomes first Jew to win 'Arab Nobel Prize': Stanford's Ronald Levy says Saudis deleted any mention of Israel from the bio he submitted for the prize," *Haaretz*, 16 April, 2009, at http://www.haaretz.com/jewish-world/2.209/u-s-professor-becomes-first-jew-to-win-arab-nobel-prize-1.274192; Martin Kramer, "Intra-Regional and Muslim Affairs," in Haim Shaked and Daniel Dishon, eds., *Middle East Contemporary Survey, Volume 8, 1983–1984*, Tel Aviv: The Shiloah Center for Middle Eastern and African Studies, 1986, p. 166; and "Which Awards are Well Known? Why?," *Computational Complexity: Computational Complexity and other fun stuff in math and computer science from Lance Fortnow and Bill Gasarch*, 19 March 2009, at http://blog.computationalcomplexity.org/2009/03/which-awards-are-well-known-why.html.

87 Peter Harrigan, "Rays of Light and Brightness: The King Faisal International Prize," *Saudi Aramco World* 51:5, September/October 2000, pp. 32–39.

88 The Diwani script is a cursive style of Arabic calligraphy that came to prominence during the reign of the early Ottoman Empire (16th and early 17th centuries), invented by Husam al-Rumi and reaching its height of popularity under Süleyman I, also known as Süleyman the Magnificent (r. 1520–1566). Whether the adoption of the Diwani script to draft each laureate's certificate was attributable to the late Queen 'Iffat is not possible to determine, although the link between her native land and her nation was inescapable. The script is as decorative as it is communicative, distinguished by the complexity of the line within the letter, and the close juxtaposition of the letters within the word—all of which emphasizes 'Iffat's complex linguistic and stylistic preferences.

Center for Research and Islamic Studies (KFCRIS), which has concentrated on Islamic culture and learning. In the tradition of Ibn Khaldun, who adopted a scientific approach and based his analyses on reason, KFF efforts encouraged scientifically proven methodologies that applied the time-honored principle of cause and effect, while analogies between past restrictions and present challenges were highlighted to better serve the nation, and economic conditions that affected everyday life scrutinized to improve living conditions for the majority. It must be added that because he emphasized reason in judging history and social events, Ibn Khaldun was falsely accused of refuting conventional religious knowledge, allegedly wishing to substitute faith with rational philosophy. As a devout Muslim, Ibn Khaldun relied on scriptures to focus his observation and reflection. Inasmuch as he referred to the Holy Qur'an, such as this passage [2:164]—

> Behold! In the creation of the heavens and the earth; in the alternation of the night and the day; in the sailing of the ships through the ocean for the benefit of mankind; in the rain which God sends down from the skies; and the life which He gives therewith to an earth that is dead; in the beasts of all kinds that He scatters through the earth; in the change of winds and the clouds which they trail like slaves between the sky and the earth;—(here) indeed are signs for people that are wise and think

—one is loath even to entertain the idea that the Tunisian engaged in idolatry. More accurately, Ibn Khaldun remarked that the role of religion was to unite Arabs—as well as other believers—by benefiting humankind through concrete development programs. Because he pointed out that injustice, despotism, and tyranny were—and still are—clear signs of the downfall of the state, Ibn Khaldun wished to rely on man to make the necessary corrections which could better serve the nation. On matters of faith, he relied on metaphysical philosophy—which he thought a true gift of revelation—to sharpen his wits.

Both King Faysal and Queen 'Iffat would certainly concur with the Tunisian.[89] As avid readers, they were known to delve into the classics and kept a copious library in their home. In fact, grandchildren received many books as gifts, in several languages, which must have broadened

---

[89] For details on the Tunisian sociologist, see Ibn Khaldun, *The Muqaddimah, An Introduction to History*, Tr. Franz Rosenthal, Bollingen Series XLIII, Princeton: Princeton University Press, 1967, 3 Vols. An abridged and edited version is also published under the title of *The Muqaddimah: An Introduction to History*, Princeton: Princeton University Press, 1981.

their worldview. Just like early Muslims who encouraged advanced scholarship and sophisticated artistic abilities, the Sa'udi royal couple engaged in mastering the latest information, and wished to see young men and women throughout the country equip themselves with techniques and innovative methods across a broad range of disciplines, including literature, philosophy, architecture, art, music, and especially the sciences. For them, Islam was the inspiration that gave their mission a purpose, for they both knew that Sa'udis needed to unleash their individual creativity to succeed. The Queen, in particular, was aware that girls needed to satisfy their thirst for knowledge if they were to fulfill their role as the educators of new generations. Significantly, the Prophet Muhammad himself had exhorted his followers to read and learn, as reported in a well-known *hadith* attributed to both Al Bayhaqi and Al Tabarani, but King Faysal bin 'Abdul 'Aziz and Queen 'Iffat Al Thunayan chose to interpret the saying in the broadest sense.[90] "Seeking knowledge is an obligation upon every Muslim," declared the Prophet according to Al Tirmidhi, which essentially meant that all knowledge, and not just *'Ilm al-Shar'i* (religious knowledge), was incumbent upon every believer. Islam was not simply a mechanical faith that commended believers to pursue minimum quests for knowledge but a belief that encouraged the faithful to fulfill their duties and embark on every learning opportunity possible. In other words, it was incumbent on a believer to acquire, to the best of their abilities, more than the minimum amount that every Muslim, whether male or female, was required to know.

Of course—and it is important to reiterate the point—this obligation cannot be limited to a specific gender or a class of people in a particular community. Rather, it is as much of an obligation on women as on men, on young as on old, on rich and poor. Indeed, the Prophet referred to the Holy Scriptures when advocating the quest for knowledge with the verse: "God will elevate to high ranks those that have faith and knowledge among you" [Qur'an 58:11]. Hence the King and Queen seldom hesitated in pursuing education programs, even when ultraconservative traditionalists opposed the pace of change. The monarchs persisted,

[90] Neither Al Bayhaqi nor Al Tabarani were as celebrated as the six leading interpreters of Islam—Al Bukhari, Al Muslim, Abu Dawud, Al Tirmidhi, Al Nasa'ih, and Ibn Majah—but both men were major Sunni *'Ulamah* following the Shafi'i School. Abu Bakr Ahmad Ibn Husayn Ibn 'Ali Ibn Musa al-Bayhaqi (994–1066), known as Imam Al Bayhaqi, and Abu al-Qasim Sulayman Ibn Ahmad Ibn Al Tabarani (873–970) were respected by their peers for their erudition and impeccable intellectual and spiritual credentials. The Iraq-born Ibn Khallikan (1211–1282), a leading Kurdish Shafi'i scholar, considered both to be his lifelong teachers.

funding the creation of libraries, saving rare manuscripts, encouraging exhibitions, and organizing and attending lectures—all to provide more easily navigable paths along which succeeding generations could travel in their own search for knowledge.

King Faysal Center for Research and Islamic Studies (KFCRIS)

Naturally, the martyred monarch's legacy was perhaps most visible at the King Faysal Center for Research and Islamic Studies, which preserved and promoted Islam's heritage. In fact, the Foundation adopted a broad agenda that mixed philanthropy with service to the nation, which highlighted the monarch's vision that was certainly shared by his spouse.

A subsidiary of the King Faysal Foundation, KFCRIS highlighted the leadership and humanism of the late King by promoting Islamic civilization and supporting cultural and scientific activities in an academic environment. This institution, which was established in 1983 and is located within the premises of the Foundation in Riyadh, houses a vast and rapidly growing library that is open to researchers, as well as a collection of rare manuscripts including hundreds of hand-copied Qur'ans of immense value to scholars. A complete electronic database assists investigators who were either part of the visiting researcher program or communicated with KFCRIS staff members. A comprehensive photographic collection—as well as clippings of dated newspapers, magazines, and journals, and rare foreign documents including a nearly complete copy of American and British archival materials pertaining to Sa'udi Arabia—is also available. KFCRIS preserves Arab and Muslim heritages by promoting manuscript preservation, as well as contributing to the cultural enrichment of the Kingdom by holding lectures that address critical topics, both contemporary and historical. The Center publishes six print items, *Al Faysal*, *Al Faysal Scientific*, *Al Faysal Literary*, *Linguistic Studies*, *Islam and the Contemporary World*, and the *KFCRIS Bulletin*, as well as the *Islamic Civilization Magazine*, which is only available online.[91]

The King Faysal School

In addition to the KFIP and the valuable work underway at the KFCRIS, the Foundation sponsors the King Faysal School, whose goal is to develop youngsters through a rigorous national and international

---

[91] According to the Center, the total number of resources available by December 2009 totaled 736,278, including books, manuscripts, documents, paintings, pictures and antiques, all of which—with the exception of rare items that can only be examined on premises—were available to both walk-in researchers and other visitors.

program of study. Students attain academic excellence based on a foundation of faith, knowledge, and work, to help create a sustainable and peaceful world through intercultural understanding and respect. With a school motto that reads, "Faith, Knowledge and Work," it fits the vision shared by the King and Queen.

Established in 1991 as a non-profit institution with a limited enrollment of approximately 350 primary students, the school had doubled in size by 1997, and now includes preschool, primary, intermediate, and secondary grades. The school allows students to concentrate on their education in an aesthetically attractive campus with 14 buildings and athletics playing fields in what is one of the most important academic projects yet sponsored by the Foundation. All facilities have been built in a style that harmonizes with that of the Diplomatic Quarter in the capital city, where the school is located. The school was founded to achieve ambitious educational and academic goals that place great emphasis on faith and loyalty in service to both crown and country. Its curriculum aims to develop students' innate abilities in the spiritual, academic, and cultural domains, while paying due heed to Islamic values and traditional Arab identity. These carefully calibrated goals help students develop a sound character, as well as modesty, sobriety, and a strongly moral code of behavior which in turn enable qualities of self-reliance, responsibility for actions, constructive competition, and leadership to emerge.

Notably, unlike its counterparts elsewhere in the country, classes start early in the morning and finish late in the afternoon five-and-a-half days a week. This full-day program includes extracurricular activities that complement the curriculum set by the Sa'udi Ministry of Education. In 1994, backed by a royal decree, the school converted to the International Baccalaureate program of international education, which raised standards even higher. By adopting such a plan, administrators settled on what was an uncommon approach in the country, namely to distance education from rote learning and develop appropriate curricula that graduated well-rounded individuals ready to tackle university-level courses. But above all, it was important to find a solid balance between traditional values and modern education, and the Faysal School supported the two without compromising either. An active calligraphy club, for example, counterbalanced classes that taught the latest in computer technology. Remarkably, the school also boasts a civics course, which was so successful that the Ministry of Education made the subject mandatory in all Sa'udi schools.[92]

---

[92] For additional details on the school, see its web page at http://www.kfs.sch.sa/en/tabid/188/Default.aspx.

Al Faysal University

One of the newest projects of the Foundation was the Al Faysal University, established in 2002, even if it did not welcome students until September 2008. Importantly, the institution stood out among Sa'udi universities because of its emphasis on the sciences. Building on the success of previous academic endeavors, the university reflects the Foundation's strong commitment to learning; family members situated the campus on the grounds of the late King Faysal's palace in Riyadh. The serene surroundings in the center of the capital make the location ideal for academic pursuits that truly honor the former monarch. Rather than keep the vast palace complex closed, trustees saw to it that the purpose-built facilities, with the capacity to accommodate up to 4,000 students, could use many existing buildings. By remodeling a few buildings and equipping them with up-to-date facilities, the university could boast four college teaching buildings, sports facilities, a conference center, and student centers all on one site. The university is specializing in the fields of business, engineering, life sciences, and medicine in this current first phase, while investigating the development of a knowledge-based economy as yet another potential faculty area. All engineering programs are based on those established by the American Board of Engineering and Technology (ABET), the primary accrediting board for engineering in the United States, which set standards at a high initial level. As part of undergraduate and graduate courses, students gain valuable work experience through the university's internship programs, which combine research with service that benefits the Kingdom. By stimulating the development of a knowledge-based economy, graduates are expected to avail themselves of specific opportunities that transform them into lifelong learners. Rather than recruit haphazardly, the board of trustees has forged academic and research alliances with world-leading institutions such as Harvard Medical International, the Massachusetts Institute of Technology, and the University of Cambridge. It has recruited top-notch academics and invited leading specialists to offer regular courses in various departments. By refusing to rush into higher education—devoting nearly six years to putting everything in place—Al Faysal University trustees emphasized what they were looking for over the long term. Using the latest technologies, they intended to create a niche university that promoted research, the feed that nurtures true development. Although the inauguration of the state-of-the-art, US$ 10 billion King 'Abdallah University of Science and Technology (KAUST) opened its doors in 2009 near Jiddah, that institution's focus was on energy and the environment, as well as the biosciences, bioengineering, applied mathematics, materials, and computer sciences. It is important to note that KAUST emphasizes postgraduate education.[93] Al Faysal University did not compete with KAUST, a coeducational university—the first in Sa'udi Arabia—whose first batch of slightly over 800 students entrusted to 67 faculty members hailed from over 30 countries. Al Faysal is also a coeducational research and teaching university, but its emphasis is on graduating Sa'udi practitioners, not only potential innovators. Unlike KAUST, which aspires to rival Cambridge, Kharagpur, or MIT, Al Faysal aims to produce fewer theoreticians and more hands-on scientists. It aims to graduate the cadre of excellent professionals the Kingdom will require as it develops into a world-class economy.

Prince Sultan College for Tourism and Business

Under the umbrella of Al Faysal University came the Prince Sultan College for Tourism and Business in Abhah, a non-profit private college accredited by the Ministry of Higher Education. Teaching in a predominantly English-language medium, the college fosters a balanced approach between the practical and academic spheres. Established in July 2001, the college operated campuses in both Abhah, the capital of Asir Province, and Jiddah. Abhah boasts a temperate climate in a mountainous region that includes sheltered valleys and fertile plains. A prime tourist destination, Abhah was also chosen as the site of the college—nestled within a resort area that offers a spectacular view overlooking the Abhah Dam Lake—because of potential employment opportunities for its graduates. Inasmuch as the development of the booming tourism sector requires both the creation of appropriate infrastructure and the training of qualified personnel, the college is well placed to meet this growing need. Sa'udi Arabia's evolving tourism and hospitality as well as Hajj & Umrah services sectors will create thousands of new positions over the next few years for graduates qualified according to innovative standards that remain true to local traditions but are equally at ease with foreign cultures. It is the goal of this hands-on institution to offer all the skills needed—both the theoretical variety in the classroom and the professional placements offsite—for working in this burgeoning industry.

A MEASURE OF PROGRESS

Few would deny that Dar al-Hanan and Effat University have made a significant contribution to the history of Sa'udi Arabia. While many

[93] For additional details on KAUST, see its dedicated webpage at http://www.kaust.edu.sa/.

worked to ensure success, Queen 'Iffat looked to a particularly high marker to measure whatever achievements were recorded, probably comparing them with her own early experiences in Constantinople and, after she returned home to Sa'udi Arabia, the enthusiastic investment she made to transform her new environment.

Speaking at the 12 May 2012 Effat University Commencement, Isobel Coleman, a Senior Fellow and Director of the Civil Society, Markets and Democracy Initiative at the New York-based Council on Foreign Relations, quoted the Egyptian poet Hafiz Ibrahim—who famously declared: "A mother is a school. Empower her, and you empower a great nation,"—as she reflected on the challenges faced by the graduates lined up in front of her. Although she did not make the link with the founder—something that every student was eminently aware of—her presentation touched upon several key developments in Sa'udi Arabia. The well-known author commented that graduates were "well placed to be at the forefront of [some of the many] changes [coming to the Kingdom]." "You will need to find ways to maintain the richness of your heritage and the aspects of your culture that make you proud," she underlined, "while at the same time navigating the currents of change and actively shaping a new future."[94] These were certainly accurate assessments, although Coleman's blog reportage a few days later concentrated on the festivities rather than the painful realities that students confronted. On her Council on Foreign Relations electronic discussion post, she admiringly reports that the graduation ceremony

> was hardly the staid affair [she] expected. Colorful klieg lights lit the way of arriving parents and dignitaries; forget 'Pomp and Circumstance'—the more than two hundred graduates and faculty paraded in to a pulsating techno beat, while stage fog swirled to dramatic effect. The array of high-heeled shoes under the graduates' sky-blue abayas was breathtaking—everything from six inch high, hot-pink platform wedges, to cowboy boots, to the latest snakeskin and metallic Manolo Blahniks." "What really impressed me," she continued, "was the energy and passion of the graduates. The president of the student government in her speech exhorted her fellow graduates—in a chant of 'yes, we can'—to change the world around them. Married at the age of twenty, she also thanked her husband for not 'putting her in a cage' and allowing her to pursue her dreams. (She exuded such determination that I can guess he didn't have much of an

[94] Isobel Coleman, "Commencement Remarks—Effat University," Jiddah, Sa'udi Arabia, 12 May 2012, at http://www.susris.com/2012/06/21/effat-university-graduates-challenged-to-shape-Kingdoms-future-coleman/.

> alternative.) The alumni speaker, who had been the valedictorian of the class of 2006, spoke of her sense of accomplishment in getting her Master's degree in England and building her career, but noted that she was most proud of passing her driver's test in the U.K. That elicited particular cheers from the crowd.[95]

Even if the cheering was illustrative of the 2011 effort to lift the driving ban for Sa'udi women, most were happy with their accomplishments and looked forward to rewarding employment opportunities. Many were aware that their struggles would be difficult as confirmed in a study conducted by Booz and Co., a global management and strategy consultation, which showed that over 75 percent of female university graduates in the Kingdom were unemployed.[96] Still, many were hopeful that they, as Effat graduates, would find good jobs because of their areas of specialization and because they were far better prepared than many colleagues attending other universities. At least one observer concluded that employment basically depended on the grades a graduate received, believing that it was "much easier" for those with better marks "to find a job." Ahmed al-Bahkalai, head of the Jazan branch of the Sa'udi Human Rights Commission, articulated this view in a widely circulated report.[97]

Others chimed in with equally pertinent comments. Elham Hassan, a psychologist, argued that receiving a diploma and then failing to find a job had "a very negative impact on both individuals and society," especially since "families see education as an investment because they know that their children will later work and help them with expenses," she

---

95 Isobel Coleman, "Effat University on the Forefront of Change in Saudi Arabia," New York: Council on Foreign Relations, 15 May 2012 ("Democracy in Development Blog") at http://blogs.cfr.org/coleman/2012/05/15/effat-university-on-the-forefront-of-change-in-saudi-arabia/.

96 The Booz Report, which was published in 2010, was devastating as it homed on the 15 percent of the Sa'udi national labor force that was comprised of women. "Sweeping reforms will have to be introduced to the national educational system as a major step in preparing Saudi women for competitive jobs," it acknowledged. While the report recognized that women's participation rate in the labor force tripled between 1992 and 2010—going from 5.4 percent to 14.4 percent—it also noted that "simply getting a degree does not guarantee employment: 78.3 percent of unemployed women are university graduates, and more than 1,000 have a doctorate degree." See Booz & Company, *Women's Employment in Saudi Arabia: A Major Challenge*, 30 March 2010, at http://www.booz.com/me/home/what_we_think/40007409/40007869/47902935?pg=0&tid=39979829.

97 "High Unemployment Among Saudi Female University Graduates," *Al Arabiya News*, 11 June 2012, at http://www.alarabiya.net/articles/2012/06/11/220016.html.

opined. Jamila al-Eissa, a professor of history at the University of Dammam, disagreed that one of the reasons why women faced high unemployment rates was due to their specializations, which concentrated on the humanities, emphasizing that there were several institutions that certainly needed teachers in those specializations, but that many graduates were neither interested in teaching careers nor, a far more serious problem, were they anxious to relocate away from family and friends. She recommended alternatives for history, geography, even Arabic language majors, by looking into media, tourism, and local government positions, all of which were certainly valid options. Eissa provided a solid explanation for female unemployment, stressing that what was lacking was "a defined plan of the distribution of university graduates among different institutions. Thorough studies have to be conducted in order to determine the needs of the Saudi job market and accordingly decide where to make the best use of each specialization," she concluded.[98]

At least one foreign observer was equally pessimistic, assessing that Riyadh's successful "King ʻAbdallah Foreign Scholarship Program," which since 2005 has encouraged students to earn degrees in over 33 countries including China, India, Britain, Australia, and, of course, the United States, was now burdened with nearly 192,592 returning graduates looking for employment.[99] While the government pressed private-sector companies to replace some of their eight million foreign workers with these grantees, few apparently were scrambling to fill available posts, both because of the low pay for most of the positions held by expatriate workers and, equally important, because of a classic problem that pervades society whereby relocation poses a serious challenge to families that prefer cohabitation to separation. Nevertheless, the entire enterprise was a work in progress and could not be evaluated when so little time had passed, while fresh opportunities are increasingly available for those who wish to embark on new adventures. To be sure, demands for good wages—not necessarily the high wages that many journalists were only interested in reporting—continue to preoccupy decision makers, but what is far more critical is to change the private sector's outlook to give educated citizens the opportunities they need to excel.

Despite the overall pessimism, there are bright spots that encourage Saʻudi educators and business leaders to emulate Effat University in placing its graduates in relevant positions, especially with international companies that have invested in the Kingdom and need competent employees. Inasmuch as global trade is conducted in the English

---

98 *Ibid.*

99 David B. Ottaway, *Saudi Arabia's Race Against Time*, Washington, D.C.: Wilson Center [Middle East Program Occasional Paper Series], Summer 2012, pp. 4–5.

language, and since Effat graduates are steeped in the medium on top of their engineering or business expertise, for example, many are prime candidates for such positions. Indeed, it may be safe to posit that while the gears of change turn rather slowly in the Kingdom, they turn regularly and with precision. Queen 'Iffat's foresight in choosing English as the language of instruction in her university was nothing if not a stroke of genius. Her early efforts to push for the introduction of foreign-language instruction in public schools were derided, but the process was engaged in and both English and French were made available. Although French was dropped in state schools, English remained and in 2003 was introduced to the sixth grade. Even if that decision was deemed sufficient at the time, rapid changes led to an acceleration of the process, as Riyadh ordered the pace to move forward. Despite a law being passed that imposed the use of Arabic as the primary language in all commercial and business dealings, including utility bills, advertising, and all sorts of contracts and insurance certificates, authorities understood that English language skills were also essential.[100] Towards that end, beginning in 2015 English language is slated to become part of the fourth-grade curriculum, which is further confirmation that the late Queen was right all along.[101]

Naturally, this was a contentious issue then as now, with many decrying the 'foreignization' of young Sa'udis, though few could deny its usefulness. To be sure, many complained that the country was not equipped to make such dramatic leaps—with additional requirements for qualified teachers, up-to-date textbooks, and supplemental materials to be created—but Effat University stood out as a beacon on the hill in response to these critics. Not only was the wherewithal available for these measures, the instruction was of the highest possible quality, the result of hard work on the part of all those responsible.

In addition to the language debate, another concrete sign of the impact that Effat University has had on the rest of the country was the decision reached by King Sa'ud University (KSU) in Riyadh to launch a drama course in 2009.[102] This initiative was so important that it deserves a dis-

---

100 "Saudi Arabia Makes Arabic Language Mandatory in all Business Dealings," *Al Arabiya*, 17 September 2012, at http://english.alarabiya.net/articles/2012/09/17/238539.html.

101 Abdullah Obaidallah Al-Ghamdi, "English Language Classes to be Rolled Out in Schools Kingdom Wide as Planned: Official," *Saudi Gazette*, 2 August 2012, at http://www.saudigazette.com.sa/index.cfm?method=home.regcon&contentid=20120823133800.

102 Iman al Khaddaf, "Drama to be Taught in Saudi Arabia for the First Time," *Al-Sharq Al-Awsat*, 24 June 2009, at http://www.aawsat.com/english/news.asp?section=7&id=17188.

cussion simply to confirm what else was possible. Considered the first of its kind, the KSU program encouraged male as well as female students to learn about the dramatic arts, with the goal of training and encouraging young Sa'udi filmmakers and technicians to develop an innovative, indigenous cinema industry. According to Professor Fahd Al Khereiji, Head of the Mass Media Department at KSU, the drama course was meant to be an alternative to the department's Theatrical Arts unit. Indeed, the shift towards drama aimed to achieve academic development and cover many different types of television, theatrical, and cinematic arts. The Professor added that the Theatrical Arts unit was somewhat restricted and not embraced by students, who saw limited employment opportunities associated with it. "Drama is more comprehensive than theatre," Al Khereiji stressed, insisting that local production companies required qualified Sa'udi technical cadres to work in film production and cited Western universities fulfilling similar goals as useful role models.[103] When the Professor was asked whether women would be allowed to join the drama course, Al Khereiji declared, "What applies to the male students applies to the female students." Queen 'Iffat was probably smiling on this most remarkable and natural comment which so amply illustrated her ambitions for everyone. In fact, KSU admitted 25 female students to drama courses in 2009–2010, and looked forward to being able to offer a Master's degree within a few years, to cater to additional needs.

Reportedly, this unprecedented step by the KSU Mass Media Department coincided with the projection of the Rotana-produced film *Manahi* at the King Fahd Cultural Center in Riyadh, a premiere attended by large audiences of different ages.[104] Proceedings went to cancer

---

103 *Ibid.* Professor Al Khereiji highlighted that the Mass Media Department, the first academic media studies department in the Gulf region, wished to promote and develop media cadres and, towards that end, encouraged students to study modern fields such as electronic journalism. The Mass Media Department at the university launched its own channel on YouTube in 2009, where several students' work was uploaded, including interesting "weekly reports" that summarized university activities. Another feature was the "Train Journey" documentary, which related the history of the media department and highlighted former students who had gone on to secure employment.

104 *Manahi* [Voyages] was a popular movie based on the successful character developed by the comedian Fayiz al-Malki. The story revolves around a *badu* who lives on the outskirts of Riyadh, who travels to Egypt in search of workers to toil on his farm and look after his camel and sheep businesses. While in Cairo, he accidentally gets entangled in a family feud between two clans, and since the trip is his first outside of the Kingdom, his naiveté leads him to get involved in several funny adventures. The movie's trailer is available at
http://www.youtube.com/watch?v=GOOl6mQjhJc.

patients via the Sanad Children's Cancer Support Society and the Sa'udi Cancer Society, though the very idea of screening a movie in the Kingdom, albeit in a private capacity, was a novelty.[105] Ironically, there were many cinemas throughout the Kingdom in the 1970s, as the medium was not then considered to be un-Islamic. Indeed, while the very idea of movies was perceived to be contrary to Arab tribal norms, improvised movie halls in Jiddah and Makkah operated as late as the early 1980s. Most of the films were from Egypt, India and Turkey, although a few Lebanese and Syrian films were screened as well, without government intervention. At the height of the Islamic revival in the 1980s, however, as a political response to an increase in religious activism in the

[105] Of course, not only were movies screened in the Kingdom, some were even made and remarkably, at least in one instance, the exercise turned out to be highly beneficial. In the early 1950s, an intensive effort was launched in the Eastern Province to combat the number one public enemy, the fly. Although a massive mosquito eradication program proved to be highly effective in reducing the incidence of malaria throughout the region, the insecticide DDT alone was not sufficient to reduce the fly population. Government officials contacted ARAMCO to see what could be done to alleviate conditions. Given overall poor public hygiene, the authorities understood that an entirely fresh, educational approach was required to change people's behavior, something that was easier said than done. ARAMCO officials knew that flies transmitted various diseases, including trachoma, which was then a major problem throughout the Arabian Peninsula. What the company proposed was ingenious.

It was eventually decided to produce a ten-minute film in Arabic entitled *al-Thubab* (The Fly), a task that was entrusted to Richard Lyford, a New York filmmaker. When it was ready, the documentary was screened via mobile projection units in the market places of Qatif as well as in various villages on the fringes of Hofuf. Most inhabitants were curious—and probably watching their first ever movie—but after a while, audience members learned how to limit the damage caused by buzzing pests. ARAMCO hired Lyford again to produce a film about water, *Miyyah*, which was equally successful. Then in 1954, when it was decided to produce a feature film about Sa'udi Arabia, Dick Lyford was once again asked to direct it. The result was *Island of the Arabs*, which told the story of early geologists who landed in Jubayl and started exploring in the desert. This feature was not an Oscar winner but told the story of the country and its founding leader, 'Abdul 'Aziz bin 'Abdul Rahman Al Sa'ud, and how he conquered Arabia after a daring raid on Riyadh in 1902. The movie was filmed at a decrepit fort in Hufuf that Prince Sa'ud bin Jiluwi, then the Governor of Al Hasah Province, provided along with "hordes of extras from the ranks of his bodyguards and various retainers as well as the horses from his personal stables." Not only was *Island of the Arabs* broadcast in movie theaters throughout the region, it was also shown multiple times on Sa'udi television every year on 23 September, the Kingdom's National Day. See Tim Barger, "The *Island of the Arabs*," ARAMCO Expats, 28 August 2012, at
http://www.aramcoexpats.com/articles/2012/08/the-island-of-the-arabs/.

aftermath of the 1979 Makkah Mosque takeover, Riyadh closed all cinemas and theaters.[106]

Of course, such projections occurred in university settings without interruption given that exposing students to a variety of cultures is an essential part of the purpose of higher education. At Effat University, as at Dar al-Hanan, drama productions were also a routine occurrence. The late Queen appreciated these efforts, attended many performances, and encouraged young women to make creative contributions. For her as well as her offspring, education was an entire package, composed of various ingredients each of which needed careful attention because the development of a mind was at stake. Queen 'Iffat would have been pleased to learn that, following the post-2005 reform initiatives introduced by King 'Abdallah bin 'Abdul 'Aziz, and for about a week in December 2008, the Rotana entertainment group, controlled by Prince al-Walid bin Talal bin 'Abdul 'Aziz, showed *Manahi* to rapturous audiences in Jiddah and nearby Ta'if. The screenings, which were approved by the provincial governor, Prince Khalid al-Faysal, sparked hopes that Sa'udi Arabia would soon allow public cinemas once again. In the event, conservative religious authorities objected, although Shaykh Ibrahim al-Gayth—then Head of the Commission for the Promotion of Virtue and the Prevention of Vice—finally conceded that "a movie could possibly be acceptable if it serves good and is suitable under Islam." The comments were made two days after the same cleric branded movies "an absolute evil," which led al-Gayth to clarify: "I did not say that we reject all cinema, but I said that we were not consulted during the organization of these movie showings."[107]

Because movie projections were limited to academic settings, and since the vast majority of Sa'udis relied on television and videos to fill their free time, a wave of fresh demands rose to alter existing conditions. The daily Arabic-language newspaper *Riyadh* carried a shrewd editorial in late August 2012, under the title "Naqisnah Sinamah" [All We Miss is Cinema], which called for the establishment of entertainment centers instead of limiting choices to street cafés. A few days later, an opinion maker printed an essay in the widely read pan-Arab daily *Al-Hayat* in which he unabashedly demanded cinema—"Nuridu Sinamah!" [We

[106] [Yael?] Admon, "Revival of Cinema Sparks Debate in Saudi Arabia," Inquiry and Analysis Series Report No. 595, Washington, D.C.: The Middle East Media Research Institute (MEMRI), 11 March 2010, at http://www.memri.org/report/en/0/0/0/0/0/0/4027.htm.

[107] "Saudi Arabia: Going to the Movies for the First Time in Decades, *The Los Angeles Times*, 23 December 2008, at http://latimesblogs.latimes.com/babylonbeyond/2008/12/saudi-arabia—1.html.

want cinema!].[108] In both essays links are made with the country's customs and traditions, while narrow interpretations of religion, which have heretofore limited such innovations, are rejected. The shrewd *'uqal al-'uqla* [commentator] makes the point that whenever a proposition is made—including, for example, allowing women to drive or reintroducing movie theaters in the Kingdom—predictable outcries insist that these are contrary to Islam. He points out that women drive and everyone goes to the movies in other Muslim countries without disastrous moral consequences. Moreover, he confirms that many Sa'udi women drive in neighboring countries, and that most Sa'udi citizens see movies during their travels without losing an iota of their faith. His brave essay concludes by making an economic case for why the availability of public cinema would neither impinge upon nor detract from daily responsibilities. Simply stated, the author affirms that those who do not wish to go to the movies are free not to, while those who wish to accompany their families and children should be able to do so as well. Inasmuch as he reminds the reader of the fate that befell the introduction of satellite dishes in the 1980s—which was sharply opposed by some, although, in the end, the phenomenon became widely accepted—the astute analyst confirms the view that Sa'udi society is rapidly changing. This article represents a small step forward but a sign of progress nonetheless. Gradual in its approach but firm in its content, such a development would have been precisely to the liking of real reformers like 'Abdul 'Aziz, 'Abdallah, Faysal, and 'Iffat, all of whom wished to see the Kingdom make steady advances.

TO EDUCATE FOR GOD AND COUNTRY

Because of unwavering commitments by both King Faysal and Queen 'Iffat, the royal couple's offspring embarked on various education projects of their own both to honor their parents' legacies, as well as fill in those lacunae that remained. Princess Sarah al-Faysal, for example, established the Madrasat al-Tarbiyyah al-Islamiyyah in Riyadh, a private primary school that housed a nursery to care for the young children of working mothers, which has since evolved into a model institution. A

[108] Mish'al al-'Anzi and Asmahan al-Ghamdi, "Naqisnah Sinamah" [All We Miss is Cinema], *Riyadh*, Number 16133, 25 August 2012, at http://www.alriyadh.com/2012/08/25/article762625.html; and 'Uqal al-'Uqla, "Nuridu Sinamah!" [We want cinema!], *Al Hayat*, 30 August 2012, p. 10, at http://alhayat.com/home/Print/430389.

similar private school, the al-Faysaliyyah, was created to cater to young boys. Speaking at Princeton University in 2006, Prince Turki al-Faysal reflected on his parents' legacy on education—especially since they and their successors recognized that oil wealth was a finite resource—to underline the family's core concerns. Prince Turki emphasized that Sa'udi elites understood that the "best and infinite resources" of the Kingdom were its people and that it was an obligation "to educate and train . . . youth[s] in new areas where they can develop, grow and innovate," if Riyadh is to diversify its economy and improve the quality of life for all citizens. Towards that end, under the auspices of the King Faysal Foundation, significant efforts were made to invest in various institutions, at the head of which were Effat College and Al-Faysal University.

King 'Abdallah bin 'Abdul 'Aziz was equally mobilized, aiming to see Sa'udis make the types of contributions to humanity that once distinguished the Arab world during its Golden Age. Whether in astronomy, mathematics, agriculture, medicine, or architecture, Arab scholars once provided the world with advances in knowledge that underpin the achievements of the modern age, though recent centuries have been far less productive. Still, that era was in the past, and thus it behooves contemporary leaders to join the long-distance race to contribute to humanity's common cause. Towards that end, Prince Turki emphasized that his and his family's interests were precisely in doing that, not just for the immediate family or only for Sa'udi citizens, but for as many needy youngsters as possible. He recalled how his parents had wanted he and his siblings to receive a world-class education and to be exposed to, and gain an understanding of, the diversity of the world that was then available through the experiences they had in private institutions such as the Hun Preparatory School in Princeton or the Montreux School in Switzerland. Likewise, he and his brothers and sisters wished for all Sa'udis to be afforded the same opportunities, and hence they had committed themselves to three critical steps to achieve this goal: first, to gradually upgrade the country's educational system, including the removal of "what might be perceived as intolerance from old textbooks," focusing on critical thinking, math, and sciences, all without neglecting true Islamic values. Second, to invest a significant portion of the country's resources in its educational system to prepare citizens for life and work in a modern global economy. And third, to broaden "the horizons of [Sa'udi] citizens and emphasize the value of cultural exchange." Prince Turki evoked an ancient Arab proverb—"What is learned in youth is carved in stone"—to stress the values by which one made basic decisions in life and how one worked with others. Faysal and 'Iffat wanted their offspring to study overseas, "to learn, make friends, and experience foreign cultures," which was also the mission Riyadh embarked upon on a larger scale after the oil boom, both to acquire critical knowledge and to become part of the community of nations.[109]

Such exposure to a variety of cultures and international knowhow notwithstanding, what Faysal and 'Iffat wanted was to create solid educational opportunities at home, their primary motivation for embarking on the variety of educational programs they set up for both men and women. Others may have embarked on identical efforts, but the happy coincidence of 'Iffat Al Thunayan's return to Makkah and her marriage with Faysal bin 'Abdul 'Aziz essentially meant that Sa'udi society's developmental rudder was in safe hands. Faysal and 'Iffat relied on God but they also believed in hard work. In a particularly moving conversation about her parents Princess Latifah al-Faysal remembered how her mother relied on her faith above all else, sincerely believing that on the Day of Judgment God would demand that both men and women should account for their deeds. "Queen 'Iffat was a faithful woman," the Princess underlined, "but I think that her faith was closely associated with deeds. Although she prayed and taught us how to worship, one could not help but witness how she practiced her faith too. She just insisted that it was a duty to do one's best, especially when given the opportunity to do something worthwhile."[110] According to Robert Lacey, Queen 'Iffat "took her inspiration from a famous collection of verses" from the Holy Qur'an, which he listed as follows:

> For Muslim men and for Muslim women . . .
> For men who believe and for women who believe . . .
> For men who speak the truth and for women who speak the truth . . .
> For men who persevere in righteousness and for women who persevere in righteousness . . .
> For men who are humble and for women who are humble . . .
> For men who give charity and for women who give charity . . .
> For men who fast and for women who fast . . .
> For men who guard their modesty and for women who guard their modesty . . .
> For men who praise God and for women who praise God . . .
> For all of them,
> God has prepared forgiveness and a vast reward.[111]

---

[109] In 2006, Sa'udi Arabia allocated 26 percent of the state budget to general and higher education, as well as to technical and vocational training. Many schools, colleges and universities were either updated or created from scratch. See "Transcript of Prince Turki's speech at Princeton," 7 December 2006, at http://www.saudiembassy.net/archive/2006/speeches/page2.aspx.

[110] Interview with HRH Princess Latifah al-Faysal, Jiddah, 12 October 2010.

[111] Lacey, *op. cit.*, p. 367.

Naturally, such a belief rested on the notion that men and women were equal before the Lord—who alone could sit in judgment—a view fully shared by King Faysal, who instinctively understood that no man should usurp a woman’s rights or responsibilities. Moreover, he affirmed that no man should object to any woman’s desire to achieve whatever goal she set out for herself, even if he also expressed reservations that were the product of age-old traditions which had forged the character of the peoples of the Arabian Peninsula. To be sure, these fine sentiments were theoretical perspectives until supported by concrete actions on the ground, but both Faysal and ‘Iffat shared the view that from those with abundant means to provide, much should be demanded—and thus it was their duty to act. Not only were Dar al-Hanan and Effat College the two shining stars in the late Queen’s educational universe, ‘Iffat’s own Sa‘udi Renaissance Movement, al-Nahdah al-Sa‘udiyyah, provided free classes in major cities to combat adult female illiteracy, ran health clinics and dispensaries with classes in hygiene and childcare, and funded a variety of programs that sought to close the knowledge gap that once existed between boys and girls, and men and women, as well as between the privileged and the disadvantaged. As discussed in the next chapter, while government agencies have since assumed many of the duties carried out by health clinics and charitable organizations created under ‘Iffat Al Thunayan’s initiatives, the very idea of providing such services in the first place came from her. Today, Riyadh’s efficient means of dispensing these services may be taken for granted, but the precedents set by the *Turkiyyah* ought not be forgotten. Her *nahdah*, in cooperation with the ministries of Education and Labor and Social Affairs, filled critical voids when no such government services existed. Sa‘udi women assumed responsibilities and acted as role models for each other—not only to empower themselves as necessary but also to enhance their self-worth at a time when that was just what this reborn nation needed.

4

Health Priorities for a Growing Population

'Iffat Al Thunayan was the ideal spouse for a conscientious leader anxious to bring about as many changes as he could over as short a period as possible. Faysal was a consummate leader who knew what his country's limitations had been when resources were scarce, and assumed great fiduciary responsibility on behalf of his nation after oil income began flooding in, so as to maximize every riyal invested in providing sorely needed socio-economic services to as many deserving recipients as possible. Between 1932 and 1953, when the founder reigned, Sa'udi Arabia had pursued myriad projects, ranging from basic housing to providing medical facilities, and embarked on numerous infrastructure projects throughout the vast country. There had been little time or money at this point in the nation's history to devote to socio-economic improvements, with most Sa'udis relying on their family support systems to survive as they gradually adjusted to the massive changes coming their way.

After 1953, the pace of change accelerated thanks to increasing oil revenues and, more importantly, the return to the country of the first wave of indigenous Sa'udis to have studied abroad, who were now entrusted with the duty of building the nation. While education was a priority that kept the country's leaders up at night, with limited manpower it was impossible for the government to look after every need. Though the country's tribal and clan support systems functioned relatively well, accelerated urbanization meant that former *badu* populations squatted in poorly devised cities that grew helter-skelter. Social services were minimal, save for religious institutions that provided some charity contributions, especially around the annual 'Id al-Fitr and 'Id al-Adhah holidays. Charitable organizations in the contemporary sense were rare indeed, except in those instances when the founder, or one of the senior princes, made an occasional contribution. Simply stated, the *badu* relied first and foremost on their survival skills to look after both their own needs and whatever requirements their relatives may have had in those often difficult conditions.[1] It was a given that proud men never begged, preferring to go hungry rather than stoop to the indignity of beseeching charity. Likewise, women received minimal assistance, but could at least rely on each other in extended families and clans to fend for token rations.

Conditions were thus far from ideal, and both the ruler and his entourage were amply aware of what ailed Sa'udi society. That much was well understood, and hence King 'Abdul 'Aziz bin 'Abdul Rahman never let one of his visitors leave empty-handed, aware that such assistance allowed his followers to survive the dire circumstances many faced. Every individual who paid his respects to the ruler was fed and allocated some type of aid before leaving the "palace." It was a given that such audiences existed both to grant allegiance (*bay'ah*) to the founder—who was glad to receive such legitimizing support—and to fulfill the supplicant's minimal desires. Of course, as the number of urbanized Sa'udis increased, such access posed its own set of problems, which could not always be satisfied. Still, the monarch was a generous leader though he also knew perfectly well what was happening all around him. In the words of one respected historian, "generosity and hospitality are real pleasures to an Arab, in addition to being enjoined by his religion; and it is no part of perfect generosity to consider whether one's beneficiaries deserve it. ['Abdul 'Aziz] could not have curtailed his gifts because tradition demanded them, and because his power partly depended on them, but he would not have curtailed them if he could, [because] . . . He enjoyed them."[2] Naturally, the founder's successors practiced identical policies, although their *majlise*s were more limited, as the greater demands on their time restricted their availability. Consequently, advisors, ministers, and, in time, bureaucrats assumed some of the governance burdens placed on Al Sa'ud officials. At times, the wheels of government worked well and provided what was necessary, though more often than not efforts were haphazard. In the inharmonious environment of the 1940s, 1950s, and early 1960s, many went without, something of which 'Iffat Al Thunayan was all too aware.

---

1 There is an abundance of details on the harsh conditions that pertained during the first few decades of the 20th century throughout the Arabian Peninsula. For a glimpse, see Leslie McLoughlin, *Ibn Saud: Founder of a Kingdom*, London: Macmillan, 1993; Haifa Alangari, *The Struggle for Power in Arabia: Ibn Saud, Hussein and Great Britain, 1914–1924*, London: Ithaca Press, 1998; and Geoff Simons, *Saudi Arabia: The Shape of a Client Feudalism*, New York: St. Martin's Press, 1998.

2 David Howarth, *The Desert King: The Life of Ibn Saud*, London: Quartet Books, 1980, p. 111.

The purpose of this chapter is threefold: first, to discuss the various philanthropic societies that emerged in the nascent Kingdom, the result of both religious injunctions and social necessities; second, to address the requirements of disabled adults and children, who were seldom provided with the care they desperately needed; and third, to evaluate how the country's health institutions emerged and then evolved. Because Princess 'Iffat arrived in Makkah with her disabled aunt, Jawharan, someone she had first taken care of when still a youngster in Constantinople, her views were largely colored by her aunt's situation. As discussed below, 'Iffat Al Thunayan worked to eliminate the huge taboos that existed around disabled individuals in Arabia—throughout the Arab World, for that matter—rejecting the prevailing attitude that the only rule to be applied in harsh desert conditions was survival of the fittest. While she appreciated existing values, whose conventional wisdom was that only healthy persons could function, travel long distances, and endure intolerable desert conditions, Princess 'Iffat nevertheless was aware that Sa'udis faced a serious dilemma. Although no health facilities worthy of the name existed in the early 1930s, intra-family marriages still produced birth deformities, leaving vulnerable disabled people living with families who barely tolerated them beyond providing basic care. She courageously launched new programs to address the specialized attention such people required, attempting to eliminate the taboo and provide adequate long-term services for the disabled. The chapter closes with an assessment of what Jawharan's own life represented for the future Queen, who loved and respected her aunt just as much as she honored and admired her mother.

PHILANTHROPIC SOCIETIES

In earlier times Arab women, including those in Sa'udi Arabia, worked hard looking after their families even when many confronted unmistakable prejudices in what was undoubtedly a paternalistic society. Outside of their immediate families, notwithstanding occasional fortunate access to a member of the ruling family, there were few opportunities for additional economic support where this was sorely needed. Employment, and consequently financial independence, was rare, though that calamity was at least gender-neutral. Many *badu* men required employment assistance, and while the National Guard, or perhaps the regular armed forces, hired a few, many others led idle lives supported by subsidies. Of course, conditions were dire for women as well, so to help alleviate some of the known shortages in the nation's capital,

Princess 'Iffat organized the al-Nahdah Philanthropic Society for Women in Riyadh.

Al-Nahdah Philanthropic Society for Women

Inspired by her daughter Sarah, who first had the idea of looking after the growing number of women requesting assistance, 'Iffat did not hesitate in ensuring that whatever was needed would be made available. Established in the capital, al-Nahdah brought together the future Queen and her two eldest daughters—Sarah al-Faysal and Latifah al-Faysal—as well as Muzaffar Adham ['Iffat's sister] and Samirah Khashoggi.[3] It was the first charitable women's organization dedicated to empowering women socially and economically through specific projects and programs. From the very beginning, an effort was made to build on volunteer efforts for general social service, even if over time the institution developed into a charitable institution committed to women's social and cultural development. Guided by *Shari'ah* rules, the women who came to al-Nahdah for basic assistance—most were provided with free sustenance—presented something of a dilemma. Beyond immediate benevolent contributions, the founders understood that the high level of illiteracy among the women seeking help required attention. If conditions were to change, they reasoned, it was important to tackle the root of the problem and not simply feed those in need; it was important to teach them how to fend for themselves. Towards that end, it may be accurate to conclude that long before the Ministry of Social Affairs had adopted various programs to combat illiteracy in the Kingdom, it was al-Nahdah and several sister institutions that set the pace. Once authorities had

---

[3] Samirah Khashoggi (1935–1986) was the daughter of Muhammad Khashoggi, one of King 'Abdul 'Aziz bin 'Abdul Rahman's personal physicians. Her brother Adnan and her sister Suhayr [Soheir] were practically raised in the al-Faysal household, and Adnan attended Victoria College in Egypt with several leading princes. In 1954, Samirah married Muhammad al-Fayid [Fayed], the Egyptian tycoon she met in Alexandria, and gave him Dodi. The marriage lasted two years although Samirah separated from al-Fayid just months after Dodi was born. She died of a heart attack in 1986 at the age of 51 and Dodi was killed in a Paris car accident along with Diana, Princess of Wales, on 31 August 1997. Soheir is a well-known Arab writer with three major novels to her name: *Mirage*, *Mosaic*, and *Nadia's Song*. For a list of the first "founders," see Salmah Muta' al-Khudayrih, *Masirat Jami'at al-Nahdah al-Nisa'iyyat al-Khayriyyah khilal Arba'in 'Aman: 1382–1422* H [The 40 Year-Long March of the Nahdah Women's Charitable Society: 1962–2002], Riyadh: Al-Nahdah Women's Charitable Society, 1424 H [2003], p. 22. The book's transliterated title and the name of the society in this instance are literal efforts, although a slight variation is offered in the text above to reflect its true philanthropic activities and—this is worth underscoring—its utilitarian vision.

taken to tackling those needs, al-Nahdah focused on the running of an orphanage, essentially to ensure that no homeless children were left to roam around the city. Over time, al-Nahdah has added a variety of social, cultural and even linguistic programs, as participants were taught basic hygiene, nursery essentials for women with newborns, cooking with modern utensils, sewing, and myriad other services.[4] Regrettably, even now few Sau'dis know about the impact of this and other, similar institutions, and even fewer are aware of Queen 'Iffat's role in seeing to it that the society flourished.

Sprawling facilities in Riyadh today offer a welcoming environment to all those anxious to benefit from al-Nahdah's programs. To say that managers run a smooth operation would indeed be an understatement as anyone who chooses to visit can see for themselves. Especially rewarding to notice is the incredible progress achieved in the sheer number of women and children who benefit from the many programs supported by the charity. While most of the projects are in social welfare and family health, gargantuan efforts have also been made over the years to look after children with special needs, as well as to introduce the early childhood education that was sorely lacking in the country before the early 1960s. Remarkably, after nearly fifty years' experience in offering social services, al-Nahdah has reached an unparalleled level, renowned for the quality and relevance of the projects it sponsors and the results that it achieves. Simply stated, in line with Queen 'Iffat Al Thunayan's wishes, al-Nahdah ensures that women are given every opportunity to become active partners in the development of Sa'udi society. The Queen wanted to empower women socially and economically, but not only by doling out financial aid to as many as possible. While she did her fair share of such philanthropy, 'Iffat Al Thunayan instructed her daughters and their friends to introduce positive changes, which meant accepting responsibility to empower recipients with the necessary skills that would allow them to hold jobs, and creating programs that generated wealth for all. As with other projects the Queen was moved to promote, al-Nahdah Philanthropic Society was founded on the principle of instilling responsibility, and especially self-reliance, in all those who benefited, whose duty it then became in their turn to contribute to the common good.

Towards that end, al-Nahdah has introduced training and self-development courses, based largely on Maslow's theory, which assumes that the life goals of every human being change according to their needs, only moving on to the next level once they have secured current requirements.[5]

---

4 Al-Khudayrih, *ibid.*, pp. 113–127.

5 Abraham Maslow first proposed his psychological theory in a paper entitled, "A Theory of Human Motivation," which was published in the *Psychological Review*

According to the theory, beyond basic physiological needs individuals in every society seek safety and security, followed by ways of satisfying their social needs, reaching comfort zones in terms of their work and, finally, achieving complete self-realization. Properly trained al-Nahdah staff members have adapted this theory to accommodate local prerequisites, with the aim of giving women tools as closely adapted to their environment as possible. Beneficiaries are, of course, provided with basic needs though they are also expected to accomplish the best to which they could aspire.

While al-Nahdah ensures that recipients receive basic requirements of food, clothing, and assistance with rent, all are expected to make useful contributions to their society, especially since the safety net created for them ensures their security. This is why al-Nahdah has been so successful, since the women are given clear incentives to improve their families' situations as well as ensure their own futures. Social workers and registered beneficiaries enjoy strong bonds not only because most realize that the financial support offered by the charity is guaranteed, but also because they can see for themselves how the projects they are engaged in help alter existing and largely unresolved social and legal problems. It is, to say the least, a successful model, one that gives each recipient a lot of belief. Importantly, the programs that motivated the first few cohorts to excel set a pattern for success that, despite inevitable limitations in literacy and basic skills, has managed to alter conditions for those involved significantly for the better.

Of crucial importance is that al-Nahdah has always been able to go about its activities with the full support of the Ministry of Labor and Social Affairs, coordinating with the authorities in those areas of the city that need priority assistance, and seldom venturing to trespass on existing state initiatives. Between 1962 and 1975, various joint ventures were launched, which benefited several poor Riyadh districts where unemployment and illiteracy were high. Of course, while government funding eventually covered a good portion of its expenses, al-Nahdah

---

50:4, 1943, pp. 370–396. Over the years his observations on the innate curiosity that human beings displayed, describing various stages of growth, led him to subdivide his theory into five categories of needs: physiological, safety, love and belonging, esteem, and self-actualization. These were the patterns of need that human motivations generally move through, based on the lives of exemplary individuals. Interestingly, he rejected the reliance of studies that concentrated on mentally challenged individuals, writing that "the study of crippled, stunted, immature, and unhealthy specimens can yield only a cripple psychology and a cripple philosophy." See Abraham Maslow, *Motivation and Personality*, New York: Harper and Row Publishers, 1954, p. 236.

started off with generous stipends from Princesses Sarah and Latifah and other family members, as well as grants allocated by wealthy contributors. Typically, Princess 'Iffat encouraged her daughters to follow her own approach by donating anonymously.[6] In 1976–1977, for example, the Tradiyyah district of the capital received special attention, as al-Nahdah volunteers offered every imaginable type of aid. The only proviso that recipients pledged to honor was to enroll their children in school, where their progress was followed by social workers entrusted with their supervision.

Among the many training services provided by the center were literacy classes and, in advanced stages, Arabic, English, and French, as well as typing courses. In 1978, the first women's library in Riyadh was formally established, followed by a solid program that introduced Braille reading and writing for the visually impaired. This was followed by a nursery lodging, vocational training and rehabilitation for those with special needs, the raising of awareness about cultural, health and social issues in the capital city's Faysaliyyah district, and the creation of emergency residential shelter for families in dire need, including battered women. Within a decade, in 1987, al-Nahdah had established Renaissance Schools from birth until the age of 21 for those with Down's Syndrome—all geared to vocational rehabilitation.[7]

By 1995, a center specializing in Sa'udi heritage had come into existence to preserve the authenticity of the country's customs at a time of rapid socio-economic changes that ushered in rapidly modernizing trends.[8] Although the Kingdom's founders were persuaded that they ought to embrace modern industrial methods to improve the lives of Sa'udi citizens, they were also aware of the ravages that foreign influences, beamed through powerful mediums like television, could inflict on local traditions. Utility clothing, including sports outfits that allowed youngsters and their mothers to gain useful mobility, were acclaimed by recipients. Apparel such as blue jeans and tank tops was also accepted since such universal garments were eminently practical. Still, as attested to by the nearly 5,000 traditional pieces of clothing, jewelry, and various

[6] Characteristically as well, Princesses Sarah and Latifah did not want to elaborate on their critical roles in the Foundation during the interviews conducted for this book, although another source confirmed their active participation. Interview with Sabah Yassin, granddaughter of Shaykh Yusuf Yassin who served King 'Abdul 'Aziz bin 'Abdul Rahman as Minister of Foreign Affairs, and who is also active with the Jiddah-based charity.

[7] Al-Khudayrih, *op. cit*, pp. 40–51.

[8] The photographs reproduced in the color plate section (after page 168) are but a small sample of the many artifacts assembled at the Society.

personal items collected and displayed in a permanent museum, *badu* mores produced their fair share of practical outfits, too. In fact, an elegant and critical aspect of al-Nahdah's plans concentrated on the preservation of these cultural artifacts, perhaps as a reminder to all those toiling at the philanthropic institution, along with its many visitors, of exactly what were the norms the foundation wished to uphold. Naturally, although the priority was to promote female employment, the Kingdom's cultural heritage was seldom neglected, as the latter strengthened the sense of what needed to be done in the contemporary sphere without ignoring or forgetting the conditions under which such development ought to happen.

The Women's Charitable Society in Jiddah

It was not long before al-Nahdah's success in Riyadh led to the establishment of the Jam'iyyah al-Nisa'iyyah al-Khayriyyah [The Women's Charitable Society] in Jiddah. Inaugurated by Princess 'Iffat on 17 June 1963, its objectives included anti-illiteracy and sewing classes for women, and also the establishment of a maternity and a childcare center.[9] Over the years this institution has welcomed many women who were in desperate need of help, but rather than simply hand out perpetual subsidies, its directors decided to transform recipients into productive citizens and residents. While many recipients were Sa'udis, a larger group included non-Sa'udis—many from African countries—who came to the Hijaz for pilgrimage and simply stayed on. To better cater to these needs, the organization was divided into two sections: one looking after divorced women and the other dealing with small families facing challenging circumstances.

Divorce was not and is not taboo in the Kingdom, but those divorcees who lacked education were expected to fend for themselves. Often, divorced women needed vocational training, which was made available through various programs, while their children were looked after in crèches. Disadvantaged families also presented challenges, with basic assistance—rations of sugar, flour, cooking oil, and other staples—being routinely provided. As families grew and overpopulation became a genuine problem, the Society introduced a limit on the number of mouths it catered to within a single family—limited to six—although extensive assistance, ranging from housing to education, was provided to members within that family. However, it was steadfast in refusing to assume responsibility for a seventh member, and went as far as to drop the entire

[9] "Women's Charitable Society in Jeddah Inaugurated," *Al Madinah Al Munawwarah*, 18 June 1963, as cited in Parssinen, *op. cit.*, p. 163.

The al-Faysal Family

1. HRH Princess Hayfah al-Faysal, one year old.

2. HRH Princess Sarah al-Faysal holding her sister, HRH Princess Lulwah al-Faysal, 1947.

3. HRH Princess Latifah al-Faysal, 3 years old, 1941.

4. HRH Sarah al-Faysal, 2 years old, and Ibrahim Bayk, Asia Al Thunayan's husband, 1937.

5. HRH Prince Sa'ud al-Faysal, 9 years old, St. Moritz, Switzerland, 1949.

6. HRH Prince Muhammad al-Faysal, 7 years old, HRH Prince 'Abdul Rahman, 3 years old, and HRH Princess Sarah al-Faysal, 8 years old [right to left], 1943.

7. HRH Prince Sa'ud al-Faysal in traditional garb, 7 years old, 1947.

8. HRH Prince Sa'ud al-Faysal, probably 4 or 5 years old, with his father, King Faysal.

9. HRH Prince Turki al-Faysal and his brother HRH Prince Bandar al-Faysal, undated photo, most probably from when they were 9 and 12 years old, respectively.

The Sa'udi Royal Family

10. King Khalid bin 'Abdul 'Aziz, r. 1975–1982.

11. King Fahd bin 'Abdul 'Aziz, r. 1982–2005.

12. King Faysal bin 'Abdul 'Aziz, r. 1964–1975.

13. Prince Sultan bin 'Abdul 'Aziz, Heir Apparent, 2005–2011.

14. Prince Salman bin 'Abdul 'Aziz, Heir Apparent, 2012–.

15. HRH Amr bin Muhammad al-Faysal, Jiddah, 2009.

17. Surrounding King Faysal are HRH Prince Fawwaz bin 'Abdul 'Aziz, and two future rulers, Fahd and 'Abdallah, offering Hajj prayers at Makkah, 1973.

16. HRH Prince Turki al-Faysal, 2011.

18. Kings Khalid, Faysal, Fahd and 'Abdallah performing a reenactment of the war dance known as the *'Ardhah*, 1972 [left to right].

19. Faysal as Heir Apparent, 1955.

20. Faysal at 14 years old in 1919.

The Al-Nahdah Philanthropic Society for Women, Riyadh

21. An award that recognized al-Nahdah's contribution to the city's social welfare.

22. Al-Nahdah maintains a pottery crafts division to teach skills that enhance local traditions.

23. Traditional *abayas* from the Najd region sewn by al-Nahdah volunteers.

24. Traditional *abayas* from Najd.

25. A view of the principal building of the society built according to Najdi customs.

The Dar al-Hanan School

26. A young pupil, early 1960s.

27. Young children at school.

28. An early Dar al-Hanan school bus.

29. The original Dar al-Hanan Building. The smaller building was used as a dormitory for students from other parts of the country.

30. A typical classroom, *circa* early 1960s.

31. Students at a school reception, academic year 1959–60.

32. A full classroom, *circa* early 1960s.

33. Pupils preparing for a school bazaar, early 1970s.

34. The science laboratory, 2010.

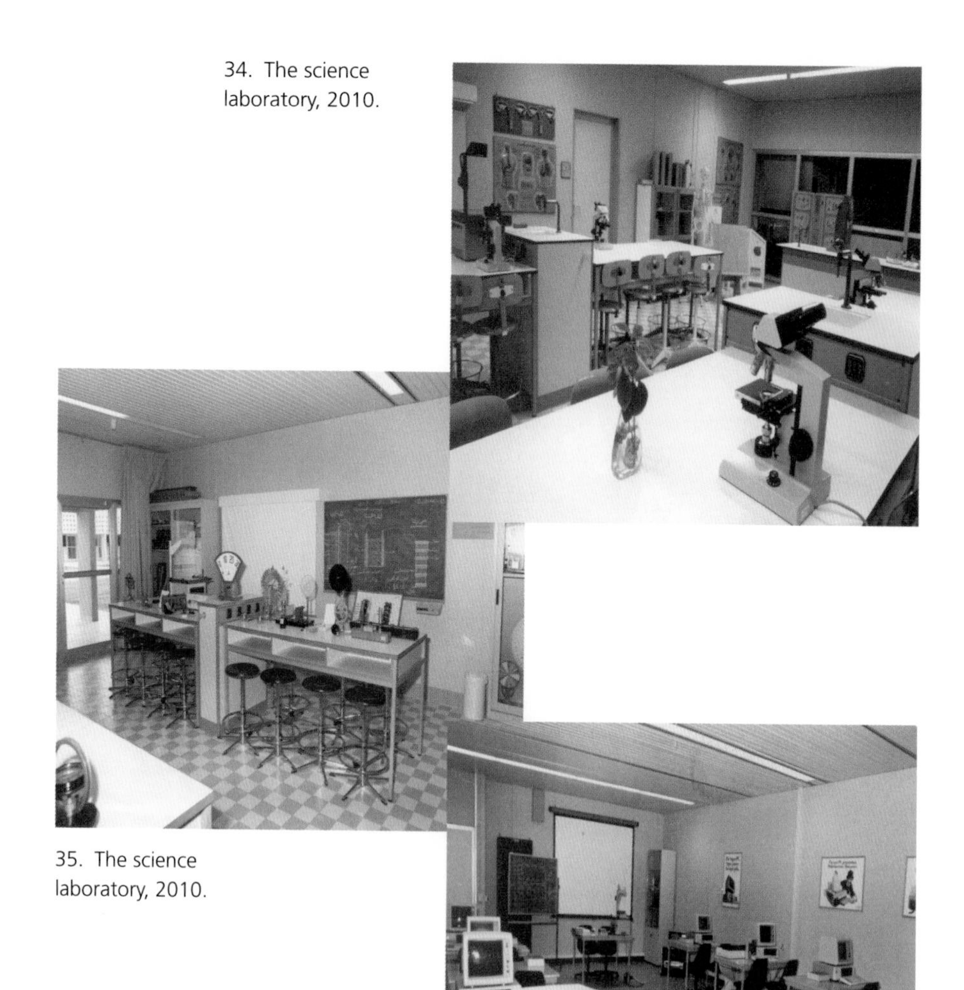

35. The science laboratory, 2010.

36. The computer room, 2010.

37. A school bus, with the inscription: "Exclusive for the transportation of Dar al-Hanan Students," 2010.

38. Students testing electrical equipment in the science laboratory, *circa* 1985.

39. A view of the Dar al-Hanan courtyard, 2010.

40. The main entrance to the school, 2010.

41. An elementary classroom, 2010.

42. The science laboratory, 2010.

43. The science laboratory, 2010.

44. The elementary school playground, 2010.

45. The administration building, 2010.

46. Al-Madrasah al-Numuzajiyyah [Model School for Boys] in Ta'if, mid-1940s.

The King Faysal School/Al Faysal University

47. Students at the King Faysal School in Riyadh, 2012.

48. King Faysal's Palace in Riyadh which was converted into the principal building at the newly inaugurated Al Faysal University.

49. University Mosque, the College of Science, and the Administration Building [left to right], which was the Riyadh home shared by King Faysal and Queen 'Iffat.

50. College of Science Main Entrance.

51. The College of Science.

Effat University, Jiddah

52. Staff members in front of the university's administrative building, 2009.

53. Students on a basketball court, 2009.

54. Students leaving the Department of Architecture [top]; The College of Business [bottom], 2009.

55. A baccalaureate robe at Effat University. The Arabic calligraphic logo spells out 'Iffat, a name that denotes 'integrity' and 'uprightness'.

King Faysal Specialist Hospital and Research Center

56. An aerial view of the hospital complex in Riyadh.

57. City view of Riyadh with the hospital complex in front, the iconic Faysaliyyah Tower near completion in the background and the Kingdom Tower, which houses the Four Seasons hotel, under construction to the left, alongside the capital city's famed King Fahd Road.

58. The hospital North Tower Building.

The Sa'udi Royal Family and International Dignitaries

59. HRH Sa'ud al-Faysal and UN Secretary-General Ban Ki-moon with the Board of Directors of the King 'Abdallah Bin 'Abdul 'Aziz International Center for Interreligious and Intercultural Dialogue (KAICIID), Vienna, Austria, 13 October 2011.

60. HRH Sa'ud al-Faysal with religious dignitaries at the inauguration of the King 'Abdallah Bin 'Abdul 'Aziz International Center for Interreligious and Intercultural Dialogue (KAICIID), Vienna, Austria, 13 October 2011.

61. King Faysal in Istanbul on an official visit to return to the Queen's birthplace, 1966.

62. King Abdallah, Commander of Sa'udi Arabian National Guard, early 1960s.

63. U.S. President Barack H. Obama and King 'Abdallah bin 'Abdul 'Aziz Al Sa'ud, at Rawdat Khuraym in Sa'udi Arabia, 28 March 2014.

64. U.S. Secretary of State John Kerry with King Abdallah at the latter's desert encampment Rawdat Khuraym near Riyadh, 5 January 2014.

65. President Franklin D. Roosevelt meets King 'Abdul 'Aziz bin 'Abdul Rahman Al Sa'ud on board the USS *Quincy* (CA-71 – Cruiser Armored) in the Great Bitter Lake, Egypt, 14 February 1945. The King is speaking to the interpreter, Colonel William A. Eddy, USMC., while Fleet Admiral William D. Leahy, USN, the President's Aide and Chief of Staff, is at left.

66. President Dwight D. Eisenhower and then Vice President, later President Richard Nixon, are shown with their host, King Sa'ud bin 'Abdul 'Aziz, at a dinner event given by the Arabian monarch at the Mayflower Hotel, Washington D.C., 1957.

67. Then Heir Apparent Faysal bin 'Abdul 'Aziz with U.S. President John F. Kennedy, The White House, Washington, D.C., 1962.

68. King Faysal with French President Georges Pompidou, Elysee Palace, Paris, 1973.

69. Egyptian President Jamal [Gamal] 'Abdul Nasir, Heir Apparent Faysal, King Hussayn bin Talal [of Jordan], Alexandria, Egypt, 1964.

70. King Faysal at the Al-Aqsah Mosque in Jerusalem, with the Mufti Al-Hussayni to his left, and King Hussayn of Jordan to the extreme left. Prince Nawwaf bin 'Abdul 'Aziz is to the monarch's right, 1966.

family if another child was added to its number. In this way, the charity promised to provide quality assistance while building self-esteem and a sense of conscientiousness among recipients.[10]

Women's Associations

This philosophy was very much in line with Queen 'Iffat's preferences, as she maintained that the needy should be given every assistance imaginable, with everyone stepping up to the proverbial plate. Over the years, thousands received such assistance, at significant cost to the State as well various charitable institutions. In 2011 alone, the Women's Charitable Society budget topped SR 30 million [US$ 8m] simply for looking after 2,600 families in the city of Jiddah. Of course, this was but one charity, and many similar institutions have been created elsewhere, even if in the post-9/11 period the very idea of charities in Sa'udi Arabia was mistakenly identified by Americans as a source of tension. Sadly, vitally important organizations like the Women's Charitable Society or the Iktifa' Women's Charitable Society, among others, were lumped together with groups allegedly funding extremists. When Washington pointed its finger at the Al-Haramayn Islamic Foundation, allegedly because it maintained "direct links" with 'Usamah bin Ladin, the ban stunned everyone. Dozens of charities were so labeled, as carefully earned reputations were smeared, often with devastating consequences. Still, Sa'udis resisted the blame game, continued to assist needy institutions, and remained true to their vocations.

Fully funded charities thus empowered needy women to live decent lives and, rather than rely exclusively on their families or the state, most learned new trades and earned incomes to support themselves. This did not mean that Sa'udi women were encouraged to neglect established traditions or family links. On the contrary, the chief purpose was to eliminate hurdles that denied women more fulfilling methods by which to contribute to their families by learning how to function in a rapidly modernizing society. "My mother insisted," Princess Sarah al-Faysal emphasized, "that every person who received assistance ought to remove the cloak of shame from their faces. She wanted a recipient to accept temporary assistance because of circumstances but to also acquire skills to repay society in even better ways."[11]

Scores of charitable foundations have emerged in the past few decades, including the 'Abdul 'Aziz Bin Baz charity foundation offering social and humanitarian services; the Charity Committee for Orphans'

---

[10] Interview with Nisrin Al-Idriss, Director of Public Relations, Women's Charitable Society, Jiddah, 20 March 2011.

[11] Interview with HRH Princess Sarah al-Faysal, Riyadh, 13 October 2010.

Care [Insan] and the Aytam charity organization, both of which offer care services for orphans and poor children in Sa'udi Arabia; the Disabled Children's Association that helps children with limited mobility all over the Kingdom; the Sa'udi Spina Bifida Support Group; the Sa'ad Al Sani' Centre for Communication Disorders; the Kafil Organization, which looks after children with special needs; and, of course, the Sa'udi Red Crescent Society, the country's leading humanitarian organization offering voluntary services and assistance whenever needs arise. For its part, the Alwaleed [Al-Walid] Bin Talal Foundation provides humanitarian assistance to various women's organizations, with a dedicated emphasis on female empowerment programs that include the development of the handicrafts sector, support for training and employment efforts, tie-ups with women's centers and associations, and awareness and education projects focusing on health and human rights. Towards that end, the King Faysal Foundation supports the Faysaliyyah Women's Charitable Society, now chaired by Princess Fahdah bint Sa'ud, among other institutions.[12]

Charities, including women's organizations, play a vital role in contemporary Sa'udi society. They stand as one of the foundations of Islam, which commands the faithful to give alms to the needy. Most have now become "service-providers of housing, health, education, social and housing benefits, and disability provisions. Particular companies or individuals set up some of these foundations, including Al-Rajhi Banking, or the better-known Prince Walid bin Talal or Abdul Latif Jamil Foundations. The umbrella charities, such as Al-Birr, have expanded as well, leading to serious progress being recorded in this area since the early 1960s.[13]

ASSISTANCE TO THE DISABLED

A 2004 medical study, based on a survey carried out by a team of physicians at King Sa'ud University in Riyadh to ascertain the prevalence, distribution, and determinants of disability among children under 16 years of age in Sa'udi Arabia, concluded that the total disabled popula-

[12] Alwaleed bin Talal Foundation, "Women's Empowerment Projects," at http://www.alwaleedfoundations.org/saudi-arabia/category/womens-empowerment/?project.

[13] For comprehensive information on different charity associations in the Kingdom, see Caroline Montagu, "Civil Society and the Voluntary Sector in Saudi Arabia," *The Middle East Journal* 64:1, Winter 2010, pp. 67–83.

tion in the Kingdom was approximately 60,000 in 2000.[14] Although published in a specialized medical journal that was not widely read among ordinary citizens, medical statistics compiled by the Ministry of Health for their annual reports offer comparable information on disabilities including numbers, types of injuries and/or disabilities, the total number of the amputee population, and geographical distributions across the vast country. People with disabilities receive better health care services in the 21st century than in the last decades of the 20th, as entire institutions have been created from scratch to assist disabled people so that as many as possible can gain employment, including those discussed above under various al-Nahdah programs. Despite gargantuan efforts, the overall penetration is still limited, given that the very idea of disability existing in Sa'udi society—which is sometimes the result of close family intermarriages—is still a taboo subject. Were it not for members of the ruling family—whose leaders supported public and private organizations and facilities for people with disabilities—as well as donations from wealthy families in the Kingdom, conditions would be dire.

To be sure, significant progress has been recorded during the past few decades as specialized organizations such as hospitals of the Sa'udi National Guard and the regular armed forces, along with private philanthropic institutions, have stepped in to look after adults as well as children with various physical and mental disabilities. While specialist organizations remain extremely sensitive about statistics regarding people with disabilities, the *East Mediterranean Health Journal*, cited above, stands out for its clarity in trying to estimate what were vastly underreported data. Of course, Queen 'Iffat wanted charitable institutions to develop the infrastructure needed to care for the disabled, but she also wanted improved services for individuals.[15] But, above all, what

[14] M.B. Al-Hazmy et al., "Handicap Among Children in Saudi Arabia: Prevalence, Distribution, Type, Determinants and Related Factors," *East Mediterranean Health Journal* 10:4–5, July–September 2004, pp. 502–521. For an equally interesting perspective, see Salah I. Al-Gain and Sami S. Al-Abdulwahab, "Issues and Obstacles in Disability Research in Saudi Arabia," *Asia Pacific Disability Rehabilitation Journal*, January 2002, at http://www.aifo.it/english/resources/online/apdrj/apdrj102/arabia.pdf.

[15] During the past few decades, the Ministry of Education operated the Nur Institute for the Blind, the Amal Institute for the Deaf and the Institute for the Intellectually Disabled [names as translated by the ministry]. Meanwhile, the Ministry of Labor and Social Affairs operated Career Rehabilitation Centers in Riyadh, Ta'if, and Damman, Social Rehabilitation Centers for the Severely Disabled in Riyadh, al-Ahsah, and Madinah, Comprehensive Rehabilitation Centers in five regions, the Institute for Paraplegic Children in Riyadh and Ta'if, and Social Welfare Centers for the elderly in seven major cities.

she wanted and worked to achieve were laws that protected disabled individuals in a variety of areas.

Towards that end, the earliest law addressing the rights of the disabled was signed in 1969 when the Labor Code was amended through a royal decree (Number M/21) which emphasized labor rights and, for the first time in the country's history, detailed vocational rehabilitation for people with disabilities. This was followed by the Labor and Workman Law, also in 1969, which established institutions necessary to provide vocational training services, ostensibly to facilitate employment opportunities. In 1973 the Council of Ministers passed a new resolution, Number 407, which allocated monthly allowances to the disabled if they participated at one of the recently created disabled training centers. It was not as simple as it sounded, for stepping out in public was a major undertaking for many who did not want to expose themselves to scrutiny. Within a year, however, a follow-up resolution, Number 715 [1974], provided rehabilitation for paraplegics, epilepsy patients, and those who required medical care under the supervision of the Ministry of Health, measures supported by King Faysal himself as he toured the country and inaugurated various facilities; the same legislation also established mother and childcare centers affiliated to the Ministry of Health, for taking care of pregnant women and children. A policy of the General Department of Rehabilitation was issued under Royal Decree Number 129 [1976], whose purpose was to approve the creation of special programs for those who could be vocationally trained and set other programs for those who were not fit to work by giving them special medical and psychological rehabilitation. In addition to the comprehensive assistance extended under these laws, an annual donation of SR 30,000 [US$ 8,000] was made to people with disabilities by the Council of Ministers Resolution Number 219 in 1980, which was administered by the General Department of Rehabilitation under the Ministry of Labor and Social Affairs. A year later, those who qualified and their companions received 50 percent discounts on all government-owned transportation services, including ships, airplanes, trains, and buses, according to Council of Ministers Resolution Number 187 [1981]. Other laws were added to this list with the Council of Ministers Resolution Number 85 for 1997 establishing the Persons with Disabilities Services Coordination Committee, which harmonized donations to the disabled and their families and prepared public awareness programs to raise awareness and conduct research into ways of preventing disability.[16]

[16] For additional details on the legislative history discussed in this paragraph, see Planning and Evaluation Department, *Country Profile on Disability Kingdom of Saudi Arabia*, Tokyo: Japan International Cooperation Agency, March 2002, at

Year after year, Riyadh improved the special services it provided to the disabled through rehabilitation centers, which totaled 29 by 2002, caring for some 8,000 beneficiaries. In addition to the services provided to groups with special needs through institutions, the ministry also provided non-institutional care services such as the foster family program, the in-family assistance program for paralyzed children, and the disabled assistance program. In 2002, beneficiaries in these programs numbered 90,000, which did not include those receiving similar assistance from Non-Governmental Organizations (NGOs).[17]

In fact, Riyadh recognized that NGOs, which in 2001 numbered 226 throughout the country—of which 204 catered to men while only 22 looked after women—undertook a wide range of activities. An estimated 55,000 special-needs children had been educated, trained, and participated in rehabilitation programs. Childcare programs had benefited 97,000 other children, while nearly a million received some type of health care. Of these, approximately 17,000 received care services adapted to the disabled and the elderly. NGOs were also active in ensuring that charity housing and housing improvement programs were available for nearly 11,000 individuals.[18] More recently, according to the Ministry of Economy and Planning, beginning in 2007 Riyadh adopted a comprehensive policy for surveying its disabled population every five years, to identify characteristics of the disabled in terms of size, type of disability, and proliferation, precisely to avoid pitfalls and to respond in a better way.[19] The Kingdom's "Ninth Development Plan" acknowledged that in 2008 the country provided 7,820 Sa'udis with comprehensive rehabilitation at designated centers for the severely disabled, 2,509 of whom were women.[20]

As these statistics reveal, Sa'udi Arabia established numerous rehabilitative services for people with disabilities over a short period of time. A majority of these programs "offered physical, occupational, speech and hearing therapy as well as prosthetic and orthotic services within the

---

http://siteresources.worldbank.org/DISABILITY/Resources/Regions/MENA/JICA Saudi_Arabia.pdf.

17 Kingdom of Sa'udi Arabia, *Eighth Development Plan 2005–2009* [1425–1430 H], Riyadh: Ministry of Economy and Planning, January 2005, pp. 311–312, available at http://www.mep.gov.sa/themes/GoldenCarpet/index.jsp;jsessionid= B67F3 24E6 C88F5A03412C80BCEC8CF32.alfa#1346424735935.

18 *Ibid.*, p. 312.

19 Kingdom of Sa'udi Arabia, *Ninth Development Plan 2010–2014* [1431–1435 H, Riyadh: Ministry of Economy and Planning, January 2010, p. 679, available at http://www.mep.gov.sa/themes/GoldenCarpet/index.jsp;jsessionid=B67F324E6C88 F5A03412C80BCEC8CF32.alfa.

20 *Ibid.*, p. 339.

existing modern and sophisticated health care service system and infrastructure."[21] Rehabilitation programs and facilities became integral parts of modern health care delivery services and, to fulfill the express wishes of successive rulers, were made available to all citizens and residents. Several specialized medical centers such as the King Faysal Specialist Hospital and Research Centre, and the King Khalid Eye Hospital, discussed in the next section of this chapter, stand as among the most modern health facilities in the world. With respect to disabled patients, the "Prince Sultan City for Humanitarian Services," which includes multidisciplinary rehabilitation programs on an unprecedented scale in the Arab World, accommodates individuals who have suffered severe strokes, traumatic injuries, congenital anomalies, or are at an advanced age with geriatric ailments such as dementia.

Although most Sa'udis now take the existence of such facilities for granted, the very idea of caring for the disabled in the 1940s and 1950s, when proper hospitals and clinics were still in their infancy, sounded preposterous to some. Few of these services existed when Princess 'Iffat proposed that the government of Sa'udi Arabia establish social rehabilitation centers, which were sorely needed even if few had the vision needed to create them. Because of narrow cultural views, Riyadh delayed plans to embark on such programs, though limited financial resources at the time did not make the government's task any easier. In the event, as initial projects were delayed, the Princess established her own social welfare institutions, which addressed the educational and health needs of those at risk. Over time, the Ministry of Labor and Social Affairs provided various services to those outside the remit of social institutions, but these were mostly financial in nature, to help parents cope with additional expenses or, if they could afford to take their charges abroad, to care for them in Europe or perhaps in nearby Lebanon. Most adults with disabilities were cared for at home even if such assistance was minimal. A few lucky children were enrolled in specific rehabilitative programs, albeit abroad, entailing drawbacks such as separation from their parents. In the late 1960s and early 1970s, several government programs funded the rehabilitation of disabled children in Lebanon, which was then one of the few Arab countries offering such services. Su'ad al-Juffali and her husband, the late Shaykh Ahmad al-Juffali, first encountered some of these Sa'udi children when a group walked by their garden in the picturesque resort village of Brummana in Lebanon.[22] Until then they had no knowledge that such programs existed—albeit outside of the Kingdom—

[21] Country Profile on Disability Kingdom of Saudi Arabia, *op. cit.*, p. 14.

[22] Interview with Su'ad Hussayni al-Juffali, President, Board of Trustees, Help Center, Jiddah, 7 November 2010.

but as discussed below that encounter led them to create the renowned Help Center, which is one of Jiddah's brilliant jewels. For while financial assistance from the state was generously given, a more pressing need was vocational rehabilitation programs that could challenge youngsters to aspire to do their best. But how were such severe intellectual disabilities to be addressed and, more importantly, what kinds of programs were required to help parents cope with their disabled children?

The Help Center

One of Sa'udi Arabia's most successful business leaders, Shaykh Ahmad 'Abdallah al-Juffali (1924–1994), was keenly aware of what needed to be done in his country. Born in Makkah into a prominent Najdi family that originated in 'Unayzah (in the Al Qasim Province)—a city that lay south of the provincial capital of Buraydah and north of Riyadh—Shaykh Ahmad, as he was known, was a born entrepreneur who in the 1940s founded the Juffali Group which has since secured many critical infrastructure projects. It was one of his companies that built the first power utility plant in the Kingdom, while other companies he owned won concessions in telecommunications, transportation, information technology, and air-conditioning, as well as in many other manufacturing and engineering projects. Whether it was the Brummana encounter that triggered the philanthropic bug on such a large scale in Shaykh Ahmad is difficult to determine, although he was well-known for periodic bouts of philanthropic activity throughout his life. In 1985, however, he and his wife founded "The Ahmed Al-Juffali Foundation (AJ Foundation)" to offer specific assistance to segments of society that were most in need, as well as to support the financing and operation of the Help Center. For nearly three decades, the AJ Foundation has continued to finance the center and provide support to more than 5,000 families with children with complex needs, though mere numbers do not even begin to tell the story.

The Help Center began operations in November 1985, when the number of families seeking assistance highlighted that special services required by their children were simply not available either in Jiddah hospitals or in the regular school settings many attended. It became clear that children with special needs required trained therapists who understood the complexities of each child's particular problems and could devise specific programs to help them live happy lives, gradually allowing them to integrate with the community and function as independent people. During the period from 1985 to 1995, the center operated out of a modest villa in Jiddah, though it also soon became clear that the available facilities were inadequate. To meet future challenges and to create a more or less permanent home for the institution, in October 1993

Shaykh Ahmad al-Juffali laid the founding stone to the 43,000-square-meter state-of-the art premises in one of Jiddah's most prestigious neighborhoods, close to the Corniche and surrounded by several palaces. Two years later, the first children arrived at the new center, which had the capacity to welcome several hundred. In 2011, nearly 375 children were enrolled at the Help Center, attended to by 150 specialists and devoted staff members.

Rather than see the children as "handicapped," the Help Center relies on a holistic approach to the development and education of its students, which focuses on both the child's functions (i.e. articulation, memory, and motor functions) and a full-fledged motivation program that offers all the stimuli and information needed to help each individual to use his/her acquired skills in living an independent and ordinary life. Known as the Bavarian Curriculum, this approach is also referred to as "Individual Corrective Therapy," which incorporates children into the mainstream school curriculum rather than isolating each child in his own orbit. By integrating children with intellectual disabilities in as complete an education environment as possible—one that emphasizes cultural and religious values, behaviors, and practices—disability itself becomes a secondary concern. Having looked around carefully for best practice, Help Center therapists used these methods—developed for German schools facing similar challenges—with adjustments to reflect Sa'udi cultural norms, customs, and beliefs. They have kept the Bavarian model's three components: *Developmental Education* that focuses on sensory-motor skills, speech/language needs, and thinking processes; *Social Skills* that assist each child in being self-reliant as well as able to communicate; and *Subject-based Areas*, including religious studies, basic stimulation, elementary science, computer skills, arts and crafts, drama, sports, domestic science/cooking, and, whenever possible, pre-reading and pre-writing as well as reading and writing. But what they have added has been equally valuable, gradually changing local taboos that inhibited children with behavior, attention, and concentration problems in an environment that traditionally was not well-known for its tolerance of the disabled. The tasks given to these children are not easy and remain a daily struggle, but every visitor leaves the Help Center amazed by the incredible progress that most of them display.

Su'ad Hussayni al-Juffali and her husband wanted to give back to their community and country, though it must be emphasized that their vision and plans grew partially out of their interactions with 'Iffat Al Thunayan and Faysal bin 'Abdul 'Aziz, as well as Princesses Sarah and Latifah. In fact, the couples were neighbors in the rather small community that was Makkah at the time, which included a few other leading families such as the Pharaons, the Jamiliyyahs, and the Sharifiyyahs.

When Su'ad first arrived as a young bride, she was quickly accepted into the small group through her cousin Nafisah Hussayni's friendship with the Queen, precisely so that she would not have to endure the sort of integration problems that 'Iffat herself had previously experienced.[23] As a 21-year old bride, Su'ad befriended the Queen's eldest daughter, Sarah—who was the same age—as well as Princess Latifah, and later recalled how the doors of the palace were swung open to receive her when she arrived in Sa'udi Arabia in 1955. "Princess Sarah was one of my best friends in Makkah," said Su'ad al-Juffali, and "Queen 'Iffat was a very attractive woman who immediately took you into a different world whenever you were in her presence. She just knew everything about me and my family—not just the fact that I was Ahmad's wife—and wanted to gain as much information as possible about Lebanon,

[23] The Hussayni, or Husayni, family was one of the most prominent Palestinian dynasties in Jerusalem, Palestine, and several members held critical political positions such as the Grand Mufti of Jerusalem. Hajj Amin al-Husayni was allegedly pro-German during World War II, though his pro-Axis broadcasts on Nazi radio stations were largely the result of his anti-British policies as opposed to any strong ideological affiliation with the Nazi regime. Muhammad Amin al-Hussayni was the Grand Mufti and President of the Supreme Muslim Council, an important Sunni institution (Hanafi School) even if most Palestinians followed the Shafi'ih School of Law. Perhaps the most prominent leader was 'Abdul Qadir al-Hussayni, who died in the prime of his life, at 41, as he defended Jerusalem in the battle of Al Qastal a few days before the establishment of the State of Israel. The son of Musa Qazim Pasha al-Hussayni, one of the commanders who led the early struggle in Palestine from 1919 to 1933, and who in turn died in 1934 after being injured in a demonstration protesting British connivance with the Zionists, Musa Qazim Pasha put up a stiff resistance. For his part, 'Abdul Qadir and his men scored important hits on the Jaffa–Jerusalem road, retaliating for Jewish attacks on several nearby villages. The Hussaynis are the descendants of the Imam Hussayn bin 'Ali and migrated to Jerusalem in the 12th century after Saladin successfully drove the Crusaders out of the Levant. Over the centuries, they earned a reputation as true defenders of the city, and rebelled against the Egyptian governor, Muhammad 'Ali, when the latter served the Ottoman Empire. Diehard Arab nationalists, they led the resistance movements that emerged against the Young Turk government after 1908, and were vocal opponents of the British Mandate government as well as early Zionist immigrants, culminating in the first Arab–Israeli war in 1948. It was in that year that most of the clan relocated to Lebanon, Jordan, and several Arab Gulf countries. Still, several family members continued to live under occupation in the Old City, though several Hussayni girls were married to prominent Lebanese and Sa'udi men. For additional details on the Hussayni family, see Ilan Pappé, "The Rise and Fall of the Husainis (Part 1)," *The Jerusalem Quarterly*, Issue 10, Autumn 2000, pp. 27–38; and idem, "The Husayni Family Faces New Challenges: Tanzimat, Young Turks, the Europeans and Zionism, 1840–1922, (Part II)," *The Jerusalem Quarterly*, Issue 11–12, Winter–Spring 2001, pp. 52–67.

where I grew up, and my ancestral homeland, Palestine." When asked to comment on the Queen's personality, her eyes lit up as if her memory banks had been recharged: "One was struck by her outstanding personality and incredible memory," she insisted, since "Queen 'Iffat just knew how to talk and put you at ease. She reminisced about her youth in Turkey, which was the ultimate point of compassion, sharing with you how one might feel when one is uprooted from a familiar environment. You were in the presence of a queen, no doubt about that, and not because she was in a Lanvin dress, or because she was surrounded by what passed for luxury in those days, but because of her fantastic presence."[24]

Yet what also impressed Su'ad al-Juffali was the Queen's truly serious side, one that was in a hurry to improve living conditions all around her. For example, at annual gatherings for Palestine, the Queen would make generous donations, especially since she knew that an entire welfare system was desperately needed in the Occupied Territories as well as in surrounding countries. She encouraged fashion shows and bazaars to raise funds, and was a silent founding member of the Dar al-Tifl al-'Arabi fil-Quds [The Jerusalem House of the Arab Child] established by Hind al-Hussayni after she had rescued 55 orphaned survivors of the 9 April 1948 Dayr [Deir] Yassin Massacres, when the small village of roughly 600 people was attacked and 107 were killed. Hind brought the children to Jerusalem and converted her grandfather's mansion into an orphanage to house them and, over the years, accepted many more foundlings in need of shelter. At one point, Queen 'Iffat personally supported several of the estimated 1,200 Palestinian orphans at the Jerusalem House, though she seldom discussed these matters in public. "One year, she gave the equivalent of a million dollars in today's value [2010] to the orphanage," recalled Su'ad al-Juffali, "and she continued to provide financial assistance to this institution until the year she passed away."

As Shaykh Ahmad's bride blossomed and became a philanthropist in her own right, she received a rare training from 'Iffat Al Thunayan. Indeed, the very idea of a welfare society in Sa'udi Arabia germinated in her presence, as the down-to-earth Queen encouraged her ladies to do good. An outsider to the family, al-Juffali was still able to observe who were the Queen's friends and ladies-in-waiting. "She had no entourage per se," Su'ad al-Juffali affirmed, "but she had her preferred women who used to visit her nearly every day. It must be stressed, moreover, that few women in town ever let go of her, and no one ever turned her back on

[24] Interview with Su'ad Hussayni al-Juffali, President, Board of Trustees, Help Center, Jiddah, 7 November 2010.

the Queen, even if differences of opinion inevitably arose." "It's hard to believe," she acknowledged, "but the Queen had a knack to bring everyone together. She was tolerant and patient but did not suffer fools and told them to shape up, reminding each and every one how lucky they were to be in the situations they were in. Above all else, she just wanted the women around her to do things and not just lounge around. Remarkably, she was like her aunt, Jawharan, who was also a strong woman, despite her disability, and I was impressed by the way the aunt was integrated in the Queen's circle."[25]

Whether the seeds for a Help Center were planted in Su'ad al-Juffali's mind in this period in the late 1950s is difficult to say, and she herself could not answer such a question. What she was sure about was the impact Jawharan had on her. Here was a disabled individual fully accepted in the Queen's growing *majlises* and always given a prominent place at her niece's insistence. There was always a place set aside for the wheelchair that Jawharan used, and it was the most natural thing for someone to wheel her in whenever she wanted to join in. Just seeing that done in this still very conservative society was incredibly significant, something that could not but leave an impression, even if indirectly.

Given the friendships that blossomed between the Faysals and the Juffalis, it was natural that Su'ad's own daughter, Mahah, would enroll at Dar al-Hanan. "What an unbelievable experience," Mahah al-Juffali acknowledged, "and I remember very vividly when we did not have to wear a veil. We wore skirt uniforms and actually carried handkerchiefs," she confirmed, "enjoying a full and active student life." What stood out for the many "half-bred," as she identified the many mixed family offspring, "was a true international environment in which we coexisted and learned, we the children of so many settled and settling families in and around Jiddah." Mahah went to the United States to attend college, first at Wellesley where she could not handle the snow and bitter cold, and then at Mills in Oakland, California, "a unique institution where many of my friends and acquaintances asked me ignorant questions, including whether I lived under a tent or had a camel."[26] Cultural shocks notwithstanding, it was at Mills that Mahah discovered child psychology and decided to make it her career, aware of her parents' project back in Jiddah. Mahah started her own family after graduating in 1978, but the needs of the community, never far from her mind, eventually called on her to act. "Our goal was and is not to look after every disabled Sa'udi child," she said, "but to offer the highest-quality care we can think of for

---

[25] *Ibid.*

[26] Interview with Mahah al-Juffali, Executive Director, Help Center, Jiddah, 8 December 2010.

those that come to us. We are, hopefully, a model for others to emulate, for it is critical to think of a setting that accompanies these children over a long period of time so that they can integrate in society and function as best as possible. We want to entrust these kids to qualified teachers and therapists—and I want to emphasize the qualified part, for that makes all the difference in the world."

Mahah's learning experiences at Dar al-Hanan were not limited to reading and writing but included a large amount of time given to the arts. It was probably these experiences that provided the inspiration to create a similar environment at the Help Center through an affiliation with VSA ["Very Special Arts"].[27] "We have come a long way since the establishment of VSA Arts—Kingdom of Saudi Arabia [VSA Arts—KSA] back in 1994," avowed Mahah, "but this association allows our students to express as they discover and explore through the arts." Volunteers at the Help Center, aiming to emulate what was one of the top global institutions for assisting disabled people, followed the template of VSA Arts International. They established a special network of six voluntary offices around the Kingdom to expand activities to cover each and every region of Sa'udi Arabia. Programs were offered in creative writing, dance, music, and visual arts, not just to encourage these educational programs to help people with special needs develop learning skills, but also to allow them to acquire independence and self-esteem, as well as to enhance their well-being by boosting their confidence. The results were truly miraculous.

Equally important was the post-graduation phase that many of these children experienced, which was before the major incentive for Su'ad al-Juffali to donate her old family home to create an "alumni club for the Help Center." Going by the name Dirat Ajdady [My Forefathers' Dwelling], it took a full year to convert the former home into a suitable venue for Help Center alumni, but this too was a major accomplishment as it introduced into Sa'udi society the idea that adults with intellectual disabilities required social, recreational, leisure, and sports activities just like the rest of the population. The facilities of this social "club span over two floors and consist of a fully equipped arcade games room, a gymna-

[27] Founded in 1974 by Jean Kennedy Smith, the former U.S. Ambassador to Ireland, as a means by which individuals with disabilities could learn through, participate in, and enjoy the arts, VSA, at one time the world's leading international non-profit organization for disability arts, was then known as the National Committee—Arts for the Handicapped before it merged in 2010 with the John F. Kennedy Center for the Performing Arts in Washington, D.C. For additional details on VSA, the international organization for disability arts, and its various activities see its dedicated webpage at http://www.kennedy-center.org/education/vsa/.

sium, arts and craft room, electronic games room, silkscreen printing facilities, wood workshop, barber and beauty salon, outdoor pool, basketball court, and football pitch."[28]

Although the Help Center is a non-profit organization, it focuses on improving the quality of life of individuals with intellectual disabilities by creating opportunities to learn, live, work, and play in a safe environment. After 2009, sheltered workshops for soap and candle making were set up at the Dirat Ajdady club to further empower young adult graduates, in order that everyone might live as full a life as possible. Moreover, as a philanthropic non-governmental institution dedicated to the welfare of youngsters and aspiring adults, what the founders aimed for was to integrate children fully and for them to assume their rightful places in society. In other words, the first mission was to eliminate existing taboos regarding those suffering from intellectual disabilities—often accompanied by physical disabilities—and to stop the regrettable epithets that literally turned these people into social outcasts. Of course, this is precisely what 'Iffat Al Thunayan encouraged everyone to do and what her daughters and sons continue to advocate. As the very creation of the Help Center illustrated, the late Queen's message echoed far beyond her immediate surroundings—a sure sign of success.

The Maharat Center

The Help Center has not been the only institution to make a significant contribution to what is a burgeoning Sa'udi civil society, as dozens of institutions have emerged to meet local requirements in recent years. One that deserves special attention is the Maharat Center in Jiddah, which from the outset has refuted the argument that people with learning disabilities are simply lazy. Rather, its educators and psychologists have always understood that early intervention produces positive results, as they have set out to identify children and young adults with learning disabilities; designed and implemented individualized skills development programs; and equipped families, schools, and other caregivers with the necessary skills and support to enable their children's development. This has been routine in many developed countries for a number of decades but is relatively new in the Kingdom, where poor readers and listeners, or even impulsive or distractible children, have traditionally been neglected. Most of these youngsters possess normal to high intelligence, though they frequently suffer from low self-esteem, their academic and social endeavors having been negatively received over a long period of time.

---

[28] For additional details on the Help Center and its various activities see its dedicated webpage at http://www.helpcenter.med.sa/index.php/helpcenter_e/e_home/.

Established in 1994 by Nadia Alireza, whose parents were also pioneers, the Maharat Center filled a critical void in the city.[29] In establishing Sa'udi Arabia's first center dealing with specific disabilities, following her own mother's motto, Nadia wanted to ensure that every child achieved their full potential so as to become a successful member of society. Her mother, Marianne Alireza, is an American Catholic of Polish descent who left behind her beloved California when she moved to Sa'udi Arabia in the mid-1940s, having married a Sa'udi man she met at college. Soon introduced to Princess 'Iffat, who characteristically made her feel welcome in what must have been strange new surroundings, Marianne had in fact already met Faysal bin 'Abdul 'Aziz in San Francisco when the latter represented his country at the inaugural United Nations conference. Marianne's husband, 'Ali Alireza, who hailed from one of the Kingdom's most important merchant families, had also been a delegate and when he invited Prince Faysal for dinner, Marianne had been beside herself, not knowing how to welcome her guest in their modest home.[30] In the event, Faysal enjoyed his dinner, and shocked Marianne by keeping her first-born, Hamidah, "on his lap for half an hour and astonished [her] by discussing at great length such things as infant feeding schedules, sleeping habits, the age at which solid food is

---

[29] Nadia's parents, 'Ali and Marianne Alireza, were one of the first mixed couples in the Kingdom. They met in a California college and Marianne lived in Sa'udi Arabia for many years before she and her husband divorced. She moved back to Jiddah a few years ago to be near her children. For additional details on the center, see its dedicated webpage at http://www.maharat.org/index_en.htm.

[30] The House of Alireza (also known as Bayt Zaynal) is one of the oldest family businesses in Sa'udi Arabia; the founder, Zaynal Alireza, started trading from Jiddah in 1845. Over the years, the businesses moved from the importation of foodstuffs, textiles and other merchandise to the acquisition of agencies for the shipping lines that carried these commodities. After 1932, the Hajih 'Abdallah Alireza and Company emerged as a major company helping to develop the country, holding the Ford Motor Co. dealership, and involved in the distribution of petroleum products, telecommunications contracts, and various shipping concerns. In view of its long business standing in the Kingdom, the company received the commercial registration number "1"—for obvious reasons a source of pride. It has thus played a significant commercial role in the Kingdom's development, including the installation of the first broadcasting and radio telegraph system, the supply and installation of the first automatic telex exchange, and then a computer-controlled electronic exchange for the Ministry of Post, Telegraph and Telephone. In time, the management and operation of the Jiddah Sea Port was entrusted to the company along with various other projects including installation of the first hyperbolic navigation system for the Ports Authority, the creation of a computer center for the National Information Centre, a land mobile radio system, flight information display systems at the King Fahd International Airport in Dhahran, and several similar projects. The company's capital

given, and when a child usually gets its first teeth."[31] This was not the only time the Foreign Minister interacted with the family, as their paths crossed again repeatedly, especially during long crossings of the Atlantic Ocean aboard the *Queen Mary* when in the immediate postwar period both Faysal and 'Ali were obliged to travel frequently to America. It was, perhaps, a sign that he missed his own children during these long journeys that he considered those of his aides and associates as family, too. Marianne was a friend of the Prince and Princess, enjoying a closeness she passed on to her offspring, all of whom maintained the best of ties with the al-Faysals. Nadia Alireza, in particular, benefited from the support that Princess Lulwah al-Faysal extended by serving as the President of the Maharat Center's board of trustees, along with Princesses Hayfah al-Faysal, Sarah al-Faysal, Albandari bint Khalid, Hassah bint Khalid, and Mudhi bint Khalid. The current composition of the board illustrates the esteem in which members of the ruling family still hold the Alirezas.

Beyond extending moral and material assistance to the Maharat Center, everyone involved appreciated the valuable work that specially trained psychologists were engaged in, as they sought to correct learning disabilities among an increasingly youthful society confronted with the challenges of modernization. Nadia, who exudes gentleness, has applied what many preached. She is a hands-on executive with a mission, akin to what her mother's good friend, the late Queen 'Iffat, exhorted an entire generation to become. "It's amazing how the Queen motivated us," she recalled, "always trying to push us to do far more than we could possibly accomplish. Queen 'Iffat was a born leader, in the true sense of the word, and I frankly do not see many like her around our part of the world."[32] Marianne Alireza, a woman of exquisite taste and impeccable grace, listened carefully to her daughter but added, "Queen 'Iffat was a gracious and correct woman. She kept track of what went on around her and seldom missed a beat. She was a master observer and was gorgeous in every sense. As Americans say, 'she was with it,'" according to her friend, some-

---

base has expanded significantly since 1960, reaching SR 130 million (US$ 34.7 million) in 2003. At the end of 2007, its reserves equaled 100 percent of its paid-up capital, and shareholders' equity amounted to SR 379 million (US$ 101 million). For additional details on the company, see Michael Field, *The Merchants: The Big Business Families of Saudi Arabia and the Gulf States*, Woodstock, New York: The Overlook Press, 1985, pp. 13–47; see also the company webpage at http://www.alireza.com/.

31 Marianne Alireza, *At the Drop of a Veil*, Boston: Houghton Mifflin Company, 1971, p. 21.

32 Interview with Nadia Alireza, Executive Director, The Maharat Center, Jiddah, 6 November 2011.

one "who wanted to address core problems in the country. When she saw something wrong and could do something about it, she never hesitated."[33] "This is, I think, her real legacy for the Kingdom," Marianne observed. "She certainly knew that unique opportunities came her way and concluded that the whole thing would be such a waste if she were to simply mind her business and let others make decisions at her behest. We were all mesmerized by her desire to do something and, naturally, pushed our own children to emulate her. When Nadia saw a need to help children with learning disabilities, it was nearly automatic that she would invest in such a project. That's what everyone learned from 'Iffat."

HEALTH INSTITUTIONS

Traditional Muslim theology offers contradictory views about contagious diseases like the plague, believing them to be either a mercy and a martyrdom from God for the believer as well as a punishment for the infidel, or a phenomenon coming directly from God and therefore not contagious. As a result, Muslim doctors and scientists have often had a difficult time in reconciling these tenets since transmissible illnesses were too serious to be left to the clergy. Over the centuries, millions of pilgrims from around the Muslim world have brought a variety of contagious diseases to the Hijaz, which naturally wreaked havoc in every community. As mentioned in Chapter 1, pilgrims from Mesopotamia (modern Iraq) and elsewhere brought cholera to Makkah in the Spring of 1831, and nearly 3,000 pilgrims returning from the Holy City to other communities in the Peninsula died of the disease. Makkah was thereafter regularly invaded by cholera epidemics until about 1912 when strict measures were taken to prevent recurrences. Most visitors were quarantined for a short period of time in specially built facilities, with no exceptions allowed even for members of the ruling family, notwithstanding that they probably enjoyed a higher standard of living. Poor hygiene and overall poverty essentially meant that the nascent Kingdom lacked basic health facilities at the time of its creation, a problem that was universally acknowledged, even as the founder and his advisors sought quickly to create the institutions that would cater to local needs.

Health care for the Kingdom's population has improved steadily since then, with a full-fledged ministry now providing primary health care

[33] Interview with Marianne Alireza, author of *At the Drop of a Veil*, Jiddah, 6 November 2011.

services through a vast network of nearly 2,000 clinics throughout the country, where an effective even if cumbersome referral system provides curative care for all. In 2014, approximately 220 hospitals, several with technologically advanced specialist services whose standards rival European counterparts, cater to every conceivable need. Most of these facilities operate on a *pro bono* basis, though a range of private facilities have emerged in recent years, some of which are of superior quality and could easily compete with government-run services.

In addition to the Ministry of Health national health care system, three additional layers of care providers exist today in Sa'udi Arabia—the Ministry of Defense and Aviation (MODA), the Ministry of Interior (MOI), and the Sa'udi Arabian National Guard (SANG) operations—all of which run separate health facilities that cater to members of the organization and their extended families. As discussed above, the Ministry of Labor and Social Affairs controls institutions for the disabled and custodial homes for orphans, which also include some degree of medical care. Other autonomous government agencies accommodate basic health services in their day-to-day activities. The Ministry of Education, for example, has provision to offer primary health care to students, while the General Organization for Social Insurance and General Presidency of Youth Welfare provides health services at sports facilities for certain categories of the population. The Royal Commission for Jubayl and Yanbu makes available health care for its employees and residents at the two industrial cities of Jubayl and Yanbu. Saudi Arabian Airlines operates its own health care facilities while several universities that house medical colleges or hospitals, specialist curative services, and medical education and training programs also look after their own employees. In sum, the vast network of public and private health care institutions that have emerged over recent decades has ensured that any Sa'udi can receive the medical attention they need. It was not always the case and although complaints as to the quality of health facilities and care abound, few can deny the commitment of the Sa'udi government in financing the majority of these institutions. Likewise, while in the past it was a fact of life that most Sa'udi patients who required specialized attention were routinely transferred to European or American hospitals, the several national tertiary care referral hospitals that have since been created in the Kingdom have eliminated the need for most of these arduous transports. One such institution, the King Faysal Specialist Hospital and Research Center (KFSHRC), was directly tied to Queen 'Iffat's vision; another, the King Khalid Eye Specialist Hospital (KKESH) in Riyadh, was inspired by the work of the KFSHRC, even if the KKESH today is unrivaled in the developing world. Both deserve special attention.

King Faysal Specialist Hospital

The King Faysal Specialist Hospital and Research Center (generally known as the Takhasusih [Specialist] in the Kingdom) was established in Riyadh on 450,000 square meters of land donated by the late monarch, who laid its cornerstone in 1970; the current total area occupied by the hospital complex is 920,000 square meters. A smaller sister facility in Jiddah was inaugurated in 1981 and carries the same name. In many ways the very creation of this hospital answered the growing call to create a premier health institution that catered to a wide range of needs so as reduce the number of patients needing to be transferred to European and American hospitals for vital treatment. While it was still under construction in 1973, Riyadh signed an agreement with the Hospital Corporation of America (HCA), the world's largest operator of private hospitals—based in Nashville, Tennessee—to manage the nascent establishment. Regrettably, King Faysal died on 25 March 1975, before the hospital was inaugurated, though King Khalid was present for the opening ceremony of the 120-bed hospital a few months later. The HCA agreement stayed in place until 1985, when operations as well as all administrative responsibilities were transferred to a local team by then confident that it could offer the same level of care.

Though a relatively small facility when it opened its doors, by 2011 the Takhasusih had grown into a 936-bed tertiary care hospital staffed by approximately 7,000 professionals drawn from 63 different nationalities. Over the years, and in addition to properly trained health-care workers, state of the art equipment was added to transform existing facilities into a truly modern hospital. By all accounts, it was the capital city's premium hospital, offering advanced care to the ruling family as well as to thousands of Sa'udis referred there from smaller institutions across the country.[34]

Inevitably, a large number of foreign workers are employed at the hospital, which, in order to meet its many needs, is obliged to recruit more senior personnel than the Kingdom can hope to train. In 2011, Sa'udi residents and fellows on the staff totaled 703, which represented some 54 percent of the total, while from the 46 percent of expatriates, 16 percent were U.S. or Canadian citizens and 11 percent were Europeans. The nursing staff totaled 1,942, of whom 18 percent were from Canada and 11 percent from the United States, with the balance from the United Kingdom, other European countries, Australia, New Zealand, the Philippines, Sa'udi Arabia, and elsewhere. English is the

[34] "Marahil al-Tawasu' fi-Mustashfah al-Takhasusih wa Da'm Malaki la-Mahdud" [Periods of Expansion at the King Faysal Specialist Hospital and Unlimited Royal Support], *Al-Takhasusih*, Special Edition, Rajab 1432 [June 2011], pp. 2–8.

medium of communication even if the staff rely on an army of translators to ensure that patients get the care they needed.[35] Because the hospital is the Kingdom's referral center for cancer treatment, its oncology department provides comprehensive therapy, education, and training as well as a clinical research programs. As a member of the Southwest Oncology Group (SWOG), Radiation Therapy Oncology Group (RTOG), and Canadian Blood and Marrow Transplantation Group (CBMTG), the King Faysal Hospital has spearheaded its own regional research consortiums, notably the Gulf Oncology Regional Group (GORG) as well as the Eastern Mediterranean Blood and Marrow Transplantation (EMBMT) Group, both of which look after patients in a variety of countries.

Moreover, its radiation oncology section provides advanced radiation therapy technologies, conventional radiation therapy, and stereotactic radiosurgery (minimally invasive), offering patients highly precise and effective treatment options. Equipped with the latest technological innovations, the Takhasusih offers intensity-modulated radiation therapy (IMRT) and has embarked on image-guided radiation therapy, also called radiotherapy; helical tomotherapy, the next generation of cutting-edge radiation therapy technology that provides oncologists with unprecedented abilities to deliver radiation therapy with surgical precision; CyberKnife® robotic radiosurgery, a non-invasive alternative to surgery for the treatment of both cancerous and non-cancerous tumors anywhere in the body, including the prostate, lungs, brain, spine, liver, pancreas, and kidneys; and a 4-D CT simulator, or "CAT" scanner, with special software that measures patient motion, such as breathing or movement during rest. In the last instance, by planning radiation treatment around a patient's natural movements, doctors can treat smaller tumors with great accuracy, which is especially useful for lung, breast, and some gastrointestinal cancers, where physicians can time the radiation to a special point in the breathing cycle to make the treatment more precise.

In addition to these advances, the Takhasusih has undertaken various organ transplantations, along with comprehensive care for cardiac surgeries, all of which has gained it a well-deserved reputation for excellence. Just as its founders envisaged, the hospital has led medical research during the past three decades and publishes a bimonthly English-language general medical journal, *The Annals of Saudi Medicine*, which is globally consulted. Indeed, the *Annals* publishes original articles on matters relating to medicine in Sa'udi Arabia in particular, and the

---

[35] Given that many patients were referrals from cities from across the Kingdom, the need for proficient translators was an essential service provided by the hospital.

Middle East in general, jointly with the King Sa'ud University College of Medicine and the King Khalid University Hospital.[36]

Because of the availability of specialized care at home, members of the ruling family and other high-level VIP patients now also rely on the facility even if several still consult foreign physicians. King Fahd bin 'Abdul 'Aziz, the Queen herself, King 'Abdallah bin 'Abdul 'Aziz, and Foreign Minister Sa'ud al-Faysal have all undergone procedures at the facility. Until a few decades ago, none of these comprehensive methods or procedures were available to most Sa'udis. Few grasped the meaning of these changes and even fewer realized the types of investment necessary to ensure that such facilities operated on a daily basis. More importantly, Sa'udis may have taken it for granted that such first-rate hospitals exist in their country, not realising that such world-class facilities arose directly from the specific visions of Faysal and 'Iffat and their determination to see them realised. The late Queen passed away after fatal complications following an operation at the Takhasusih in Riyadh. She was fully aware of and accepted the risks involved in her surgery, but was not afraid to undergo the procedure. She was also perfectly satisfied with the care she received at the hospital, at ease at the facility not only because it was close to her residence—the palace that today houses Al-Faysal University—but because she knew that she would not receive better care anywhere else in the world. That was her legacy, too—to ensure that Sa'udis were well served at home, taken care of by local physicians trained to the highest international standards.

King Khalid Eye Hospital

If the Takhasusih stands out, several other hospitals have also contributed to the much-improved level of health care provision across the Kingdom, with the King Khalid Eye Specialist Hospital among the most renowned. Designed to be a large health institution offering high-quality specialized services for ophthalmology and eye surgery, King Khalid is one of only a handful of similar research centers to be found anywhere in the world, with establishments in Germany, Japan, and the United States being comparable in standard to the service offered by the Sa'udi hospital. No visitor to this facility operated by the Ministry of Health could fail to be impressed with the superior ophthalmic care delivered to patients at its sprawling facilities, a level of excellence that extends through its outreach programs to the rest of the country.[37]

---

[36] Most of the information in this section was gathered first-hand during a tour of the King Faysal Specialist Hospital in Jiddah on 19 March 2011.

[37] Much of the information in the section was based on a comprehensive tour of the hospital on 29 March 2011. Dr. 'Abdallah 'Abdul 'Aziz al-Salman, the Director

Though many Sa'udis have come to know of the King Khalid Eye Specialist Hospital since it opened in December 1982, few outsiders know of its existence, or that both inpatient and outpatient care are available to treat a broad spectrum of eye diseases, ranging from infectious to inflammatory illnesses, and covering trauma injuries, tumors, and retinal disorders as well as restoration of sight through cataract surgery and corneal grafting. King Khalid Eye Hospital is affiliated with the Johns Hopkins University School of Medicine, located in Baltimore, Maryland, one of the world's premier health care institutions, which allows for routine exchanges among specialists. Naturally, few Sa'udis can begin to imagine what promoting and supporting such a research vision entailed, especially in a rather sophisticated branch of medicine like ophthalmic care. Physicians at the hospital conduct various investigations with colleagues around the world, including clinical trials to collect specific information about therapeutic outcomes in the treatment of common ophthalmic disorders in the Kingdom. In 2003, for example, the Anterior Segment Division established the first formal research program for the systematic examination of one specific area of clinical concern. The Cornea Transplant Study Group focuses on graft survival and visual outcome after corneal transplantation as well as the identification of risk factors that affected the prognosis. Similar study groups are planned in the areas of glaucoma, retinal diseases, pediatric ophthalmology, strabismus (a condition in which the eyes are not properly aligned with each other), and oculoplastics (orbital surgery that reshapes the area in and around the eye, often performed to correct or treat a medical condition or an injury).[38]

King Khalid Eye Hospital has also conducted epidemiological studies that have been central in planning the allocation of eye care resources in the Kingdom, including the 1984 study, *National Study of Causes of Blindness*, and the 1999 study, *National Study of Causes of Blindness in the Elderly*. Current research focuses on the prevalence of congenital disorders, such as cataract and glaucoma; genetic disorders, such as keratoconus (degeneration of the structure of the cornea) and macular corneal dystrophy in young patients; diabetic retinopathy in middle-aged Sa'udis; and cataract, glaucoma, and macular degeneration in older

---

of Protocol, Public Relations and Information, was kind enough to accompany me on a tour of various departments, as he introduced me to dozens of physicians and health practitioners and made sure that I visited both the eye banks as well as the laboratories where Sa'udi technicians designed individual eye sockets for patients ravaged by cancer or disfigured in major accidents.

[38] For a complete list of these activities, see Kingdom of Saudi Arabia, *King Khaled Eye Specialist Hospital Annual Report* 2010, Riyadh: Ministry of Health, 2010.

Sa'udis. Such information was deemed necessary in the planning the allocation of resources across various facilities including King Khalid Eye Hospital and other, regional medical centers, as well as in reassessing the residency training requirements of the Kingdom to meet developing trends in ophthalmic disease. Starting in 1988, the hospital set up a tumor registry to catalog and review the incidence of tumor pathology being managed at the facility. Demographics and International Classification of Diseases for Oncology (ICD-O) categories were systematically recorded for the purposes of education, research, adjunct medical record management, and incident reporting to the National Cancer Registry of Sa'udi Arabia. Between 1983 and 31 December 2005, the tumor registry has had a cumulative total of 3,072 entries, comprising 1,197 (39%) malignant and 1,875 (61%) nonmalignant tumors.

The hospital's eye bank provided donors' tissues for Sa'udi and non-Sa'udi patients who were candidates for corneal transplant, epikeratoplasty (which involves the placement of a preshaped corneal tissue lens on the surface of the patient's cornea), graft of the scleral or white of the eye, and amniotic membrane transplantation surgeries. The chief purpose of the eye bank is to fight corneal blindness by providing corneas and other tissues on behalf of the citizens of Sa'udi Arabia. Corneas are either imported or retrieved from local donors, all of whom are screened and their tissues evaluated according to strict medical standards, notably, those drawn up by the Eye Bank Association of America (EBAA). Retrieval of local corneas and evaluation of imported corneas are tasks performed by eye bank specialists, all of whom are certified by the EBAA. And in a departure that represents a new concept in the country, the eye bank also promotes local donations through donors' cards, brochures, news releases, articles, and educational programs. It works closely with the Sa'udi Center for Organ Transplantation (SCOT), the EBAA, Tissue Banks International, the International Federation of Eye Banks, Vision Share, and European Eye Banks, to meet local and regional needs. Once corneas, eye globes, scleras, biolenses, and amniotic membranes are received, they are evaluated for their suitability for transplantation, and if approved are made available for operations.

The inclusion of the King Khalid Eye Specialist Hospital in a discussion about health care in the Kingdom is important for two reasons. In the first instance, the initial measure of excellence set by King Faysal and Queen 'Iffat at the Takhasusih was high, leading others, such as the King Khalid, to follow suit. Lessons were quickly absorbed among those involved as healthy competition emerged among government officials and philanthropists in the drive to equip the country with premium health facilities. Of course, some of this competition was personal, as philanthropists tried to outdo one another. Likewise, not every project turned out to be as successful as the Takhasusih or the King Khalid Eye Hospital, with prestige projects falling by the wayside when they simply could not provide adequate care. Nevertheless, vigorous rivalries, even those of the "to-impress" variety that led to grandstanding projects of one kind or another, raised the overall standard of the country's health institutions. The second reason why the Faysal–'Iffat initiative was worthy of emulation was because everyone could see the results for themselves. Queen 'Iffat certainly knew that Sa'udi Arabia could afford to send patients to European and American hospitals, but had enough foresight to conclude that any country wishing to be truly self-sufficient should seek to create its own infrastructure and develop indigenous professional expertise.

Both of the examples discussed above met these two conditions, to pursue excellence and rely on philanthropists to invest in the country's health facilities, as Riyadh strengthened its core health policies, a process that was neither culturally well established nor cost-free. Few Sa'udis appreciated the determination that such ventures required, to see major investments come to fruition in the form of a top-notch health care system that has become the gold standard for the region.

Health Awareness in the Kingdom

Health-related topics were once taboo in the Kingdom, and issues that dealt with disabilities or cancer or other debilitating diseases were seldom broached. For years, such conversations were usually held only in times of sorrow. Hardly any woman mustered the courage to voice any concerns she may have had before about breast cancer, for instance, given the inviolable norms traditionally associated with a woman's body. Cancer in general, and breast cancer in particular, simply never came up as a topic of discussion.

Yet, like people everywhere, few Sa'udis were left untouched by cancer. Even in the West, until quite recently individuals diagnosed with cancer have often been embarrassed to talk about their predicament, even within their own families, and this lack of communication has often translated into poor support mechanisms at a time when a patient needed all the help they could muster. In Sa'udi Arabia, this posed an even greater challenge, not only because few social support systems existed—at least until very recently—but also because the local culture prevented people from seeking the kind of assistance that could make a difference. More often than not, breast or prostate cancer patients and their immediate family members simply accepted a physician's prognosis and were embarrassed to ask questions as to the options available to treat the disease. Regrettably, because the majority of Sa'udi women were reluctant to undergo regular mammograms and even fewer men were proactive in seeking prostate examinations, many cases went undiagnosed until it was too late. Breast cancer examinations to detect a lump, whether performed by a trained technician or self-administered, require little technical expertise but are essential in catching the cancer before it grows beyond the stage where it is still treatable. Prostate cancer diagnosis is a bit more complicated though routine blood tests can at least raise the red flag long before the disease begins to metastasize. Unfortunately, few Sau'di women muster the courage to submit to the necessary annual physicals and follow-ups, the main reason why breast cancer has remained the most diagnosed form of cancer in the Kingdom, accounting for 13.8 percent of all cancers and 26 percent of cancers among women in 2007, according to a study by the Saudi Cancer Registry.[39]

Although the Sa'udi Cancer Society has encouraged debate on this sensitive question, a full-fledged conversation was not broached until 2011, when Princess Hassah bint Trad al-Sha'alan lent her support. As the wife of the Custodian of the Two Holy Mosques, King 'Abdallah bin 'Abdul 'Aziz, and as the Honorary President of the proactive Zahra Breast Cancer Association, Princess Hassah has been able to mobilize a large group. The ruler's spouse was joined by Princess Rimah bint 'Abdallah bin 'Abdul 'Aziz, a daughter of the ruler, who was also active in the cause, Princess Hayfah al-Faysal bin 'Abdul 'Aziz, and Princess Rimah bint Bandar bin Sultan Al Sa'ud, who pledged: "Let it be known that henceforth, ignorance is no longer an excuse and no woman should be allowed to be left to suffer in silence."[40] These were not idle words, but while the 10 October 2011 National Awareness Campaign to Combat Breast Cancer was inaugurated under great fanfare in Riyadh to coincide with International Breast Cancer Awareness Month, this has not been a routine event. Sa'udi women, including princesses, have not been used to taking the lead in health matters, which in the case of a taboo subject like breast cancer represents a very bold step. Whether the goal of the Zahra Breast Cancer Association was simply to educate women and young girls by providing basic education on this serious health issue could not be

---

[39] Haya S. Al-Eid, BDS, DFE, CTR, *Cancer Incidence and Survival—Report: Saudi Arabia 2007*, Kingdom of Saudi Arabia, Ministry of Health, Saudi Cancer Registry, 2010, at http://www.scr.org.sa/reports/SCR2007.pdf, pp. 17–18.

[40] In October 2011, over 5,000 Sa'udi and expatriate women created the world's largest human pink ribbon in aid of breast cancer awareness in Jiddah, during an event organized by the Riyadh-based Zahra Breast Cancer Association. See, Saudi Arabia News and Updates, "Saudi Pink Ribbon Breaks Guinness Record," 28 October 2011, at http://www.a1saudiarabia.com/24490-saudi-pink-ribbon-breaks-guinness-record/.

determined in the absence of conclusive declarations. Suffice it to say that social and cultural barriers are gradually giving way. Even older women are now willing to consider physical examinations, though administrators at the Zahra Breast Cancer Association are still encountering some reticence. Their hope is to educate young Sa'udis starting in middle or high school by introducing the subject of the disease in health, science, or biology courses. How the topic is broached, perhaps alongside discussions of various types of diseases, is still undecided. It seems inevitable, however, given the frightening statistics that reflect poor health outcomes in the country, that different attitudes will eventually prevail.

Queen 'Iffat Al Thunayan wanted students at Dar al-Hanan to study science courses because she knew that truly educated youngsters would remove fear and awkwardness from their vocabularies. She wanted her girls to grow into responsible women just as much as she banked on her boys to be trustworthy and accountable, too. It is worth recalling that her quest for health education for boys as well as girls stemmed from her hope that such knowledge would better equip both for the duties that awaited them. Awakened youngsters grew into dependable adults, she believed, and on health matters as serious as cancer, for example, an introduction to basic sciences would enlighten rather than frighten them.

THE IMPACT OF JAWHARAN AL THUNAYAN

The health-related examples cited in this chapter, ranging from the initial charities and modest health facilities to major hospitals and widespread social support mechanisms that look after the needy, are but small drops in the immense tide of change that has swept through the Kingdom since 1932. Thousands of charities, associations, medical clinics, and hospitals, which now serve Sa'udis and the millions of expatriates who toil in the Kingdom, have all emerged over a very short period of time. While it is correct to conclude that Sa'udis in general and successive governments in particular have spent lavishly to equip their country with the latest available medical gear and trained generations of health professionals to fill posts created at modern facilities, much of the progress has been due to the innate capability of Sa'udi men and women to learn and, each in their own modest way, to make a difference. To say that Sa'udis have come a long way would indeed be an understatement but one should not simply state the obvious. There have been other, less tangible reasons for this record of progress and these, too, deserve an airing.

The experience 'Iffat Al Thunayan gained in caring for a disabled aunt while she herself was still a child left its imprint on everything she tried to do for her countrymen. Care-giving can be a thankless job and while Princess 'Iffat was able to rely on other helpers after she and Jawharan reached Makkah, she had already assisted her disabled aunt for at least a full decade by then. Of course, in addition to the physical challenges involved in being a carer in defeated Constantinople after World War I, as well as the perilous boat trip to Jiddah in January 1932, the young woman may also have been grappling with complex social and emotional issues. Little is known of the attitude of Jawharan Al Thunayan toward her own disability or of how she dealt with being so dependent on her niece. Queen 'Iffat seldom talked about Jawharan's life in the Ottoman Empire, although family members noted that she struggled with her emotions as she was left to look after a woman for whom on the one hand she bore the deepest affection, but who was nonetheless entirely dependent on her. Likewise, as is the case with the vast majority of disabled individuals, Jawharan did not enjoy being dependent on others, including her niece, even after 'Iffat became a spouse of the Viceroy of the Hijaz. She was glad for 'Iffat and grateful for the additional help she herself would receive—as a result of which her quality of life would improve sharply—though she still apparently resented being dependent according to family members.

Neither Queen 'Iffat nor anyone else in the family ever thought of institutionalizing Jawharan, and she lived out her remaining days in the comfort of the Queen's house. It would have been culturally unacceptable to do otherwise. Simply stated, disabled individuals of any age were cared for by their loved ones, and few if any ever considered nursing homes as a solution. Yet the experience of being a carer, while not uncommon, awakened in the Queen a quite exceptional sense of responsibility. She knew that among severely disabled younger people, as well as seniors, many not only lived long lives but remained the responsibility of family caregivers. It was precisely because she understood the toll such duties exacted on loved ones that 'Iffat Al Thunayan raised the idea of building nursing homes for the severely disabled, although she preferred that specialized centers be created alongside them, too.

Disabled people, even those with a need for daily assistance, dread life in institutions, and this is just as much the case in most of the developing world, including Sa'udi Arabia. Institutions such as the Help Center have come to play a critical role as contemporary living pressures, especially in a segregated society, have heightened the need for alternatives. Institutionalization was and remains an atrocious way to address the needs of the disabled, and nursing homes or even live-in helpers offer intelligent alternative solutions. Fortunately for Sa'udis in such situations, for the past few decades expatriate workers have been available to take on these tasks. But long before these trends emerged, it was Queen

'Iffat who first realized the importance of devising effective health institutions and charitable organizations in the Kingdom. She knew that outside of the ruling family and the coterie of well-off citizens, the vast majority required significant assistance, especially the kind of trained help that was both expensive and difficult to come by.

Remarkably, much of her vision materialized in just a few decades, to the extent that a comparison between health conditions in the early 1930s and those in contemporary Sa'udi Arabia would not be fair—so much has changed. By pointing the system toward constant improvements, setting the bar ever higher, 'Iffat Al Thunayan encouraged many to shoulder their responsibilities. Naturally, she did not create the current health system on her own, nor did she set out the blueprints that were subsequently followed through several five-year plans. Rather, she did something better: she simply inspired her fellow citizens to spend their money wisely and acquire the knowledge to enable them to manage the health needs of a modern nation.

5

The Role of Women in the Kingdom

The position of women in Muslim societies in general and in the Sa'udi environment in particular is a complex and frequently misunderstood issue. It is certainly true that Muslim and Western views of the role of women show sharp cultural differences, but the stereotype of Muslim women as uneducated, with no rights and no opportunities, is a caricature born of malevolence. The Holy Qur'an gave women economic and social rights long before Western women attained such rights, and it would be fair to say that from the very beginning of Islam, women were granted various liberties as well as distinct privileges. At a time when few women anywhere in the world were legally entitled to inherit and bequeath property, hold their wealth in their own names even after marriage, and avoid obligation to contribute that wealth to their husband's or their family's fortunes, Islam granted them such rights. In fact, the important roles played by the wives of the Prophet Muhammad in the course of his ministry contradict what in the West is a popular myth that Islam undervalued the female half of humanity.

It is nevertheless true that under Islam a woman is enjoined to behave modestly in public and, as in the West until recently, is generally expected to commit herself fully to making a family home—an environment within which, incidentally, she enjoys a preeminent role. Such expectations are rather different from those now widely required of women in the West, just as the stability of family life and the security women enjoy in Muslim societies differ markedly from the conditions which women face elsewhere. That said, though it would be a mistake to think that the role of women in Sa'udi society is confined to home-making, it is also not the purpose of this chapter to identify and discuss all of the socio-cultural ills that prevent many women from reaching their potential. That literature is already vast enough, and while it contains undeniable truths, the development of the Kingdom has brought with it increasing opportunities for women in both education and employment.[1] Significant reforms were introduced during the past few decades that recognize the value of women as full members of society, with vital roles to play in the economy, and more importantly as essential partners to men as the Kingdom prepares for the many socio-economic challenges ahead.[2]

The purpose of this chapter is threefold. First, it will offer a brief discussion of how Islam perceives women, especially since 'Iffat Al Thunayan was a practicing Muslim who took her religious duties seriously. She seldom wavered from her core beliefs even as she pushed for dramatic changes in the way her daughters—indeed, all Sa'udi girls and women—behaved and were treated in the segregated country. Though extremist elements have hijacked much of this discussion in recent years, Queen 'Iffat was a modernizer in the Islamic sense of the word, which is to say she sought the optimum means of benefiting recipients and refused to see Islam as a faith that shackled women to subservience. The only kind of submission she recognized was what she owed God, a spiritual debt that applied equally to men and women. Religious obligations aside, the chapter then moves to consider her views on two important questions, namely the customary veiling of Sa'udi women and the quest for gender equality. The discussion then proceeds to a detailed assessment of the current position of Sa'udi women, focusing on judicial restrictions and the putative changes that have now been introduced, along with an evaluation of the socio-cultural limitations that caused reforms to be delayed. Finally, an effort is made to assess the roles that women play in key sectors of the economy, as the country prepares for the future. The chapter closes with an evaluation of Queen 'Iffat Al Thunayan's vision for Sa'udi women.

---

[1] The classic study on this subject is Soraya Altorki, *Women in Saudi Arabia: Ideology and Behavior among the Elite*, New York: Columbia University Press, 1988. For a more recent tome, see Eleanor Abdella Doumato, *Getting God's Ear: Women, Islam, and Healing in Saudi Arabia and the Gulf*, New York: Columbia University Press, 2000. Doumato also prepared a special report, worthy of careful attention, itemizing all of the major problems in a non-judgmental fashion. See, Freedom House, *Women's Rights in the Middle East and North Africa 2010—Saudi Arabia*, 3 March 2010, available at: http://www.unhcr.org/refworld/docid/4b99011da0.html [accessed 28 September 2012].

For an equally incisive assessment of some of the key concerns that affect women's lives in the Kingdom, see Sean Foley, "All I Want is Equality with Girls: Gender and Social Change in the Twenty-First Century Gulf," *MERIA Journal* 14:1, March 2010, pp. 21–35, at http://www.gloria-center.org/2010/03/foley-2010-03-03/.

[2] Joseph A. Kéchichian, *Legal and Political Reforms in Sa'udi Arabia*, London and New York: Routledge, 2013, pp. 43–50, 81–83 and 195–196.

WOMEN IN ISLAM

When the father of the Prophet, 'Abdallah, died two months before Muhammad was born, no one could have guessed that his mother, Aminah bint Wahb, would also pass away as the little boy neared his sixth birthday. It was the kind of tragedy that was once all too common in the harsh conditions throughout the Arabian Peninsula—one which, regrettably, denied the Prophet the parental nurturing he would otherwise have enjoyed. That task fell to two other men: first, his grandfather, 'Abdul Mutalib, who raised Muhammad for two full years; second, his paternal uncle, a well-known Makkahan merchant by the name of Abu Talib, in whose household the boy became a young adolescent and finally a distinguished man. Muhammad traveled to Syria with his uncle on several occasions, and it was on one of these visits that a Nestorian monk, whose name was reported to be Sergius Bahirah, foretold the nine-year-old's prophetic destiny.[3]

Muhammad, having grown into a handsome young man, was recruited by a wealthy businesswoman, Khadijah bint Khuwaylid, who was also known as the *tahirah* (virtuous). It was she who eventually proposed marriage after a period when, despite their age difference (she was 40 and he 25), the young Muhammad had won over Khadijah after demonstrating his moral values and impeccable loyalty. Sadly, none of the seven children (four girls and three sons) Khadijah gave the Prophet survived, which prompted Muhammad to look after 'Ali, his first cousin and the son of his uncle, Abu Talib. He also adopted Zayd, a slave whom he freed (manumission), so that a semblance of family life existed around him. The pious Khadijah was the first Muslim to accept the Prophet's teachings, believing him when he revealed how the archangel Gabriel appeared and dictated the Holy Scriptures. She also accepted the Qur'an as the word of God.[4] Khadijah died in 619 after a marriage that had lasted twenty-five years. Loyal until the end, Muhammad did not take a second wife when Khadijah was alive, considering her virtue to be boundless. Reflecting on his spouse, he reportedly said: "She believed in me when I was rejected. When they called me a liar, she proclaimed me truthful. When I was poor, she shared her wealth with me."[5] Years later, 'Ayshah, whom the Prophet would also love, apparently wondered about

---

[3] William Montgomery Watt, *Muhammad: Prophet and Statesman*, London and New York: Oxford University Press, 1961, pp. 1–2.

[4] Resit Haylamaz, *Khadija: The First Muslim and the Wife of the Prophet Muhammad*, London: Light, Inc., 2008. See also Deepak Chopra, *Muhammad: A Story of the Last Prophet*, New York: HarperOne, 2010, pp. 94–105.

[5] This attribution is cited in various sources. See, for example, "Lady Khadija: The

this first marriage, in a moment of jealousy asking Muhammad: "Was [Khadijah] not old, and has not Allah given you a better one in her place?" "No," replied Muhammad, "there can never be one better than her; she believed in me when others ridiculed me, she helped me when I was persecuted by the world."[6]

As the life of the Prophet was widely known and religiously taught in Muslim schools, 'Iffat Al Thunayan herself recognised the similarity of the Prophet's life and the fate that befell Faysal, who lost his own mother, Tarfah bint 'Abdallah bin 'Abdul Latif Al al-Shaykh, when he was five months old. Of course, Faysal's father was the founder of the modern Sa'udi state, while his mother was an Al al-Shaykh. Coincidentally, the future monarch was tutored in Islam by his maternal grandfather, Shaykh 'Abdallah bin 'Abdul Latif Al al-Shaykh (1848–1921), a leading Sunni Muslim scholar in Sa'udi Arabia in the late 19th and early 20th centuries, and probably the single most important influence on his life. 'Iffat Al Thunayan could not help but draw parallels as she recounted to her children between her own life and those of prominent spouses of the Prophet—the fates that befell them and her—though she was too discreet to discuss these topics in public.

Although young and attractive, 'Iffat Al Thunayan was not jealous of Faysal's previous wives, recognizing tribal customs that necessitated frequent marriages with daughters of warriors who were defeated in battle, to secure strategic family allegiances. Like Cleopatra, who was both brilliant and beautiful, 'Iffat Al Thunayan was a risk taker. Yet, unlike the last of the Ptolemies, whose allegiances were temporary and selfish in the extreme, Queen 'Iffat displayed utmost loyalty to her immediate family and the ruling establishment. Early on, she understood that one had to forgo and sacrifice in this life to accomplish one's objectives and, when the opportunity was given, one had to work tirelessly to reach those goals. She was persuaded that Sa'udi women would achieve their rights when they empowered themselves to learn and contribute, tactfully introducing fundamental changes in what was a traditional society, while at the same time holding their heads dignified and high.

Even if conditions were poor, beginning in the early 1940s Sa'udi authorities pushed for improved education and, after the oil-boom of the

First Believer and Helper of Islam," islamicoccasions.com, at http://www.ezsoftech.com/islamic/khadijah.asp.

[6] See Mumtaz Ahmad Faruqui, *Anecdotes from the Life of The Prophet Muhammad*, Dublin, Ohio: 1997, originally published by the Ahmadiyyah Anjuman Isha'at Islam, Lahore, Pakistan, 1925. The conversation is also available in Abdul Hameed Siddiqui, *Sahih al-Muslim*, Book 31, Chapter 12, Numbers 5965–5975, at http://www.shariahprogram.ca/Hadith/Sahih-Muslim/031.smt.html.

1970s, invested in major programs intended to empower as many as possible. If the goal was to build a robust economy, this required an educated class. As discussed earlier, Islam encouraged learning, and Queen 'Iffat ensured that those who wished to could gain access to every level of education. After Dar al-Hanan, women seldom looked back and towards the end of the 20th century surpassed men in school enrollment, literacy, and even educational achievement in the Kingdom. This point was reiterated by the queen's daughter, Princess Lulwah al-Faysal, who frequently responded to questions about the poor conditions supposedly faced by Muslim women in general and Sa'udi women in particular:

> Well, if they were to listen only to the media they would think that the women in Saudi Arabia are completely suppressed, not educated, and don't have any jobs. The reality is that while education started for men in 1960, it started for women just two years later in 1962. Actually, prior to the start of the Ministry of Education there already were schools for women, private schools, including Dar-Al-Hanan, which my mother opened in 1955. . . . You should also know that at that point in our history we were a country of 5 percent literacy and at the moment we're a country of 5 percent illiteracy. That shows how far we have come in just 70 years—even less if you consider that formal education started 50 years ago. It's not just Americans who are not familiar with these facts. We're asked about the same things in other places, too. I don't know why. Now I'm not saying that we're angels or perfect—there are some families that are stricter with women. However, education for women has never been taboo since it was accepted in 1962. From the moment the public schools opened for women, they have never closed down.[7]

The Princess could just as easily have added that Islam commended both men and women to learn even if Sa'udis were also encouraged to have large families, with few seeing contradictions between these two goals. Nevertheless, compatibility issues existed, especially within conservative circles. Many saw modern education as a threat and, in the politicized environment of the Muslim world during the second half of the 20th century, Riyadh certainly concluded that the best method for preventing the unrest caused elsewhere by socialist prophets, religious congregants, or even Arab nationalists was to put on the brakes. Faced

[7] Saudi–US Relations Information Service (SUSRIS), "Building Bridges: A Conversation with Princess Loulwa Al-Faisal," 2 June 2005, at http://www.susris.com/2005/06/02/building-bridges-a-conversation-with-princess-loulwa-al-faisal-2/.

with epochal developments such as the February 1979 Islamic Revolution in Iran, the November 1979 seizure of the Grand Mosque in Makkah, and the Soviet invasion and occupation of Afghanistan in December 1979, Riyadh chose to reinforce Islamic values in the Kingdom. To be sure, Sa'udis were confident that improved conditions at home would strengthen the country's credentials abroad, and that Islam offered the best hope for addressing the many challenges that confronted the country. Moreover, by insisting on stricter interpretations of the faith enforcing a total segregation, the authorities argued that they were successfully addressing the concerns of the majority. Instead of investing in technological advances, the state fell back on conservative values, preferring these to a variety of "isms." Towards that end, to bolster this commitment King Fahd bin 'Abdul 'Aziz gave far wider latitude to the Commission for the Promotion of Virtue and the Prevention of Vice to enforce Muslim morality regarding women in all public settings.[8]

By all accounts, the country took a sharp turn in a far more conservative direction as once gender-integrated institutions, such as buses, offices, and recreational areas became rigidly segregated. The monarch authorized the construction of parallel buildings, and whole sections of communities arose just for women, an economically counterproductive move given the exorbitant costs. Still, the measures satisfied conservative 'Ulamah who believed that local norms were thus protected. To general consternation, Riyadh even curtailed opportunities for single Sa'udi women to study abroad, which undid some of the progress recorded under previous reigns.[9] Among many new restrictions, authorities enforced the *mahram* regulation, forbidding women from working outside of education and health sectors or, if they managed businesses, making sure that the requirement for male guardianship was applied. Severe travel restrictions were also announced, a petty and pointless move given that those who could afford to travel were well off and could circumvent any bans.[10] Of course, it is worth repeating that none of these restrictions contributed anything to Islamic observance, since Sa'udi

---

[8] Eleanor Doumato, "Gender, Monarchy, and National Identity in Saudi Arabia," *British Journal of Middle Eastern Studies* 19:1, 1992, pp. 34–39. See also, Eleanor Doumato, "The Saudis and the Gulf War: Gender, Power, and Revival of the Religious Right," in Abbas Abdelkarim, ed., *Change and Development in the Gulf*, New York: Palgrave Macmillan, 1999, pp. 184–210.

[9] Doumato, "Gender, Monarchy, and National Identity," *ibid.*, p. 41.

[10] Munira Fakhro, "Gulf Women and Islamic Law," in Mai Yamani, ed., *Feminism and Islam, Legal and Literary Perspectives*, New York: New York University Press, 1996, p. 257.

women were invariably virtuous and frowned upon unethical behavior. Nevertheless, by emphasizing the need to enforce personal status laws, clerics intensified conservative sensibilities. Although most women wore modest clothes, often covering their hair with a veil, a new trend emerged as even professional women took to wearing a *niqab* and gloves.

Customary Veiling of Sa'udi Women

In many ways, no question was as sensitive as that of the veil, as Islam recommended both men and women to wear modest attires. For complicated socio-economic and perhaps political reasons, some Muslim women removed their *hijabs* in the 1920s and 1930s, which caused a sensation wherever it occurred.[11] As discussed earlier, 'Iffat Al Thunayan wore a *hijab* in public but seldom in private, in keeping with her view that the garment was of limited use. Although she did not rebel against the veil, which she did not wear in Constantinople during her youth, 'Iffat Al Thunayan nevertheless respected local norms. In that sense, she was not like Hudah Sha'rawy and Sayzah Nabarawi, two brave Egyptian women who, upon their return from Rome in 1923, removed their veils at the Cairo train station. Still, it is worth noting that throughout much of Muslim history only relatively well-off women have worn the garment, since only the upper classes could in fact afford to keep complex households where the lady (or ladies) of the house could entertain. This was the ultimate irony of the *hijab*, for inasmuch as such homes were expensive to maintain, only those with the means to do so could keep several wives and could ask their spouses to don expensive veils.

Even fewer could afford to engage in the type of multiple courtships for which 'Abdul 'Aziz bin 'Abdul Rahman was renowned. Naturally, women from princely households veiled themselves whenever they stepped out, which distinguished them from women from far more financially modest backgrounds who could not afford the luxury of leisurely lives, but who were called upon to toil for a living. Peasant women often wore a mere shawl, sometimes decorated with a few coins—their sole independent wealth—that covered portions of their hair but never their faces. More importantly, a woman wearing a shawl to cover part of her hair was a customary phenomenon not a religious requirement, and this too was lost on clerics. In fact, the best evidence explaining social norms throughout the Levant, and especially in Egypt, was the fact that in public most Jewish and Christian women wore attire

---

[11] For a good introduction, see Fadwa El-Guindi and Sherifa Zuhur, "Hijab," *The Oxford Encyclopedia of the Islamic World*, Oxford and New York, 2009, Volume 2, pp. 399–403. See also Fadwa El-Guindi, *Veil: Modesty, Privacy, and Resistance*, Oxford and New York: Oxford University Press, 1999.

that was similar to their Muslim counterparts. Of course, Christian nuns wore veils as well, something that seems ageless in European history and continues to flourish in Slavic societies in the 21st century. Were the veil a religiously imposed garment in Islam, hardly any other women in what were then fairly mixed environments would have practiced the "fashion," irrespective of what revisionists claim in the literature. According to Lucie Duff-Gordon, a well-known British traveler who visited Upper Egypt in the mid-1800s, Coptic women were far more conservative in their traditions and wore the veil more often than their Muslim counterparts.[12] This, and similar anecdotal evidence gathered over the decades, but especially in the incredible 20th century, supports the notion that wearing the veil was a social practice, with little or no religious requirement associated with it.

Towards the end of the 18th century, several Egyptian writers ventured the ultimate political call to elevate a woman's status in society, insisting that educating women would serve everyone. In 1899, Qasim Amin (1863–1908), the Alexandria jurist best known for his advocacy of women's emancipation and one of the founders of the Egyptian national movement, published *Tahrir al-Mara'ah* [The Liberation of Women] in 1899 and an even more powerful sequel, *Al-Mara'ah al-Jadidah* [The New Woman], in 1900, in which he discussed how the low social and educational standing of Egyptian women negated the country's intrinsic values and forced it to submit to European socio-political authority.[13] Egypt's, and consequently the Arab world's, "first feminist" opined that the aristocratic Egyptian women who were kept as prisoners in their homes led lives akin to those of slaves, a status that was to be rejected henceforth. By advancing strong arguments from religious scholarship, Amin concluded that women should develop intellectually to be competent, precisely to bring up the nation's children in ways that would enhance their worth and the collective self-confidence of the entire nation. Towards that end, he called for the removal of the veil, forced upon women by challenged men who, allegedly, feared modernization and progress.

---

12 Lucie Duff-Gordon, *Letters From Egypt*, London: CreateSpace [An Amazon.com Books-on-Demand Project], 2012, [originally published in 1863], pp. 17, 20 and especially 32.

13 Qasim Amin, *Tahrir al-Mara'ah* [The Liberation of Women: Two Documents in the History of Egyptian Feminism], translated by Samiha Sidhom Peterson, Cairo: American University in Cairo Press, 2000 [first published in 1899], and idem, *Al-Mara'ah al-Jadidah* [The New Woman: A Document in the Early Debate on Egyptian Feminism], translated by Samiha Sidhom Peterson, Cairo: American University in Cairo Press, 1995 [first published in 1900].

Amin was neither the first nor the last sage to offer such an interpretation of Arab and Muslim women. In 1894, Morcos Fahmy had written a highly controversial play under the title *A Woman in the Orient*, which urged Arab women to give up wearing the veil and called for the free mixing of men and women. The young Coptic writer eventually published his play as a book, *Woman In the Middle East*, which drew the ire of many Islamists then as now. Nonetheless, leading modernizers such as Rifa'ah Al-Tahtawi, Qasim Amin, Hudah Sha'rawy, Aminah Al-Sayyid, and Nawwal Al-Sa'dawy, among others, all believed that basic emancipation was necessary to harvest women's talents. In Egypt as in the Ottoman Empire, the first signs of change came about as a new generation took conscience of what it was that defined gender. Beyond equality of the sexes, serious questions touching on education, early marriages imposed on non-adult children, and a dislike for polygamy, among similar concerns, preoccupied writers who wished to break the traditional holds that tended to strangulate the Muslim realm. Hudah Sha'rawy was at the forefront of the changes that altered her country.[14] During a visit to Paris, Hudah purchased an entirely new, Western wardrobe that suited her well. Yet she acquired something far more valuable, an awakened nationalism that she would put to good use in Cairo upon returning home.

On an otherwise ordinary day in 1908, as Hudah Sha'rawy was convened to the palace to meet with Princess 'Ayn al-Hayat to participate in a reception to honor Lady Cromer, everything changed. Princess 'Ayn al-Hayat, wife of Sultan Hussayn Kamal, had summoned Cairenese elites to thank the British Consul-General's wife for the establishment of a medical dispensary. But Hudah Sha'rawy declined, causing the Princess to seek to find the reason behind her non-attendance. A few days later, while the two women sat together, Hudah explained that it was out of the question for her to honor the spouse of Lord Evelyn Baring Cromer for her deeds, no matter how honorable, because she was the spouse of an "occupier." Instead, Sha'rawy said, it was up to Egyptian women to be at the forefront of social and charitable ventures; she then pleaded with the Princess to support her in launching such initiatives. It was a daring proposition but the idea appealed to the Sultan's wife, who encouraged Hudah to create such an institution. Remarkably, and perhaps for the first time in contemporary Egyptian history, a prenatal care facility was established to cater to women from all walks of life, looking after those who needed assistance irrespective of financial means

[14] For a look at this world, see Huda Shaarawi, *Harem Years: The Memoirs of an Egyptian Feminist, 1879–1924*, translated by Margot Badran, New York: The Feminist Press at the City University of New York, 1987.

or religious beliefs. The benevolent establishment, created in 1909 and known as the Mabarrat Muhammad ʻAli al-Kabir [Muhammad ʻAli the Great Philanthropic Association], eventually grew into one of Cairo's largest hospitals and acted as a center for several outreach clinics throughout Egypt. In November 1914, after yet another visit to France—more precisely to Vittel where Hudah's son Muhammad was recuperating from depression—she created the Intellectual Association of Egyptian Women, which invested in the development of upper- and middle-class Egyptian women's intrinsic capabilities given how limited their access was to educational institutions. In 1923, she founded the Egyptian Feminist Union (EFU), which had about 250 members at its height, focusing on women's suffrage, increased education for women, and changes in the personal status laws. On her return from Rome in 1923, Shaʻrawy removed her veil in public as she stepped out of her car at the Cairo train station. Women who were there to greet her were shocked by her bold move, but several applauded while a few even emulated her in what was a public act of defiance. Her audacious act notwithstanding, Shaʻrawy always argued for a gradualist approach to removing the veil, even if the times required drastic actions. Indeed, removal of the veil was never on the Egyptian Feminist Union's agenda, since it was primarily the wealthiest women in society who wore it. Instead, she wished to focus on women's rights as described in the Holy Qur'an, to further advance the Muslim woman, who, she concluded, needed to be as well educated as her Jewish and Christian neighbors in Egypt. Above all, what truly interested her—the subject to which she devoted so much time—was the Egyptian woman's economic and political roles in society.

Shaʻrawy owed little to her husband, ʻAli, save his unadulterated support of the nationalist movement alongside the great Saʻad Zaghlul (1859–1927), who served as Prime Minister from 26 January 1924 to 24 November 1924. Zaghlul was many things but above all else a nationalist who, along with his wife Safiyyah—the daughter of Mustafa Fahmy Pasha, the Egyptian cabinet minister, and two-time Prime Minister of Egypt—was the individual who literally defined anti-British sentiments though in a way that did not reject many of the values of Western modernization. Safiyyah Zaghlul, a feminist and revolutionary in her own right, saw in Hudah Shaʻrawy a political soulmate. Together, the two women contributed to the Egyptian nationalist struggle, as beginning in 1919 they mobilized upper- and middle-class women to organize against the British. Within a year, Hudah had become the President of the Wafd Party Women's Central Committee but was seriously disappointed when the new independent government barred women from the opening of the Egyptian Parliament in 1920. Shaʻrawy led a delegation of women to picket the opening, and submitted a list of 32 feminist, social, and nationalist demands to the men gathered to determine the fate of the new nation. By 1924—that is, after Sha'rawy had concluded that entrenched traditions were difficult to change—she had resigned from the Wafdist Central Committee so as to devote the rest of her time to the EFU. Even if progress was limited, Zaghlul and others were no longer shy of appearing in public with their spouses. Moreover, it is important to note that the unveiled Safiyyah Zaghlul, who became known as the "mother of the nation," was often seen participating in open fora.

For her part, Hudah Sha'rawy devoted the rest of her life to publishing and speaking: first, starting in 1925, with the feminist French-language magazine, *L'Egyptienne* [The Egyptian Woman], produced for elite ladies; and then, after 1937, using the same title for the Arabic-language *al-Misriyyah*, which catered to a wider audience. *Al-Misriyyah* was, in truth, the first woman's magazine that made its way to Sa'udi audiences, including to 'Iffat Al Thunayan, who was a regular consumer of its impeccable coverage. What distinguished this magazine from other publications was its intellectual breadth, and it was above all for this reason that Sha'rawy was appointed to lead the 1938 Conference of Oriental Woman, which condemned British and Zionist political activities in Palestine. For this wholly committed woman, who stood as a role model to many others throughout the Arab World, there was an indubitable association between feminism and Arab nationalism on the one hand and the awakening of a postcolonial desire for citizenship on the other. To say that she was ahead of her time would indeed be an understatement as she deplored the creation of the League of Arab States in 1946, maintaining that the League was just half a league since it only included half of the Arab nation.[15]

The Quest for Gender Equality

Of course, Hudah Sha'rawy was only one among several feminist Egyptians down the centuries who have changed their country, in her case being ambitious enough to seek political office. Like many of her female ancestors, she added to Egypt's long and distinguished legacy, even if serious challenges have emerged in recent times. Sa'udi women have been equally distinguished in leaving their mark on society,[16]

---

15 Gilbert Sinoué, *12 Femmes d'Orient qui ont changé l'Histoire*, Paris: Pygmalion, 2011, p. 144.

16 Dalal Mukhlid al-Harbi, *Prominent Women from Central Arabia*, Reading, UK: Ithaca Press, 2008. See also Stig Stenslie, "Power Behind the Veil: Princesses of House of Saud," *Journal of Arabian Studies: Arabia, the Gulf, and the Red Sea* 1:1, 2011, pp. 69–79.

supporting their men on battlefields, and advising, albeit discreetly, on a slew of socio-political concerns. Like many of her predecessors, including the powerful wives of King 'Abdul 'Aziz bin 'Abdul Rahman Al Sa'ud, 'Iffat Al Thunayan seldom displayed the slightest interest in high office, and was content to be the woman who stood by her monarch, the love of her life. Though to many of her contemporaries she was simply the *Turkiyyah*, Princess 'Iffat knew what she wanted for her country, and worked tirelessly to accomplish as much as she possibly could. Still, like Hatshepsut, 'Iffat was not interested in monumental accomplishments but more concrete and down-to-earth goals that would serve those in need. In a way, she resembled the exceptional Egyptian Pharaoh-Queen, who wanted to communicate with her people, or at least to establish with them what could possibly unite them. Though peerless, the two queens shared something else, and that was their immense patience. That quality, perhaps more than any other, allowed both to surmount significant odds and to transform hostile environments into positive settings.[17]

It is also possible to compare 'Iffat Al Thunayan to Shajarat al-Durr, the Cherkess beauty who conquered Al Salih in 1238 when the Ayyubi leader received the help of Mamluk notables who overthrew Al Salih's brother, Al 'Adil, and asked him to rule Egypt. Although Al Salih's reliance on the Mamluks signaled the end of the Ayyubi dynasty, Shajarat al-Durr's son, Khalil, died when the young boy was only six years old, a tragedy that truly consumed the young Queen. Yet her courage and determination, which proved critical as she fought against the sixth Crusades after her husband died of tuberculosis, were legendary.[18] That was also the case with 'Iffat, who did not allow her husband's assassination to deflect her from the mission she had set out on: to empower Sa'udi women and establish key educational institutions, for which she fought tooth and nail. Shajarat al-Durr was a Sultanah as well as the "Queen of Muslims," while Queen 'Iffat was the only Queen the Kingdom of Sa'udi Arabia recognized as such since all other wives of monarchs were known as princesses. It is worth repeating that 'Iffat Al Thunayan sought a different kind of gender equality, one that allowed women to make useful contributions to their nation while enjoying the fruits of their labor within the confines of traditional environments.

In 1962, that is, when the government of the Kingdom of Sa'udi Arabia undertook the introduction of a national education program for girls, few envisaged the progress that would be made. Remarkably, by

---

[17] Sinoué, *op. cit.*, pp. 183–207. Several of Queen 'Iffat's granddaughters emphasized her immense patience, describing how she would endure impertinence simply because she wanted something concrete in exchange, which she often secured.

[18] Sinoué, *op. cit.*, pp. 324–336.

the mid-1970s about half of Sa'udi girls were attending school, and five years later—that is, by the early 1980s—education was available to all Sa'udi girls. What had come to pass over the short span of a few years was truly epochal, and by 1980 the country boasted six universities for women while other universities fielded separate sections for women. Under the reign of King Fahd, further encouragements for women to take active roles in public as well as in private spheres were fairly common, even if social conditions worsened. In terms of employment, however, women have gradually come to play more active roles in teaching, medicine, social work, and broadcasting. Of course, over the years significant financial resources have been devoted to education, with the number of private schools reaching nearly 1,000 as long ago as 1985, comprising more than 8,000 classrooms handling around 200,000 students. Importantly, while most leadership positions in the field of education were held by men for most of contemporary Sa'udi history, on 14 February 2009 King 'Abdallah bin 'Abdul 'Aziz appointed Nurah al-Fayiz, then an official at the Saudi Institute for Public Administration, as the Deputy Minister responsible for women's education.

While a commitment to equal political rights has yet to come to the Kingdom, the theoretical right to vote was finally secured in 2011 after King 'Abdallah issued the necessary decrees that authorized women to participate in scheduled municipal elections in 2015. Likewise, while little progress has been made in the equal status family law, the support of the ruling family introduced positive changes in specific areas in health affairs. Naturally, because women's empowerment requires democratic and participatory spaces, senior members of the family have long emphasized the need to create institutions that will assume the necessary burdens. In that regard, though a few decades ago few NGOs played any significant role in the country, more and more have contributed to the growth of civil society in recent years. The challenge of achieving gender equality, still some way in the future, was always self-evident to Queen 'Iffat, who addressed intrinsic weaknesses by creating sustainable networks and alliances in support of a national agenda that served both men and women.

WOMEN IN SA'UDI ARABIA

The explosion of literacy and global communications facilitated conditions under which more Muslims could aspire to be *fatwah*-issuing scholars, a source of authority that is complex and confusing; the result has been hundreds of thousands of rulings in various countries. As the vast majority of *fatwahs* issued by *'Ulamah* touched on social practices, inevitable abuses pullulated, some falling into a comical realm that dishonored the faith. For example, Shaykh 'Abdul Muhsin Al 'Ubaykan, one of the country's leading scholars, opined that a man who entered a house and came in contact with the womenfolk there should be made symbolically related to the women by drinking milk from one of the women. Although his 22 May 2010 *fatwah* precluded any sexual relations between the man and the donor woman, the ruling was immediately derided by most and rejected for its trivial approach, calling on the *'alim* to focus instead on much more significant concerns.

This was not the first time such a bizarre ruling had come to light. On 22 May 2007, 'Izzat 'Attiyyah was disciplined by Al Azhar University officials in Cairo after he issued a *fatwah* calling upon women to breastfeed their male colleagues, ostensibly because such a relationship offered a way around the mixing of the sexes in the workplace. Another ruling, this time in Somalia, prohibited female Muslims from watching World Cup soccer games (since men wore shorts), while a Malaysian *fatwah* asserted that Muslims should not do yoga on account of the various physical positions required in the exercises. One in Pakistan forbade polio vaccination because it was a Western plot to harm Muslims. There have been, to say the least, thousands of similar examples, and the vast majority have dealt with women.

As the frequency of such rulings increased, various officials confronted the ire of public scrutiny, which included international pressure from several governments. King 'Abdallah bin 'Abdul 'Aziz was not amused by such frivolities as occurred in Sa'udi Arabia, which, regrettably, gained momentum after the mid-1990s. Disappointed by the level to which such homilies had descended, on 17 January 2009 he assembled about 170 scholars for a major International Conference on Fatwah and its Regulations, lamenting that "the Islamic world has been plagued by an extremely negative phenomenon, which is the tendency to deliver *fatwas* by unqualified persons, especially on satellite television channels, the Internet and other modern channels of communication." "Issuing ill-considered *fatwas* without following any criterion," underscored the King, "offers biased, ignorant, extremist or careless individuals the opportunity to pose as religious experts qualified to issue *fatwas*."[19]

Permission to issue *fatwahs* was henceforth limited to senior scholars, presumably vetted for their expertise, a decision that irked some and pleased others. The Sa'udi Minister of Islamic Affairs, Endowments,

---

[19] Caryle Murphy, "Fatwa Chaos," *The Majalla*, 23 August 2010 at http://www.majalla.com/eng/2010/08/article55110707.

Preaching, and Guidance, Shaykh Salih bin 'Abdul 'Aziz Al al-Shaykh, called upon all preachers who appeared on television shows to obtain permission from the Kingdom's Mufti, Shaykh 'Abdul 'Aziz bin 'Abdallah Al al-Shaykh, before issuing religious decrees to the public. In the event it was unclear whether Shaykh Yusuf al-Ahmad, a professor at the Imam Muhammad bin Sa'ud University in Riyadh and a controversial scholar who had previously defied government policies, heeded the minister's call. In fact, after the Makkah conference on *fatwahs*, Shaykh al-Ahmad audaciously issued a ruling that ignored the ruler's decree. He even went so far as to forbid the employment of women as supermarket cashiers, a move Riyadh supported allegedly because such work was part of a "Westernizing" project that intended to end the segregation of women in the workforce. Overconfident in more ways than one, Shaykh al-Ahmad blatantly opposed the opening of the King 'Abdallah University for Science and Technology (KAUST), the Kingdom's first co-educational facility, and otherwise seldom missed an opportunity to seize an opportunity as he insisted on doctrinaire positions instead of backing important strides made by his countrymen and women. He was arrested on 7 July 2011 after posting a video message on YouTube in which he criticized the long-term detention of security suspects without charge or trial, triggering one of the most ironic chapters in contemporary Sa'udi domestic affairs as Human Rights Watch rushed to his assistance.[20] The organization called for his release and, because Shaykh al-Ahmad criticized the arrests of women who went to the ministry on 2 July 2011 and on "previous occasions to protest, peacefully, the long-term detention of their male relatives," previous critics became his allies. Paradoxically, even his fiercest opponents, Sa'udi women who debated the scholar's convoluted views on the Internet, rallied to his cause as many rejected yet another attempt to silence a maverick voice. Although few saw Shaykh al-Ahmad as a natural ally, the support he gained is one of the best illustrations of the convoluted ideas about the role of women extant in the Kingdom, with few choosing to remember one of the Shaykh's truly out-of-this-world proposals: to demolish parts of the Grand Mosque in Makkah and subsequently construct separate floors for women in the house of worship—all so that men and women would be physically prevented from *ikhtilat* (gender mixing) during *tawwaf* (circumambulation) and prayer.[21]

---

20 Human Rights Watch, "Saudi Arabia: Free Islamic Scholar Who Criticized Ministry," 14 July 2011, at http://www.hrw.org/news/2011/07/14/saudi-arabia-free-islamic-scholar-who-criticized-ministry.

21 It was unclear when or whether the Shaykh received a pardon, though information about his scholarship is nearly impossible to locate.

How Sa'udi women reached this point when so much progress was accomplished between 1932 and 2014 is a question of critical relevance to the main subject of this study. What did the renewed emphasis on segregation mean for the gradual progress that Sa'udi women had enjoyed, which has seen painstaking efforts to improve education and health services, and, above all else, has begun to provide them with the wherewithal to contribute to their country's prosperity and well-being?

The key concerns for securing opportunities revolved around lifting existing judicial restrictions as well as various socio-cultural limitations, although the creation of extensive separate public spheres, which Sa'udi officials believed were signs of progress, played an equally important role. The development of women-only public spaces in recent years has been perceived as an enhancement mechanism, even a religiously sanctified step, as clerics and civilians institutionalized women-only public environments. This policy has been controversial to say the least, especially because segregation has focused on the question of how women participated in everyday life, as many more have entered the workforce. Parallel to opinions delivered by religious scholars and, strangely, the primary driving forces behind the institutionalization of segregation, have been demands made by women. While some have opposed the practice of gender segregation, others have encouraged such a policy, thinking that, putting aside the impractical aspects that segregation inevitably leads to in a rapidly modernizing society, such practices protect them from predators in the form of untrustworthy men. Indeed, those who have favored segregation in the Kingdom have not been opposed to modernization, even if the creation of parallel worlds has posed gargantuan logistical problems. Rather, they genuinely believe that the conservative society is better served by full separation of the sexes, effectively meaning the development of two Sa'udi Arabias that only meet in the home.

Judicial Restrictions and Putative Changes

Queen 'Iffat Al Thunayan accepted segregation though she worked to enhance women's rights within the practices of the faith, which meant—for all practical purposes—that Sa'udi women would see their roles properly defined in the country's judicial system. She did not wish to see access to justice decided on the basis of gender and wanted institutions in place to secure rights and define responsibilities for both men and women. In short, what she wanted, and worked towards, was an end to discrimination based on gender. To her credit, sharp improvements or, perhaps more accurately, promises for improvements were made in women's access to courts and their rights as citizens, and these require careful attention.

Although several articles in the 1992 Basic Law required that Riyadh premise its legitimacy on justice, consultation, and equality in accordance with *Shari'ah*, the latter—as practiced in the Kingdom—did not offer equality to women, particularly regarding family law.[22] In fact, while the overwhelming majority of Muslim women throughout the world were provided with legal protection at this time, Sa'udi women were considered as legal minors under the control of their *mahram* (closest male relative), with strict legal restrictions on their personal behavior that, obviously, did not apply to men. The Hay'at al-Amr bil-Ma'ruf wal-Nahi 'an al-Munkar [Commission for the Promotion of Virtue and Prevention of Vice] oversaw public moral behavior, including very conservative dress and carefully controlled interactions between men and women—a severe regime the like of which does not exist in other Muslim countries. In addition to the *mutawa'in* (those who cause obedience), several enforcement mechanisms for accusing and detaining suspects existed parallel to the religious police, with no uniform application of the law. In a largely patriarchal and even hierarchical society, privileges favored men over women, and especially elites over commoners.

Even before he acceded to rulership in mid-2005, then heir apparent 'Abdallah bin 'Abdul 'Aziz pushed for the adoption of a royal decree that affirmed the principle of equality between men and women in all matters relating to Sa'udi nationality, although a key restriction remained in place which denied a woman the right to pass citizenship to her non-citizen spouse and children.[23] The ruler proposed an amendment to this decree in 2005, which stipulated that under certain conditions the law would grant non-Sa'udi spouses and/or children nationality. A further amendment in 2007 clarified additional changes although the law still contained certain restrictions.

Perhaps the most dramatic legal change of recent times was the post-2001 global requirement that travelers display a full facial photograph in official documents. Sa'udi women were exempted from affixing their photos in passports and Queen 'Iffat was no exception (see Appendix II

---

[22] For a good introduction to this sensitive subject, see Maha A. Z. Yamani, *Polygamy and Law in Contemporary Saudi Arabia*, Reading, UK: Ithaca Press, 2008, especially pp. 127–162.

[23] Royal Decree number M/54 (29 Shawwal 1425 AH), in "Consideration of reports submitted by States Parties under article 18 of the Convention, Combined initial and second periodic reports of States Parties: Saudi Arabia," United Nations, Committee on the Elimination of Discrimination Against Women, CEDAW/C/SAU/2, 07-29667 [E]120507 230507, 29 March 2007, p. 16, at http://daccessdds.un.org/doc/UNDOC/GEN/N07/296/67/PDF/N0729667.pdf?OpenElement.

for a copy of her diplomatic documents). At home, no women were issued with identification cards of any description, much less ones that displayed photographs; it remained a taboo subject. Ironically, Ottoman identification cards did not carry photographs either, as illustrated by the Queen's original civil status documents (see Appendix III). Nonetheless, global realities imposed specific requirements on Riyadh and, to his credit, Prince Nayif bin 'Abdul 'Aziz Al Sa'ud, then Minister of the Interior, pushed for precisely such a document. In 2002, women were thus allowed to apply for their own individual civil status cards rather than, as in the past, needing to endure having a legal identity only as a dependent on their *mahram*'s documents. Moreover, in 2008, women were allowed to receive their civil status papers without their guardian's permission and, starting in September 2012, could travel within the Gulf Cooperation Council territories using their smart identity cards without an exit letter or a passport.[24] This decision, an avowal that times were changing, gave women a travel privilege that was previously confined to men, though they still required permission from a *mahram* to travel abroad.

If the Ministry of the Interior altered its regulations and adapted to contemporary requirements, the courts nevertheless dragged their feet, posing inevitable problems as Sa'udi society experienced dramatic economic and social changes. Inasmuch as the vast majority of women still require the presence of a male relative or a male lawyer to represent them, fair judgments were, at least for those involved in such cases, rare. Beyond their intimidating atmosphere, all Sa'udi courts are under the direct authority of male adjudicators, posing serious handicaps especially in those cases dealing with family matters where the *mahram* is also the husband. Women who appear in court are of course fully covered, to satisfy the *ikhtilat* prerequisite, with judges facing the unhappy prospect of reaching conclusions without as much as seeing a woman's face in a divorce or child custody case. Few moderators see the inherent contradictions in such adversarial trials. To make matters worse, women are at a further disadvantage in the existing legal system because the testimony of a man is equal to that of two women, whereas, for the purpose of compensation in accidental death or injury cases, a woman's worth is calculated at half that of a man.[25]

[24] Awad al-Maliki, "Saudi Women Can Obtain ID Cards without Guardian's Permission," *Al Madinah*, 4 March 2008. See also Habib Toumi, "Saudi Women Allowed GCC Travel on Smart IDs," *Gulf News*, 18 September 2012, at http://m.gulfnews.com/news/gulf/saudi-arabia/saudi-women-allowed-gcc-travel-on-smart-ids-1.1078030.

[25] Yamani, *op. cit.*, pp. 133–134.

These socio-legal conditions were centuries old, although serious reforms were introduced beginning in 2003, when Riyadh created the King 'Abdul 'Aziz Center for National Dialogue and started to incorporate many of the recommendations vetted through its cathartic sessions.[26] One of the most memorable dialogues was held between 12 and 14 June 2004 in Madinah, the capital of the first Islamic state, on women's rights and their roles within society. This was no ordinary conversation as the Chairman, Shaykh Salih bin 'Abdul Rahman al-Hussayn, acknowledged. He pleaded for mutual understanding between men and women, advising everyone to abandon the competitive views which had grown up around this issue, which reflected the acute tensions that had arisen in the conservative social environment of the Kingdom. The cleric also added that society was obliged to treat women justly, in line with *Shari'ah* obligations and regardless of local customs. Conservative elements among the audience listened incredulously.[27] Female speakers did not mince their words when their turn came to articulate a variety of views. Dr. Salihah al-Hulays, who taught at Umm Al-Qurah University, promptly dismissed calls for equality between men and women, while other women participants insisted that women faced genuine challenges and that these should be addressed candidly. "How come we see all these injustices being committed against women if women faced no real problems?" asked Dr. Hanan al-Ahmadi, from the Institute of Public Administration in Riyadh.[28]

It is worth recalling that the second dialogue held in Makkah supported the role played by women in Sa'udi society, even if the more interesting question was the recognition that attitudes towards women were changing, as participants settled on nine recommendations to alert decision makers to their basic needs. Importantly, two of the nine suggestions made to the authorities were exceptional in tone as well as substance, with one claiming that intrinsic ties between a husband and wife should be founded on piety, guardianship, obedience, and consultation. It boldly stated that "guardianship" ought not to be interpreted to mean control, or to negate a woman's jurisdiction over herself; but rather that obedience meant only within the limits of what was good and was not akin to slavery—words that resonated loud and clear. Equally valuable was the recommendation made to Riyadh that all legislation ought

---

26 Kéchichian, *Legal and Political Reforms*, *op. cit.*, 62–108.

27 Abdul Wahab Bashir, "Madinah Forum on Women Calls for Respecting Tradition," *Arab News*, 14 June 2004 at http://archive.arabnews.com/?page=1§ion=0&article=46787&d=14&m=6&y=2004.

28 *Ibid.*

to reevaluate the position of women involved in litigation, which also called on courts to plan for the establishment of specialized family affairs courts that took into consideration the special circumstances of women, as well as suggesting that courts should set up departments that accommodated female litigants as they recorded or lodged their complaints.[29]

Remarkably, controversial debates as to whether women ought to have the right to present the cases of their clients in *Shari'ah* courts were finally settled in late 2012, when women were granted the right to litigate in a courtroom.[30] Because Queen 'Iffat was a staunch supporter of marriage but did not oppose divorce when a couple could no longer provide a healthy environment in which to raise their children or were otherwise incompatible, these recent changes would certainly have pleased her. She accepted separations in extreme cases, and though she believed that a woman ought to respect her husband, she also expected reciprocity.[31]

The late Queen would have been even more pleased to learn that King 'Abdallah bin 'Abdul 'Aziz announced that women would be allowed to vote and run for office in local elections beginning in 2015 and, equally important, promised that women would henceforth gain access to the judiciary. This late 2011 proposition was not a simple reform to enact, because, while the monarch's word is the law of the land, Sa'udi kings have almost always ruled by consensus not by diktat. Indeed, 'Abdallah knew that women who attended law school beginning as recently in 2006 were still being denied the right to practice, which has limited their employment opportunities to the women's sections of law firms and government offices.

In time, however, female attorneys are expected to appear in a court of law, and though the King knew that female attorneys were not allowed to argue cases before a court as lawyers, an undetermined number have recently been allowed to argue cases in court as the "legal representatives" of other women.[32] These were important steps, yet they stood

---

[29] Kéchichian, *Legal and Political Reforms*, *op. cit.*, pp. 81–83.

[30] Khadijah Bawazeer, "Divorce in Saudi Arabia," *Saudi Gazette*, 10 October 2012, at http://www.saudigazette.com.sa/index.cfm?method=home.regcon&content ID=20120507123571. See also Katy Watson, "Winning the Case for Women in Work: Saudi Arabia's Steps to Reform," *BBC News*, 13 December 2012, at http://www.bbc.co.uk/news/business-20697030.

[31] These views were confirmed in two separate interviews with HRH Princess Lulwah al-Faysal, Jiddah, 17 October 2010, as well as HRH Princess Al-Bandari bint 'Abdul Rahman al-Faysal, Riyadh, 15 October 2010.

[32] "New Law will End Male Dominance in Saudi Courts," *Arab News*, 10 February 2010, at http://www.arabnews.com/node/337642; see also Joe Avancena, "Saudi

without the necessary rules and regulations that certified the profession of female attorneys in the country, and it was to remedy such deficiencies that the monarch backed a plan to reform the court system by allowing women to argue cases on child custody, divorce, and other family-related issues as a first step, all of which were universally recognized as long overdue. At the time of writing, however, those special courts for women were still under development, though few doubted that they would become reality.[33] In time, misgivings that women would sit as judges in family courts and that family law may well be standardized to avoid the arbitrary opinions of individual male judges will gradually dissipate. Reports circulated in late 2012 that nearly 300 Sa'udi women lawyers "expected to be licensed to argue clients' cases in courtrooms in the near future," although the move was not formally approved at the time of writing; that said, the day is close when such practices will become routine.[34]

As important as these contemplated changes are, still in abeyance is a written penal code that would enable those men and women subject to arbitrary arrest and detention, at least to defend themselves in accordance with *Shari'ah*. This is a problematic challenge for a legal clause that would, by its very definition, deny adjudicators the right to interpret the law and determine arbitrary punishments. Cases of poor judgments fill the dockets and, increasingly, a plethora of videos and documents available on the World Wide Web add insult to injury. While a few legitimate cases may well have necessitated the kind of sentences that keep order in society, many more were poor examples that can only be attributed to overzealousness. Alleged sorcery and witchcraft cases, both of which were frowned upon in the Kingdom, do not deserve the kind of attention that Sa'udi judges have allocated to them. By drawing attention to such cases, the entire world knows about them and this adds to the catalog of negative opinions held by others about the Kingdom, based on

---

http://www.saudigazette.com.sa/index.cfm?method=home.regcon&contentID=2010030265001. For an interesting report on women attorneys arguing cases, see "Female Lawyers Seek Justice," *Saudi Gazette*, 23 June 2011, at http://www.saudigazette.com.sa/index.cfm?method=home.regcon&contentID=20110723105845.

33 Muhammad Humaidan, "Women Lawyers Call for Expediting Rules to Streamline their Practice," *Arab News*, 27 November 2011, at http://www.arabnews.com/node/399363. See also Dina Al-Shibeeb, Saudi Women Aim to Practice Law, Traditionally a Male Domain," *Al Arabiya News*, 23 April 2011, at http://www.alarabiya.net/articles/2011/04/23/146400.html.

34 Jumana Al Tamimi, "Saudi Courts May Soon have Women Lawyers: Delay in Government Decision not Justified, but Ceiling of Expectations Rising," *Gulf News*, 5 October 2012, p. 14.

unrepresentative examples that border on the ridiculous.[35] Women are easy targets, especially as regards the crime of *khulwah* (the illegal mixing of unrelated men and women). In more conservative parts of the country, a man and a woman having dinner in a restaurant, or sharing a taxi, or even meeting for business, could invite the potentially severe wrath of the law. Inevitably, anecdotal evidence quickly spreads through the media, all of which has further complicated the monarch's task of introducing genuine legal reforms.[36]

None of this was new, with such episodes having been recorded in Sa'udi annals since 1932. Queen 'Iffat Al Thunayan knew about a number of cases and objected to the abuses, wisely contending that they were evidence the Commission for the Promotion of Virtue and Prevention of Vice needed to be made properly accountable. Her friends and allies in this endeavor included King Faysal, when he was alive, and after his death, Prince Nayif bin 'Abdul 'Aziz Al Sa'ud, the Minister of

---

[35] For two such cases that received prominence, see *The Ismailis of Najran: Second-class Saudi Citizens*, New York: Human Rights Watch, 2008, at http://www.hrw.org/sites/default/files/reports/saudiarabia0908web.pdf, especially pp. 50–52 and 75–76. See also "Woman Convicted of 'Sorcery' is Beheaded in Saudi Arabia," *The Daily Mail*, 13 December 2011, at http://www.dailymail.co.uk/news/article-2073181/Saudi-Arabia-authorities-behead-woman-sorcery.html; "Woman Faces Death Penalty for Witchcraft after 'Casting Spell on 13-year-old Shopper'," *The Daily Mail*, 19 April 2012, at http://www.dailymail.co.uk/news/article-2131967/Woman-faces-death-penalty-witchcraft-accused-casting-spell-shopper-13.html; "Saudi Man Executed for 'Witchcraft and Sorcery'," *BBC News*, 19 June 2012 at http://www.bbc.co.uk/news/world-middle-east-18503550; Ryan Jacobs, "Saudi Arabia's War on Witchcraft: A Special Unit of the Religious Police Pursues Magical Crime Aggressively, and the Convicted," *The Atlantic*, 19 August 2013, at http://www.theatlantic.com/international/archive/2013/08/saudi-arabias-war-on-witchcraft/278701/; and Michael Schulson, "Will Saudi Arabia Execute Guest Workers for 'Witchcraft'?," *The Daily Beast*, 29 March 2014, at http://www.thedailybeast.com/articles/2014/03/29/indonesia-workers-in-saudi-arabia-are-on-trial-for-witchcraft-some-facing-the-death-penalty.html.

[36] In February 2008, a 37-year-old American businesswoman named Yara—a mother of three whose Jordanian parents had raised her in conservative Salt Lake City, Utah—was arrested by officials of the Commission for the Promotion of Virtue and Prevention of Vice in Riyadh for sitting at a table in public with a male colleague, who was also arrested. At the Malaz prison, Yara reported that she was taken "into a filthy bathroom, full of water and dirt." "They made me take off my clothes and squat and they threw my clothes in this slush and made me put them back on," she said. Eventually she was taken before a judge who told her: "You are sinful and you are going to burn in hell." After signing a confession, she was released to the custody of her husband." See Sonia Verma, "Religious Police in Saudi Arabia Arrest Mother for Sitting with a Man," *The Times* (London), 7 February 2008, at http://www.reli

the Interior, who issued several decrees over the years requiring Commission authorities to turn over custody of any detainee to the regular police. Whether such decrees were carefully enforced is impossible to verify although the late Queen was known to intervene with senior male family members whenever she heard of a case that involved Commission officials. Her brother-in-law, King 'Abdallah bin 'Abdul 'Aziz, shared 'Iffat Al Thunayan's apprehensions and was literally infuriated after *mutawa'in* guards refused firemen the authorization to enter a girls' school in Makkah in 2002 [that would place them in *khulwah*], which cost the lives of 15 children. He was likewise exasperated by the nonchalant 2007 dismissal of the "Qatif Girl" rapists verdict, which finally prompted the ruler to dismiss senior officials, and introduce wholesale reform measures that certainly did curtail Commission freedoms. Still, no member of the religious police force was ever punished for these crimes, for fear of upsetting domestic tranquility.

Mercifully, Commission leaders realized that nonchalant behavior was no longer acceptable, and that the enforcers' powers would be clamped down upon to curb their excesses. Routine functions like arrests and interrogations would no longer be their domain, and alleged culprits would henceforth be handed over to other state bodies. In a remarkably frank interview, Shaykh 'Abdul Latif bin 'Abdul 'Aziz Al al-Shaykh confided that growing anger among Sa'udis objecting to aggressive behavior by the *mutawa'in* had led him to introduce these latest reforms.

---

gionnewsblog.com/20554/islamic-extremism-42. In March 2008, two Sa'udi women—along with two men, a Sa'udi and an Indonesian—were arrested as they were leaving a rest house located close to al-Salam Recreation Center in Manhal, east of Abhah, for being in a state of *khulwah*. See Hayat Al-Ghamdi, "Vice Cops Arrest Four in 'Khulwa' Charges in Abha Rest House," *Arab News*, 10 March 2008, at http://arabnews.com/node/309724. But the case that upset many involved 75-year-old Khamisa Sawadi, a Syrian married to a Sa'udi, who was convicted of *khulwah* in March 2009 and sentenced to 40 lashings, four months in jail, and deportation after the religious police found her alone with two young men—reportedly her late husband's nephew and his friend bringing her loaves of bread. See Badea Abu Al-Naja, "Khulwa Sentence Against Elderly Widow Causes Uproar," *Arab News*, 11 March 2009, at http://www.arabnews.com/node/321891. For more recent and equally comical fare, including a claim that men and women exchanging e-mails could be committing *khulwah* which, strangely, redefined bizarre, see Yusuf Muhammad, "Arab Resident Arrested for *khulwa*," *Arab News*, 17 February 2014, at http://www.arabnews.com/news/526996; and Steph Cockroft, "Is Online Dating a Sin? Saudi Cleric Says that Men and Women Using the Internet to Talk is Religiously Forbidden," *The Daily Mail*, 29 May 2014, at http://www.dailymail.co.uk/news/article-2643019/Is-online-dating-sin-Saudi-cleric-says-men-women-using-internet-talk-religiously-forbidden.html.

The YouTube video uploaded from a mobile phone, which showed a religious policeman ordering a young woman to leave a mall because of her makeup, went viral and seriously hurt the country's reputation. Another incident caused a fatal car crash when *mutawa'in* elements chased a man who refused to turn his radio down. In this last instance, of course, the clergyman was deeply embarrassed and, two weeks into his job, "banned volunteers from serving in the force," while in April 2012 he "warned that those found to have harassed people would be punished."[37] What was increasingly obvious was that Riyadh was no longer in the mood to tolerate the overzealous application of what *mutawa'in* troops undertook in the course of their duties, which was why a new armory of measures to curb their powers was announced, though one wondered whether the necessary training would also be pursued as the Commission introduced a new code of practice.

Socio-Cultural Limitations and Future Challenges

Queen 'Iffat and members of her family accepted the graduated pace of legal reforms, even if she and they preferred that Sa'udi men accelerate their deliverance from age-old norms, which no longer fulfilled the needs of a rapidly modernizing Muslim nation state. As discussed in chapters three and four, rather than forcing the issues that concerned her, the Queen emphasized socio-cultural changes, including the right to education and health care, among others. Still, all Sa'udi women confronted traditions of segregation that limited their capacity for self-expression, and it was only the Queen's innate genius for gentle persuasion that circumvented many of the roadblocks in front of her. In fact, it would be fair to say that the noticeable changes that have occurred during the past few decades were partly the result of her initiatives, especially those concerned with social values.

To begin with, by emphasizing education for girls early on, Queen 'Iffat ensured that a woman's presence was not only tolerated but also accepted. Increasingly, young women earned the right to maintain a public life, especially as educators and health providers, two professions that certainly suited them well but that also brought them in contact—even if veiled—with men, even the most conservative of whom were obliged to

[37] "Saudi Arabia Religious Police Chief Announces New Curbs," BBC News, 3 October 2012, at http://www.bbc.co.uk/news/world-middle-east-19819791. See also Abdullah al-Bargi, "Haia Chief for Shorter Prayer Break, *Arab News*, 1 January 2014, at http://www.arabnews.com/news/501741 and Manal Al Sharif, "Rein in the Saudi Religious Police," *The New York Times*, 11 February 2014, http://www.nytimes.com/2014/02/11/opinion/rein-in-the-saudi-religious-police.html.

concede the educator's or the caregiver's worth. Women filled indispensable staff positions at public hospitals, were entrusted with the education of youngsters—both boys and girls—and appointed to high-profile private positions in the business community. A few were elected to chambers of commerce positions or mixed-gender business organizations.[38]

Equally important, by underlining areas where they could make a difference, women showed the determination to become truly valuable and no longer to tolerate discrimination and violence against them. Through her welfare societies, Queen 'Iffat looked after many battered women, which led to the creation of an entire network of effective socio-cultural institutions that in their turn protected those who were abused. In time, the Ministry of Social Affairs became fully engaged in implementing social awareness campaigns on domestic violence, as it hired professional counselors, physicians, and law-enforcement officers trained to recognize and deal with cases of domestic violence.[39] As discussed earlier, women's access to health care and the freedom to make independent decisions regarding their health and reproductive rights were no longer an exclusively male monopoly. Although many Sa'udi hospitals refused treatment without guardian consent, many others were now aware of life-threatening challenges to women and ill children, especially when absentee fathers were nowhere in sight. In addition to serious ethical challenges, hospital administrators faced additional financial burdens as insurance companies insisted on the type of care that did not escalate costs, which was often a critical issue in life-and death conditions. Increasingly, hospitals in the Kingdom permitted women to consent to their own treatment, as well as those of their children if proper insurance was available. Most Sa'udis took for granted the current, state-

---

[38] For a good iteration of this point, see Marie-Gabrielle Palau, *Leaders of Saudi Arabia*, Paris, France: Omnia International SARL, 2008. This book lists dozens of business and political leaders, including several prominent women, most of whom were photographed.

[39] For a key piece of original research on this important social question, see, Abdulaziz A. Albrithen, "Alcoholism and Domestic Violence in Saudi Society," Doctoral Dissertation, Liverpool, UK: University of Liverpool, September 2006, at http://faculty.ksu.edu.sa/aalbrithen/Documents/Ph.D. Thesis.pdf. See also, The National Family Safety Program, *Domestic Violence and Child Abuse and Neglect in Saudi Arabia*, Riyadh: National Guard Health Affairs, n.d., at http://nfsp.org.sa/index.php/component/phocadownload/category/7-2012-04-03-11-28-16?download=53:2012-04-03-11-11-38; and A.A. Tashkandi and P. Rasheed, "Wife Abuse: A Hidden Problem—A Study Among Saudi Women Attending PHC Centres," *La Revue de Santé de la Méditerranée Orientale* 15:5, 2009, pp. 1242–1253, at www.emro.who.int/emhj/1505/15_5_2009_1242_1253.pdf.

of-the-art, government-funded medical care available to every citizen, but the dramatic improvements in this sector, and especially in the balanced allocation of health care resources between men and women, were the result of painful choices made in the 1950s and 1960s. It is worth repeating that model clinics and modern hospitals came into existence because of specific policies first established under Kings Sa'ud and Faysal, and it has behooved successive generations to recognize that available facilities were built neither haphazardly nor on the cheap.[40]

By all accounts, sharp improvements were recorded in the percentage of safe births, most of which were attended by skilled health personnel, even if the infant mortality rate was 18 per 1,000 live births in 2010 for children under five and 15 per 1,000 live births for infants, with the maternal mortality ratio in 2010 stood at 24 per 100,000 births.[41] In 1970, these figures had been very high, with infant mortality at that time running at 185 per 1,000 births and maternal mortality hovering at around 40 per 1,000. Of course, women received better health care but the extent to which they were free to participate in and influence community life, policies, and social development has been somewhat limited until recent years. In part because of Queen 'Iffat's sustained efforts to create the institutions that nurtured such activities, family life—ranging from education to health and business issues—has created numerous opportunities for those who wished to avail themselves of such services. Consequently, and gradually, many women teachers, social workers, physicians, journalists, university professors, and investors, have begun to influence policies and social development programs.

Another significant concern for women has been the disproportionate ways in which they are affected by poverty in comparison with men. Of

---

[40] Consequently, according to the 2011 United Nations *Human Development Report*, life expectancy in the Kingdom of Sa'udi Arabia stood at an average of 74.35 years [74.1 in 2013, although the discrepancy was within the margin of error], with males averaging around 72.37 years and women around 76.42 years. See "Saudi Arabia Life Expectancy at Birth," IndexMundi, at http://www.indexmundi.com/saudi_arabia/life_expectancy_at_birth.html.
Life expectancy at birth was 53.9 years in 1970 and was even lower in the 1930s and 1940s. Kingdom of Saudi Arabia, *Human Development Report 2002*, Riyadh: Ministry of Economy and Planning, 2003, at http://hdr.undp.org/en/reports/national/arabstates/saudiarabia/Saudi%20Arabia_2003_en.pdf, pp. 34, 47; and United National Development Program, *Human Development Report 2011: Sustainability and Equity—A Better Future for All*, New York, UNDP, 2011.

[41] United National Development Program, *Human Development Report 2013: The Rise of the South—Human Progress in a Diverse World*, New York, UNDP, 2013, p. 167 [available at http://hdr.undp.org/en/2013-report].

course, the primary reason for this lopsided disadvantage is past employment limitations. With restricted access to transportation, women are effectively shortchanged, since entrepreneurship requires a minimum level of mobility. Moreover, because of legal conditions, many women have abandoned the hope of gaining full control over their destinies, especially if they choose to work outside the home. This concern is made even more complicated when a woman is the second, third, or even the fourth wife, which seriously curtails her sense of proprietorship in her home. Inasmuch as such factors affect the economic well-being of women, and often prevent those facing economic hardship from taking care of themselves, the issue leaves a legacy on society at large. This is one of the reasons why Queen 'Iffat did not advocate for change outside government-sponsored channels, because she understood that meaningful social change would only come through a change in the law. While she strongly believed in and supported the creation of institutions that protect women, granting them human and political rights, she nevertheless understood that nothing would be accomplished through abrupt decisions.

WOMEN AS ROLE MODELS

As discussed above, segregation—that is, women-only public spaces—and *ikhtilat* were related to the discussion about *tamkin* (empowerment) and *nuhud* (rise), terms that were used in the 2005 *Arab Human Development Report* on Arab women.[42] More often than not, every initiative or strategy that aimed to strengthen the *tamkin* of Sa'udi women seemed to be determined by top-down efforts that, logically, raised several fundamental questions. Despite the undeniable progress recorded since 1932, it is reasonable to ask whether the Sa'udi woman is perceived as a role model in her environment and what role religion plays in women's ideas about contemporary conditions? In other words, in the light of Queen 'Iffat's legacy, it is fair to wonder whether and how women speak about the role of women in the Kingdom today? Equally important, what is the contribution that women are expected to make to the country's economic prosperity, especially as Riyadh seeks increasing influence in the world?

Economic Solutions for a G-20 Member

The Gini coefficient, developed by the Italian statistician and sociologist Corrado Gini early in the 20th century, introduced a zero to one

[42] United Nations Development Programme, *Arab Human Development Report*

scale, where zero represents perfect equality among genders, that is, exactly equal income or the same legal rights. A Gini coefficient of one (100 on the percentile scale) expresses maximal inequality across the different values, that is, one person among the population has all the income. One recent estimate puts the Gini coefficient factor for Sa'udi Arabia at 0.32.[43] While inequality may have become somewhat worse since the 1980s oil boom, essentially because of a sharp increase in the total numbers of people and Riyadh's limited capacity for absorbing them, King 'Abdallah bin 'Abdul 'Aziz has introduced decisive steps to alleviate poverty and enhance personal incomes. In 2002, the then heir apparent visited a poor neighborhood in Riyadh, and was livid at what he saw. This, more than any anecdotal evidence, stiffened his resolve for addressing intrinsic problems long before the uprisings that rocked the Arab World starting in late 2010.[44] To remedy such conditions, the ruler introduced concrete steps to expand rural development, increased social security expenditures, and promoted a comprehensive national housing program. Over the course of the past few years, but especially in 2011, Riyadh has allocated nearly $200 billion dollars for various projects, and improved public services, including subsidized education, health, and housing. Job market opportunities have improved as well, and while unemployment concerns persist—especially because of the presence of a large expatriate population now numbering over 8 million—an overall upturn has been noted. The 2013 UNDP *Human Development Report* ranked Saudi Arabia 32nd out of 103 developing countries with respect to the "Human Poverty Index" (with an index value of 14.9 percent), and the "Gender Development Index" ranked the county at 128th world-wide (with a score of 0.76) with respect to treatment of women, based on 2010 data. These scores reflect better access for women to education and health in recent years, even if large sections of the job market that remain inaccessible presumably still require close attention.

In fact, more than a lack of access, the problem stems from a certain mindset that does not consider women as economically potent.

2005: Towards the Rise of Women in the Arab World, New York: United Nations Publications, 2005.

[43] Kirk-Dale McDowall-Rose, "Saudi Arabia—Why It's Different to Dubai and Why It's a Good Bet," *IBM Strategy and Transformation*, 27 July 2012, at https://www-304.ibm.com/connections/blogs/gbs_strategy/entry/saudi_arabia_why_its_different_to_dubai_why_its_a_good_bet1?lang=en_us.

[44] "Change and Reform: A Conversation with Khaled Al-Seif," Saudi–US Relations Information Service/SUSRIS, 22 January 2012, at http://susris.com/2012/01/22/change-and-reform-a-conversation-with-khaled-al-seif/.

Thousands of currently unemployed Sa'udi women are ready and willing to work and could easily be employed by the Kingdom's private sector. If carefully planned, female participation in the workforce could comfortably reach 40 percent, a figure that would mean an increase in GDP of $17 billion per year, possibly adding $58 billion in revenues to Sa'udi companies on the back of significant increases in productivity, engagement, and innovation. One research organization has estimated that in 2011, around 385,000 well-educated Sa'udi women were available to join the market, but were not currently being utilized. Moreover, the same analysis suggests that the private sector has the capacity to employ at least 7 million female Sa'udi workers, which represents a huge figure in a population that hovers around the 30 million mark.[45]

It must be emphasized that most Sa'udi women need to work to support their families, and in that regard a number of local, homegrown businesses signal a rise in female entrepreneurship. The latest craze is the many cupcake shops that have sprung up throughout the Gulf region, hacking at teenage consumers' "slimming diets and gnawing at their fat budgets." Sa'udi shopping malls have embraced the phenomenon, as "Cupcake Entrepreneurs" have become role models. Beyond the immediate returns that come from running your business, young educated women face the real prospect of unemployment, which is why many have turned to "satisfying the insatiable cravings of cupcake fanatics as one among several other ways of keeping busy, earning money and achieving some social notoriety."[46] Of course, this is just a single example, but in highlighting the changing face of business innovation in the Kingdom, it deserves some careful attention. By making a leap into innovation, whether selling cupcakes or anything else, in a culture where a full-time job is the dream of the majority these entrepreneurs have demonstrated that they could contribute to their society on their own terms. To be sure, the vast majority of these women are professionals seeking job satisfaction as well as security, even if becoming an entrepreneur represents an incredible cultural leap for most. Whether the business is selling cupcakes, burgers, or vintage handbags is not relevant. Remarkably, highly educated women want to be involved in businesses they like,

---

45 "Saudi Companies Could Easily Employ Thousands More Saudi Females, Says Report," at http://www.ameinfo.com/saudi-companies-easily-employ-thousands-saudi-313807.

46 Hasan Tariq Alhasan, "The Gulf's Cupcake Entrepreneurs: Facing Unemployment, Educated Young Gulf Women are Abandoning Innovation and Catering to an Urge to Consume," *The Guardian*, 3 October 2012, at http://www.guardian.co.uk/commentisfree/2012/oct/03/gulf-cupcake-entrepreneurs.

because not everyone can become an engineer, a physician, or a lawyer. Many have the passion for baking cupcakes, designing jewelry, or sewing garments, and pursuing their passions as entrepreneurial opportunities ensures financial success as well as creative satisfaction. Women suffer more from joblessness than men, constituting up to 75 percent of job seekers in Sa'udi Arabia precisely because of the cultural mindset that still pigeonholes them into stereotypical roles. Courageous entrepreneurs, on the other hand, are determinedly showing that not only can they make the necessary adjustments, they can also have satisfying careers, and add to the country's overall prosperity, too.

'Iffat Al Thunayan and Sa'udi Women

Queen 'Iffat attempted to create a secure modernizing environment for Sa'udi women, to enable them to articulate ideas about society, contribute to their communities, and enjoy the fruits of life as far as possible. She also worked hard to share her own perspectives, which revolved around loyalty to crown and country, at a time when Sa'udi nationalism was not clearly defined. In short, she worked to empower those who wished to be stronger, pushed for an institutionalization process to the hilt, and encouraged active mentalities in those who had previously been reticent or timid. As such, she was a true modernizer—one who did not fit the classic model of copying the example of others but who adapted to circumstances as necessary, governed by a keen understanding that "society need[ed] in a sense a homogeneous culture in which people" were "inducted to be able to do business with each other."[47] This approach did not mean that the search for a relevant modernity was necessarily the search for secularism, or give credence to the idea that Islam and modernity were incompatible. In fact, her entire life proved that the search for material and spiritual progress were indeed compatible, as, for example, in her legitimizing of women-only public spaces through reference to Islamic doctrine. Neither did it mean that she accepted a second-class status. On the contrary, she viewed segregation as necessary in the conservative public milieu, but rejected restrictions on *ikhtilat* in private. The Queen's objective was to add *tamkin* and *nuhud* whenever possible, so that Sa'udi women could benefit from what was offered to them.[48]

For 'Iffat Al Thunayan religion was a central feature of Sa'udi modernity, along with technological innovations that improved quality of life.

---

[47] Charles Taylor, "Nationalism and Modernity," in John Hall, ed., *The State of the Nation: Ernest Gellner and the Theory of Nationalism*, Cambridge: Cambridge University Press, 1998, pp. 191–218. The quote is on page 193.

[48] Interview with HRH Princess Sarah al-Faysal, Riyadh, 13 October 2010.

Cars and planes were innovations not to be found in the Holy Scriptures but all Muslims, including pious Muslims, accepted both without any reservations. Scientific progress, ranging from medicine to space exploration, was also welcomed, since denying such progress was ignorance and truly un-Islamic.

In the last years of the 20th century and the first decade of the 21st, Islam embraced the computer, the Internet, and assorted digital telephones, which were not *haram* because they transmitted the Word of God. To be sure, there was room for abuse, but the instruments themselves were not to blame for human behavior. This was at heart the late Queen's perspective, one that built on the notion that everyone should be open to innovation and rely on his conscience to do good and inflict no harm to oneself or to others. In other words, material progress—including progress for women—was not only possible but also worthy of encouragement as long as it occurred within the limits and framework set out by Islam and its interpretations. She was certainly persuaded that modernization incorporated material and spiritual dimensions and that these two were mutually compatible. Of course, Queen 'Iffat did not reject Westernization, and while she observed well-established distinctions between modernization and Westernization, she nevertheless appreciated that Muslims, including Muslim women, could benefit from some of the freedoms the West took for granted.

To be sure, she rejected copycat behavior with respect to morals that reached the Peninsula through various media outlets. She also rejected the secularism of the West, which encouraged a separation between religion and state. But she did not abhor Western clothes or food, for example, and while she did not agree with the Western women's liberation movement that arose during the 1970s, the late Queen could still see in it a lot of positive aspects from which Sa'udi women could benefit. In this respect, she was not only referring to cars, planes, cameras, air conditioning, or even the current wave of Internet-driven social networks, but to serious advances in the sciences. For her, a modern Islamic country, which she certainly considered Sa'udi Arabia to be—or to be on its way to becoming during her lifetime—needed access to the scientific knowledge that Western societies were in the forefront of developing. Even more importantly—and this provides another example of her tireless search to introduce scientific knowledge among Sa'udi women—'Iffat Al Thunayan did not believe, even for a moment, that skilled men and women would be preoccupied with each other while engaged in serious work. Rather, she maintained that they could easily concentrate on their work, and that *ikhtilat*, at least at that level, was a secondary concern. She trusted modern citizens, both men and women, to make scientific discoveries that added to humanity's vast and growing knowledge base, rather than being fearful of each other's company. She certainly had no problems whatsoever if a woman chose to wear a *hijab* in such circumstances, though she also believed that professional colleagues respected themselves and each other far more than most people believed.[49]

This attitude is noteworthy in demonstrating what Queen 'Iffat wanted for women in the Kingdom—namely, that Sa'udi Arabia should not simply become a modern country in the material sense but should develop the wherewithal of a modernizing society in acquiring intellectual and social values that emphasized quality of life while still obeying the faith. By its very nature, the Kingdom was a mixed society which included very conservative, underdeveloped regions as well as more progressive, ultramodern environments. Both aspects made up the whole, but it was nearly impossible to impose similar values on all. Thus the Queen concentrated on empowering women to become cultured, informed, and, especially, educated in science subjects, having faith that from such support would come serious scientific contributions. For her, a cultured young woman was someone who knew herself well, could articulate thoughts, and interact with everyone with grace. Someone who learned how to think and talk with poise, someone whose self-esteem was high, and who could mingle with anyone anywhere. Similarly, a well-educated woman was someone who not only gained knowledge but could effectively use what she had learned to improve herself and those around her. This did not mean that acquiring erudition precluded such a person from being religious, faithful, and confident in her sacred duties. On the contrary, she thought that a modernizing Sa'udi woman was better able to participate in her society, while upholding local traditions and, especially, her faith. A well-developed contemporary mind was compatible with religion and its dogmas even if in some quarters these were seen as conservative.

Consequently, her ideal modernizers were individuals like Dr. Sahar Al Dawsary, the Executive Director and Chief of Pediatrics and Neonatology at the Saad Specialist Hospital in Al-Khobar, or Dr. May Al Khunayzi, Executive Director at the same facility.[50] The list was truly long and included Dr. Nahid Tahir, the Founder and Chief Executive Officer of the investment bank Gulf One, certainly considered to be one of the Kingdom's key financial institutions. A Dar al-Hanan graduate, the financial economics laureate not only earned a doctorate but was the first woman to be hired by the National Commercial Bank (NCB), where she worked with nearly 4,000 men. The investment institution she then

---

[49] Interview with HRH Princess Masha'il bint Turki al-Faysal, Riyadh, 14 October 2010.

[50] Marie-Gabrielle Palau, *op. cit.*, pp. 68–69 and 132–133.

set up, which specialized in infrastructure and industrial projects, turned a profit after its very first quarter as it pursued the motto of adding value to the Kingdom.[51] Another name is Hayat Sindi, a Sa'udi researcher who was appointed by the United Nations Educational, Scientific and Cultural Organization (UNESCO) as a Goodwill Ambassador to support science education, especially among young girls. According to Irina Bokova, the Director-General of UNESCO, Hayat's nomination was "in recognition of her work to create an ecosystem of entrepreneurship and social innovation for scientists, technologists and engineers in the Middle East and beyond." The nomination also acknowledged "her efforts to bring the youth closer to innovators and her dedication to the ideals and aims of the organization," testimony that Queen 'Iffat's investments had paid off handsomely.[52] The number of professional women who have made serious contributions to Sa'udi society is vast and growing exponentially. Many have functioned within the narrow cultural confines of the *hijab* but have functioned rather well all the same. The overwhelming majority succeeded in their endeavors and succeeded in discarding imposed burdens because their contributions were deemed essential. This, perhaps more than anything else, was the legacy of Queen 'Iffat as she hoped that Sa'udi women would accomplish extraordinary acts in the most ordinary ways.

❖

Because of their unique relationship, it may be safe to conclude that Queen 'Iffat Al Thunayan and King Faysal bin 'Abdul 'Aziz shared a joint vision, which focused on empowering both men and women to contribute to the growing prosperity of the Kingdom. More importantly, the Queen's mission after the monarch passed away did not end, even if his successors assumed their fair share of responsibilities. 'Iffat Al Thunayan knew that his legacy was intrinsically tied to hers, and vice versa, and never did anything to jeopardize either. She knew that her late husband was not the type of person who indulged her for the sake of

---

[51] *Ibid.*, 274–275.

[52] Hayat, who was born in Makkah in 1967, has made major contributions to point-of-care diagnostics—medical testing at or near the site of patient care—and, specifically, has designed a biochemical sensor with thermo-elastic probes known as the Magnetic Acoustic Resonance Sensor (Mars). Hayat holds a pharmacology degree from King's College in London as well as a doctorate in biotechnology from the University of Cambridge. See Habib Toumi, "Saudi Scientist Chosen UN Goodwill Ambassador: Hayat Recognised for Outstanding Efforts to Bring Youth Closer to Innovators," *Gulf News*, 2 October 2012, at http://gulfnews.com/news/gulf/saudi-arabia/saudi-scientist-chosen-un-goodwill-ambassador-1.1083788.

pleasing a spouse—though he clearly loved her deeply—but because he seriously wanted to see Sa'udi women participate fully in society. He knew, as she did, that the country needed every individual's skills, and was also cognizant that those skills required development. To say, therefore, that the royal couple formed a harmonious duopoly sharing deep convictions about the future of the country would be perhaps the best way of describing their benevolent union.

6

From the Hijaz to Najd

Although the foundations of the Third Sa'udi State, the contemporary Kingdom of Sa'udi Arabia, were laid on 15 January 1902, when 'Abdul 'Aziz bin 'Abdul Rahman Al Sa'ud reclaimed regions that had belonged to his ancestors, what would ensure the state's eventual political success was in fact the 1744 alliance that had united the Al Sa'ud with the Al al-Shaykh. 'Abdul 'Aziz was a leader in every sense of the word, a statesman who transformed the tribal conglomerates scattered throughout the Arabian Peninsula into the present country, a task that was as difficult to accomplish as the alliance set up by his predecessors. Thousands, perhaps hundreds of thousands, welcomed and accepted his leadership because it ensured genuine security and was based on *Shari'ah* law. His followers trusted him as they would his successors, not only because 'Abdul 'Aziz bin 'Abdul Rahman and his sons knew how to command, but also because the Al Sa'ud aimed to marry power with justice. Of course, there was also a core understanding that a nation is not "invented" with the stroke of a pen or at the end of a sword, but that its building and prosperity depend on hard work even if the environment is hostile to anything but mere survival.

Equally important, and despite facile commentaries that have chosen to ignore the roles played by women in Sa'udi society, it is valuable to note that the founder was not a misogynist. On the contrary, he was well aware of the women educators and warriors who filled local history narratives, even if few outsiders were aware of such contributions. Beyond the traditional female companions of the Prophet, many Najdi women contributed significantly to their environments, even though most recorded histories opted to overlook them.[1] In fact, several Central Arabian women earned their fame by composing poetry, which was memorized and passed on orally from one generation to the next. Many

---

[1] Little biographical information on women is found in the classic sources on the area, most of which concentrate on depicting history from a male perspective that, naturally, was neither unusual nor unique to Sa'udi Arabia. See, for example,

others played unifying roles as they married into key tribes, unions that for practical purposes strengthened Najdi harmony. A recent biography provides detailed data on 52 women, who lived between the eighteenth century and 1953, and who were truly influential in shaping the history of the leading tribal families that combined forces to create the successive Kingdoms of Sa'udi Arabia.[2]

Importantly, the volume included entries for, among others, al-Jawharah bint Faysal bin Turki Al Sa'ud, the founder-ruler's aunt, who acted as a *consigliere*; Turfah bint 'Abdallah bin 'Abdul Latif al-Shaykh, King Faysal's mother; Hussah bint Ahmad bin Muhammad al-Sudayri, the woman who married 'Abdul 'Aziz twice and gave him seven sons as well as seven daughters, amongst whom were King Fahd and heir apparents Sultan, Nayif, and Salman; al-Jawharah bint Turki bin 'Abdallah Al Sa'ud, the woman who saved Muhammad bin Sa'ud [r. 1742–1765] from an assassination attempt; and Nurah bint 'Abdul Rahman, the founder-monarch's eldest sister, who inspired the young Prince to return from Kuwait to Riyadh.[3] Yet remarkably it did not include an entry on 'Iffat Al Thunayan, despite her being a contemporary of King 'Abdul 'Aziz bin 'Abdul Rahman Al Sa'ud.[4]

Inasmuch as this remarkable woman became Queen in a country that has seen strong female characters leave their mark on what was a paternalistic society, what 'Iffat Al Thunayan added was a presence and a spirit that truly distinguished her from most other women who have made an impression on Sa'udi life. Like other very strong women in

---

Hussayn Ibn Ghannam, *Tarikh Najd* [The History of Najd], Beirut, Lebanon: Dar al-Shuruq, 1994 [it is important to note that Ibn Ghannam was a disciple of Muhammad bin 'Abdul Wahhab]. See also, Muhammad bin 'Umar al-Fakhiri, *Al-Akhbar al-Najdiyyah* [Reportage on Najd], Riyadh: Matabi' Jami'at al-Imam Muhammad ibn Sa'ud al-Islamiyyah, n.d.; and 'Uthman bin 'Abdallah Ibn Bishr, *'Unwan al-Majd fi Tarikh Najd* [The Sign of Honor in the History of Najd], Riyadh: King Abdul Aziz Public Library for the Wazarat al-Ma'arif al-Sa'udiyyah [Ministry of Education], 2002.

2 Dalal Mukhlid al-Harbi, *Prominent Women from Central Arabia*, Reading, UK: Ithaca Press [in association with the King Abdul Aziz Foundation for Research and Archives], 2008.

3 Muhammad bin Sa'ud [r. 1742–1765] is the correct Ibn Sa'ud as recorded in local sources, a moniker that is mistakenly—and often—attributed to 'Abdul 'Aziz bin 'Abdul Rahman [r. 1932–1953], the founder of the Third Kingdom.

4 As someone who did not seek the limelight, one of the reasons why so little was publicly known about the late Queen was due to her strict adherence to local norms, which essentially relegated women to the private sphere. Still, because of her immense contributions, it is critical to draw as accurate a picture as is possible, to better assess 'Iffat Al Thunayan's role in nurturing the Sa'udi nation.

Arabia, 'Iffat defined an outlook, set markers, identified goals, anticipated challenges, applied diplomatic skills, cajoled the reticent, emancipated the reserved, invested in men and women, and expected to see results not only from her own work but also from that of all those who had toiled to rebuild the nation. Her numerous achievements, some of which have been described in previous chapters, illustrate the depth and breadth of her influence throughout the vast country from the time she first set foot on its soil in January 1932 until she passed away on 17 February 2000. While the future Queen devoted the early years of her married life to raising her children, her presence next to the Viceroy of the Hijaz, who became heir apparent and eventually monarch, was equally valuable as she enthused Faysal in some of his most epochal decisions. Far from being a power couple in the Westernized sense, the Faysal–'Iffat complement was focused on delivering sorely needed socio-economic reforms in a rapidly developing country, one that required the creation of advanced institutions of learning and more efficient health care facilities, two major areas of concern to which Queen 'Iffat devoted huge amounts of time and energy, and whose improvement was carefully coordinated with her husband.

The purpose of this chapter is to highlight the Queen's unflinching spirit in the years after her husband was murdered, to better assess how earnestly she worked to preserve the Al Sa'ud legacy bequeathed by the founder and his successors. Although 'Iffat Al Thunayan's role is often overlooked in this process, in reality she played a larger part than many assumed. The discussion below focuses on the sources that mobilized her willpower, especially her core beliefs and, equally important, her understanding of the roles that women were called upon to play in Sa'udi Arabia. The chapter closes with an analysis of the late Queen's reliance on family values and how those sustained her in the last journey back to Najd.

WOUNDED BUT NOT BROKEN

'Iffat Al Thunayan lived with Faysal bin 'Abdul 'Aziz "for 43 years and 20 days," as she was fond of reminding her guests after he was murdered on 25 March 1975. Naturally, his death and the way it came about received extensive media coverage, although family stoicism prevented public displays of grief. Distraught Sa'udis took to the streets of Riyadh as soon as they heard the news, surrounding the hospital where the King's remains lay, wailing and screaming their sorrow. As numerous heads of state rushed to Sa'udi Arabia to attend the funeral, hardly anyone mentioned the impact that the murder had had on the Queen and immediate family members. Princess Lulwah recalled seeing her mother crouched on the floor as she rushed through the palace doors, sobbing, "They took him away, they took him away." It was a devastating moment that became permanently etched on everyone's mind as 'Iffat Al Thunayan measured the senseless act and its consequences, aware that the assassin was a deranged family member.[5]

Impact of Faysal's Death

What followed was a period of mourning, both official and private, which saw a variety of new faces emerge on the political scene. Heir apparent Khalid bin 'Abdul 'Aziz was elevated to the rulership, seconded by Prince Fahd bin 'Abdul 'Aziz who, as the new heir to the throne, assumed the extraordinary burden of governorship from his ailing brother. Both King Khalid and heir apparent Fahd were affected by the tragedy, with the monarch crying openly as his fallen brother's remains were buried. They paid customary condolence calls to the devastated Faysal family, including separate visits to Queen 'Iffat, who commiserated with her brothers-in-law. The calls were exceptional because they went beyond the usual protocol. In fact, it was the Queen's well-established open-house policies—practiced with rare generosity—that compelled a sitting monarch and senior members of the family to make the move to her home, which she naturally reciprocated. Yet it was also the first time in recorded history in the Kingdom when such high-level visits had been undertaken, affirming 'Iffat Al Thunayan's sway on senior Al Sa'ud figures. In other words, the most powerful authorities in the Kingdom acknowledged Queen 'Iffat Al Thunayan's significant contributions in setting clear parameters for the family code of behavior, accepted by everyone as a mark of affection and respect. What was even more touching was the genuine warmth that all senior male members displayed towards her, not only out of deference to their fallen brother,

---

[5] Joseph A. Kéchichian, *Faysal: Saudi Arabia's King for All Seasons*, Gainesville: University Press of Florida, 2008, pp. 192–197. As various conspiracy theories associated with this tragedy were purposefully overlooked in my political biography of the late monarch, the following may shed light on the longstanding debate. See Robert Dreyfuss, " Discover Plot against Saudi Arabia: Murder of Faisal Tied to U.S.-Based British Intelligence Network," *Executive Intelligence Review* 5:50, 26 December 1978, pp. 45–46; Robert Lacey, *Inside the Kingdom: Kings, Clerics, Modernists, Terrorists, and the Struggle for Saudi Arabia*, New York: Viking, 2009, p. 94 [which includes the bizarre sentence: "If you did not go to prison in the reign of King Faisal, you would never go to prison," which may be misunderstood as implying that dissidents were routinely jailed for their opinions between 1964 and 1975].

but also because they accepted her as a sister whose contributions had been equally critical. All witnessed, and were impressed by, Faysal's deference to 'Iffat in his *majlis* throughout his life. Few could forget how often she attended these gatherings, when each and every half-brother became aware of her valuable contributions to their discussions. Moreover, on these occasions, "Faysal was not arrogant towards her," nor did he ask her simply to observe. "On the contrary, he was patient and wanted to learn from her," confirmed their son 'Abdul Rahman al-Faysal, "though she seldom imposed herself and knew when to add value; but when she did speak everyone paid attention."[6] Although less often after 1975, both Kings Khalid and Fahd consulted Queen 'Iffat on key matters, confided in her on family concerns that required her intercession, and asked for her advice in significant policy areas that affected Sa'udi women. King Fahd, who was close to his brother Faysal and who visited the palace often during his youth, sought his *ukhti*'s [sister's] input on many issues. "She was not his mother but could have been," affirmed 'Abdallah Al-Ghamdi, a pillar among all palace employees who was privy to the family's private affairs.[7] She was perceived, even in a largely paternalistic environment, as the most senior person, the *primus inter pares* among her Al Sa'ud peers.[8] That was the legacy that 'Iffat left to her extended family, whose members understood quite well the strength of the Faysal–'Iffat alliance, one that stood as a model for others to emulate.

After a period of several weeks, the grieving Queen faced specific choices now that her beloved companion was no longer alive. Although her sons, daughters, dozens of grandchildren, and numerous friends and acquaintances both in Sa'udi Arabia and throughout the world doted on her, 'Iffat knew that the time was right to reorganize her life under these new circumstances. This awareness sharpened her focus on the need to serve her husband's memory and, equally important, to continue her own contributions to their shared unfinished business. In other words, Queen 'Iffat refused to throw in the proverbial towel after King Faysal's death, preferring to channel her energies into what she believed he would certainly want to have seen achieved. It would have been easy simply to retire and enjoy family life, but that would have been uncharacteristic of this larger-than-life figure. Still, she did not rush into action, choosing to take time to reflect on what steps to take next. Towards that end, she retreated to her Paris apartment on the Avenue Foch, where she re-exam-

[6] Interview with HRH Prince 'Abdul Rahman al-Faysal, Riyadh, 13 October 2010.
[7] Al-Ghamdi worked as the Palace Manager for nearly three decades and earned the Queen's trust. Interview with 'Abdallah Al-Ghamdi, Jiddah, 7 November 2010.
[8] Interview with HRH Princess Hayfah al-Faysal, Jiddah, 16 October 2010.

ined her priorities over the course of several months. It was in the French capital that ‘Iffat's sons and daughters gathered regularly around her to devise a plan to honor their father. While she did not coach them to take any specific actions or give instructions on what needed to be done, and although the idea to establish the King Faysal Foundation germinated in the mind of her stepson, Prince Khalid al-Faysal—aided by the input of his half-brothers and half-sisters—there can be little doubt that ‘Iffat Al Thunayan set in motion the grander scheme to create an institution worthy of the martyred ruler. She knew how to motivate and how to think big and she seldom settled for the average.

Her home along the Avenue Foch, perhaps the most expensive residential avenue in the French capital, abutted the nearby Bois de Boulogne, its second-largest park, affording ‘Iffat Al Thunayan an unparalleled level of tranquility. An avid hiker who purchased fashionable walking shoes from the famed Avenue de la Grande Armée store Au Petit Matelot, not far from her *maison particulier*, Queen ‘Iffat was well-known throughout the neighborhood. Everyone called her “La Reine” [The Queen] whenever they spotted her walking around during her daily exercises. She spent a full year in Paris, decompressing from the heavy burden that weighed on her shoulders by going out to museums with the two companions who were always by her side, as they had been in the Kingdom: Sitt Mu‘allah, the Turkish companion whose family, related to the former sultans in Turkey, had found refuge in Paris after the collapse of the Ottoman Empire; and Sevgi Khanum, the Turkish lady-in-waiting who was her link with her past. She went to Megève, the popular ski resort near Mont-Blanc in the French Alps, though the 1976 trip was too painful to bear and she left after only a few days. This was one of the few places that she and King Faysal could enjoy visiting together, as, while he was not a skier, the relaxing atmosphere had always allowed them some private moments. The Queen did not share these memories with her companions, but the association was too painfully evident to be missed. However, this was a rare withdrawal, as ‘Iffat Al Thunayan kept up a full schedule, though it seems likely that there were other occasions on which she may have had cause to reflect on her former married life, even during what was a full schedule of trips she and members of the family took throughout Europe—traveling by car to various countries, visiting capitals as well as smaller boroughs, attending classical music concerts, and going to the movies—in addition to the scores of visitors paying their respects whom she welcomed to her Paris home. King Hussayn of Jordan called on her whenever he was in France, and he and Queen Noor dined frequently at her house. Countless Sa‘udi visitors stopped by, all shepherded by ‘Abdul Rahman al-Faysal, who kept his mother company and looked after her needs.

Paris was a home from home, the place where her youngest daughter, Princess Hayfah, had been born and where her physicians practiced. Queen 'Iffat suffered from emphysema, a chronic obstructive pulmonary disease—one of the most common lung diseases and one which involves destruction of the organ over time—along with various heart problems. With medication, both sets of conditions were treatable, even if the stress associated with Faysal's demise complicated her overall health. Beyond the daily walks, the Queen kept physically busy, as the Paris dwelling boasted a unique garden. This was where she spent a great deal of time pruning roses with the utmost care, an activity that allowed her to relax, while mending her increasingly fragile body. On the advice of her son-in-law, Prince Bandar bin Sultan, the Sa'udi who was so well attuned to American affairs, she traveled to Houston, Texas in 1980 to consult Dr. Michael E. DeBakey (1908–2008). This renowned American cardiac surgeon, the son of Lebanese immigrants to Lake Charles in Louisiana, operated on her but without performing a transplant. She was not ready for a cumbersome artificial heart, still an experimental device in the late 1970s, preferring instead to rely on medication to alleviate her pain. The postoperative recovery in her Paris home was sufficient, although she also spent time at her brother's British estate outside of London.[9]

No doubt during her convalescence she reflected on her sons and daughters and dozens of grandchildren and wished to see them all thrive. Most excelled, and she was especially proud both of Sa'ud and Turki, respectively Minister of Foreign Affairs and long-time Chief of Intelligence. Yet 'Iffat also understood that Faysal's demise altered the pattern of family visits by Fahd, Sultan, 'Abdallah, Nayif, and Salman, among others. Preoccupied with their respective duties and responsibilities, visits by her brothers-in-law became less frequent, limited to special occasions or holiday obligations. This was understandable but the Queen instituted a new rule, which stipulated that wherever she happened to be, those sons and daughters as well the many grandchildren who were in town should gather for dinner at her house. This was her way of keeping the family united and, in the words of 'Abdul Rahman al-Faysal, she became the magnet that "drew all of us to her house almost every night."[10]

---

9 She was a frequent flyer on Shaykh Kamal Adham's legendary 1962 Boeing 720s that first flew with Western Airlines and carried the HZ-KA1 and HZ-KA4 registration numbers. In addition, the Queen frequently flew in her brother's Hawker Siddeley HS-125-600 B (HZ-KA2) as well as a Falcon 20 (HZ-KA3) that hopped across the English Channel.

10 Interview with HRH Prince 'Abdul Rahman al-Faysal, Riyadh, 13 October 2010.

Preserving the Al Sa'ud Legacy

'Iffat Al Thunayan's influence went beyond her immediate family, as countless friends and acquaintances were also drawn to her. Her mother and aunt, when they were alive, formed a core group. Her half-brother and half-sister, along with their offspring, added a second layer. Sons, daughters, physicians and attorneys, leading Hijazi family members, and dozens of friends enlarged the entourage. It was a grand circle that literally encompassed the small but close Makkah society, later to be further engorged with Jiddawi additions that swelled numbers into the few hundred. With rare exceptions, the Queen was almost always accompanied by a small group of devoted friends who kept her company, allowing her to evaluate what was taking place in Sa'udi society. By creating a "court," Queen 'Iffat empowered the Al Sa'ud in ways heretofore unimagined, something that was not done consciously but that certainly reinforced the stability and cohesiveness of the ruling family.

After a year in France, 'Iffat Al Thunayan returned to the Kingdom, where King Khalid bought her a new house in Jiddah and her sons settled on a new dwelling in Riyadh. She could not return to the homes she had shared with Faysal, and while she had always liked to live on the second floor, both of her new residences boasted gardens that were generously filled with her favorite roses. Visitors often found her in her gardens, walking among plants she regularly pruned, an activity that afforded her much-needed exercise. Family members stopped by daily, bringing with them news of the world, though she seldom abandoned the voracious reading habits that occupied her for several hours each day. She surely missed her chess games with Faysal, which the couple had been fond of playing even before they were married. Family members recalled 'Iffat's prowess at the game, which she often won, leaving Faysal agape. While he graciously conceded, the regular games illustrated his pride in her intrinsic abilities, which she strove to develop even further. Faysal was not so proud as to refuse sound advice, and his character was such that he always wanted to learn more.[11] This open-mindedness of his, perhaps more than any other characteristic, shaped her own desire to support and improve on the Al Sa'ud legacy. By emphasizing that members of the ruling family were duty-bound to contribute, 'Iffat signaled her intention to continue Faysal's legacy.[12] The monarch had been loath to remain in the dark and so was his spouse. When in 1958 the Kingdom's economy suffered its worst crisis, for example, Faysal had understood that he

---

[11] Interview with HRH 'Amr bin Muhammad al-Faysal, Jiddah, 5 October 2010.

[12] 'Iffat insisted that the family was too valuable to wither. When King Khalid once informed her that he had dismissed Musa'id bin 'Abdul 'Aziz from the Ministry of

needed to know what ailed the country's finances and, towards that end, brought in a Pakistani scholar, Anwar 'Ali, to head the Central Bank [1958–1974] as well as teach him the basics of economics over the course of two intensive weeks.[13] Likewise, when 'Iffat wanted to address the country's health conditions, she took tutorials from the palace physician to familiarize herself with circumstances throughout the country. "Faysal did not feel shame to learn from anyone, which was probably her influence on him," and neither did 'Iffat, "who prized scientific knowledge as the best means to improve quality of life on the Arabian Peninsula."[14] From their chess games to the attention to detail they paid in their grandest social undertakings, which enabled them both to reach sound decisions, the Faysal–'Iffat duo was a model to emulate, even if leading scholars—especially religious 'Ulamah—were available to add their own interpretations.

Of course, 'Iffat Al Thunayan knew her country's history but was persuaded that it was not enough simply to glorify the past, lest one repeat errors galore. It was important to update the Al Sa'ud legacy, not only by restoring old buildings—though she asked Faysal to do precisely that in Makkah when she first arrived in 1932—but in creating fresh legacies that would be based on competence and productivity. For the urbanized and rather sophisticated young woman, someone who read a great deal and was aware of what else was going on in the world, the Al

---

Finance, the Queen was upset, telling the King: "Your brother [Faysal] appointed him and trusted him. You need to preserve our family's values. You need to keep your brothers in positions of authority, not to rely on mere appointees to object to your decisions." Interview with HRH Prince Bandar al-Faysal, Riyadh, 28 March 2011.

[13] The Kingdom's Central Bank, the Saudi Arabian Monetary Agency (SAMA), was created in 1952 on the heels of the US/Saudi Security Agreement. By 1958, SAMA was run by Anwar 'Ali, who later became an advisor to King Faysal. 'Ali had been Chief of the International Monetary Fund's Middle East Department, and recruited three Western bankers as SAMA advisors, who came to be known as the Three Wise Men or White Fathers. These Western bankers, the most powerful of whom was John Meyer, Jr., Chairman of Morgan Guaranty's International Division and later Chairman of JP Morgan, funneled SAMA petrodollar royalties into Morgan Guaranty accounts, and called the shots with 'Ali serving as Faysal's eyes and ears. In turn Morgan served as a well-paid investment counselor to SAMA. Anwar 'Ali's son even landed a job at Morgan Guaranty. See Ron Chernow, *The House of Morgan*, New York: Atlantic Monthly Press, 1990, p. 606. See also Dean Henderson, *Big Oil & Their Bankers In The Persian Gulf: Four Horsemen, Eight Families & Their Global Intelligence, Narcotics & Terror Network*, CreateSpace Independent Publishing Platform (amazon.com), 2010, pp. 45–68.

[14] Interview with HRH Prince 'Abdul Rahman al-Faysal, Riyadh, 13 October 2010.

Sa'ud were poised to excel. She was a diehard nation-builder, someone who valued the past but who also drew succor from her intrinsic desire to do better so as to empower the current generation and plan for the next. It was towards this end that she decided to invest in the 'Imarat al-Malikah [The Queen's Building] in Jiddah—then a city spread out with low-rise apartment complexes and a few villas—not to generate income but to set an example of what was expected of the Al Sa'ud. The decision to fund the construction of the first tower building in the Kingdom was something of an eye-opener and, at 24 stories, the skyscraper reflected her desire to aim for bigger and better facilities that embodied the grandeur of her overall vision. Naturally, she was aware of the building's financial potential though she first wanted the structure to stand as a model for others to emulate. For years, the edifice dominated old Jiddah, and it still stands as a reminder of what was intended by its construction. Yet, even if many more towers have been raised over the course of the past few decades, her initiative was meaningful in more ways than assumed. At a time when many invested overseas, 'Iffat wanted to set the example that Sa'udis must invest at home.

To her credit, Queen 'Iffat used part of the proceeds that the commercial facility generated to support charity work, instructing her lawyer to pay anonymously for funerals, weddings, and other social events. Hussayn Shukri—who handled the family's private affairs and who, long before his retirement, trained his son, Dr. Kamal Hussayn Shukri, to assume the burden—would be instructed to prepare cashier's checks and have them discreetly delivered to those most in need. "She spent millions per year this way and she continued to do this for decades," he revealed, "and I wish I could tell you the real figures but hardly anyone would be able to tell you. Believe me," he affirmed, "when I tell you that we disbursed hundreds of millions over nearly five decades."[15] By practicing what she preached, the Queen fulfilled her dreams of becoming the missing link between the poor and the rich, and she encouraged her offspring to do likewise. Her attorney brought in various advisors who told her where financial assets could be invested and their revenues multiplied, all to create a stable stream of income that would be independent of state coffers. In fact, her wise investments helped to do what needed to be done, becoming a method she relied upon after 1975 when her relationship with the state changed. In the post-1975 period, 'Iffat Al Thunayan managed her portfolio carefully, precisely to guarantee the large income that she required for the myriad charity organizations she supported along with literally thousands of individuals whom she also helped. True to her track record, her last attorney confirmed that "she

[15] Interview with Hussayn Shukri, Esq., Jiddah, 21 October 2010.

worked with all of her advisors,” and gave specific instructions as to the types of investments she preferred. Indeed, the late Queen personally examined revenue statements on a more or less regular basis and, in a most remarkable development, never opted to associate herself with a business partner.[16] Hers was a strict investment portfolio earmarked for specific programs in the Kingdom and key charities in the Arab world. Though she never became one of the richest Sa‘udis, ‘Iffat Al Thunayan was nevertheless one of its largest donors, a legacy that confers honor and prestige on the ruling family. No one summarized this preference better that Hayfah bint Sa‘ud al-Faysal, the erudite English Literature Professor at King Sa‘ud University:

> My grandmother thought in terms of power. She could read power, though she recommended that we delve into sciences. She admired strong women and wanted us to be achievers. She inspired all of us and me in particular and taught me not to be offended easily. Tactful and Socratic in her approach, neither melodramatic nor ideological, she knew what power was. It was much more than political, military, or even financial might. For her, it was all about what one did with the opportunities thrown into one’s lap, and she knew precisely how to preserve and protect her family interests.[17]

HEALED BY WILLPOWER

As discussed earlier, ‘Iffat Al Thunayan was aware of her family’s history and benefited from her Al Sa‘ud ties in being able to learn more of its past record, both its glorious as well as its infamous past. She certainly knew of the rise of two significant previous Kingdoms and the internecine warfare that had decimated key tribes on the Arabian Peninsula. She had read testimonies that described the harsh environment that was Najd after the mid-1500s, when widespread intolerance, especially towards Ottoman troops that occupied large sections of both the Hijaz and Hasah provinces, mobilized various tribal confederations to oppose usurpers. Indeed, because strict followers of Unitarian creeds

16 Interview with Dr. Kamal Hussayn Shukri, Esq., Jiddah, 29 March 2011. I thank Dr. Shukri for sharing a copy of the late Queen’s last will, reproduced in Appendix V, which specified that a third of all her estate would be allocated to supporting various charities.

17 Interview with HRH Princess Hayfah bint Sa‘ud al-Faysal, Riyadh, 16 October 2010.

[deriving from Wahhabi traditions] perceived the Ottomans as lax—practicing their Muslim faith in what some interpreted as un-Islamic fashion, drinking, smoking, and otherwise misinterpreting religious precepts—the die was cast. If "Wahhabis, who were the more warlike, declared the lives and property of their antagonists to have been forfeited by religious infidelity and applied themselves to execute the sentence," their profound distrust of "false" Muslims colored many relationships.[18] Early followers of Shaykh Muhammad bin 'Abdul Wahhab had opposed the Sharifs of Makkah, whose pecuniary interests were well established, thereby planting the seeds of decades and even centuries of antagonisms. It was only after the 1744 Al Sa'ud–Al Shaykh alliance that a level of order was imposed in this chaotic environment, something which Faysal and 'Iffat not only knew quite well but which motivated them to do all they could to preserve the Kingdom lest the country's mosaic unravel.

'Iffat was a devout believer who fully appreciated the role the Al Sa'ud had played in preserving Islam's holiest cities, Makkah and Madinah. Equally important, she understood the immense duties that fell on their shoulders and, as a key figure, specifically on her own. After all, she first went to Makkah to perform *hajj*, an obligation she took seriously, and that act of pilgrimage permanently changed her life. Nevertheless, it is important to note that 'Iffat was first exposed to the Sunni Hanafi school of thought, practiced throughout the Ottoman Empire, a background which probably colored the "*Turkiyyah*" label she attracted upon arriving in Makkah. Of course, due to the Ottoman influence in Makkah, Hijazi courts issued decrees under both the Hanafi and Shafi'i schools until at least 1927, whereas the Al Thunayan and the overwhelming majority of Najdis followed Hanbali teachings. Devout Sunni Muslims tolerated each other's interpretations, which is not to say that misunderstandings did not arise but that outside of scholarly disputes few focused on what divided believers. 'Iffat and Faysal were aware of non-Hanbali jurisprudence even if they and the entire country followed Hanbali construal after 1932; indeed, it is critical to note that their shared traditions were firmly rooted in Hanbali values. At no time did the late Queen question her core beliefs, without a doubt drawing succor from her Al Thunayan tribal roots even if she seldom chose to focus on the narrower interpretations of Hanbali teachings. Her faith and willpower were such that she knew how to rely on the essence of the former and the depth of the latter.

[18] J.G. Lorimer, *Gazetteer of the Persian Gulf, Oman, and Central Arabia*, Calcutta: Government Printing Office, 1915, Reprinted in Shannon, Ireland: Irish Universities Press, 1989 (in six volumes), Volume 1, Part 1B, p. 1052.

Core Beliefs and Norms

Queen 'Iffat's personality did not change over the years and in her religious observance, too, she remained the faithful believer she had always been. Although the young teacher transformed herself with relative ease into the spouse of the Viceroy of the Hijaz, circumstances made her one of Makkah's most important residents, gathering in her house all who needed a friendly ear to which they could address concerns or vent criticism. Yet not only was she willing to listen, relying on her innate skills to quickly translate demands into actions, the mere fact that she was in the Holy City compelled her to adopt a set of moral, religious and social norms that she used as a guide throughout her life. Religious authorities were frequent guests in Faysal's dwelling, and 'Iffat was meticulous in her public behavior and always deferential. She performed her pilgrimage rites and practiced her faith with diligence and piety. Those who recalled her youthful charms as a relatively cosmopolitan girl nurtured by one of the most vibrant cities in the world were amazed at her ability to adapt to the much stricter codes of the Hijaz. "She listened carefully and seldom spoke at first, observing those counseling the Viceroy and seeking his input on a variety of subjects," from which it may be safe to conclude that she committed herself to practices as she witnessed them.[19] Inevitably, as her interests expanded 'Iffat saw the need to adopt far more tolerant customs. When clerics objected to expanded education programs for both boys and girls, 'Iffat fell back on Qur'anic teachings that encouraged and even demanded that the faithful be educated. She helped define education, and when that failed to accomplish the desired results, she resorted to Qur'anic injunctions that required Muslims to expand their knowledge. When a cleric argued that girls should not be exposed to advanced studies, she enlightened them by discussing the power of the influential women who helped the Prophet achieve some of his most memorable triumphs. Above all else, what she wanted was for Sa'udi women to roll up their sleeves and help build the nation, for she knew deep in her heart that the country could not advance if half of its population remained relatively idle. More important, she also stressed that such participation was a religious duty, for the Lord Almighty called on all believers to work in earnest. In other words, it is safe to conclude that the Queen practiced her faith the way it was intended rather than selecting those features that empowered the few. She expected little else from those around her. Still, it is important to ask how she reacted to extremism as deviant interpretations steadily crept into Sa'udi Arabia, and what she thought of those who hid their waywardness behind *Shari'ah* law.

---

[19] Interview with HE Ahmad 'Abdul Wahhab, Jiddah, 20 October 2010.

The rise of religious extremism throughout the Muslim world as well as in Sa'udi Arabia is a complex question that deserves a careful analysis of Cold War politics, the impact of the creation of Israel [with its mantra of Jews as the Chosen People], Arabs throughout the Middle East suffering the consequences of mistaken development policies and, perhaps as important as any other factor, the profound political and economic repercussions of dictatorships, often supported by the West, that strangled whatever freedoms existed in their respective countries. Overcautious initiatives denied many sorely needed socio-economic reforms, and, as discussed earlier, it took gargantuan royal efforts to introduce the key changes that would improve the lives of millions in the Kingdom. Political debates were limited, though successive rulers pushed genuine development projects. King Faysal was certainly a conservative ruler, though Riyadh quickly authorized massive infrastructure investments as soon as oil resources allowed. The monarch seldom hesitated in ushering in valuable changes that enhanced quality of life, as he balanced local needs with the country's rapid development requirements, two aims which for many within the Kingdom were contradictory. He was ably assisted in these endeavors by his spouse, the overwhelming majority of the Al Sa'ud, and a rapidly growing intelligentsia, an increasingly significant segment of society whose members understood the action that was necessary to bring the Kingdom into the 20th century. Still, notwithstanding many social advances in the battle of ideas, the arena was left wide open to voices that fell back on narrow religious norms, sometimes as champions of extremism. In 1968, the Sahwah al-Islamiyyah (Islamic Awakening) began, in the name of God, as a "nonviolent, symbolic, apolitical movement that confined its activities to individual acts, such as listening to tapes of the Qur'an."[20] At first, clerics refrained from demanding political changes, though it was not long before that protocol was breached.[21] The event that brought dramatic changes was the 1979 assault on the Holy Mosque in Makkah, which profoundly altered the country's socio-religious scene.[22]

After the insurrection of Juhayman al-'Utaybi, a relatively docile population accepted what was presented to it in the name of Islam, which

---

[20] Abdullah F. Ansary, "Combating Extremism: A Brief Overview of Saudi Arabia's Approach," *Middle East Policy* 15:2, Summer 2008, pages 111–142.

[21] Mishari Al-Zaydi, "An Interview with Sheikh Abdul-Mohsen Bin Nasser Al-Obeikan," *Al-Sharq Al-Awsat*, 24 May 2005, at http://www.asharq-e.com/news.asp?id=85.

[22] Joseph A. Kéchichian, "The Role of the Ulama in the Politics of an Islamic State: The Case of Saudi Arabia," *International Journal of Middle East Studies* 18:1, February 1986, pp. 53–71; idem, "Islamic Revivalism and Change

meant that extremist voices could and did find refuge in the Kingdom. Beyond its violent message, however, the Juhayman vision was neither superficial nor simplistic, but threatened internal stability by presenting arguments wrapped in strict *Shari'ah* law. His religious devotion aside, what 'Utaybi and his supporters rejected was the authority of the Al Sa'ud, viewing members of the family as abusers of wealth and power. Even worse, 'Utaybi—and, it may be safe to assume, others who came after him and preached similar messages—alleged that the Al Sa'ud did not rule according to the Qur'an. In fact, while fair criticisms towards the Al Sa'ud could indeed be made, the notion that the ruling family did not rule according to *Shari'ah* was preposterous. The extremists based their beliefs on narrow interpretations of the Qur'an and selected *Hadiths*, given that so many proponents lacked any knowledge of Islamic jurisprudence.[23] Nevertheless, *takfir* ideologies gained popularity because they justified *jihad* not only against atheist Soviets in Afghanistan between 25 December 1979 and 15 February 1989 but also at home ever since. Regrettably, an entire generation of gullible young men have participated in such *jihad*, with extremists manipulating them at will.

Ten days after the Holy Mosque in Makkah was liberated from Juhayman al-'Utaybi's desecration, Queen 'Iffat asked Prince Turki al-Faysal to drive her there so that she could see for herself what had happened. Dakhil Allah al-Harthy, who looked after palace affairs, recalled that the Queen cried when she saw the damage. She performed *'Umrah* during her four-hour-long visit and returned totally dejected at what she had witnessed.[24] Shaken to her bones, she wondered how

---

in Saudi Arabia: Juhayman Al-Utaybi's 'Letters' to the Saudi People," *The Muslim World* 70:1, January 1990, pp. 1–16. For more recent discussions of these events, see Yaroslav Trofimov, *The Siege of Mecca: The Forgotten Uprising in Islam's Holiest Shrine and the Birth of Al Qaeda*, New York: Doubleday, 2007, and Thomas Hegghammer and Stephane Lacroix, "Rejectionist Islamism in Saudi Arabia: The Story of Juhayman al-'Utaybi Revisited," *International Journal of Middle East Studies* 39:1, February 2007, pp. 103–122, and Joseph A. Kéchichian, *Legal and Political Reforms in Sa'udi Arabia*, London: Routledge, 2013, pp. 163–174.

23 Martin Kramer, "Fundamentalist Islam at Large: The Drive for Power," *Middle East Quarterly* 3:2, June 1996, pp. 37–49; see also Abdul Rahman ibn Mualaa al-Luwaihiq al-Muitairi, *Religious Extremism in the Lives of Contemporary Muslims*, Denver, Colorado: Al-Basheer Company for Publications and Translations, 2001; Masood Ashraf Raja, "Muslim Modernity: Poetics, Politics, and Metaphysics," in Gabriele Marranci, ed., *Muslim Societies and the Challenge of Secularization: An Interdisciplinary Approach*, Aberdeen: Springer, 2010, pp. 99–112; and Mostapha Benhenda, "Liberal Democracy and Political Islam: The Search for Common Ground," *Politics, Philosophy & Economics* 10:1, February 2011, pp. 88–115.

24 Interview with HE Dakhil Allah al-Harthy, Jiddah, 25 November 2010.

devout Muslims could engage in such wanton violence and destruction, and asked her son to keep her informed on the progress of Riyadh's investigation. She recalled the many conversations she had held with leading clerics over the years and how she had invariably tried to convey the message that the Kingdom's modernizing steps were always compatible with the faith. She refused to kowtow to those who wanted to keep Sa'udis locked in narrow-minded environments, and instead worked to improve everyone's standards of living, allowing the faithful to contribute without having to concede one iota of their beliefs. She had insisted down the years that everyone should assume responsibility for their actions and obey the laws of the land. She once told Shaykh Nasir bin Hamad al-Fahd, who at first refused to provide theological justification for the introduction of television in the late 1960s: "Have you not sworn allegiance to the State and how could you now disobey the monarch when it has been shown that radio and television transmit the Word of God?"[25] This was vintage 'Iffat, who understood—perhaps better than most—that even Sa'udi officials within the ruling family as well as those in the religious establishment were receptive to social forces that sought to make things easily digestible. In fact, she herself became such a force on key issues, and seldom abnegated the duty to exercise her will, especially when the ideas proposed were compatible with her core beliefs and the customs of the Al Sa'ud. Of course, the fact that Faysal stood by her made all the difference in the world, but so did her own determination to accept nothing short of success. While both Faysal and 'Iffat compromised to get things done, and while both equally stood their ground to advance the interests of the nation as a whole, she herself shone by focusing on the politically and doctrinally sensitive area of women's education.

Women in Islam

When 'Iffat Al Thunayan wanted to persuade shaykhs to allow women in the classroom, she cajoled them by saying: "Would Faysal do something against the teachings of Islam?"[26] At a family gathering in early 1980, she expressed her rejection of the Juhayman al-'Utaybi takeover of the Holy Mosque in Makkah, opining that the alleged revolutionary was wrong to abjure state authority, and reaching the inevitable conclusion that his actions hurt Islam.[27] The late Queen had gradually become a "master-observer" of Sa'udi society and, aware of her role, she did not let anything or anyone prevent her from advancing

---

25 Interview with HE Ahmad 'Abdul Wahhab, Jiddah, 20 October 2010.
26 Interview with HRH Prince 'Abdul Rahman al-Faysal, Riyadh, 13 October 2010
27 Interview with HRH Princess Sarah al-Faysal, Riyadh, 13 October 2010.

the interests of the nation. She was never a slave to be "emancipated," though she silently suffered for a long time in being pejoratively labeled the *Turkiyyah*; but she always relied on her willpower and her faith to pull her through difficult times. In the words of Marianne Alireza—a contemporary emigrant who adapted to her new environment and who sometimes accompanied the young Princess on her European outings—'Iffat succeeded even if "Sa'udi society did not allow for a powerful woman to shine."[28] "This elegant and feminine woman was a devout Muslim who was generous with her compliments—though her best ones were almost always delivered in Turkish—and bighearted with those who could hardly imagine her vision for the nation," added Alireza. She rejected cheap mercantilism and insisted that a faithful individual could and ought to be as elegant as possible. "No one liked me when I came in wearing my high heels," she told one of her granddaughters, "but I ignored them and later on became friends with most. They started copying me when they saw that I did not deviate from my religious obligations."[29] To be sure, she was not a feminist in the contemporary sense of the word, since she accepted the role of women in the conservative country, but she never compromised on a woman's right to education and, equally important, on her right to become a contributing member of Sa'udi society.

As discussed above, Queen 'Iffat never wore revealing clothes but was impeccably attired and donned a veil in public. Her dresses were fitted with long sleeves because that was a way to respect Islamic traditions in the Kingdom. She wore designer outfits when she was at official functions or attending wedding parties, appropriately perfumed with the latest Christian Dior scent, along with her own legendary *joie de vivre*.[30] Marianne Alireza summed up her elegance best when the Californian recalled that the late Queen was "gorgeous in every sense of the word." Marianne's daughter Nadia, a woman who left her mark on Sa'udi

---

[28] Interview with Marianne Alireza, Jiddah, 6 November 2010. Born Likowski, in 1945 Marianne moved from the San Francisco Bay Area in the United States to Jiddah with her husband, 'Ali. Her book is a treasure trove for those curious about life in the Kingdom long before it entered its modernizing phase, including keen observations on members of the Al Faysal. See Marianne Alireza, *At the Drop of a Veil*, Boston: Houghton Mifflin Company, 1971.

[29] Interview with HRH Princess al-Bandari bint 'Abdul Rahman al-Faysal, Riyadh, 27 March 2011.

[30] The Queen often wore her hair in a chignon that enhanced her elegance. On the other hand, she seldom donned fancy jewelry, although she favored white diamonds and wore a string of pearls around her neck. Despite her wealth, she kept a modest collection and was known to wear the same dozen items of jewelry, on a regular basis. Interview with HRH Princess Lulwah al-Faysal, Jiddah, 25 October 2010.

society in her own right by operating one of the most effective learning centers in Jiddah, offered an even more graceful observation. "Young Sa'udi women who wear the *niqab* today stand in direct contradiction with what Queen 'Iffat aimed to achieve for the Kingdom," she reflected, "which was to remain religious without falling by extremist waysides.[31] One could be elegant, love the arts, enjoy Umm Khulthum songs, and even watch the occasional Latin American *telenovela* on television without losing one's faith. One could wear high heels and be presentable without abandoning religious norms. And one could certainly look after household animals, especially her favorite Persian cats, without distancing oneself from daily prayers. 'Iffat Al Thunayan did all of these and other things without ever abandoning her principles and core beliefs. What upset the Queen more than anything else—and she would let her interlocutor have a piece of her mind on the matter as appropriate—was rigidity and absolutism, which she considered un-Islamic.

It is in this context that her views on women ought to be evaluated, including perspectives on the roles women ought to play in the country's religious establishment, aware that the Hay'at Kibar al-'Ulamah [Council of Supreme Scholars] almost always rejected the appointment of women to positions of prominence. To better ascertain these views, in addition to members of the family who kindly answered various questions on the matter, at least a dozen graduates of Dar al-Hanan and Effat University were interviewed to evaluate the impact that advanced education opportunities have had on women in Sa'udi Arabia.[32] All agreed that the late Queen emphasized the necessity of developing each individual's inherent skills to help them assert their identity and strengthen their character. Towards that end, everyone believed that 'Iffat Al Thunayan wanted them to "modernize but not Westernize," and always to operate within the confines of clearly defined socio-religious boundaries that respected Sa'udi norms. Her goal was not to create a female army that would revolutionize Sa'udi society but gradually to appease those who failed to see

---

[31] Interview with Nadia Alireza, Jiddah, 30 March 2011. In addition to running the Maharat Learning Center, discussed in Chapter 4, Nadia Alireza was one of the founders of the Mansoojat Foundation, a UK-registered charity established by a group of Sa'udi women "with a passionate interest in the traditional ethnic embroidery and costumes of the Kingdom of Sa'udi Arabia." See www.mansoojat.org for additional details.

[32] This section is based on interviews conducted in Jiddah, with Muluk al-Shaykh, Safanah Sayjani, Sarah Sharaf, Rottana Khayat, 'Arij Abu Zarifah, Nisrin al-Idriss, Munah al-Fadli, and Wad Abu Zunadah. In addition, I benefited from extensive conversations on this subject with Mahah al-Juffali, Dr. Nahid Tahir, Dr. Hayfah Jamal al-Layl, and HRH Nurah bint Turki al-Faysal.

value in whatever contributions women could and were willing to make. Her objective was to establish the foundations of a stronger nation, one that drew succor from the innate talents of each and every member of society, no matter how limited. Critically, what was remarkable about such a perspective was its timing, made at a time when the Kingdom's income was far less than it would become in the post-1974 period, and long before Riyadh had earned its reputation as the world's leading petroleum exporter.[33]

It must also be emphasized that although several scholars have recently seen the need to include women in the Kingdom's highest deliberative religious organization, the 17 scholars sitting on the Council of Supreme Scholars—all of whom were appointed by royal decree for four-year terms—considered the very idea of women sitting on the Council as both controversial and unnecessary. Qays al-Mubarak and ʻAbdul Rahman al-Zunaydi, respectively Professor of Islamic Jurisprudence at King Faysal University and Professor of Islamic Culture at King Muhammad bin Saʻud University, recently opined that women should be included among their ranks, in particular to alleviate any sentiments of embarrassment that some female members of society felt when submitting their concerns to the Council for advice and resolution.[34] Inasmuch as both believe that men and women ought to mingle in scholarly gatherings because of existing precedent dating back to the Prophet's time, it was natural for them to make the leap, emphasizing that women justices would help improve whatever commentaries the Council offered to the faithful. Of course, such views have been unpopular in this paternalistic society throughout the centuries, though the Kingdom's religious elites have been increasingly subjected to bouts of genuine reform. Still, as recently as 2008, a leading member of the Council, Shaykh ʻAbdallah bin Maniʻ, quoted the Prophet in rejecting any such considerations, a move which spoke volumes. In the event, Shaykh Maniʻ and others fell back on a well-known *Hadith* that attributed the following to the Messenger: "No People shall succeed if ruled by a woman," even if the context in which the Prophet uttered those words was narrowly political not social, and dealt with a specific interaction with Persia.[35]

---

[33] I am grateful to Dr. Tahir for this perspective. Interview with Dr. Nahid Tahir, Founder and Chief Executive Officer, Gulf One Investment Bank, Jiddah, 27 March 2011.

[34] Yaser Ba-ʻAmer, "Council of 'Supreme Scholars' Rejects the Appointment of Women," *Islam Online*, 15 March 2008, at http://politicalislam.org/Articles/PI%20549%20Women%20appointment%20Rejected.pdf

[35] Kéchichian, *Legal and Political Reforms*, *op. cit.*, p. 50.

Be that as it may, Islam recognized women's rights and duties in clearly defined terms, which were often neglected. Because a woman may have children and become a mother, it is written that "paradise lies under her feet," something that not even conservative clerics could refute. In an authentic *Hadith*, the Prophet was asked on four separate occasions: "Who is the one most worthy of my care?", to which he responded, "your mother" the first three times before adding "your father" in the fourth. According to the Scriptures, God further admonished man to respect woman, when he revealed: "Your Lord has decreed that you worship none but Him and that you be kind to your parents. When one or both of them attains old age in your life, say not to them a word of disrespect, nor repel them but address them in terms of honor" [Surat al-Isra' (17:23)]. It is worth highlighting that several passages in the Holy Qur'an remind believers that men and women are equals [Surat al-Shurah (42:49), Surat al-Rum (30:21), and Surat Al-Baqarah (2:187)]. Even more critical, there is little or nothing in *Shari'ah* that suggests women are impure, because a believer can never be tainted. "Whoever works righteousness," revealed the Creator, "whether male or female, and has faith, verily, to him will We give a life that is good and pure, and We will bestow on such their reward according to the best of their actions" [(Surat al-Nahl (16:97)]. According to the Holy Qur'an, therefore, divine commands apply equally to both men and women, and the latter's responsibilities in faith are exactly the same as those of the former.

As a faithful woman, Queen 'Iffat Al Thunayan applied the prescriptions that defined her beliefs: to perform her prayers, pay Zakat duty, fast during Ramadan, and perform Hajj if possible. As revealed by the Lord: "Believers, men and women, are guardians, one of another: they enjoin what is just, and forbid what is evil," [Surat al-Tawbah (9:71)] which was why 'Iffat Al Thunayan strove to do good and forbid evil in the work she and her family undertook to improve their community's welfare. When particularly vexing interlocutors tried to derail her projects, the Queen fell back on the Holy Scriptures, reminding one and all that the Qur'an addressed everyone, men and women, on an equal footing:

> "The Muslim men and Muslim women, the believing men and believing women, the worshipping men and worshipping women, the truthful men and truthful women, the pious men and pious women, the alms-giving men and the alms-giving women, the fasting men and fasting women, the men who are chaste and the women who are chaste, the men who remember Allah much and the women who do likewise, Allah has prepared a forgiveness and a great reward for all" [Surat al-Ahzab (33:35)].

In her view it was thus inimical to argue for the exclusion of women from playing key roles in society and occupying leadership positions in government, including in sensitive areas—all so as to better serve the nation.

In a political setting, therefore, officials were called upon to obey God's laws as well as those devised by mankind to preserve earthly harmony. Nevertheless, the Queen recognized that if Muslim women reached positions of authority elsewhere throughout the realm, stretching from the Atlantic to the Pacific, it was the result of emancipation and education. An Egyptian female adjudicator needed to be a qualified practitioner before sitting in judgment of worldly affairs, while an Indonesian airline pilot needed a license to command a passenger aircraft. Both would need to overcome their alleged weaknesses due to child-bearing and menstruation—a natural occurrence which does not incapacitate—though their professional qualifications would be the key determining factor in assessing the competence their respective professions demand. Similarly, Queen 'Iffat Al Thunayan wished to see Sa'udi women gain the proficiencies that opened doors, both to fulfill life goals in their chosen fields and to make useful contributions to the nation. Of course, objectors have seldom failed to point towards alleged female weaknesses though in truth such arguments hid a deeper agenda that stems from the continuous power struggle in which men engage, including confrontations that pit the religious establishment against those who wish to limit such absolute authority. In the case of Sa'udi Arabia, in recent years a new generation of more assertive men and women have supported key reforms precisely to eliminate opposition that purports to preserve social harmony when, in reality, it simply keeps the nation weak.

Changing ingrained patterns of behavior, however, is easier said than done, but it behooves the Sa'udi religious establishment to heed calls towards moderation made by senior government officials. In fact, various cases of Sa'udi women who have rejected excessive intrusions in their lives by members of the Commission for the Promotion of Virtue and the Prevention of Vice have filled newspaper pages and online social networking sites. Such stories illustrate that times are changing, as an increasingly educated population refuses to kowtow to stale notions, claiming psychological, physical, and even material damage from commission officers for breaching the limits of their authority.[36]

[36] There are many reports that address various concerns on this sensitive topic. The following selection of recent examples give a flavor: Reuters, "Saudi Women Complain Over 'Militant' Kin Detention," 16 July 2007, at

Ironically, to finally address some of the "pressing needs" that confronted the Commission, hiring women to serve it was deemed worthy even if the ultimate purpose was not clear.[37]

Educated Sa'udi women insist that Queen 'Iffat's efforts meant that their "characters were formed to uphold Sa'udi values—to perform under duress, to be faithful, generous, and to display our pride in our culture." In the words of Nahid Tahir, one of the Kingdom's most successful investment bankers, who has a doctorate in financial economics from Lancaster University in Britain, "we were trained at Dar al-Hanan to become strong and to believe in ourselves."[38] This Madinah-born and Houston-educated professional did not hesitate to emphasize what she felt it meant to be a Sa'udi: "someone who accepted modernization while upholding our core values." Mahah al-Juffali, the Muir College graduate who also earned her high-school degree at Dar al-Hanan, confirmed that "Queen 'Iffat's glow wrapped us every time she came to visit what was truly an international atmosphere in Jiddah. We did not realize it at the time, and while there may not have been a grand scheme to empower most graduates, the education we received was truly unique."[39] "We used to wear skirts to school," she recalled, "but after 1979, long dresses became the norm. Still, while our wardrobe changed, the openness that Cécile Rushdy and her staff offered, based on Queen

---

http://www.reuters.com/article/2007/07/16/idUSL16763366; Ebtihal Mubarak, "Commission Responds to Umm Faisal Lawsuit," *Arab News*, 3 February 2008, p. 2; "Saudi Women Complain of Discrimination, Abuse: UN Official," *Emirates 24/7*, Dubai, 13 February 2008, at http://www.emirates247.com/eb247/news/saudi-women-complain-of-discrimination-abuse-un-official-2008-02-13-1.214867; "World Report 2012: Saudi Arabia," New York: Human Rights Watch, 2012, at http://www.hrw.org/world-report-2012/world-report-2012-saudi-arabia; "Saudi's Religious Police Reject 'Doll' Cover: Publisher," *Al-Ahram Online*, 13 March 2013, at http://english.ahram.org.eg/NewsContent/2/8/66772/World/Region/Saudis-religious-police-reject-doll-cover-Publishe.aspx; Olog-Hai, "Is Your Name Now 'Banned' in Saudi Arabia?," *The Belfast Telegraph*, 15 March 2014, at http://www.freerepublic.com/focus/chat/3133577/posts; and Rima al-Mukhtar, "Women's Visits to Hospitals Without Male Guardians Banned," *Arab News*, 14 February 2014, at http://www.arabnews.com/news/525696.

Marianne Alireza, who was 82 in 2010 when I interviewed her, shared how a Commission member [Mutawa'] reprimanded her because her head was not covered while sitting on the beach. "I gave the poor fellow a piece of my mind," she declared, adding: "He walked away without being ashamed of his behavior though he should have been." Interview with Marianne Alireza, Jiddah, 6 November 2010.

37 Badria Al-Bishr, "Saudi Religious Police Women . . . a 'Pressing Need?'," *Al-Hayat*, 31 December 2012, at http://alhayat.com/Details/467592.

38 Interview with Dr. Nahid Tahir, Jiddah, 27 March 2011.

39 Interview with Mahah al-Juffali, Jiddah, 8 December 2010.

'Iffat's specific instructions, did not change. The mission—and it was a mission for us, too—was to emancipate our intellect. In that respect, I think that both succeeded."[40]

The mission thrived in more ways than many assumed. To take one example, Hayfah Jamal al-Layl and her two siblings, the daughters of a police officer from Madinah, all three of whom attended Dar al-Hanan, were gifted students who went on to university, earned degrees, taught at leading institutions, and, in the case of Dr. Hayfah, assumed the presidency of Effat University—thereby becoming the first female Sa'udi university president. What she learned at Dar al-Hanan was leadership, intermixed with lifelong lessons that have never left her, which embraced the whole person. "We studied very hard," Dr. Hayfah recalled, "but we also learned about how to enjoy our lives. Believe it or not, we used to have annual plays and even staged a 'Dance Fever' to honor John Travolta, though our final ceremonies always revolved around 'Ardhah [traditional Sa'udi] dances."[41] Inspired by Queen 'Iffat, and recruited by Princess Lulwah al-Faysal to transform the college into the renowned university it became in a very short time period, Dr. Hayfah recognized that the late Queen's mission was magical. "We work and work and work and when we're done, we work some more, for that is our mission," she stressed, "but we also strive to work in earnest to develop our students' intellect to allow them to shine as well as succeed. Every year, our students help out at the Jiddah Economic Forum, which is now a recognized international gathering, and it is truly astounding the compliments that our graduates receive from all who attend. Sa'udis and non-Sa'udis see for themselves the professionalism that young students achieve, and this, above all else, would have made the Queen happy. This is my mission, really," Dr. Hayfah concluded, "and there is nothing in the world more satisfying than to receive news from our successful graduates who keep on adding value to this nation."[42]

Eternal optimists, university presidents everywhere tend to vaunt their graduates, programs, and assorted achievements. Dr. Hayfah Jamal al-Layl is no exception even if her case stands out because she has operated against the odds in a country that still officially practices segregation, and where women's education is a recent achievement. Dar al-Hanan and

---

[40] Interview with Mahah al-Juffali, Jiddah, 23 October 2010.

[41] Interview with Dr. Hayfah Jamal al-Layl, President, Effat University, Jiddah, 12 December 2010. Dr. Hayfah earned both a Master's and a Doctoral degree in Public Policy from the University of Southern California, in Los Angeles, and started her academic career at the King 'Abdul 'Aziz University, where she became a Dean.

[42] Interview with Dr. Hayfah Jamal al-Layl, Jiddah, 16 March 2011.

Effat University graduates are like their counterparts everywhere, young and full of life, anxious to achieve miracles and jump through whatever challenges rise up in front of them. Yet, in this case as well, assorted conversations conducted in the course of this study have revealed dramatic sociological transformations that one seldom encounters on the Arabian Peninsula.[43]

Muluk al-Shaykh, who was born in Jiddah and attended Effat College—before it became a formal university in 2009—because her father wanted "her to study, not just marry," became an early graduate in communications. She was shocked on career day when potential employers interviewed her and she was "so proud to actually function as a whole person in this society." "Dr. Hayfah spoke to us about Queen 'Iffat," she recalled, "and I along with most of my friends were curious since we really did not know that much about her." "It was at Effat that I learned how to think critically and, encouraged by friends and teachers, submitted one of my opinion essays to *Sayyidaty* [a popular women's magazine], which accepted it. I felt liberated and thus became a columnist. Still, I knew that I needed to add to my knowledge capabilities and thus applied for an MBA program, and earned a fresh degree. It was as if I were on a mission," Ms. Al-Shaykh emphasized, a statement which certainly fits the pattern of Effat graduates.[44] Because Sa'udi society is conservative and, for most families, two incomes are required to ensure a good standard of living, young women like Ms. Al-Shaykh complain about jobs, lack of the right to drive, and the impediments to starting their own businesses, though many recognize that 9 to 5 schedules—which few practice—are also necessary to succeed. Most seek financial independence and, through Queen 'Iffat's efforts, many have been able to break through barriers, thereby enabling other young educated women to thrive, even if conditions remain neither easy to deal with nor risk-free.

Safanah Sayjani was 17 years old when she first attended Effat and, as a resident in one of the college's dorms, she cried all night as her family was in distant Sharjah (United Arab Emirates). "All of us were lonely," she clarified, "and really not prepared to become college students." Safanah was born in Riyadh, though her family hailed from the Makkah region, so she was familiar with conditions in the Kingdom. Still, the experience was shocking, "as living conditions in the dorms were not ideal." She revealed that she wrote a letter to the Jiddah daily

[43] These subjective observations are also based on a series of lectures delivered at various universities throughout the Gulf Cooperation Council region during the past few decades, numerous meetings with young graduates, and extensive conversations with hundreds of youths.

[44] Interview with Muluk al-Shaykh, Jiddah, 12 March 2011.

'*Ukaz*, complaining about poor facilities, which were rapidly fixed. "By voicing my opinion, I ensured that we had air-conditioning in our rooms, which further boosted my self-confidence. At Effat, I can honestly say that I learned how to take risks, but they had to be smart ones, and I am a better person today because of the opportunities I've had there."[45] When asked how she related to Queen 'Iffat's legacy, Ms. Sayjani unhesitatingly responded: "I am what she wanted Sa'udi women to be. I have a voice, am active, and I can think for myself even if I live in a conservative society whose norms I embrace. I am a stronger woman because of her," the young woman concluded. This is not the first time that such bold statements have been uttered by young Sa'udis, though what stands out in this testimony is the acknowledgment that women, as well as many men, are now willing to speak out. To be sure, Sa'udis are reserved with strangers, but seldom hesitate to offer their views. When prompted by a tangential remark that asks a difficult question, instead of skirting around the substance younger Sa'udi women no longer hesitate to offer an opinion as to what ails their society and what needs to be fixed to free the nation from its putative doldrums. "People nowadays even talk about confronting taboos. When I hear a member of the *Hay'at al-Amr bil-Ma'ruf wal-Nahi 'an al-Munkar* [Commission for the Promotion of Virtue and Prevention of Vice] telling me to 'cover up,' I ask: show me something in the Qur'an that says I should wear a *niqab*," affirmed Ms. Sayjani. The mere fact that such responses are so freely offered illustrates the level of change underway in society, although Ms. Sayjani was quick to add, "What we must really do is to educate our men, because they have to accept that we do not need to ask their permission to do something with our lives." She cited the examples of successful Sa'udi institutions like the Kingdom Holding Company, run by Prince Walid bin Talal bin 'Abdul 'Aziz, and the King 'Abdallah University of Science and Technology [KAUST], where educators welcomed women in their midst, as ideal paradigms for the country. "We must step up to the plate," she insisted, "and assume our roles. If Queen 'Iffat were alive when [Jiddah] flooded in 2009 [when 77 people were killed], you can be sure that she would have done something about it, and we must learn from her example to get our hands dirty if we want to take care of our own."

No matter how energetic such comments may be, they pale in comparison with the vigorous awareness that Sa'udi Arabia ought to open up, because it can no longer afford to depend solely on past values. Sarah Sharaf, whose mother knew 'Iffat Al Thunayan and who attended Princess Lulwah's wedding, spoke of how often her mother spoke to her

[45] Interview with Safanah Sayjani, Jiddah, 12 March 2011.

and her siblings about the Queen. "For my mother, Queen 'Iffat was a grandiose figure, someone who valued contact with foreign representatives and who did not discriminate against Arabs seeking refuge in the Kingdom. As a recomposed family of Palestinians and Egyptians we were outsiders, but the Queen would have none of that. My mother always reminded us that we were made welcome by the *Turkiyyah*, who knew what it meant to be ostracized."[46] At Effat College, Ms. Sharaf learned to speak near-native English—"a gift to those of us who considered ourselves part of the larger world"—and to strengthen her character. "We gained confidence through hard work," she opined, "and to conduct real research that allowed me, a professional translator, to perform at an internationally acceptable level." Ms. Sharaf never turned in her library card and continued to use the university's facilities "because we still do not have public libraries that fill this need." Five years after her graduation she still felt attached to the institution. "It's difficult to leave and although I have done consulting work at the German-Sa'udi Hospital, [and at] ARAMCO [the state oil company] as well as at KAUST, I am now involved with a nearby *'umrah* organization that looks after foreign pilgrims that visit the Holy Cities. I now live close to my family and to Effat. Sa'udi women will change this country for the better." Ms. Sharaf underscored the roles played by women in the fields of *hajj* and *'umrah*, something that was not accepted just a few years ago, "which serves pilgrims and grants us the opportunities to become financially independent." Adopting a work ethic is consequently seen as a positive feature, because, as this erudite young woman emphasized, "we do not need to be at war with men but to really become their partners. Just like Faysal and 'Iffat were."

"We must reach a level that should let a woman walk or drive or do whatever it is she is doing and not be bothered by a man," insisted Rottana Khayat. Here was yet another constatation that the male view of women in the Kingdom ought to evolve so as to "respect us beyond our roles as wives and mothers."[47] "That day will come when we will eliminate the many contradictions and double standards that exist in our society," she clarified, "simply because the whole world is changing and we just cannot remain in our closed environment." Queen 'Iffat Al Thunayan cautioned young Sa'udis, both men and women, to modernize without necessarily becoming Westernized, and it was remarkable to hear her voice echoed in these conversations. "Although we need the right educational tools to succeed," added Ms. Khayat, "we must end

[46] Interview with Sarah Sharaf, Jiddah, 13 March 2011.
[47] Interview with Rottana Khayat, Jiddah, 14 March 2011.

narrow-minded interpretations that degrade our religion. Islam is glorious," she hammered, "though you would not get that impression by reading Western reports on how our Hay'at behaved, often degrading and threatening us. Can you imagine wearing gloves in this heat so as not to display our nail polish? What does that have anything to do with my belief in the Almighty. Queen 'Iffat taught us to be impeccable ladies, making sure that we were feminine because that's our nature, but to also remain faithful to His Word." "Our model," she concluded, "is the Faysal–'Iffat paradigm. They are not our Anthony and Cleopatra or Romeo and Juliet versions," she clarified, "they were better because they truly trusted each other and worked hard to improve this nation." Moreover, echoing this commitment in her own life, Ms. Khayat further confirmed that she was preparing an advanced degree in psychiatry so that, in time, she could practice her skills, "because 'Iffat's legacy on us is quite simple, really: we need to work hard to add value for the next generation."

The effort might indeed take an entire generation, "or at least 50 years," according to 'Arij Abu Zarifah, a married Effat graduate in business administration who wanted to work after she and her husband had been blessed with three sons. "My husband gave me a choice," she confided: "Work or me. I chose work and although my former husband now regrets his hastiness, he did not understand that for me to be a better wife and mother, I truly needed to improve myself and become productive."[48] This Effat College student learned various hands-on skills as she volunteered at the local hospital, and eventually accepted a human relations position with a major medical facility under construction, but what she also learned in the process was to do the job herself instead of relying on others. She hoped that women would secure equal legal rights in the workforce and become active members of society, "for that is the only way we are going to ensure our nation's progress," she declared. "In time," Ms. Zarifah added, "Sa'udi men will understand that women can be tremendous assets, and I strongly believe that Queen 'Iffat will look down from heaven one of these days and smile at us after we reach our inevitable internal harmony."

Social harmony was certainly one of the late Queen's lifelong objectives, as she invested heavily in women's benevolent associations along with charities that catered to battered women and those with special needs. Nisrin al-Idriss, the Press Director for the Jiddah-based Jam'iyyah al-Khayriyyah [Benevolent Association], organized a visit to the organization's premises—where women were asked to cover their faces in my presence—to showcase some of its activities. "We assist divorced women

[48] Interview with 'Arij Abu Zarifah, Jiddah, 19 March 2011.

and look after needy families," she explained, "as a full healing process is gradually introduced to help as many as possible. We teach women survival skills while their infants are in crèches, and though we have a lot of volunteers, many of our current initiatives are entrusted to professionals. We want to restore family harmony and as 75 percent of the women who walk through our doors are Sa'udis, it is incumbent on us to alleviate whatever suffering we can identify."[49] In 2010, for example, the Jam'iyyah looked after 2,600 families in Jiddah, which was not a negligible figure, on a budget of 30 million riyals [US$ 8m]. Ms. al-Idriss recognized that the organization could not turn down the needy and, indeed, looks after foreign *hajjis* who leave infants in its care, but its chief mission is to restore harmony among members of broken Sa'udi families, in line with what Queen 'Iffat Al Thunayan prescribed. "To really address our core problem, which is to teach useful skills to lower middle-class women who find themselves in such dire conditions, we need to persuade the *mahrams* that a nurse assistant who works in an honorable fashion is nothing but a blessing. We are making progress," she elucidated, "since we now have clear boundaries as to what kind of assistance we give: Families must have no more than six children and the women ought to accept training. If she does not come to her classes, and after a short reprieve, we drop them. Same for kids, if a woman has a seventh child and wants to be on the dole, we no longer accept them in our programs."[50] Remarkably, gradual harmonization seems to have settled in at the Jam'iyyah, the result of increased awareness that each individual must take responsibility for her actions.

The daughter of a Yemeni woman who received help from the Jam'iyyah in 1967, Munah al-Fadli has seen first-hand what the organization does for local women who require assistance. Ms. Al-Fadli, now a matriarch in her own right, kindly answered many of my questions on Queen 'Iffat, whom she had known personally. She confirmed that 'Iffat Al Thunayan was a doer. Over a cold soft drink, which she served herself in her modest home outside of Jiddah, al-Fadli elaborated: "She was warm and did not talk a lot but she did a lot quietly. She did not want just to hand out help. No, that was not her style. She wanted the women that required our aid to learn a trade and earn a legitimate salary."[51] In 1967 or 1968, at a time when the Jam'iyyah had been operational for no more than five years, only the basics were provided, but "the Queen wanted to change that." In addition to classes and marketable skills, women were taught how to sew, cook, practice hygienic habits to raise

---

[49] Interview with Nisrin al-Idriss, Jiddah, 20 March 2011.
[50] *Ibid.*
[51] Interview with Mona al-Fadli, Jiddah, 22 March 2011.

their children, and otherwise take care of themselves so as to better look after their families. "Our 'Iffat was happy when she saw results and for 37 years, I served the Jam'iyyah because of her. She was a real *malikah* [queen] and though she was kind as a mother, she insisted that her own daughters follow in her footsteps to really change the lives of many Sa'udi women." Ms. Al-Fadli also affirmed that while the late Queen drew strength from Faysal, " . . . what she carried inside of her, and what she honestly wished to share with all of us, was to know the difference between *ghalat* and *'ayb* [what may be wrong vs. what is shameful]."

This insight was corroborated by Wad Abu Zunadah. A computer science graduate from Effat College, the Jiddah native, whose mother taught English Literature at King 'Abdul 'Aziz University, recalled her orientation session on the day preceding classes. "We were not told to do this and not to do that. There was no effort to portray our actions in terms of what might be perceived as being wrong or shameful, though faculty and staff members took pains to instill in us the necessity to preserve our 'reputations' as Effat girls and women."[52] Ms. Abu Zunadah, who accepted a position of assistant to the Effat Dean of Student Affairs, did not foresee an immediate elimination of segregation though she believed that after a period of time, "perhaps two generations, we will change." "When I meet a man I like," she stated, "I will sit with him and try to figure him out, especially to evaluate his limitations. He will need to be honest with me and I will not rush into a lifelong decision. That's the challenge Sa'udi women face: we ought to learn to be patient and not rush into an alliance that may be weak. Queen 'Iffat was lucky in that she had Faysal but she also taught us to assume our social duties with poise. She believed in God, Faysal, and in herself, and we ought to follow in her footsteps by holding on to our faith, relying on trustworthy partners—but, above all, we must be true to ourselves."

STRENGTHENED BY FAITH

Because of the many difficulties she confronted during the first sixteen years of her life in Constantinople, Queen 'Iffat Al Thunayan was forced into situations that privileged young girls seldom face, which perhaps explains her unique character. One of her granddaughters realized that the Queen "was 'geared' to succeed as she planned like a political strate-

[52] Interview with Wed Abu Zunadah, Jiddah, 23 March 2011.

gist and executed like a military tactician."[53] Though she carried herself as a Queen, 'Iffat drew succor from her faith, and passed those core values to family members.

The Character of a Lioness

"She raised me," said Ahmad 'Abdul Wahhab—whose father was brought up in Istanbul and married a Cherkess wife, and who in turn became neighbors with the Al Thunayan—and "she will always have a special place in my heart."[54] The family came to Makkah to work for the future Queen, but when Ahmad's father died when the boy was only 12 years old, the then Princess looked after him, too. Over time, and given his vast knowledge of Arab affairs and incredible memory with faces and names, Ahmad became the Chief of Protocol for the Diwan. In addition to Faysal, he served both Kings Khalid and Fahd before retiring. Inasmuch as Ahmad 'Abdul Wahhab witnessed history, his recollection of Queen 'Iffat's composure revealed the making of a rare human being on the Arabian Peninsula, unprecedented in her scope and reach. Indeed, after Faysal became King, 'Iffat Al Thunayan assumed a vastly expanded role, as she received Queen Elizabeth, Margaret Thatcher—before and after she became Prime Minister in 1979—and the Iranian Empress Farah Diba when these prominent personalities visited Sa'udi Arabia. Invariably, she also left strong impressions on each one of them, which contributed greatly to Sa'udi diplomatic efforts.[55] She accompanied King Faysal on several official visits, including one to France where she attended a formal reception at the Elysée Palace. Everyone noticed the sparkle in her eyes and the smile on her face that had so mesmerized Faysal from the start and that truly affected all those who knew her.

At ease among royalty just as much as among the *badu*, Queen 'Iffat made it a point always to know what was going on all around her. She read, inquired, followed up, paid special attention at her husband's *majlises*, asked many questions each and every time a senior Al Sa'ud family member visited (both males and females), listened carefully, instructed her attorney to follow up as necessary, and shared her views with her offspring and grandchildren. To say that she knew a lot would

---

53 Interview with HRH Princess Nurah bint Turki al-Faysal, Jiddah, 12 December 2010.

54 Interview with HE Ahmad 'Abdul Wahhab, 20 October 2010.

55 'Iffat Al Thunayan seldom abused her privileged position and rarely traveled on government jets. For the most part, she flew on her brother Kamal Adham's planes or, when accompanied by HRH Prince Turki al-Faysal when he was Head of the General Intelligence Directorate, on the latter's official aircraft. More often than not, she was accompanied by family members, which meant there were no bodyguards.

indeed be an understatement. 'Iffat Al Thunayan was also up to date with the latest developments in the art and music world. Her interests varied and, in addition to poetry and traditional Arabic music, contemporary painting fascinated her. Salvador Dalí intrigued her as did the latest French artists in Montmartre, the Parisian community that had been home to dozens of renowned painters, including Claude Monet, Vincent van Gogh, Pablo Picasso, Raoul Dufy, and Amedeo Modigliani, along with the best of the younger generation such as Gen Paul. A genuine lover of fine art, she encouraged her own grandchildren to try painting for themselves and, whenever she saw talent, encouraged it.[56]

Of course, what interested the Queen more than any other subject was the Kingdom's politics and the fate that befell the Al Sa'ud of ruling the country. Her diplomatic finesse became increasingly advanced as she met regularly with senior officials and key ministers, spoke with them often, and instructed each to follow up on particular concerns. An avid observer of developments at home, she gave these officials her honest opinion and, while never forgetting that Faysal was ruler, issued carefully tailored pleas to meet whatever needs required Riyadh's attention. Naturally, she wanted Faysal to shine, and never looked for glory for herself but strove to make him the great monarch he became. Always so attentive to his image, Queen 'Iffat made it a lifelong cause to ensure that her spouse was free from daily preoccupations, to better concentrate on the nation's business. She sewed his *thobes* [garments] and introduced the collar worn by most Sa'udi males today. More important, she discussed with Faysal the details of their children's education and took upon herself the required follow-up both at home and overseas. Above all else, she ensured that Faysal was not burdened with ordinary chores and did not trouble him with mundane matters. Of course, the monarch doted on his partner, and did not voice objections but a particular episode illustrates the kind of relationship that developed between them, one based on mutual respect and consideration. According to 'Abdallah al-Ghamdi, who worked at the palace and looked after the Queen's travel needs in

[56] One of the late Queen's granddaughters, HRH Princess Lulwah bint Bandar bin Sultan bin 'Abdul 'Aziz once showed her one of her paintings, which reminded the Queen of the work of a famous artist. Princess Lulwah was amazed by her grandmother's memory and the details she provided on her favorite painters. The young woman gave her grandmother a composition of her own that was prominently displayed in the Queen's Parisian home. After 'Iffat Al Thunayan passed away, Princess Lulwah "inherited" the painting, which, the young woman insisted, "will never be sold or given to anyone under any circumstances." Interview with HRH Princess Lulwah bint Bandar bin Sultan bin 'Abdul 'Aziz, Jiddah, 16 October 2010.

his capacity as a controller at the Jiddah airport for over three decades, Faysal once arrived home and noticed two brand-new Mercedes-Benz cars parked in front of the entrance. The incident occurred in 1967, at the height of the austerity programs that the King had introduced to put the Kingdom's economy on a better footing, measures which severely curtailed domestic spending, including expenditures by members of the ruling family. Faysal asked about the cars and was told that they were gifts from the Queen's brother, Kamal Adham, an answer which seemed to satisfy him.[57] However, Al-Ghamdi revealed that 'Iffat Al Thunayan noticed that Faysal had made inquiries, though, with characteristic discretion, he did not bring up the subject in public. Without missing a heartbeat, she immediately instructed that the cars be stored, and no one ever saw them again. She must have concluded that he did not approve, and though he said absolutely nothing to her, "she knew." She told her brother about it, but neither Kamal Adham nor Faysal bin 'Abdul 'Aziz ever raised the issue again.

Al-Ghamdi's explanations touched on yet another of the Queen's characteristics, which was to trust her employees and look after them in exceptionally generous ways. But she expected certain standards in return, for instance, requiring every staff member—male as well as female—to be impeccably dressed, both at home and whenever they accompanied her during her overseas trips. When 'Abdallah al-Ghamdi once walked into Kamal Adham's home near London wearing jeans and a jacket, she called him close to her and told him to go and get a decent suit. "I want you and all Sa'udis to be presentable in public," he remembered her telling him, a wish with which he immediately complied. "I never wore jeans in her presence after that episode," affirmed al-Ghamdi. For his part, Dakhil Allah al-Harthy, who managed the palaces for the royal couple for decades, recalled the way he was hired: "You will be on probation for three months," she told him, "and you will be looked after very well, but make sure that you are always well groomed and follow my instructions carefully, especially with guests."[58] Al-Harthy was told to feed those who stopped by the palace for lunch or dinner, and never to turn anyone down: "The palace doors must always be kept open," she told him, "and make sure that nothing is thrown away, for there is always someone in need who must be cared for." After his probationary period ended satisfactorily, the Queen told al-Harthy to see Prince Turki al-Faysal to regularize his stay as a permanent employee, which he remained until her death.

---

57 Interview with 'Abdallah al-Ghamdi, Jiddah, 7 November 2010.
58 Interview with Dakhil Allah al-Harthy, Jiddah, 25 November 2010.

Some three hundred individuals worked for Queen 'Iffat Al Thunayan over the years, and she instructed al-Harthy to look after each and every one. For this purpose she received sufficient income from her investments in the Jiddah 'Imarat al-Malikah and the Bahr al-Ahmar Hotel, both of which she owned. As al-Harthy confirmed, she never received a state subsidy to cover these expenses,[59] telling him on one occasion, "I did not ask for state handouts under Faysal and I am not going to now," which meant that she needed to be an astute investor to ensure a steady income. Remarkably, 'Iffat Al Thunayan taught her staff loyalty, not only through her generosity but also by instilling in them a sense of pride in their work. "We were never made to feel that we were mere servants to a monarch and his family, but were made to assume responsibility for those who represented the image of our nation," avowed al-Harthy, who summed up his feelings best when he declared, "We felt we were serving the Kingdom because she truly represented the country."

Queen 'Iffat knew most staff members personally and gave each one holiday gratuities. Most saw her as a "grandmother," and appreciated her generosity, though she insisted that they take their work seriously. Many remembered her iconic beauty, even at an advanced age, comparing her looks to those of the legendary Hollywood actress Rita Hayworth.[60] Most considered her a role model, someone who stood out in society and who seldom compromised on principles that defended the interests of her nation.

The Return to Najd

"Sa'udi Arabia was lucky that she came back from Turkey," said Princess Hayfah al-Faysal, echoing her brother Sa'ud, who added, "God willed it."[61] "She united us," declared 'Abdul 'Aziz bin Turki al-Faysal, fondly remembering 'Id al-Fitr celebrations when the Queen gathered together most of her offspring to further reinforce family ties. "The holidays always presented opportunities to meet cousins who would

---

[59] In her last will and testament the Queen allocated a third of her wealth to the charities she supported throughout the years. The front page of the will is reproduced in Appendix V.

[60] As she grew in age and required the care of a live-in nurse who administered massages, Queen 'Iffat's demands diminished, though her infectious smile was never far from her face. "She made it a point to know me and ask about my family," said Christina Epolito, who looked after her during the 1990s. Interview with Christina Epolito, Jiddah, 16 October 2010.

[61] Interviews with HRH Hayfah al-Faysal, Jiddah, 25 October 2010, and HRH Prince Sa'ud al-Faysal, Riyadh, 26 October 2010.

assemble in Warfield in the English countryside, the home that Kamal Adham placed at his sister's disposal whenever she wanted to be in London."[62] As cousins flew in from the Kingdom, the United States, from wherever their parents were assigned, they would all gather to be with a doting grandmother who acted as "the glue that kept the family together." "As times passed," 'Abdul 'Aziz bin Turki al-Faysal added, "we would actually cherish those times more than many assumed, not only because we knew that we would all spend some time together, but also because many of us realized the meaning of belonging to the Faysal family." Such gatherings served additional purposes, too, as 'Iffat Al Thunayan caught up with her grandchildren, inquiring about their schools and other interests, and offering solicited as well as unsolicited advice. It was as if she was on a mission to instill in the youngsters what she had successfully managed to inculcate in her own offspring, namely, to be proud of their heritage without being arrogant. She cautioned the younger but rapidly growing boys and girls to be careful of their duties, encouraging them to be aware of the role that their grandfather had played in the country's history and always to serve Sa'udi Arabia rather than simply help themselves to its bounty on account of their station in life. She once told Rimah bint Bandar bin Sultan to "always watch the impression you leave and be as sharp as you possibly can, for you never know who might be paying attention or watching you."[63] Several other family members elaborated on this theme, which highlighted the Queen's eagle-sharp focus on what really mattered in life: to be both morally as well as intellectually honest.

After King Faysal bin 'Abdul 'Aziz passed away, Queen 'Iffat decided to dedicate her life to her country, which took its toll on her health. She suffered from a heart ailment for several years and first consulted the renowned American cardiologist Michael Ellis DeBakey in Houston, with whom she became friends.[64] After those first consultations in Texas, DeBakey visited 'Iffat Al Thunayan in Paris, where the famed heart surgeon solicited her financial assistance towards the building of a hospital in Monte Carlo. According to Ahmad bin 'Abdul Wahhab, the

---

[62] Interview with HRH Prince 'Abdul 'Aziz bin Turki al-Faysal, Jiddah, 23 October 2010.

[63] Interview with HRH Princess Rimah bint Bandar al-Faysal, Riyadh, 26 October 2010. Princess Rimah recalled a visit when she was wearing fashionably torn jeans, which the Queen did not approve of, and which elicited the following remark: "I would have never looked like this when I was your age," which spoke volumes without being disparaging, something that "grandma specialized in."

[64] Michael Ellis DeBakey (1908–2008) was born as Michel Dabaghi in Lake Charles, Louisiana to Lebanese immigrants Shakir and Rahijah Dabaghi. DeBakey,

Queen agreed to help on the condition that the hospital be built in Sa'udi Arabia, telling the American: "I congratulate you and I will help you but only if you do it in my home."[65] "This was her identity, it was in her blood, and not only was one of her ancestors a ruler of Riyadh; she felt a Sa'udi and made those around her feel so too. She knew how to shine in Faysal's glow but it was also her extensive polishing," as the conversations she held with Dr. DeBakey illustrate. Aware that such an undertaking required indigenous manpower to help create the type of facilities envisaged by the Houstonian, the Queen fully supported her husband when he instructed Dr. Sayyid 'Ali Rif'at, a physician who had married her sister Muzaffar, to help create the King Faysal Specialist Hospital, which now maintains facilities in both Riyadh and Jiddah, both of which offer international standards of care.

Specialists at the hospital followed her condition on a regular basis, eventually recommending heart surgery, which she opted to undergo. When the time came to go through with this serious procedure, 'Iffat Al Thunayan fully understood the risks associated with surgery, especially given her advanced age. Several months before she went to the hospital,

---

who anglicized the family name, developed the roller pump that became an essential component of the heart-lung that allowed the continuous flow of blood during operations, which in turn allowed surgeons to perform open-heart surgeries. DeBakey was one of the first physicians to perform coronary artery bypass surgeries and, in 1953, performed the first successful operation that removed excess materials from inside the carotid artery [Carotid Endarterectomy], a remarkable effort. A pioneer in the development of an artificial heart, DeBakey was also the first physician to use external heart pump in a patient successfully, and pioneered the use of Dacron grafts to replace or repair blood vessels. He is credited with developing the Mobile Army Surgical Hospitals (M.A.S.H.) concept for the United States military, which saved thousands of lives during the Korean and Vietnam conflicts. DeBakey devoted considerable time to national advisory committees and to consultancies in several European, Arab, and Far Eastern countries, where he helped establish health care systems. In a detailed obituary in *The New York Times*, Lawrence K. Altman wrote that DeBakey, "the oldest of five children of Lebanese-Christian immigrants who moved to the United States to escape religious intolerance in the Middle East," credited "much of his surgical success to his mother, Raheeja, for teaching him to sew, crochet, and knit." His parents, who hailed from Marja'un, Lebanon, chose Cajun country because French was spoken there, as it had been in their native land of Lebanon. See Lawrence K. Altman, "Dr. Michael E. DeBakey, Rebuilder of Hearts, Dies at 99," *The New York Times*, 13 July 2008, at http://www.nytimes.com/2008/07/13/health/12cnd-debakey.html. See also Philip A. Salem, M.D., "Michael DeBakey: The Real Man Behind the Genius," *Al-Hewar: The Center for Arab Culture and Dialogue*, at http://www.alhewar.net/Basket/Salem_Debakey.htm.

[65] Interview with Ahmad 'Abdul Wahhab, 20 October 2010.

she distributed her favorite art pieces, figurines, lace dresses, and numerous *objets* she had collected over the years to her daughters, step-daughters, and granddaughters. "It was not easy seeing her suffer towards the end of her life as she was in obvious pain," confirmed Princess Hayfah al-Faysal, but having had exhaustive consultations via satellite with Houston, she decided to have the operation.[66] A few days before her scheduled procedure, ʻIffat Al Thunayan gathered most of her children and grandchildren into her hospital suite in Riyadh to advise them on life's key features. The hospital scene was sad but Princess Nurah bint Turki al-Faysal recalled how it also resembled ʻId gatherings when ʻIffat Al Thunayan would dote on her grandchildren and distribute gifts. She was happy when everyone was around her. "Remember who you are," she told them, "be cautious and always remember that you carry Faysal's name."[67] Everyone in the room weighed the gravity of the moment but they were happy to be with her and listen to her advice, which was quite simple. "You should always be together," she told her offspring.[68] She confided to her daughter Princess Latifah, "I hope that my mind will not leave me," as she did not want to be beholden to any of her children.[69] Of course, she was not the possessive type and always encouraged her daughters to assume their fair share of responsibilities too, which she applied to herself.[70] As family members worried about her condition at the Riyadh hospital and even considered soliciting independent medical advice, the Queen reprimanded those close to her who wanted to switch physicians, resenting that they would think of treating her with such condescension even if the intention was to secure the best available care. As she was sound of mind, she insisted that she would be the only patient in the room and would make her own decisions. Her last testament the night before her operation was simple: She told her offspring to "remain humble, available, truthful with others, loving and respectful of each other, and to always be generous with those who help you make good decisions."[71] "ʻIdʻuli" [wish me well to live through

66 Interview with HRH Princess Hayfah al-Faysal, Jiddah, 16 October 2010.

67 Interview with HRH Princess Nurah bint Turki al-Faysal, Jiddah, 11 March 2011.

68 Interview with HRH Princess Sarah bint ʻAbdul Rahman al-Faysal, Riyadh, 14 October 2010.

69 Interview with HRH Princess Latifah al-Faysal, Jiddah, 12 October 2010.

70 Like many Saʻudi women, Queen ʻIffat believed that every woman ought to depend on herself, work, drive—she drove when they were in the countryside but never in the cities and encouraged young princesses to learn how to drive—and otherwise help her man.

71 Interview with HRH Prince Turki al-Faysal, Riyadh, 16 October 2011.

another 'Id], she told family members, "for she probably knew that this might be her last day alive, adding that it did not matter what happened to her."[72] Sitting up in her bed, she told everyone, "I will fight the disease, but I am ready to die if that is God's Will," as she did not like being dependent.[73] It is accurate to conclude that she was happy that she died with her senses fully intact, not in any stage of senility, and she never pretended that she deserved better care than other patients at the hospital. "She was not about to acquire a new personality," reflected Princess Lulwah, who remembered her mother's last words to her: "You must survive and excel."[74] Regrettably, the Queen did not survive the procedure and passed away on the operating table on 17 February 2000.

When she had attained her eternal peace, the hospital gradually grew quiet. Prince 'Abdul 'Aziz bin Turki and several of the late Queen's grandchildren wanted to see her one last time. "Even dead, she had a presence. I asked my father if I could go and see her and he took me in."[75] Other family members paid their respects, too, before senior members of the ruling family gathered to offer funeral prayers. These were led by then heir apparent, now King, 'Abdallah bin 'Abdul 'Aziz Al Sa'ud at the Turki bin 'Abdallah Mosque in Riyadh on 18 February 2000.[76] It fell on 'Abdallah Al-Ghamdi and Prince Turki al-Faysal to place the Queen's remains in her unmarked grave.

CONCLUSION

When 'Iffat Al Thunayan passed away, Sharifah Jalali, a heretofore little-known *Jiddawiyyah*, revealed that the Queen had supported her

---

72 Interview with Halah Rif'at, Jiddah, 24 October 2010.

73 Interview with HRH Princess Sarah al-Faysal, Riyadh, 13 October 2010.

74 Interview with HRH Princess Lulwah al-Faysal, Jiddah, 17 October 2010.

75 Interview with 'Abdul 'Aziz bin Turki al-Faysal, Jiddah, 23 October 2010.

76 "Sumu Wali al-'Ahd Yu'adi Salat al-Mayit and Yatalaqah al-Ta'azi fi Wafat al-'Amirah 'Iffat Al-Thunayan" [His Highness the Heir Apparent Performs Funeral Prayers and Accepts Condolences on the Death of Princess 'Iffat Al Thunayan], *'Ukaz*, 19 February 2000, pp. 1, 3, and 32; see also Ahmad Muhammad Badib, "Wa Matat Sayiddat al-Qulub" [The Queen of Hearts Passed Away], *'Ukaz*, 21 February 2000, p. 3; Khazimah al-'Attas and Salwah al-'Umran, "Al-Amirah 'Iffat Tamayazat bil-Insaniyyah wal-Ihtimam bi-Ta'lim al-Fatat al-Sa'udiyyah" [Princess 'Iffat Distinguished Herself through her Humanity and her Attention to the Education of the Sa'udi Girl], *'Ukaz*, 20 February 2000, p. 23; Amimah bint Musa'id bin Ahmad Al-Sudayri, "Banatuna wal-Hadath" [Our Girls and Events], *'Ukaz*, 22 February 2000, p. 20; Al-Jawharah bint Muhammad Al 'Anqari, "Wafa' li-'Iffat Tul al-Sinin"

and her family for many years.[77] It was just one disclosure that illustrated with what care and discretion the Queen looked after those most in need. Her attorney confirmed that 'Iffat kept a ledger with the names and telephone numbers of specific associations that received assistance and as she heard from her entourage or read in local papers, she anonymously instructed Hussayn Shukri to deliver financial instruments to cover medical expenses, social needs at weddings or funerals, and schooling as appropriate. When she heard of the case of a Palestinian child who needed an operation in Germany, for example, she instructed Shukri to prepare a check for half a million riyals (US$ 135,000), which was dispatched through the Rabitat al-'Alam al-Islami organization.[78] A dedicated philanthropist who gave generously at a time when such disbursements were limited, the Queen lived up to her Sa'udi roots, even if most of her assistance was of the anonymous kind. This part of her character was ingrained in her by the harsh Sa'udi environment she knew well and had had to endure in the initial years after her 1932 return, though 'Iffat Al Thunayan humanized her surroundings as she weighed the many contributions made by hundreds of thousands before her. Most Sa'udis were certainly aware of their history and seldom boasted or took credit for what they considered to be mere duties. Critically, the history of the Arabian Peninsula is a painful one, with wars and conquests that injured many; naturally, with limited resources little could be achieved before oil wealth transformed the country. For 'Iffat, who was well versed in that history, such challenges were part of the country's legacy, but she also opted to confront what ailed her society. Simply stated, because she appreciated her position among the Al Sa'ud as well as being aware of the unique opportunities that accompanied her privileged station in life, she decided not to waste them.

Hers was first and foremost a commitment to a man, Faysal, who loved and trusted her completely. In turn, she earned his confidence, and gave him a strong family that accepted their responsibility to serve the

---

[Loyalty to 'Iffat Over the Years], *'Ukaz*, 22 February 2000, p. 4; Mother . . . and the Humanity], *'Ukaz*, 27 February 2000, p. 17; Nurah al-Hamrani, "Ay Ura' Yurthiq" [Who Will Justly Honor You], *'Ukaz*, 27 February 2000, p. 30. For an emotional farewell, see Prince Turki al-Faysal, "Risalah ila Ummi" [An Epistle to my Mother], *Al-Sharq Al-Awsat*, 28 February 2000, which critics misread as a letter to the Queen Announcing the Death of King Faysal [which occurred in 1975]. See "Prince Turki Al Faisal," *Saba*, 10 September 2001, at http://www.arab.net/arab-view/article.asp?artID=23.

[77] Interview with HRH Princess Rimah bint Bandar bin Sultan, Riyadh, 26 October 2010. In the words of the Princess, "We did not realize it until much later, but Queen 'Iffat truly changed this nation one person at a time."

[78] Interview with Hussayn Shukri, Esq., Jiddah, 21 October 2010.

nation. For Foreign Minister Sa'ud al-Faysal, 'Iffat Al Thunayan was a "woman of vision, but was much more than a mother: she was a teacher, a doctor, a mentor, a friend; she established solid ties with all her children." Indeed, "She respected us and never tried to dominate us," he emphasized in what turned out to be a particularly demonstrative interview. Prince Sa'ud had tears in his eyes as he recalled his mother and the impact she had on him: "My mother had the patience of a saint and the energy of a lioness," he stated, relieved to talk about the person who passed on to him the sense of duty that she herself had practiced with a vengeance.[79]

According to Prince Bandar al-Faysal, she was proud of Sa'ud as the Prince assumed the position of Foreign Minister in 1975 after their father was gunned down, and of her youngest son, Turki. Bandar, an air-force officer with a distinguished record, believed that his brother Turki was "smart as hell," and that he worked hard to protect the nation. "Our sense of duty comes from our mother, really," offered Bandar in his formidable voice, "because she was persuaded that the Al Sa'ud must serve the nation in every capacity. If the Al Sa'ud do not serve," she once told Bandar, "power will be taken away from them, so we'd better use it or lose it."[80] This attentiveness translated into loyalty—to Faysal at first, and gradually to the Al Sa'ud and the Kingdom. Truth be told, Queen 'Iffat did not wish to collect awards for her achievements but to leave a lasting legacy, one that spoke of steady contributions to the nation—especially through various educational and health programs—which for her meant everything. "She wanted Sa'udis to be forward-looking and not bury their hands in the sand," concluded Nurah bint Turki al-Faysal, recalling that her grandmother used to tell her: "When you walk, you look forward, not backwards, and I hope that you and everyone in this country will do likewise."[81]

'Iffat was not a founder of the Kingdom, of course, but she certainly was one of its builders. She was not a bee queen but perhaps she was a

---

[79] As the interview was scheduled to take place between meetings with two visiting ambassadors, Prince Sa'ud was glad "not to talk politics" as he ushered me to the seat next to him. The interview emphasized Queen 'Iffat's sense of duty, which was clearly passed on to her sons and daughters, as a perfect example of what he meant. What quickly became apparent in the long conversation was the impact that Queen 'Iffat had had on this senior member of the family, who was glad to share personal insights on how he was raised. Interview with HRH Prince Sa'ud al-Faysal, Riyadh, 26 October 2010.

[80] Interview with HRH Prince Bandar al-Faysal, Riyadh, 28 March 2011.

[81] Interview with HRH Princess Nurah bint Turki al-Faysal, Jiddah, 11 March 2011.

builder queen. At the very least, she was a woman who grew up in relative poverty, blaming the war in the Ottoman Empire and later Turkey for robbing her of her father. From this early experience, she learned to rely on hard work to accomplish many of her goals, instilling her own work ethic in her offspring and never giving her sons and daughters cheap compliments. To be sure, she expressed pride when that was warranted, though she preferred this to come indirectly through acquaintances and friends. Undoubtedly, she was proud of her family, and especially of her country, and although she passed away in 2000, her presence is still felt today by her offspring, along with many friends and employees. Though few outsiders remember her today, in reality "she is not gone." "For us," said Sarah bint 'Abdul Rahman al-Faysal, "she is still around," and she persevered: "Not only did she love life and made you live it to the hilt, but she exuded confidence and did not show her vulnerabilities." In one of her more vivid recollections, Princess Sarah remembered how her grandmother encouraged the grandchildren to be "Aslan Gibi" [like a lion] and advised them to be achievers.[82] She told al-Bandari bint 'Abdul Rahman al-Faysal: "Leave a legacy, no matter what you do. You must do something valuable, not just live."[83] Though she was proud of all of her children, she literally admired her youngest daughter Hayfah—perhaps the one whose character most resembled hers—and was especially proud of both Sa'ud and Turki. All agreed that while many saw her as an intruder in the Al Sa'ud dynasty, the *Turkiyyah* who could never become a true *badawiyyah*, in reality she assumed the Al Sa'ud's aura and overcame various difficulties, thus earning everyone's respect.

Content with her achievements, and never bitter, she overcame the initial loneliness she felt when she arrived in the nascent Kingdom. Al-Bandari reported her grandmother telling her how she used to hide in a closet to listen to music—even if the presence of a gramophone and records indicated that music was not forbidden in Makkah—for fear of offending those who could not possibly understand why she craved civilization. King 'Abdul 'Aziz made her feel a real Sa'udi, since she was a direct cousin, which was probably why she set out to prove herself. King Faysal, the man who fell in love with 'Iffat Al Thunayan the moment he laid eyes on her, made sure that she did not feel as if she were an outsider either. Both men helped her focus to serve the nation, a mission from which she never wavered. She became a knight and if Faysal had the

[82] Interview with HRH Princess Sarah bint 'Abdul Rahman al-Faysal, Riyadh, 14 October 2010.

[83] Interview with HRH Princess al-Bandari bint 'Abdul Rahman al-Faysal, Riyadh, 15 October 2010.

proclivity for reform, she had the style to shine in all of the efforts she embarked upon, which added grace to value and guaranteed her place in the history of the Kingdom.

Appendices

I   Interviews conducted by the author
II   The late Queen's passport and various visas
III   'Iffat Al Thunayan's Ottoman identity card
IV   'Iffat's Letters to King Fahd and Heir Apparent 'Abdallah asking for support
V   Queen 'Iffat's last will

Appendix I

Interviews conducted by the author

Interviews with Al Sa‘ud family members and other Sa‘udi interviewees were carried out between early 2010 and early 2013. The interviews were all pre-arranged, and took place in Riyadh or Jiddah (unless specified otherwise). Formal positions held by members of the ruling family are not included here to avoid repetition.

Al Sa‘ud Family Members (alphabetical)

HRH Prince ‘Abdul ‘Aziz bin Turki al-Faysal
Jiddah, 23 October 2010.

HRH Prince ‘Abdul Rahman al-Faysal
Riyadh, 13 October 2010.

HRH Prince ‘Amr bin Muhammad al-Faysal
Jiddah, 5 October 2010.

HRH Prince Bandar al-Faysal
Riyadh, 15 October 2010, 28 March 2011.

HRH Princess al-Bandari bint ‘Abdul Rahman al-Faysal
Riyadh, 15 October 2010, 27 March 2011.

HRH Prince Faysal bin Turki al-Faysal
Jiddah, 23 October, 2010.

HRH Princess Hayfah al-Faysal
Jiddah, 16 October 2010, 25 October 2010.

HRH Princess Hayfah bint Sa‘ud al-Faysal
Riyadh, 16 October 2010.

HRH Khalid bin Sa‘ud bin Khalid Al Sa‘ud
Riyadh, 27 October 2010.

HRH Princess Latifah al-Faysal
Jiddah, 12 October 2010.

HRH Princess Lulwah al-Faysal
Jiddah, 17 October 2010, 25 October 2010, 27 October 2010.

HRH Princess Lulwah bint Bandar bin Sultan bin ʿAbdul ʿAziz
Jiddah, 16 October 2010.

HRH Princess Mashaʿil bint Turki al-Faysal
Riyadh, 14 October 2010.

HRH Princess Nurah bint Saʿud bin ʿAbdul Muhsin
Jiddah, 27 October 2010.

HRH Princess Nurah bint Turki al-Faysal
Jiddah, 17 October 2010, 8 November 2010, 12 December 2010, 11 March 2011.

HRH Princess Rimah bint Bandar bin Sultan
Riyadh, 26 October 2010.

HRH Prince Saʿud al-Faysal
Riyadh, 26 October 2010.

HRH Prince Saʿud bin ʿAbdul Rahman al-Faysal
Riyadh, 14 October 2010.

HRH Princess Sarah al-Faysal
Riyadh, 13 October 2010.

HRH Princess Sarah bint ʿAbdul Rahman al-Faysal
Riyadh, 14 October 2010.

HRH Prince Talal bin ʿAbdul ʿAziz Al Saʿud
Riyadh, 19 February 2013.

HRH Prince Turki al-Faysal
Riyadh, 16 October 2010, 30 March 2011, and 16 October 2011.

HH Mansour Al Thunayan
Jiddah, 22 October 2010, 19 March 2011, and 14 March 2012.

Other Sa'udi Interviewees (alphabetical)

Ahmad 'Abdul Wahab
Chief of Protocol, 1964–2005
Jiddah, 20 October 2010.

Shaykh Faysal Kamal Adham
Nephew of Queen 'Iffat, Businessman
Jiddah, 7 November 2010, 9 December 2011.

Marianne Alireza
Friend of Queen 'Iffat, Author
Jiddah, 14 September 2011, 6 November 2010.

Nadia Alireza,
Director, Maharat Center
Jiddah, 14 September 2011, 6 November 2010, 30 March 2011.

Christina Epolito
Formal Palace Staff Member
Jiddah, 16 October 2010.

Munah al-Fadli
Jam'iyyah al-Khayriyyah fi Jiddah [Benevolent Society of Jiddah]
Jiddah, 22 March 2011.

'Abdallah al-Ghamdi
Formal Palace Staff Member
Jiddah, 7 November 2010.

Dakhil Allah al-Harthy
Formal Palace Staff Member
Jiddah, 25 November 2010.

Nisrin Al-Idriss
Director of Public Relations, Women's Charitable Society
Jiddah, 20 March 2011.

Shaykh Jamil al-Hujaylan
Secretary-General of the Gulf Cooperation Council (1996–2002). Ambassador to France (1976–1999), Ambassador to the Federal Republic of Germany (1973–1976); Minister of Health in King Faysal's Cabinet (1970–1974); Minister of Information (1964–1970), and

Ambassador to Kuwait (1960–1963)
Riyadh, 19 March 2012.

Mahah Ahmad al-Juffali
Executive Director and Supervising Trustee, Help Center
Jiddah, 23 October 2010, 8 December 2010.

Su'ad Husayni [Hussayni] al-Juffali
President, Board of Trustees, Help Center
Jiddah, 23 October 2010, 7 November 2010.

Rottana Khayat
Effat University Graduate
Jiddah, 14 March 2011.

Fayzah 'Abdallah Kayyal
Dar al-Hanan Assistant Principal
Jiddah, 8 December 2010.

Hayfah Jamal al-Layl, PhD
President, Effat University
Jiddah, 12 December 2010, 16 March 2011.

Khalid Al Maeena
Editor-in-Chief, *Arab News*
Jiddah, 12 October 2010, 11 September 2011.

Raghad Musli
Effat University Graduate
Jiddah, 20 March 2011.

Halah Rifa'at
Niece of Queen 'Iffat
Jiddah, 24 October 2010.

Cécile Rushdy
President, Dar Al Hanan School
Jiddah, 12 October 2010, and 8 November 2010.

Dr. 'Abdallah 'Abdul 'Aziz al-Salman
Director of Protocol, Public Relations and Information
King Khalid Eye Hospital
Riyadh, 29 March 2011.

Safanah Sayjani
Effat University Graduate
Jiddah, 12 March 2011.

Sarah Sharaf
Effat University Graduate
Jiddah, 13 March 2011.

Muluk Al Shaykh
Effat University Graduate
Jiddah, 12 March 2011.

Hussayn Shukri
Queen ‘Iffat Attorney
Jiddah, 21 October 2010.

Kamal Hussayn Shukri, PhD
Queen ‘Iffat Attorney
Jiddah, 29 March 2011.

Safanah Sijayni
Effat University Graduate
Jiddah, 12 March 2011.

Nahid Tahir, PhD
Founder and Chief Executive Officer, Gulf Once Investment Bank
Jiddah, 27 March 2011.

Hassan Yassin
Counselor to Foreign Minister Sa‘ud al-Faysal
Riyadh, 29 March 2011.

Sabah Yassin, Member al-Nahdah Women's Charitable Society
Jiddah, 20 March 2011

‘Arij Abu Zarifah
Effat University Graduate
Jiddah, 19 March 2011.

Wad Abu Zunadah
Effat University Graduate
Jiddah, 23 March 2011.

Appendix II

The late Queen's passport and various visas

The following pages provide a small selection of the entire document. The front pages of the passport give specific reference to the late Queen's title; notable is the exemption of a photograph.

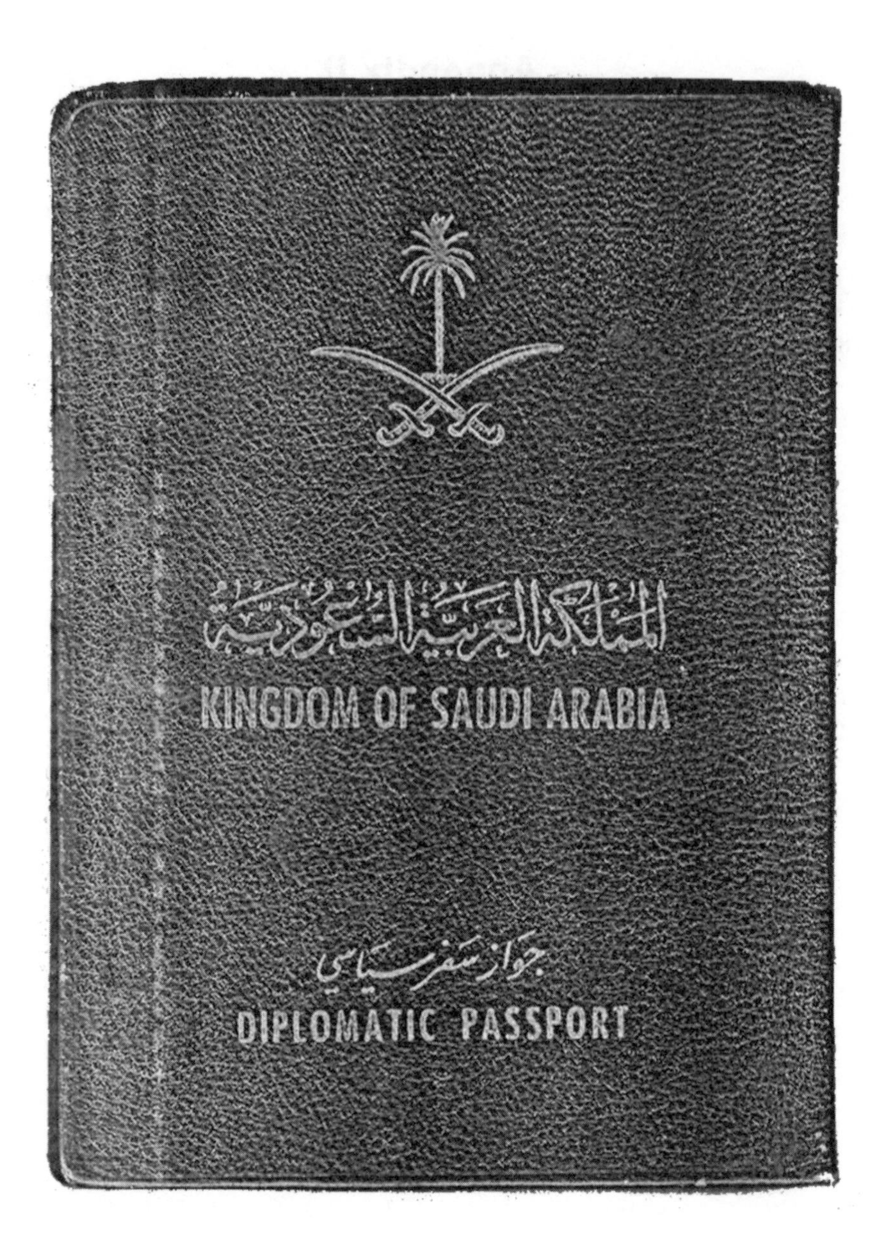
المملكة العربية السعودية
KINGDOM OF SAUDI ARABIA
جواز سفر سياسي
DIPLOMATIC PASSPORT

المملكة العربية السعودية

KINGDOM OF SAUDI ARABIA

وزارة الخارجية

MINISTRY OF FOREIGN AFFAIRS

جواز سفر سياسي

DIPLOMATIC PASSPORT

Passport No. 260-92 ٩٢-٢٦٠ رقم الجواز

اسم حامل الجواز صاحبة الجلالة الملكة عفت فيصل حرم صاحب الجلالة الملك فيصل بن عبد العزيز المعظم

Name of bearer HER MAJESTY QUEEN EFFAT FAISAL WIFE OF HIS MAJESTY KING FAISAL BIN ABDUL AZIZ LATE

-١-

تعليمات

بشأن الجواز السياسي

١ - تصدر الجوازات السياسية من وزارة الخارجية

٢ - في حالة فقد الجواز السياسي او تلفه يقتضي اشعار وزارة الخارجية في الحال، او اخطار اقرب سفارة او مفوضية او قنصلية للمملكة العربية السعودية .

٣ - يصلح الجواز السياسي الى حين العودة من السفر . وحين العودة يسلم الى دائرة الجوازات لايصاله الى وزارة الخارجية مباشرة .

٤ - تجدد صلاحية الجواز السياسي من قبل وزارة الخارجية .

٥ - لا تجوز اضافة اسم بلد جديد او اسماء اشخاص او زيادة صفحات على هذا الجواز الا من قبل وزارة الخارجية فقط .

KINGDOM OF SAUDI ARABIA

In the name of His Majesty the King

This is to require all civil and military officials in the Kingdom of Saudi Arabia, and to request the Competent Authorities in all Friendly Governments to allow bearer to pass freely without let or hindrance, and to afford him every assistance and protection.

This passport is valid until return from abroad.

Issued at JEDDAH on 16-7-1972

Minister of Foreign Affairs

-٣-

المملكة العربية السعودية

باسم جلالة الملك

اطلب من جميع الموظفين الملكيين والعسكريين في المملكة العربية السعودية، وارجو من السلطات المختصة في سائر الحكومات الصديقة ان يسمحوا لحامل هذا الجواز بحرية المرور وان يسهلوا اسباب سفره ويبذلوا له كل ما ينبغي من مساعدة ورعاية .

صدر هذا الجواز في جدة

بتاريخ ١٣٩٢/٦/٥ الموافق ١٦/٧/٧٢

ويعمل به لحين العودة من السفر .

وزير الخارجية

-٢-

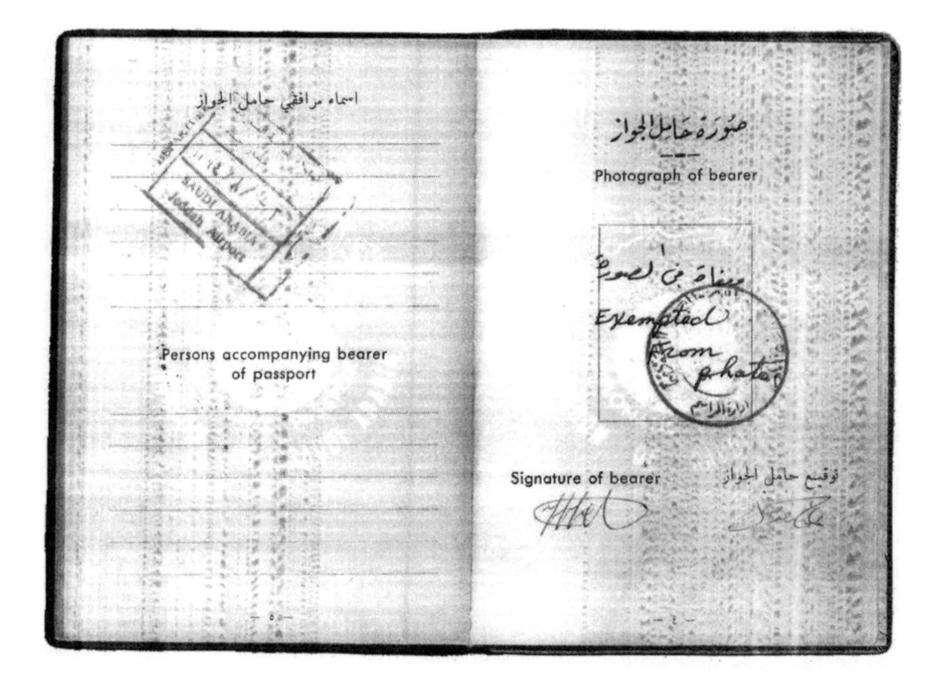
اسماء مرافقي حامل الجواز

SAUDI ARABIA
Jeddah Airport

Persons accompanying bearer of passport

— ٥ —

صورة حامل الجواز

Photograph of bearer

معفاة من الصورة
Exempted from photo

Signature of bearer

توقيع حامل الجواز

— ٤ —

Renewals التجديدات

جدد هذا الجواز في ١٣/٧/٩٢

الموافق ٢٨/٨/٧٢

Renewed on 28/8/1973

جدد هذا الجواز في ١٥/٧/٩٣

الموافق ٢/٨/٧٤م

Renewed on 3.8.1974

— ٧ —

البلاد التي يعمل بها هذا الجواز

البلدان العربية - آسيا - أفريقيا
اوربا - المملكة المتحدة -
الولايات المتحدة الأمريكية

Countries for which this passport is valid

ARAB COUNTRIES-
ASIA - AFRICA - EUROPE
U.K. U.S.A.

— ٦ —

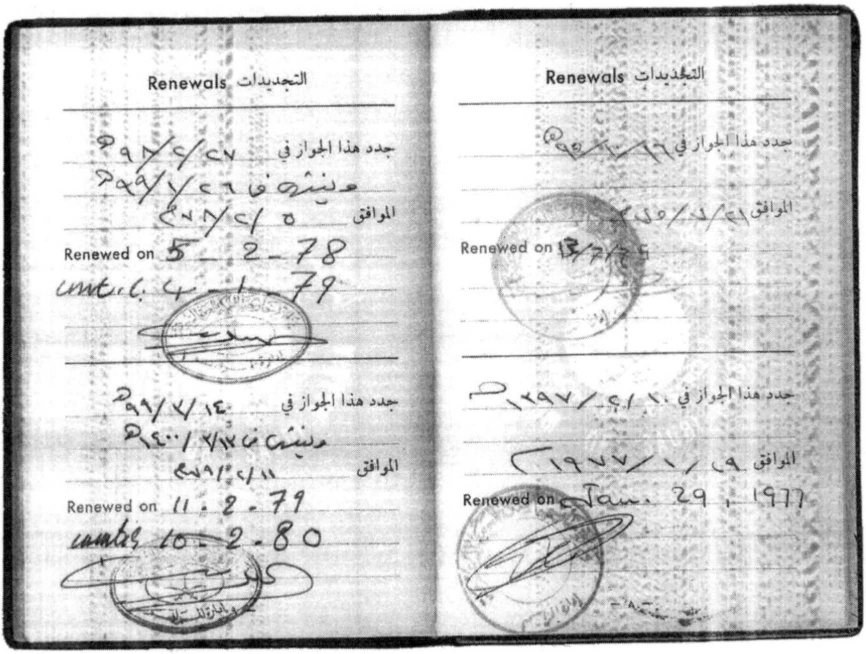

Renewals التجديدات

جدد هذا الجواز في

الموافق

Renewed on 5 - 2 - 78

until 4 - 1 - 79

جدد هذا الجواز في

الموافق

Renewed on 11 - 2 - 79

until 10 - 2 - 80

Renewals التجديدات

جدد هذا الجواز في

الموافق

Renewed on 13/7/76

جدد هذا الجواز في

الموافق

Renewed on Jan. 29, 1977

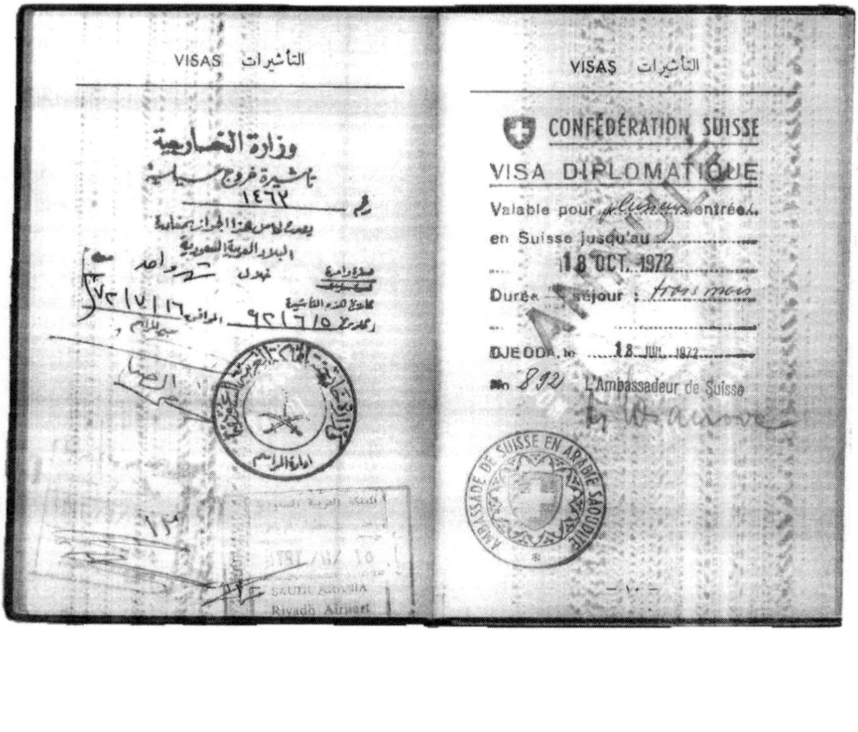

VISAS التأشيرات

وزارة الخارجية

تأشيرة خروج سياسية

رقم ١٤٦٢

VISAS التأشيرات

CONFÉDÉRATION SUISSE

VISA DIPLOMATIQUE

Valable pour plusieurs entrées

en Suisse jusqu'au 18 OCT. 1972

Durée du séjour : trois mois

DJEDDA, le 18 JUIL. 1972

No 892 L'Ambassadeur de Suisse

AMBASSADE DE SUISSE EN ARABIE SAOUDITE

SAUDI ARABIA

Riyadh Airport

VISAS التأشيرات

DIPLOMATIC VISA 366/72

Gratis
Official Courtesy

SEEN
AT THE BRITISH EMBASSY
(Consular Section)
JEDDA

Good for single journey to the United Kingdom within three months of date hereof if passport remains valid.

Date 19 JUL 1972

BRITISH EMBASSY CONSULAR SECTION 4 JEDDA

VISAS التأشيرات

VISA DIPLOMATIQUE

AMBASSADE DE FRANCE
EN ARABIE SAOUDITE

VISA No. 274
Valable pour plusieurs voyages
Aller et retour en France et un séjour de trois mois
Utilisable jusqu'au 16 décembre 1972
A Djeddah le 17 juillet 1972

24 JUIL 1972 FRANCE

AFFAIRES ÉTRANGÈRES GRATIS

AMBASSADE DE FRANCE A DJEDDAH

L'Ambassadeur de France
en Arabie Séoudite

VISAS التأشيرات

VISA DIPLOMATIQUE

AMBASSADE DE FRANCE
EN ARABIE SAOUDITE

VISA No. 519
Valable pour plusieurs voyages
Aller et retour en France et un séjour de six mois
Utilisable jusqu'au 27 AVR. 1974
A Djeddah le 28 AOUT 1973

18 OCT

L'Ambassadeur de France
en Arabie Séoudite

AMBASSADE DE FRANCE A DJEDDAH

AFFAIRES ÉTRANGÈRES GRATIS

VISAS التأشيرات

وزارة الخارجية

Jeddah Airport

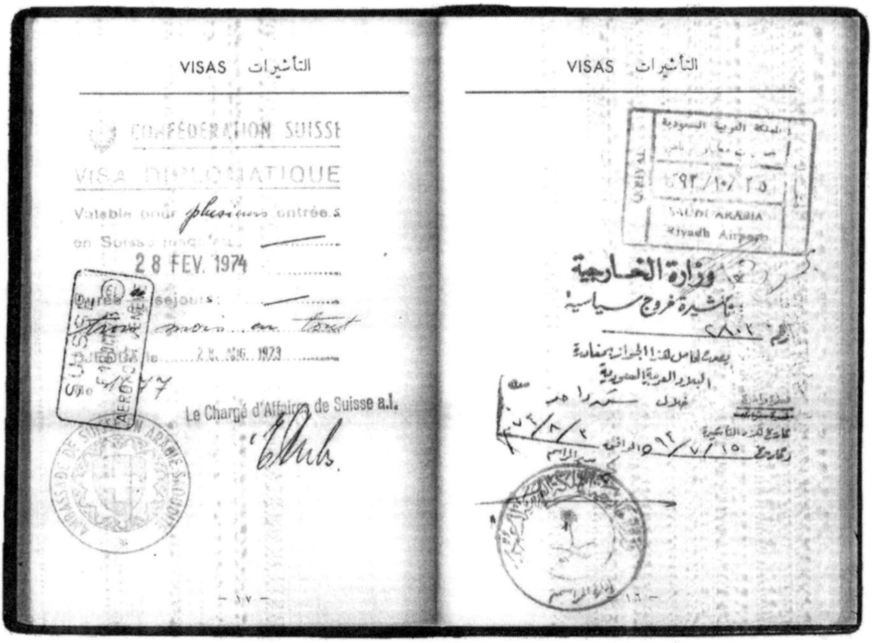

VISAS التأشيرات

CONFÉDÉRATION SUISSE

VISA DIPLOMATIQUE

Valable pour plusieurs entrées

en Suisse jusqu'au

28 FEV. 1974

Durée des séjours: trois mois en tout

Djeddah le 28. AUG. 1973

Le Chargé d'Affaires de Suisse a.i.

VISAS التأشيرات

SAUDI ARABIA

Riyadh Airport

وزارة الخارجية

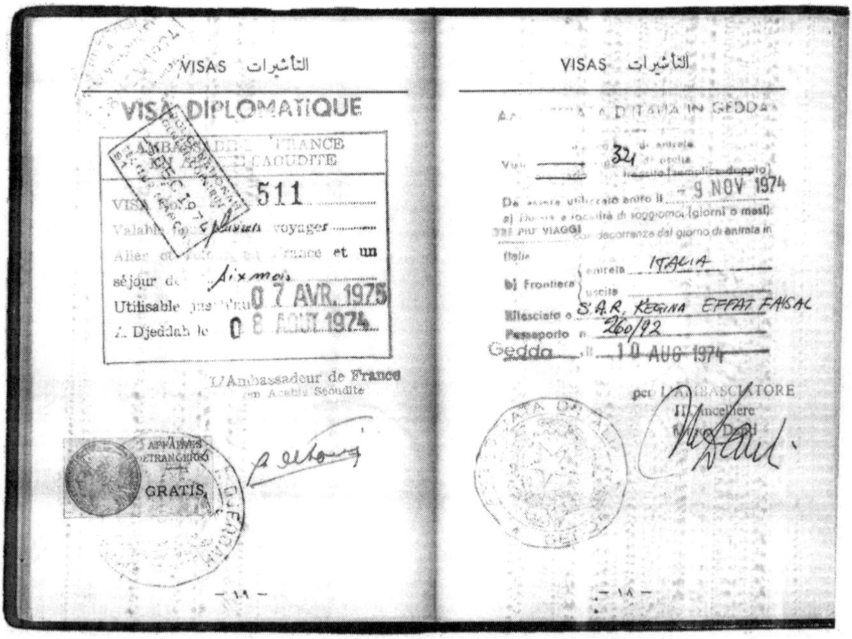

تأشيرة خروج سياسية

VISAS التأشيرات

VISA DIPLOMATIQUE

AMBASSADE DE FRANCE EN ARABIE SAOUDITE

VISA No 511

Valable pour plusieurs voyages

séjour de six mois

Utilisable jusqu'au 07 AVR. 1975

A Djeddah le 08 AOUT 1974

L'Ambassadeur de France en Arabie Seoudite

AFFAIRES ETRANGERES

GRATIS

VISAS التأشيرات

D'ITALIA IN GEDDA

321

9 NOV 1974

PIU' VIAGGI

b) Frontiera entrata ITALIA

Rilasciato a S.A.R. REGINA EFFAT FAISAL

Passaporto n. 260/92

Gedda il 10 AUG 1974

per L'AMBASCIATORE

Il Cancelliere

VISAS التأشيرات

CONFÉDÉRATION SUISSE

VISA DIPLOMATIQUE

SUISSE
E 18NOV.74
AEROPORT GENEVE

plusieurs entrées

10 FEV. 1975

Trois mois en tout

JEDDA, le 10 AUG 1974

No 1822

Le Chargé d'Affaires de Suisse a.i.

— ٢١ —

VISAS التأشيرات

VISADO DIPLOMATICO

EMBAJADA DE ESPAÑA EN YEDDAH

VISADO DE ENTRADA 90 DIAS

N.° 9A3/1974

Visto en esta embajada, válido para permanecer noventa dias en España con derecho a entrar y salir tres veces dentro de dicho plazo, a contar de la fecha de su primera entrada.

Este visado caduca, sino es utilizado a los tres meses de la fecha de su expedición.

Yeddah, a 11 AUG 1974

El Embajador de España

EMBAJADA DE ESPAÑA

El Canciller

— ٢٠ —

VISAS التأشيرات

ENTRY

المملكة العربية السعودية

جوازات مطار جدة

٢ /١٢/ ١٣٩٤

SAUDI ARABIA
Jeddah Airport

— ٢٣ —

VISAS التأشيرات

8398/74

SEEN at the British Embassy (Consular Section)

Jedda

Good for journeys to

United Kingdom

within six months of date hereof if passport remains valid.

(Signed)

Date 12 AUG 1974

BRITISH EMBASSY CONSULAR SECTION JEDDA

— ٢٢ —

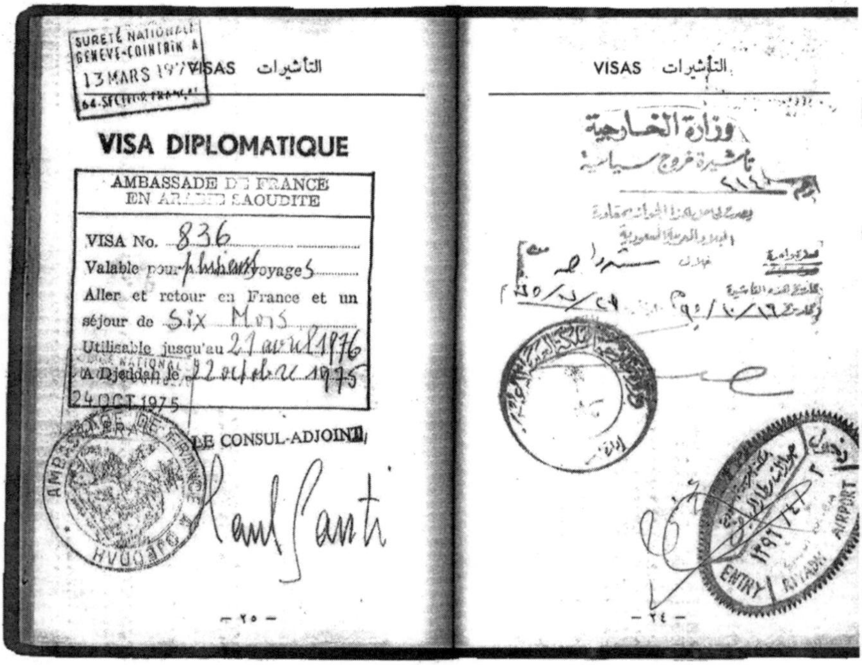

SURETÉ NATIONALE GENEVE-COINTRIN A 13 MARS 1977

VISAS التأشيرات

VISA DIPLOMATIQUE

AMBASSADE DE FRANCE EN ARABIE SAOUDITE

VISA No. 836

Valable pour plusieurs voyages

Aller et retour en France et un séjour de Six Mois

Utilisable jusqu'au 21 avril 1976

A Djeddah le 22 octobre 1975

24 OCT 1975

LE CONSUL-ADJOINT

AMBASSADE DE FRANCE

— ٢٥ —

VISAS التأشيرات

وزارة الخارجية

تأشيرة خروج سياسية

ENTRY RIYADH AIRPORT

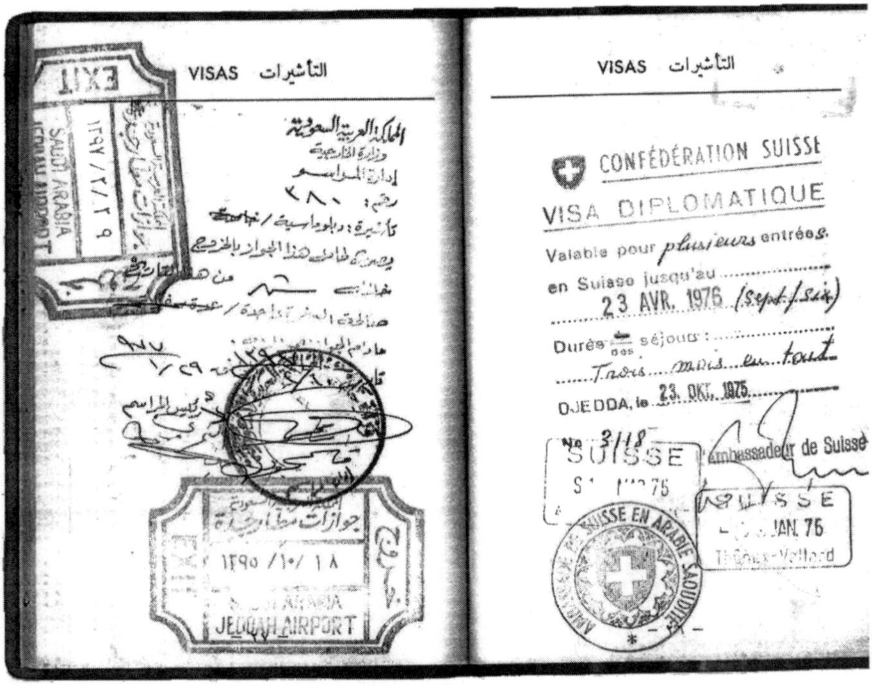

— ٢٤ —

EXIT

SAUDI ARABIA JEDDAH AIRPORT

VISAS التأشيرات

المملكة العربية السعودية

JEDDAH AIRPORT

VISAS التأشيرات

CONFÉDÉRATION SUISSE

VISA DIPLOMATIQUE

Valable pour plusieurs entrées

en Suisse jusqu'au 23 AVR. 1976 (Sept./six)

Durée des séjours: Trois mois en tout

DJEDDA, le 23. OKT. 1975.

No 3/18

l'Ambassadeur de Suisse

SUISSE

JAN. 76

AMBASSADE DE SUISSE EN ARABIE SAOUDITE

Appendix III

‘Iffat Al Thunayan’s Ottoman identity card

Queen ‘Iffat Al Thunayan’s Ottoman identity card, which provides her name, the names of her parents, Asia and Muhammad Sa‘ud, her birthday (1329 H, 1916 CE), nationality (Turkish) and religion (Muslim).

هويت جزدانى

سجل نفوس قانوننك بعض موادى

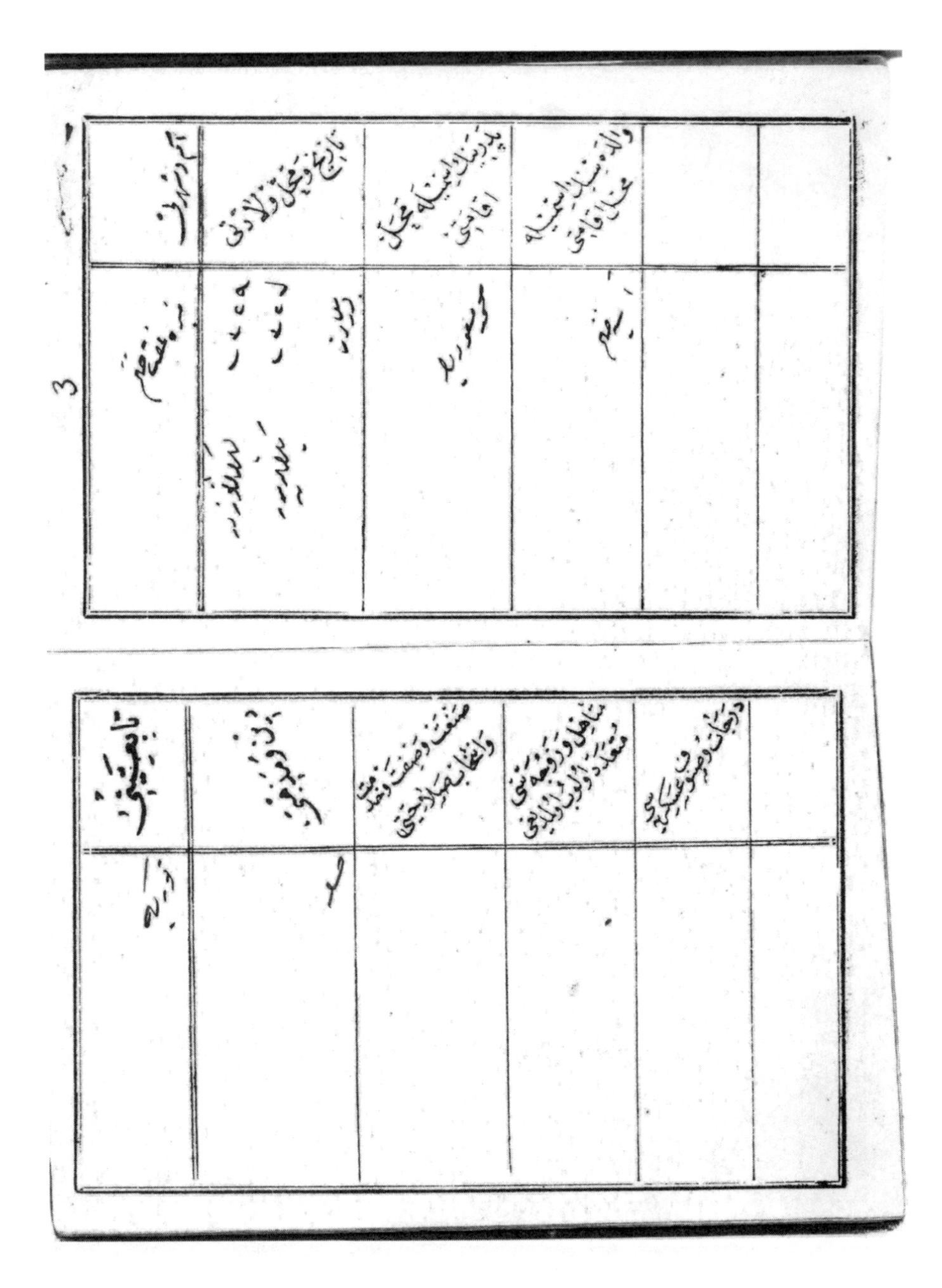

اشکال مخصوصه	
بوی	
صاچ	
قاش	
کوز	
بورون	
آغز	
بیق	
صقال	
چکه	
چهره	
رنك	
علامت فارقهٔ ثابته	

سجل نفوسه قید اولندیغی محل	
ولایتی	[illegible]
قضاسی	[illegible]
ناحیه سی	
محله و یا قریه سی	[illegible]
زقاغی	[illegible]
مسکن نومروسی	١٣
نوع مسکن	[illegible]
	[illegible]

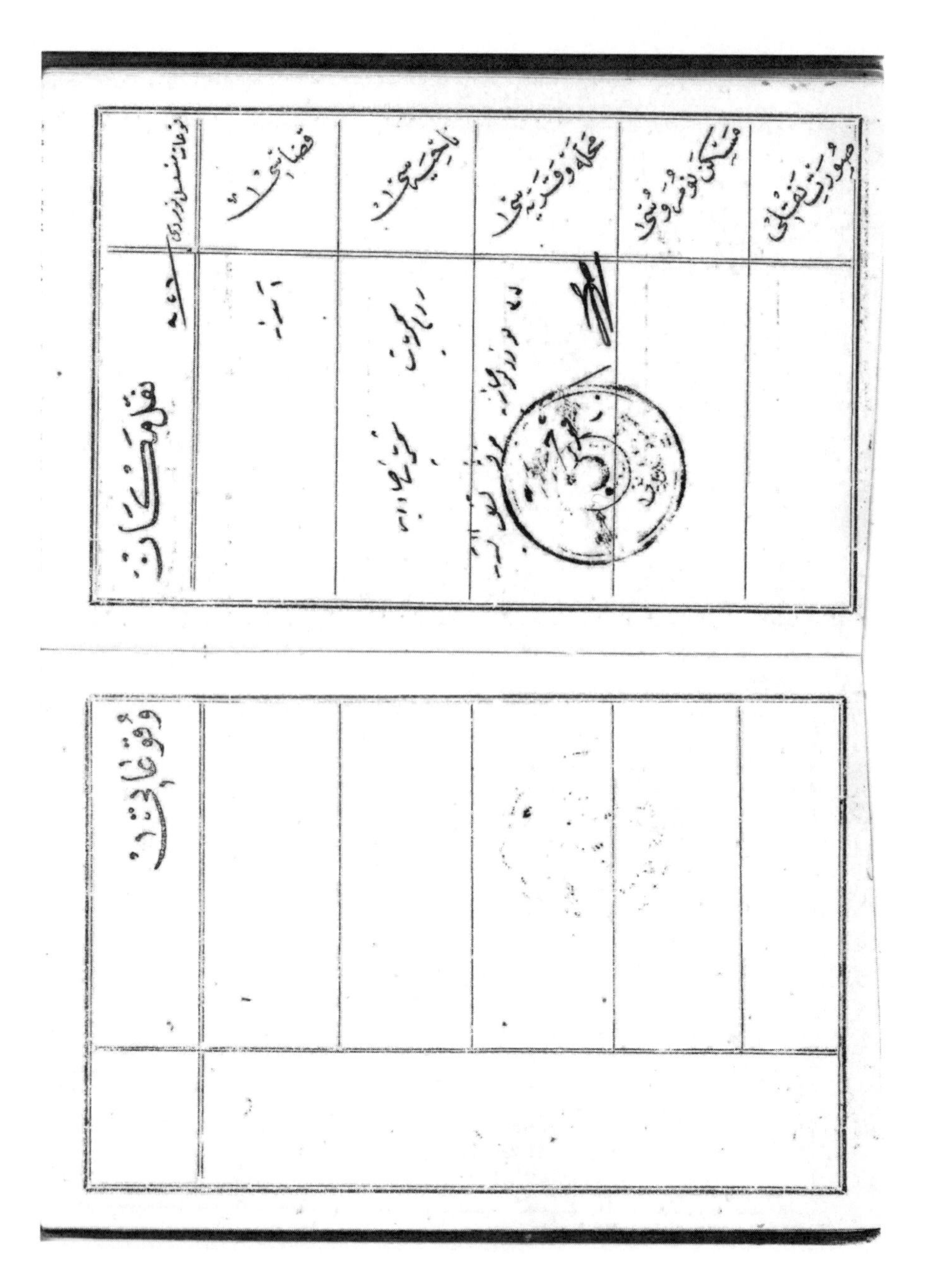

Appendix IV

'Iffat's Letters to King Fahd and Heir Apparent 'Abdallah asking for support

As discussed in Chapter 3, the queen recorded the progress achieved by women in the Kingdom under the ruler's reign; described her work with the non-profit institution and explained how she took the initiative to follow-up on a 3 June 1997 [18 Safar 1418 H] Council of Ministers decision that authorized the public sector to establish universities and colleges; and requested a license for the *'Iffat Women's College* under the patronage of the King Faysal Foundation. Both letters carry her legendary signature, 'Iffat al-Faysal, which is revelatory as it emphasizes her Faysal credentials.

بسم الله الرحمن الرحيم

المملكة العربية السعودية
قصر جلالة المرحوم الملك
فيصل بن عبدالعزيز آل سعود

الرقم ٢/١٠٩/٩٨..........
التاريخ ١٤١٠٩/١٠/٢٠٩هـ..
المرفقات ....

صاحب السمو الملكي الأمير عبدالله بن عبدالعزيز حفظه الله ورعاه
ولي العهد والنائب الأول لرئيس مجلس الوزراء ورئيس الحرس الوطني

السلام عليكم ورحمة الله وبركاته وبعد – أود أن أعرض لسموكم أنه بمناسبة صدور توصية مقام مجلس الوزراء الموقر فى جلسته المنعقدة يوم الإثنين ١٨ صفر ١٤١٨هـ الموافق ٣ يونيو ١٩٩٧م بتمكين القطاع الأهلي من إقامة مؤسسات تعليمية لاتهدف إلى الربح على أسس إدارية وعلمية وإقتصادية ومالية سليمة ، بغرض المساهمة فى تلبية إحتياجات التنمية مكملة بذلك ماتقوم به الجامعات الحكومية وتشجيع القطاع الأهلى على المساهمة فى تمويل برامج ومراكز ومنح دراسية وفق ضوابط تنظم ذلك وتسيره ٠٠٠ فقد تشرفت برفع طلب إلى مقام خادم الحرمين الشريفين ، ألتمس فيه الموافقة على إنشاء جامعة أهلية للبنات بمقر مدارس دار الحنان بجدة تحت رعاية مؤسسة الملك فيصل الخيرية ، حيث أن النظام الأساسي للمؤسسة يسمح ضمن أغراضها بإنشاء الجامعات ٠٠ وقد تم بالفعل التبرع بالأرض والمباني والتجهيزات الخاصة بهذا الكيان التعليمي – دار الحنان – والبالغ قيمتها حوالى (٣٠٠) ثلاثمائة مليون ريال إلى مؤسسة الملك فيصل الخيرية ٠

ومما يسعدني ويثلج خاطرى ياصاحب السمو أن مؤسسة دار الحنان التى كنت قد قمت بإنشائها بدافع من شعورى بولائى وواجبى نحو هذا البلد العزيز المعطاء ، وأهله الكرام ، وعرفاناً منى بما أغدقه عليّ من جميل وطيب مقام ٠٠ كانت هي أول مدرسة تفتح أبوابها لإستقبال بناتنا المتلهفات على طلب العلم والمعرفة ٠٠ وهي مؤسسة لم تسع منذ إنشائها فيما تمارسه من نشاط تربوى وتعليمى ، لتحقيق أي ربح أو منفعة خاصة ٠٠

ودار الحنان فى موقعها الجديد بمدينة جدة ، أقيمت على مساحة تبلغ حوالى تسعين ألف متر مربع ، وتتكون من عدد من المبانى المنفصلة المخصصة لأغراض مختلفة ، تحتوى على قاعات دراسية تسع (٢٠٠٠) طالبة متوفرة فيها ولها المعامل المتكاملة والمعدات والأدوات بالإضافة إلى مكتبة رئيسية ، ومسجد للصلاة ، ومركز للمهن والأشغال النسوية ، ومركز للخدمات الصحية مع مرافقه اللآزمة ، وقاعة محاضرات تتسع لعدد (٧٥٠) طالبة ، ومركز مكشوف للتربية البدنية للفتيات يتسع لعدد (١٥٠٠) طالبة ، وأيضا قاعات للألعاب الرياضية

بسم الله الرحمن الرحيم

المملكة العربية السعودية
قصر جلالة المرحوم الملك
فيصل بن عبدالعزيز آل سعود

الرقم ....
التاريخ ....
المرفقات ....

- ٢ -

المختلفة ، بالإضافة إلى صالة رئيسية للطعام ، هذا إلى جانب توفُّر سَكَن خاص للطالبات ، وسَكَن آخر للمُدرسات ، ومبانٍ أخرى مُخصصة للإدارة والسكرتارية ، إلى جانب المطبخ والمغسلة والمخازن وجراج السيارات ، وتمتلك أيضا عددا من السيارات وورش الصيانة .

كما تحتوى أيضا على مركز للأعداد للخدمة العامة والتعليم المستمر ، يُنظم دورات أكاديمية فى : تعليم أصول المحادثة والمخاطبة باللغة الإنجليزية بصفة عامة ، وما تعلق منها خاصة بممارسة أوجه النشاط المختلفة فى مجالات العمل بالتمريض ، والأعمال الإدارية .. الخ .. وكذلك فى إعداد الراغبات فى الإشتراك فى إمتحانات اللغة الإنجليزية المعروفة بـ : "توفل – بيت – إف سى إي – كيت (TOEFL-PET-FCE-KET)" .. وكذلك تعليم اللغة العربية لغير الناطقين بها (فُصْحَى كانت أو عامية) .. وغير ذلك من دراسات إسلامية لغير الناطقين بالعربية .. وأيضا التدريب على دورات كمبيوتر باللغة العربية لنُظم : "مقدمة الحاسب الآلى ، دوس ، خرائط التدفق ، معالجة الكلمات ، وإدارة قواعد البيانات / إكسس – ويندوز." .

ويُنظم هذا المركز أيضا دورات غير أكاديمية متعددة ، وكذلك " دورات تقدم بالتعاون مع مركز تعليم الكبار والتعليم المستمر بالجامعة الأمريكية بالقاهرة " ، "ودورات تقدم بالتعاون مع جامعة كمبردج فى بريطانيا" ، "ودورات تقدم بالتعاون مع المركز السعودى الفرنسى بجدة" ، "ودورات تقدم بالتعاون مع جامعة الملك عبدالعزيز بجدة" .

ولقد كان الهدف من إعداد هذه المبانى بهذه التجهيزات فى حينه على النحو المذكور ، هو الأمل فى أن تكون مقراً لجامعةٍ أهلية للبنات ، عندما يحين الوقت المناسب ... وبفضل من الله وتوفيقه فقد آن الأوان لأن يبزغ الأمل إلى عالم الحقيقة ، ويرى الضوء فى أقرب فرصة بمشيئة الله وتوفيقه .

وبتاريخ ١٤١٨/١٢/١٥هـ ، رَفَعْتُ طلباً ثانياً إلى مقام خادم الحرمين الشريفين (المرفق طيه صورة منه) ، للموافقة على تعديل مُسَمَّى الكيان التعليمى ليُصْبح " **كلية عفت الأهلية للبنات – برعاية مؤسسة الملك فيصل الخيرية** " وذلك تمشياً مع توصية مقام مجلس الوزراء بإنشاء كليات أهلية .

وتَشْمل هذه الكلية الأقسام الآتية :–

١ – قسم الصيدلة
٢ – قسم الحاسب الآلى ونظم المعلومات .
٣ – قسم اللغات والعلوم الإنسانية .. ويشتمل على شعبة علم النفس التربوى .. وشعبة رياض الأطفال .. وشعبة اللغة الإنجليزية والترجمة ، ويمكن أن يشمل شعبا أخرى مستقبلا إن شاء الله .
٤ – قسم العلوم الطبية التطبيقية ، ويشتمل على شعبة المختبرات الطبية الإكلينيكية ويمكن أن يشمل شعبا أخرى مستقبلا إن شاء الله .

بسم الله الرحمن الرحيم

المملكة العربية السعودية
قصر جلالة المرحوم الملك
فيصل بن عبد العزيز آل سعود

الرقم ....
التاريخ ....
المرفقات ....

- ٣ -

هذا وكان قد تَمّ العمل خِلال الأحد عشر شهراً الماضية لوضع توصية مجلس الوزراء الموقر مَوْضِعَ التنفيذ حيث أُعِدت الدراسات والإستشارات والخُطوات اللآزمة لذلك على النحو الآتى :-

(١) قام مكتب للإستشارات الإدارية بإجراء دراسة إستطلاعية للتعرف على إحتياجات مُجْتمع محافظة جدة لخدمات التعليم الأهلى الجامعى للبنات .

(٢) قام فريق عمل من أساتذة الجامعات بالمملكة بإعداد نظام الكلية الأساسى وهياكلها الإدارية واللوائح المختلفة ، مثل لائحة الدراسة والإختبارات – لائحة شئون أعضاء هيئة التدريس – لائحة شئون المتعاقدين – لائحة شئون الطالبات – لائحة الشئون المالية .. الخ ..

(٣) قام فريق عمل آخر من المختصين بالتعرف على تجارب وأنظمة التعليم الأهلى الجامعى فى الدول العربية ، وتم إعداد دراسة تحليلية مقارنة لبعض الجامعات الأهلية فى دول المنطقة (الإمارات العربية المتحدة – لبنان – الأردن – مصر) لتُساعد فى وَضْع التصور النهائى للكلية الأهلية بجدة إن شاء الله .

(٤) قام فريق من الإستشاريين الهندسيين بإعداد تقييم مفصل لكافة المنشآت والمرافق القائمة فى الموقع المقترح للكلية وإعداد توصياتهم بشأن تجهيزها لإستيعاب الأقسام المختلفة مع كافة متطلباتها التعليمية والتشغيلية لكل تخصص على حده .

(٥) تم أيضا إعداد الدراسة المالية والإقتصادية التى روعى فيها أنه إلى جانب التبرع الكامل بالمبانى بمنشآتها ومعداتها وتجهيزاتها الكاملة إلى الكلية ، فإن تمويل رأس المال العامل سيكون على عاتق بعضا من أبناء وطننا الغالى فى المرحلة الأولى ، وأما بعد ذلك فسيكون من التدفقات المتوقعة من دخل الكلية .

(٦) وقد تم أيضا إعداد المناهج الدراسية لأقسام الكلية المختلفة المشار إليها بعاليه .

إن الهدف إن شاء الله من هذه الكلية هو إتاحة الفرصة لعدد أكبر من المواطنات الناشئات للحصول على الشهادات الجامعية بالمناهج العلمية المتطورة والأساليب العملية الحديثة التى ستحرص الكلية إن شاء الله على توفيرها ، والتى تبتغى تهيئة وإعداد الفتاة السعودية .. الملتزمة بيقين العقيدة .. والمتحلية بسمات مجتمعنا الإسلامى العربى الأصيل .

بسم الله الرحمن الرحيم

المملكة العربية السعودية
قصر جلالة المرحوم الملك
فيصل بن عبد العزيز آل سعود

الرقم ....
التاريخ ....
المرفقات ....

- ٤ -

سمو الأمير

إنه بفضل رعاية مولاي خادم الحرمين الشريفين ورعاية سموكم الكريم لهذا الوطن الكريم وأهله ، وبفضل ماحظيت به بنات وطننا من رعاية خاصة كريمة ، يحدوني الأمل – إن شاء الله – في أن يبزغ أمل إنشاء هذه الكلية إلى عالم الحقيقة بفضل كريم رعايتكم ومساندتكم .

سدد الله خطاكم .. وجعل التوفيق حليفكم .. والله ولي التوفيق ..

عفت بنت محمد الثنيان

حرم المغفور له الملك فيصل بن عبدالعزيز

بسم الله الرحمن الرحيم

المملكة العربية السعودية
قصر جلالة المرحوم الملك
فيصل بن عبد العزيز آل سعود

الرقم ....
التاريخ ....
المرفقات ....

مولاي خادم الحرمين الشريفين الملك فهد بن عبدالعزيز سلمه الله ورعاه

السلام عليكم ورحمة الله وبركاته وبعد

فإن ماحظيت به المرأه السعودية فى عهد مقامكم الكريم من عناية خاصة من حيث تهيئة الفرص لتعليمها وتأهيلها للعمل فى المجالات المناسبة لدورها فى مجتمعنا الإسلامى ، كان له أكبر الأثر فى أن تكون المرأه السعودية مفخرة لبلدها بحصولها على أرقى الشهادات فى مختلف التخصصات وعملها فى المجالات العلمية والإجتماعية والإنسانية المتعددة فى إطار التقاليد الإسلامية الغراء التى تميز مجتمعنا السعودى .

ولقد سبق لى يامولاي أن ساهمت فى إنشاء " مؤسسة دار الحنان " بمدينة جدة كدار رعاية للفتيات اليتيمات والمحتاجات والتى إنبثق عنها أول دار علم تفتح أبوابها لإستقبال بناتنا السعوديات المتلهفات على طلب العلم والمعرفة ... وهذه المؤسسة منذ إنشائها وكما تعلمون - حفظكم الله - لاتسعى فيما تمارسه من نشاط تربوى أو تعليمى لتحقيق أي ربح أو منفعة خاصة .

وبمناسبة صدور توصية مقام مجلس الوزراء الموقر فى جلسته المنعقدة يوم الإثنين ١٨ صفر ١٤١٨هـ الموافق ٣ يونيو ١٩٩٧م بتمكين القطاع الأهلى من إقامة مؤسسات تعليمية لاتهدف إلى الربح على أسس إدارية وعلمية وإقتصادية ومالية سليمة ، بغرض المساهمة فى تلبية إحتياجات التنمية مكملة بذلك ماتقوم به الجامعات الحكومية ، وتشجيع القطاع الأهلى على المساهمة فى تمويل برامج ومراكز ومنح دراسية وفق ضوابط تنظم ذلك وتسيره .

وكما كان لى شرف إفتتاح أول دار علم للفتيات ، فإننى يامولاي - أدامكم الله - يحدونى الأمل أيضا فى إفتتاح أول جامعة أهلية للبنات بمحافظة جدة تحت رعاية مؤسسة المغفور له الملك فيصل الخيرية التى يجيز نظامها الأساسى مزاولة مثل هذا الغرض ، عملا خالصا لوجه الله تعالى دفعنى إليه شعورى بواجبى تجاه وطننا الغالى .. خاصة وأن الحاجة إلى مثل هذه الجامعة تتنامى بإستمرار مع تطور النمو السكانى ، وتزايد حاجة القطاعات الإقتصادية المختلفة بالمجتمع إلى طلب توفيرالعديد من المواطنين المتخصصين فى المجالات المختلفة من المؤهلين تأهيلا علميا عاليا .. وفى ضوء الزيادة السنوية فى أعداد الطلاب والطالبات ، الراغبين فى مواصلة تعليمهم الجامعى فإن الحاجة أصبحت ماسه فى أن ينهض القطاع الأهلى بتحمل أعباء مثل هذه المؤسسات الأكاديمية وفق ماجاء بتوصيه مقام مجلس الوزراء الموقر.

بسم الله الرحمن الرحيم

المملكة العربية السعودية
قصر جلالة المرحوم الملك
فيصل بن عبد العزيز آل سعود

الرقم ....
التاريخ ....
المرفقات ....

-٢-

والهدف إن شاء الله من هذه الجامعة هو إتاحة الفرصة لعدد أكبر من المواطنات الناشئات للحصول على الشهادات الجامعية بالمناهج العلمية المتطورة والأساليب العملية الحديثة التى ستحرص الجامعة إن شاء الله على توفيرها ، والتى تبتغى تهيئة وإعداد الفتاة السعودية ... الملتزمة بيقين العقيدة ... والمتحلية بسمات مجتمعنا الاسلامي العربي الأصيل ... حتى إذا ما إكتملت لها الأسباب ، وإجتازت مراحل التحصيل والاعداد ، كان عليها أن تشارك بعلمها وعملها ، في أي موقع يرتضيه لها ولاة أمرنا للنهوض بدولتنا المباركة .

وإذ يسمح لى مولاي أن أعرض على أنظاركم الكريمة بأن المبانى التى أنشأتها لتكون مقرا لمدارس دار الحنان قد روعي فى تصميمها وتنفيذها أن تحتوى على المنشآت والتجهيزات التى تسمح بإستيعاب مثل هذه المؤسسات التعليمية العالية ، على نحو ييسر أمر تحويلها لتكون مقرا لجامعة أهلية مكونة من عدة كليات ذات تخصصات مختلفة ، عندما يحين الوقت المناسب لتحقيق هذا الهدف السامى الكبير ..... فقد أقيمت هذه المنشآت ضمن أرض تبلغ مساحتها حوالى (٩٠,٠٠٠) تسعين ألف متر مربع بموقع متميز فى مدينة جدة ، وتتكون من عدد من المبان المنفصلة التى يمكن تخصيصها لأغراض تعليمية مختلفة ، والتى تحتوى على قاعات دراسية تسع (٢٠٠٠) طالبة تتوفر فيها المعامل المتكاملة والمعدات والأدوات اللآزمة لها ، بالإضافة إلى مكتبة رئيسية ، ومسجد للصلاة ومركز للمهن والأشغال النسوية ، ومركز للخدمات الصحية مع مرافقه اللآزمة ، وقاعة محاضرات تتسع لعدد (٧٥٠) طالبة مع جميع تجهيزاتها ، وأيضا قاعات مغلقة للتربية الرياضية المختلفة ، بالإضافة إلى صالة رئيسية للطعام ، هذا إلى جانب توفر سكن خاص للطالبات ، وآخر للمدرسات ، ومبان أخرى مخصصة للإدارة والسكرتارية ، إلى جانب المرافق الأخري المساندة لتشغيل هذه المباني وصيانتها .
ويبين التقرير الهندسي المرفق ، المدعم بالصور ، المباني والتجهيزات المشار اليها .

وها هو بفضل من الله وتوفيقه وبعد صدور التوصية الحكيمة لمجلس الوزراء الموقر ، قد آن الأوان لأن يبزغ الأمل إلى عالم الحقيقة ، ليرى الضوء علي أياديكم الجليلة فى أقرب فرصة بمشيئة الله وتوفيقه ثم بتوجيهات مولاي أدامكم الله .

هذا وقد تم العمل خلال الستة أشهر الماضية لوضع توصية مجلس الوزراء الموقر موضع التنفيذ حيث أعدت الدراسات والإستشارات التالية :

بسم الله الرحمن الرحيم

المملكة العربية السعودية
قصر جلالة المرحوم الملك
فيصل بن عبد العزيز آل سعود

الرقم ....
التاريخ ....
المرفقات ....

-٣-

(١) قام مكتب للإستشارات الإدارية بإجراء دراسة إستطلاعية للتعرف على إحتياجات مجتمع محافظة جدة لخدمات التعليم الأهلى الجامعى للبنات مع إعداد دراسة جدوي اقتصادية متكاملة لمشروع جامعه أهليه خيريه لاتهدف إلى الربح ·

(٢) قام فريق عمل من أساتذة الجامعات بالمملكة بإعداد نظام الجامعة الأساسى وهياكلها الإدارية واللوائح المختلفة ، مثل لآئحة الدراسة والإختبارات – لائحة شئون أعضاء هيئة التدريس – لائحة شئون المتعاقدين – لائحة شئون الطالبات – لائحة الشئون المالية ·· الخ ·

(٣) قام فريق عمل آخر من المختصين بالتعرف على تجارب وأنظمة التعليم الأهلى الجامعى فى الدول العربية ، وتم إعداد دراسة تحليلية مقارنة لبعض الجامعات الأهلية فى دول المنطقة (الإمارات العربية المتحدة – لبنان – الأردن – مصر) لتساعد فى وضع التصور النهائى للجامعة الأهلية بجدة إن شاء الله ·

(٤) قام فريق من الإستشاريين الهندسيين بإعداد تقييم مفصل لكافة المنشآت والمرافق القائمة فى الموقع المقترح للجامعة وإعداد توصياتهم بشأن تجهيزها لإستيعاب الكليات المختلفة مع كافة متطلباتها التعليمية والتشغيلية لكل تخصص على حده ·

(٥) جاري في الوقت ذاته اعداد المناهج الاكاديمية للتخصصات المقترحة لتكون كافة الدراسات الاقتصادية والتنظيمية والأكاديمية تحت أنظار مقامكم الكريم – رعاكم الله–.

(٦) دراسة إمكانية التعاون بين أحد الجامعات العالمية المعروفة وبين الجامعة الوليده بعد إنشائها بإذن الله ·· فضلا عن السعي إلى عضوية الجامعة فى إتحاد الجامعات العربية ، لتكون الشهادات والدرجات العلمية التى تمنحها الجامعة معادلة مع الشهادات العالمية والعربية ·

مولاي

إنه إلى جانب التبرع بكامل المبانى السابق الإشارة إليها بجميع منشآتها ومعداتها وتجهيزاتها الكاملة إلى الجامعة الأهلية المقترحة للبنات والتي تزيد قيمتها عن (٣٠٠) مليون ريال ، فإن تمويل رأس المال العامل سيكون على عاتق بعضا من أبناء وطننا الغالى فى المرحلة الأولى ، وأما بعد ذلك فسيكون من التدفقات المتوقعة من دخل الجامعة ، وذلك طبقا لما أظهرته دراسة الجدوى الإقتصادية والتى يعول عليها فى ضمان إستمرارية الجامعة بإذن الله · والتى من أغراضها عدم تحقيق أي مكاسب مادية كعائد ربحوى والإستفادة من فائض الدخل السنوى إن تحقق ذلك ، لدعم التطور المستمر للنواحى التعليمية والتشغيلية لكليات الجامعة المختلفة ·

بسم الله الرحمن الرحيم

المملكة العربية السعودية
قصر جلالة المرحوم الملك
فيصل بن عبد العزيز آل سعود

الرقم ....
التاريخ ....
المرفقات ....

-٤-

ولأنكم يامولاي رعاكم الله وأدامكم لنا راعيا وملاذا بعد المولي عز وجل قد أخذتم علي عاتقكم دعم مسيرة التعليم بكافة مراحله لجميع مواطني هذا البلد الغالي ، فأنني أتقدم بهذا الطلب برجاء أن يشملني عطفكم الدائم علينا يامولاي بالموافقة علي التصريح لي بانشاء جامعة أهلية للبنات بمحافظة جدة بمسمى :

" جامعة عفت الأهلية للبنات " ، تحت رعاية وإشراف مؤسسة الملك فيصل الخيرية ، تضم فى
المرحلة الأولى الكليات الآتية :

(١) كلية الصيدلة .
(٢) كلية الحاسب الآلى ونظم المعلومات .
(٣) كلية العمارة والتصميم الداخلى .
(٤) كلية التربية ورياض الأطفال .

وأرجو يامولاي إن شاء الله ، بعد صدور موافقتكم السامية التوجيه لوزارة التعليم العالي بانفاذ موافقتكم الكريمة ليتواكب افتتاح الجامعة مع بداية العام الدراسي ١٤١٩هـ/ ١٤٢٠هـ ، وأن تحظي الجامعة بشرف تفضلكم بافتتاحها كأول جامعة أهلية للبنات لآح أملها في عهدكم ، وبزغت الي النور بتوجيهاتكم .

والله سبحانه وتعالي ، أسأل طول العمر لمقامكم الكريم حفظكم الله وأن يسدد خطاكم ويوفقكم لما فيه الخير والرقي لهذا الوطن الغالي ومواطنيه .

عفت بنت محمد الثنيان

حرم المغفور له الملك فيصل بن عبد العزيز

Appendix V

Queen ‘Iffat’s last will

The first page of the Queen’s last will and testament, recorded at the Riyadh *Shari‘ah* Court on 1394 Safar 1394 H [13 March 1974 CE] and duly certified by the Ministry of Justice on 17 Safar 1394 H, affirms that she signed in front of a legal representative and in the presence of two witnesses, and being of sound mind, to divide her estate according to her wishes.

بسم الله الرحمن الرحيم

المملكة العربية السعودية
وزارة العدل

الصكوك الصادرة من المحاكم الشرعية

وصاية كاتب عدل

[illegible] فقد ذهبت أنا كاتب عدل بالرياض [illegible] فحضرت لدي
صاحب الجلالة الملك المعظم فيصل بن عبد العزيز حفظه الله [illegible]
[illegible] شرعاً قائلاً [illegible] أشهد أن لا إله إلا الله وحده لا شريك له وأشهد أن محمداً
رسول الله وأن عيسى عبده ورسوله وكلمته ألقاها إلى مريم وروح منه وأن الجنة حق وأن النار
حق وأن الساعة آتية لا ريب فيها وأن الله يبعث من في القبور وأوصي [illegible] خلفي
من المسلمين أن يتقوا الله ويصلحوا ذات بينهم وأن يكونوا [illegible] إخواناً [illegible] وأوصي بثلث مالي
[illegible]
[illegible] الثلث [illegible]
[illegible] وصلى الله
على نبينا محمد وآله وصحبه وسلم [illegible] عبد العزيز [illegible]
[illegible]
[illegible] وصلى الله على نبينا محمد وآله وصحبه وسلم [illegible]

١١٣٩٠
[illegible]

Bibliography

Additional materials, including newspaper citations and web links, are included as footnotes to each chapter.

Documents

Kingdom of Sa'udi Arabia. The National Family Safety Program, *Domestic Violence and Child Abuse and Neglect in Saudi Arabia*, Riyadh: National Guard Health Affairs, n.d., at http://nfsp.org.sa/index.php/component/phocadownload/category/7-2012-04-03-11-28-16?download=53:2012-04-03-11-11-38.

Kingdom of Sa'udi Arabia. *Eighth Development Plan 2005–2009* [1425–1430 H], Riyadh: Ministry of Economy and Planning, January 2005, pp. 311–312, available at http://www.mep.gov.sa/themes/GoldenCarpet/index.jsp;jsessionid=B67F324E6C88F5A03412C80BCEC8CF32.alfa#1346424735935.

Kingdom of Sa'udi Arabia. *Human Development Report 2002*, Riyadh: Ministry of Economy and Planning, 2003, at http://hdr.undp.org/en/reports/national/arabstates/saudiarabia/Saudi%20Arabia_2003_en.pdf.

Kingdom of Sa'udi Arabia. *King Khaled Eye Specialist Hospital Annual Report* 2010, Riyadh: Ministry of Health, 2010.

Kingdom of Sa'udi Arabia. *Ninth Development Plan 2010–2014* [1431–1435 H, Riyadh: Ministry of Economy and Planning, January 2010, p. 679, available at http://www.mep.gov.sa/themes/GoldenCarpet/index.jsp;jsessionid=B67F324E6C88F5A03412C80BCEC8CF32.alfa.

Kingdom of Sa'udi Arabia. Royal Decree number M/54 (29 Shawwal 1425 AH), in "Consideration of reports submitted by States Parties under article 18 of the Convention, Combined initial and second periodic reports of States Parties: Saudi Arabia," United Nations, Committee on the Elimination of Discrimination Against Women, CEDAW/C/SAU/2, 07-29667 [E]120507 230507, 29 March 2007, p. 16, at http://daccessdds.un.org/doc/UNDOC/GEN/N07/296/67/PDF/N0729667.pdf?OpenElement.

Kingdom of Sa'udi Arabia. *Al-Ta'lim al-'Ali wa Bina' al-Ma'rifah fil-Mamlakah al-'Arabiyyah al-Sa'udiyyah: Taqwim Duwali* [Higher Education and the

Building of a Knowledge Society in the Kingdom of Sa'udi Arabia: An International Calendar], Riyadh: Ministry of Higher Education, 2010 [1431 H].

United Nations Development Program. *Arab Human Development Report 2005: Towards the Rise of Women in the Arab World*, New York: United Nations Publications, 2005.

United National Development Program. *Human Development Report 2011: Sustainability and Equity—A Better Future for All*, New York, UNDP, 2011.

United National Development Program. *Human Development Report 2013: The Rise of the South—Human Progress in a Diverse World*, New York, UNDP, 2013.

Secondary Sources

The 9/11 Commission Report: Final Report of the National Commission on Terrorist Attacks Upon the United States, New York: W.W. Norton & Company, [2004?].

Admon, [Yael?]. "Revival of Cinema Sparks Debate in Saudi Arabia," Inquiry and Analysis Series Report No.595, Washington, D.C.: The Middle East Media Research Institute (MEMRI), 11 March 2010, at http://www.memri.org/report/en/0/0/0/0/0/0/4027.htm.

Ahmed, Leila. *Women and Gender in Islam: Historical Roots of a Modern Debate*, New Haven, Connecticut, Yale University Press, 1992.

Ahmed, Qanta A. *In the Land of Invisible Women: A Female Doctor's Journey in the Saudi Kingdom*, Naperville, Illinois: Sourcebooks, Inc., 2008.

Akçam, Taner. *The Young Turks' Crime Against Humanity: The Armenian Genocide and Ethnic Cleansing in the Ottoman Empire*, Princeton, New Jersey: Princeton University Press, 2012.

Akmese, Handan Nezir. *The Birth of Modern Turkey: The Ottoman Military and the March to World War I*, London: I.B. Tauris, 2005.

Aksin, Sina. *Turkey: From Empire to Revolutionary Republic—The Emergence of the Turkish Nation from 1789 to Present*, New York: New York University Press, 2007.

Alami, Jamal. "Education in the Hijaz Under Turkish and Sharifian Rule," *The Islamic Quarterly* 19:1–2, January–June 1975.

Alangari, Haifa. *The Struggle for Power in Arabia: Ibn Saud, Hussein and Great Britain, 1914–1924*, London: Ithaca Press, 1998.

Albrithen, Abdulaziz A. "Alcoholism and Domestic Violence in Saudi Society," Doctoral Dissertation, Liverpool, UK: University of Liverpool, September 2006, at http://faculty.ksu.edu.sa/aalbrithen/Documents/Ph.D._Thesis.pdf.

Alireza, Marianne. *At the Drop of a Veil*, Boston: Houghton Mifflin Company, 1971.

Allail, Haifa Reda Jamal. "The Importance of Global Dimension in Citizenship, Family & Education: A Vision for Global Peace—The Case of Effat College," delivered to the World Family Summit held in Sanya (near Hainan), China, 6–9 December 2004 [Mimeographed, in author's hands].

Almunajjed, Mona. *Women in Saudi Arabia Today*, New York: St. Martin's Press, 1997.

Alrabaa, Sami. *Veiled Atrocities: True Stories of Oppression in Saudi Arabia*, Amherst, New York: Prometheus Books, 2010.

Altorki, Soraya. *Women in Saudi Arabia: Ideology and Behavior Among the Elite*, New York: Columbia University Press, 1988.

Amin, Qasim. *Al-Mara'ah al-Jadidah* [The New Woman: A Document in the Early Debate on Egyptian Feminism], translated by Samiha Sidhom Peterson, Cairo: American University in Cairo Press, 1995 [first published in 1900].

_____. *Tahrir al-Mara'ah* [The Liberation of Women: Two Documents in the History of Egyptian Feminism], translated by Samiha Sidhom Peterson, Cairo: American University in Cairo Press, 2000 [first published in 1899].

An-Na'im, Abdullahi A. "The Position of Islamic States Regarding the Universal Declaration of Human Rights," in Peter Baehr, Cees Flinterman and Mignon Senders, eds., *Innovation and Inspiration: Fifty Years of the Universal Declaration of Human Rights*, Amsterdam: Koninklijke Nederlandse Akademie van Wetenschappen, 1999, pp. 177–192.

Ansary, Abdullah F. "Combating Extremism: A Brief Overview of Saudi Arabia's Approach," *Middle East Policy* 15:2, Summer 2008, pages 111–142.

Antonius, George. *The Arab Awakening: The Story of the Arab National Movement*, New York: Capricorn Books, 1965 [originally published by G.P. Putnam's Sons in 1946].

Arebi, Saddeka. *Women and Words in Saudi Arabia: The Politics of Literary Discourse*, New York: Colombia University Press, 1994.

Armstrong, Harold C. *Lord of Arabia: Ibn Saud, An Intimate Study of a King*, London: Arthur Barker Ltd., 1934.

Awde, Nicolas. *Women In Islam: An Anthology From The Qu'ran and Hadiths*, New York: Hippocrene Books, 2005.

Aybars, Ergün. *Türkiye Cumhuriyeti Tarihi I* [History of the Republic of Turkey, Volume 1] (in Turkish), Bornova-Izmir, Turkey: Ege Üniversitesi Basımevi, 1984.

Badawi, Jamal. *Gender Equity in Islam: Basic Principles*, Plainfield, Indiana: American Trust Publications, 2005.

Beaty, Jonathan and S. C. Gwynne, *The Outlaw Bank: A Wild Ride Into the Secret Heart of BCCI*, New York: Random House, 1993.

Benhenda, Mostapha. "Liberal Democracy and Political Islam: The Search for Common Ground," *Politics, Philosophy & Economics* 10:1, February 2011, pp. 88–115.

Benoist-Mechin, [Jacques]. *Fayçal, Roi d'Arabie: L'Homme, Le Souverain, Sa Place dans le Monde 1906–1975*, Paris: Albin Michel, 1975

_____. *Le Loup et le Leopard: Ibn-Seoud ou la naissance d'un royaume*, Paris: Albin Michel, 1955.

Bishr, 'Uthman bin 'Abdallah Ibn. *'Unwan al-Majd fi Tarikh Najd* [The Sign of Honor in the History of Najd], Riyadh: King Abdul Aziz Public Library for the Wazarat al-Ma'arif al-Sa'udiyyah [Ministry of Education], 2002.

Blanchard, Christopher M. "Saudi Arabia: Background and U.S. Relations," Washington, D.C.: Congressional Research Service, RL33533, 19 June 2012.

Bligh, Alexander. *From Prince to King: Royal Succession in the House of Saud in the Twentieth Century*, New York and London: New York University Press, 1984.

Bronson, Rachel. "Rethinking Religion: The Legacy of the U.S.–Saudi Relationship," *The Washington Quarterly* 28:4, Autumn 2005, pp. 119–137.

Bubshait, Al-Jawhara. "Saudi Women's Education: History, Reality and Challenges," in *Woman in Saudi Arabia: Cross-Cultural Views*, Riyadh: Ghainaa Publications, 2008.

"Building Bridges: A Conversation with Princess Loulwa Al-Faisal," 2 June 2005, Saudi–US Relations Information Service (SUSRIS), at http://www.susris.com/2005/06/02/building-bridges-a-conversation-with-princess-loulwa-al-faisal-2/.

Bullough, Oliver. *Let Our Fame Be Great: Journeys Among the Defiant People of the Caucasus*, New York: Basic Books, 2010.

Campbell, Kay Hardy and Nicole LeCorgne, "Effat's News Roses," *Saudi Aramco World* 58:1, January/February 2007, pp. 2–7.

Chernow, Ron. *The House of Morgan*, New York: Atlantic Monthly Press, 1990.

Chopra, Deepak. *Muhammad: A Story of the Last Prophet*, New York: HarperOne, 2010.

Coleman, Isobel. *Paradise Beneath Her Feet: How Women are Transforming the Middle East*, New York: Random House, 2010.

Cooper, Andrew Scott. *The Oil Kings: How the U.S., Iran, and Saudi Arabia Changed the Balance of Power in the Middle East*, New York: Simon & Schuster, 2011.

Cornell, Svante. *Small Nations and Great Powers: A Study of Ethnopolitical Conflict in the Caucasus*, London: Routledge, 2000.

Country Profile on Disability Kingdom of Saudi Arabia, Tokyo: Japan International Cooperation Agency, Planning and Evaluation Department, March 2002, at http://siteresources.worldbank.org/DISABILITY/Resources/Regions/MENA/JICA_Saudi_Arabia.pdf.

Darulfatwa of Australia, *Upholding the Methodology of the Master of Messengers*, Bankstown, Sydney, New South Wales: Islamic High Council of Australia, 2012.

Decker, Kristin. *The Unveiling: An American Teacher in a Saudi Palace*, College Station, Texas: Virtualbookworm.com Publishing, 2006.

Doumato, Eleanor Abdella. "Gender, Monarchy, and National Identity in Saudi Arabia," *British Journal of Middle Eastern Studies* 19:1, 1992, pp. 34–39.

_____. *Getting God's Ear: Women, Islam, and Healing in Saudi Arabia and the Gulf*, New York: Columbia University Press, 2000.

_____. "The Saudis and the Gulf War: Gender, Power, and Revival of the Religious Right," in Abbas Abdelkarim, ed., *Change and Development in the Gulf*, New York: Palgrave Macmillan, 1999, pp. 184–210.

_____. "Women and Work in Saudi Arabia: How Flexible Are Islamic Margins," *The Middle East Journal* 53:4, Autumn 1999, pp. 568–583.

_____. *Women's Rights in the Middle East and North Africa 2010—Saudi Arabia*, 3 March 2010, Prepared for Freedom House, available at: http://www.unhcr.org/refworld/docid/4b99011da0.html [accessed 28 September 2012].

Dreyfuss, Robert. "Discover Plot against Saudi Arabia: Murder of Faisal Tied to U.S.-Based British Intelligence Network," *Executive Intelligence Review* 5:50, 26 December 1978, pp. 45–46.

Duff-Gordon, Lucie. *Letters From Egypt*, London: CreateSpace [An Amazon.com Books-on-Demand Project], 2012, (originally published in 1863).

Duhaish, Abdul Latief bin. "Elementary Schools in Hijaz During the Half Century, AG 1295–1345," in Mohamed Tahir, ed., *Encyclopedic Survey of Islamic Culture*, Volume 3, New Delhi, India: 1986, pp. 35–60.

Edge, Deckle. *In the Kingdom of Men*, New York: Knopf, 2012.

Al-Eid, Haya S. BDS, DFE, CTR, *Cancer Incidence and Survival-Report: Saudi Arabia 2007*, Kingdom of Saudi Arabia, Ministry of Health, Saudi Cancer Registry, 2010, at http://www.scr.org.sa/reports/SCR2007.pdf.

Endress, Gerhard and Abdou Filali-Ansary, eds., *Organizing Knowledge: Encyclopaedic Activities in the Pre-Eighteenth Century Islamic World*, Leiden, The Netherlands: E.J. Brill, 2006.

English, Jeanette M. *Infidel Behind The Paradoxical Veil: A Western Woman's Experience in Saudi Arabia*, Bloomington, Indiana: AuthorHouse, 2011.

Erickson, Edward J. *Ordered to Die: A History of the Ottoman Army in the First World War*, Westport, Connecticut: Greenwood Press, 2000.

Al-Fakhiri, Muhammad bin 'Umar. *Al-Akhbar al-Najdiyyah* [Reportage on Najd], Riyadh: Matabi' Jami'at al-Imam Muhammad ibn Sa'ud al-Islamiyyah, n.d.

Fakhro, Munira. "Gulf Women and Islamic Law," in Mai Yamani, ed., *Feminism and Islam: Legal and Literary Perspectives*, New York: New York University Press, 1996.

Farah, Caesar E. "Nationalist Concerns for Syria: The Case of Farah Antun, Mayy Ziadah and al-Kawakibi," in Adel Beshara, *The Origins of Syrian Nationhood: Histories, Pioneers and Identity*, London: Routledge, 2011, pp. 210–222.

Al-Farsy, Fouad. *Modernity and Tradition: The Saudi Equation*, Guernsey, Channel Islands: Knight Communications, 1994.

Faruqui, Mumtaz Ahmad. *Anecdotes from the Life of The Prophet Muhammad*, Dublin, Ohio: 1997, originally published by the Ahmadiyyah Anjuman Isha'at Islam, Lahore, Pakistan, 1925.

Field, Michael. *The Merchants: The Big Business Families of Saudi Arabia and the Gulf States*, Woodstock, New York: The Overlook Press, 1985.

Findley, Carter Vaugh. "The Tanzimat," in Resat Kasaba, *The Cambridge History of Turkey*, Volume 4, Cambridge: Cambridge University Press, 2008, pp. 11–37.

Foley, Sean. "All I Want is Equality with Girls: Gender and Social Change in the

Twenty-First Century Gulf," *MERIA Journal* 14:1, March 2010, pp. 21–35, at http://www.gloria-center.org/2010/03/foley-2010-03-03/.

Fortna, Benjamin C. *Imperial Classroom: Islam, the State, and Education in the Late Ottoman Empire*, New York: Oxford University Press, 2002.

_____. *Learning to Read in the Late Ottoman Empire and the Early Turkish Republic*, New York and London: Palgrave Macmillan, 2011.

_____. "The Reign of Abdülhamid II," in Resat Kasaba, *The Cambridge History of Turkey*, Volume 4, Cambridge: Cambridge University Press, 2008, pp. 38–61.

Fraser, Flora. *Pauline Bonaparte: Venus of Empire*, New York: Alfred A. Knopf, 2009.

Freely, John. *Istanbul: The Imperial City*, New York: Penguin Books, 1998.

Fromkin, David. *A Peace to End All Peace: The Fall of the Ottoman Empire and the Creation of the Modern Middle East*, New York: Holt Paperbacks, 2009.

Al-Gain, Salah I. and Sami S. Al-Abdulwahab, "Issues and Obstacles in Disability Research in Saudi Arabia," *Asia Pacific Disability Rehabilitation Journal*, January 2002, at http://www.aifo.it/english/resources/online/apdrj/apdrj102/arabia.pdf.

Ghannam, Husayn Ibn. *Tarikh Najd* [The History of Najd], Beirut, Lebanon: Dar al-Shuruq, 1994.

Gilliot, Claude, ed. *Education and Learning in the Early Islamic World*, Farnham, Surrey, UK: Ashgate, 2012.

Goldsmith, Barbara. *Obsessive Genius: The Inner World of Marie Curie*, New York: W. W. Norton, 2005.

Goodwin, Jan. *Price of Honor: Muslim Women—Lift the Veil of Silence on the Islamic World*, New York: A Plume Book [Penguin], 1994 and 2003.

El-Guindi, Fadwa, and Sherifa Zuhur. "Hijab," *The Oxford Encyclopedia of the Islamic World*, Oxford and New York, 2009, Volume 2, pp. 399–403.

El-Guindi, Fadwa. *Veil: Modesty, Privacy, and Resistance*, Oxford and New York: Oxford University Press, 1999.

Habib, John S. *Ibn Sa'ud's Warriors of Islam: The Ikhwan of Najd and Their Role in the Creation of the Sa'udi Kingdom, 1910–1930*, Leiden, the Netherlands: E.J. Brill, 1978.

Hall, Richard C. *The Balkan Wars 1912–1913: Prelude to the First World War*, London and New York: Routledge, 2000.

Hamdan, Amani. "Women and Education in Saudi Arabia: Challenges and Achievements," *International Education Journal* 6:1, March 2005, pp. 42–64.

Al-Hamdi, Sabri Falih. *Al-Mustasharun al-'Arab wal-Siyasah al-Kharijiyyah al-Sa'udiyyah Khilal Hikm al-Malik 'Abdul 'Aziz bin Sa'ud (1915–1953)* [The Arab Advisors and the Foreign Policy of Sa'udi Arabia under the Rule of 'Abdul 'Aziz bin Sa'ud (1915–1953)], London: Dar al-Hikmah, 2011.

Hamzah, Fuad. *Al-Bilad al-'Arabiyyah al-Sa'udiyyah* [The Kingdom of Saudi Arabia], 2nd edition, Cairo: Maktabat al-Nasr al-Hadithat, 1968.

Hanioğlu, Şükrü. *Preparations for a Revolution: Young Turks 1902–1908*, New York: Oxford University Press, 2001.

_____. *The Young Turks in Opposition*, New York: Oxford University Press, 1995.

Al-Harbi, Dalal Mukhlid. *Prominent Women from Central Arabia*, Reading, United Kingdom: Ithaca Press [in association with the King Abdul Aziz Foundation for Research and Archives], 2008.

Harrigan, Peter. "Rays of Light and Brightness: The King Faisal International Prize," *Saudi Aramco World* 51:5, September/October 2000, pp. 32–39.

Hart, Peter. *Gallipoli*, New York: Oxford University Press, 2011.

Hassan, Aminuddi, Norhasni Zainal Abiddin, and Abdul Razaq Ahmad. "Islamic Philosophy as the Basis to Ensure Academic Excellence," *Asian Social Science* 7:3, March 2011, pp. 37–41.

Haylamaz, Resit. *Khadija: The First Muslim and the Wife of the Prophet Muhammad*, London: Light, Inc., 2008.

Al-Hazmy, M. B. *et al.* "Handicap Among Children in Saudi Arabia: Prevalence, Distribution, Type, Determinants and Related Factors," *East Mediterranean Health Journal* 10:4–5, July–September 2004, pp. 502–21.

Heath, Jennifer. *The Scimitar and the Veil: Extraordinary Women of Islam*, Mahwah, New Jersey: Hidden Spring, 2004.

Hegghammer, Thomas, and Stephane Lacroix, "Rejectionist Islamism in Saudi Arabia: The Story of Juhayman al-'Utaybi Revisited," *International Journal of Middle East Studies* 39:1, February 2007, pp. 103–122.

Henderson, Dean. *Big Oil & Their Bankers In The Persian Gulf: Four Horsemen, Eight Families & Their Global Intelligence, Narcotics & Terror Network*, CreateSpace Independent Publishing Platform (amazon.com), 2010.

Henze, Paul B. "Circassian Resistance To Russia," in Marie Bennigsen Broxup, ed., *The North Caucasus Barrier: Russian Advance Towards the Muslim World*, London: Hurst & Co., 1992, pp. 62–111.

Hilton, Lisa. *Queens Consort: England's Medieval Queens*, New York: Pegasus Books, 2010.

Holden, David and Richard Johns. *The House of Saud: The Rise and Rule of the Most Powerful Dynasty in the Arab World*, New York: Holt, Rinehart and Winston, 1981.

House, Karen Elliott. *On Saudi Arabia: Its People, Past, Religion, Fault Lines—and Future*, New York: Knopf, 2012.

Howarth, David. *The Desert King: The Life of Ibn Saud*, London: Quartet Books, 1965, 1980.

Hurgronje, Christiaan Snouck. "Mohammedanism: Lectures on Its Origin, Its Religious and Political Growth, and Its Present State," 1916, available online as an eBook under the Gutenberg project at http://www.gutenberg.net/1/0/1/6/10163.

Huyette, Summer Scott. *Political Adaptation in Saudi Arabia: A Study of the Council of Ministers*, Boulder, Colorado: Westview Press, 1985.

Islam, Samirah Ibrahim. *'Iffat Al Thunayan: Tarikh wa Injaz* ['Iffat Al Thunayan: History and Achievements], Jiddah: Al-Multakah al-Thaqafih, 1421H [2001].

The Ismailis of Najran: Second-class Saudi Citizens, New York: Human Rights Watch, 2008, at http://www.hrw.org/sites/default/files/reports/saudiarabia0908web.pdf.

Jacobs, Ryan. "Saudi Arabia's War on Witchcraft: A Special Unit of the Religious Police Pursues Magical Crime Aggressively, and the Convicted," *The Atlantic*, 19 August 2013, at http://www.theatlantic.com/international/archive/2013/08/saudi-arabias-war-on-witchcraft/278701/.

Jaimoukha, Amjad. *The Circassians: A Handbook*, New York and London: Palgrave Macmillan, 2001.

Janin, Hunt. *Pursuit of Learning in the Islamic World, 610–2003*, Jefferson, North Carolina: McFarland & Company, 2006.

Jawad, Haifaa A. *The Rights of Women in Islam: An Authentic Approach*, London: Macmillan Press, 1998.

Kaarthikeyan, D. R. and Radhavinod Raju. *Triumph of Truth: Rajiv Gandhi Assassination—The Investigation*, New Delhi: New Dawn Press, 2004.

Karmi, Ghada. "Women, Islam, and Patriarchalism," in Mai Yamani, ed., *Feminism and Islam: Legal and Literary Perspectives*, New York: New York University Press, 1996, pp. 69–86.

Kasaba, Resat. *The Cambridge History of Turkey*, Volume 4, Cambridge: Cambridge University Press, 2008.

Kéchichian, Joseph A. *Faysal: Saudi Arabia's King for All Seasons*, Gainesville: University Press of Florida, 2008.

_____. "Islamic Revivalism and Change in Saudi Arabia: Juhayman Al-Utaybi's 'Letters' to the Saudi People," *The Muslim World* 70:1, January 1990, pp. 1–16.

_____. *Legal and Political Reforms in Sa'udi Arabia*, London: Routledge, 2013.

_____. *Power and Succession in Arab Monarchies: A Reference Guide*, Boulder, Colorado and London: Lynne Rienner, 2008.

_____. "The Role of the Ulama in the Politics of an Islamic State: The Case of Saudi Arabia," *International Journal of Middle East Studies* 18:1, February 1986, pp. 53–71.

_____. *Succession in Saudi Arabia*, New York: Palgrave, 2001.

Kerry, John and Hank Brown, *The BCCI Affair: A Report to the Committee on Foreign Relations*, Washington, D.C.: United States Senate, 102d Congress 2d Session, Senate Print 102–140, December 1992.

Ibn Khaldun, *The Muqaddimah, An Introduction to History*, Tr. Franz Rosenthal, Bollingen Series XLIII, Princeton: Princeton University Press, 1967, 3 Vols. An abridged and edited version is also published under the title of *The Muqaddimah: An Introduction to History*, Princeton: Princeton University Press, 1981.

Al-Khudayrih, Salmah Muta'. *Masirat Jami'at al-Nahdah al-Nisa'iyyat al-Khayriyyah khilal Arba'in 'Aman: 1382–1422* H [The 40 Years-Long March of the Nahdah Women's Charitable Society: 1962–2002], Riyadh: Al-Nahdah Women's Charitable Society, 1424 H [2003].

Kinross, Lord [Patrick Balfour]. *The Ottoman Centuries: The Rise and Fall of the Turkish Empire*, New York: Morrow Quill Paperbacks, 1977.

Kishk, Muhammad Jalal. *Al-Sa'udiyyun Wal-Hal Al-Islami* [The Saudis and the Islamic Solution], Jeddah: The Saudi Publishing and Distribution House, 1982.

Kostiner, Joseph. *The Making of Saudi Arabia, 1916–1936: From Chieftancy to Monarchical State*, New York and Oxford: Oxford University Press, 1993.

Kramer, Martin. "Fundamentalist Islam at Large: The Drive for Power," *Middle East Quarterly* 3:2, June 1996, pp. 37–49.

_____. "Intra-Regional and Muslim Affairs," in Haim Shaked and Daniel Dishon, eds., *Middle East Contemporary Survey, Volume 8, 1983–1984*, Tel Aviv: The Shiloah Center for Middle Eastern and African Studies, 1986.

Lacey, Robert. *Inside the Kingdom: Kings, Clerics, Modernists, Terrorists, and the Struggle for Saudi Arabia*, New York: Viking, 2009.

_____. *The Kingdom: Arabia and the House of Saud*, London: Hutchinson, 1981.

Lawrence, T. E. *Seven Pillars of Wisdom: A Triumph*, New York: Anchor Books, 1991 [Originally published by Doubleday in 1926].

Leatherdale, Clive. *Britain and Saudi Arabia 1925–1939: The Imperial Oasis*, London: Frank Cass, 1983.

Lees, Brian. *A Handbook of the Al Saud Family of Saudi Arabia*, London: Royal Genealogies, 1980.

Lorimer, J. G. *Gazetteer of the Persian Gulf, Oman, and Central Arabia*, Calcutta: Government Printing Office, 1915. Reprinted in Shannon, Ireland: Irish Universities Press, 1989 (in six volumes).

Mansel, Philip. *Constantinople: City of the World's Desire, 1453–1924*, London: John Murray, 2006.

_____. *Sultans in Splendour*, London: Parkway Publishing, 1988.

"Marahil al-Tawasu' fi-Mustashfah al-Takhasusih wa Da'm Malakih la-Mahdud" [Periods of Expansion at the King Faysal Specialist Hospital and Unlimited Royal Support], *Al-Takhasusih*, Special Edition, Rajab 1432 [June 2011], pp. 2–8.

Maruoğlu, Sinan. *Osmanlı döneminde Kuzey Irak, 1831–1914* [Northern Iraq during the Ottoman period, 1831–1914], Istanbul: Eren, 1998.

Maslow, Abraham. *Motivation and Personality, New York:* Harper and Row Publishers, 1954.

McDowall-Rose, Kirk-Dale. "Saudi Arabia—Why It's Different to Dubai and Why It's a Good Bet," *IBM Strategy and Transformation*, 27 July 2012, at https://www-304.ibm.com/connections/blogs/gbs_strategy/entry/saudi_arabia_why_its_different_to_dubai_why_its_a_good_bet1?lang=en_us.

McLoughlin, Leslie. *Ibn Saud: Founder of a Kingdom*, Basingstoke and London: Macmillan Press, 1993.

McMeekin, Sean. *The Berlin–Baghdad Express: The Ottoman Empire and Germany's Bid for World Power*, Cambridge, Massachusetts: The Belknap Press of Harvard University Press, 2010.

Montagu, Caroline. "Civil Society and the Voluntary Sector in Saudi Arabia," *The Middle East Journal* 64:1, Winter 2010, pp. 67–83.

Mubarakpuri, Safiur Rahma. *History of Makkah*, Riyadh: Maktaba Dar-us-Salam, 2000.

Al-Muitairi, Abdul Rahman ibn Mualaa al-Luwaihiq. *Religious Extremism in the Lives of Contemporary Muslims*, Denver, Colorado: Al-Basheer Company for Publications and Translations, 2001.

Murphy, Caryle. "Fatwa Chaos," *The Majalla*, 23 August 2010 at http://www.majalla.com/eng/2010/08/article55110707.

Nasr, Seyyed Hossein. *Science and Civilization In Islam*, Chicago: Kazi Publications, 2007 [originally published in 1968 by Harvard University Press].

Notestine, Patrick Tom. *Paramedic to the Prince: An American Paramedic's Account of Life Inside the Mysterious World of the Kingdom of Saudi Arabia*, Lexington, Kentucky: BookSurge Publishing, 2009.

Ochsenwald, William. "The Annexation of the Hijaz," in Mohammed Ayoob and Hasan Kosebalaban, *Religion and Politics in Saudi Arabia: Wahhabism and the State*, Boulder, Colorado and London: Lynne Rienner Publishers, 2009, pp. 75–89.

Ottaway, David B. *The King's Messenger: Prince Bandar bin Sultan and America's Tangled Relationship with Saudi Arabia*, New York: Walker & Company, 2008.

_____. *Saudi Arabia's Race Against Time*, Washington, D.C.: Wilson Center [Middle East Program Occasional Paper Series], Summer 2012.

Özdemir, Ahmet. "Savas Esirlerinin Milli Mücadeledeki Yeri" [Prisoners of War in the National Struggle], Ankara University, *Türk Inkılap Tarihi Enstitüsü Atatürk Yolu Dergisi*, 2:6, 1990.

Öztürk, Mustafa. "Al-'Ilaqat al-Turkiyyah-al-Sa'udiyyah fi Itar 'Ahd al-Malik Faysal bin 'Abdul 'Aziz" [Turkish–Saudi Relations under King Faysal bin 'Abdul 'Aziz's Rule], in *Proceedings of the King Faisal bin Abdulaziz Al Saud Studies and Research Conference*, Riyadh, Saudi Arabia: King Abdulaziz Foundation for Research and Archives (Al-Darah), 2009, Volume 3, pp. 406–436.

Palau, Marie-Gabrielle. *Leaders of Saudi Arabia*, Paris, France: Omnia International SARL, 2008.

Pamuk, Şevket. *A Monetary History of the Ottoman Empire*, Cambridge: Cambridge University Press, 2000.

Pappé, Ilan. "The Husayni Family Faces New Challenges: Tanzimat, Young Turks, the Europeans and Zionism, 1840–1922, (Part II)," *The Jerusalem Quarterly*, Issue 11–12, Winter–Spring 2001, pp. 52–67.

_____. "The Rise and Fall of the Husainis (Part 1)," *The Jerusalem Quarterly*, Issue 10, Autumn 2000, pp. 27–38.

Parssinen, Catherine. "The Changing Role of Women," in Willard A. Beling, ed., *King Faisal and the Modernisation of Saudi Arabia*, Boulder, Colorado: Westview Press, 1980, pp. 145–170.

Patai, Raphael. *The Arab Mind*, New York: Recovery Resources Press, 2010 [originally published by Scribner in 1967].

_____. *Golden River to Golden Road: Society, Culture, and Change in the Middle East*, 2nd ed., Philadelphia: University of Pennsylvania Press, 1967.

Philby, [Harry] St. John B. *Arabian Jubilee*, London: Robert Hale Limited, 1952.

_____. *Sa'udi Arabia*, London: Ernest Benn Limited, 1955.

Pitts, Vincent J. *La Grande Mademoiselle at the Court of France: 1627–1693*, Baltimore and London: The Johns Hopkins University Press, 2000.

Pourasgari, Homa. *The Dawn of Saudi: In Search for Freedom*, Beverly Hills, California: Lindbrook Press, 2009.

Powell, William. *Saudi Arabia and Its Royal Family*, Secaucus, New Jersey: Lyle Stuart, Inc., 1982.

Provence, Michael. *The Great Syrian Revolt and the Rise of Arab Nationalism*, Austin, Texas: The University of Texas Press, 2005.

Quataert, Donald. *The Ottoman Empire, 1700–1922*, 2nd ed., Cambridge: Cambridge University Press, 2005.

Raja, Masood Ashraf. "Muslim Modernity: Poetics, Politics, and Metaphysics," in Gabriele Marranci, ed., *Muslim Societies and the Challenge of Secularization: An Interdisciplinary Approach*, Aberdeen: Springer, 2010, pp. 99–112.

Ramsaur Ernest Edmondson, Jr. *The Young Turks: Prelude to the Revolution of 1908*, New York: Russell & Russell, 1957.

Raphaeli, Nimrod. "Financing of Terrorism: Sources, Methods, and Channels," *Terrorism and Political Violence* 15:4, Winter 2003, pp. 59–82.

Al Rasheed, Madawi. *A History of Saudi Arabia*, 2nd edition, Cambridge: Cambridge University Press, 2010.

_____. *Politics in an Arabian Oasis: The Rashidi Tribal Dynasty*, London and New York: I.B. Tauris & Co. Limited, 1991.

Al-Rashid, Ibrahim. *Documents on the History of Saudi Arabia*, Salisbury, North Carolina: Documents Publications, 1976.

Riedel, Bruce. "Brezhnev in the Hejaz," *The National Interest*, Number 115, September/October 2011, pp. 27–32.

Rihani, Ameen. *Ibn Sa'oud of Arabia*, London: Kegan Paul, 2002 [originally published as *Maker of Modern Arabia or Ibn Sa'oud of Arabia: His People and His Land*, London: Constable and Co. Ltd., 1928].

Rush, A. de L. *Ruling Families of Arabia, Saudi Arabia: The Royal Family of Al-Sa'ud, Volume 1*, London: Archive Editions, 1991.

Salamah, Rania Sulayman Yunis. *Dar al-Hanan*, Jiddah: Madaris Dar al-Hanan, 1429 H [2008].

Salameh, Ghassan. *Al-Siyasah al-Kharijiyah al-Sa'udiyyah Munzu 'Am 1945* [Saudi Foreign Policy Since 1945], Beirut: Ma'had al-Anma' al-'Arabi, 1980.

Salem, Philip A. "Michael DeBakey: The Real Man Behind the Genius," *Al-Hewar: The Center for Arab Culture and Dialogue*, at http://www.alhewar.net/Basket/Salem_Debakey.htm.

Sasson, Jean. *Princess: A True Story of Life Behind the Veil in Saudi Arabia*, New York: William Morrow & Co, 1992.

_____. *Princess Sultana's Circle*, Atlanta, Georgia: Windsor-Brooke Books, LLC, 2002.
_____. *Princess Sultana's Daughters*, New York: Doubleday, 1994.
Satia, Priya. *Spies in Arabia: The Great War and the Cultural Foundations of Britain's Covert Empire in the Middle East*, New York: Oxford University Press, 2008.
"Saudi Arabia: Free Islamic Scholar Who Criticized Ministry," Human Rights Watch, 14 July 2011, at http://www.hrw.org/news/2011/07/14/saudi-arabia-free-islamic-scholar-who-criticized-ministry.
Schiff, Stacy. *Cleopatra: A Life*, New York: Little, Brown and Company, 2010.
Shaarawi, Huda. *Harem Years: The Memoirs of an Egyptian Feminist, 1879–1924*, translated by Margot Badran, New York: The Feminist Press at the City University of New York, 1987.
Sharaf, Sabri. *The House of Saud in Commerce: A Study of Riyal Entrepreneurship in Saudi Arabia*, New Delhi: I. S. Publications, 2001.
Siddiqui, Abdul Hameed. *Sahih al-Muslim*, Book 31, Chapter 12, Numbers 5965–5975, at http://www.shariahprogram.ca/Hadith/Sahih-Muslim/031.smt.html.
Simons, Geoff *Saudi Arabia: The Shape of a Client Feudalism*, New York: St. Martin's Press, 1998.
Simpson, William. *The Prince: The Secret Story of the World's Most Intriguing Royal—Prince Bandar bin Sultan*, New York: Harper, 2006.
Sinoué, Gilbert. *12 Femmes d'Orient qui ont changé l'Histoire*, Paris: Pygmalion, 2011.
Spink, Kathry. *Mother Teresa: A Complete Authorized Biography*, New York: Harpercollins, 1997.
Stenslie, Stig. "Power Behind the Veil: Princesses of House of Saud," *Journal of Arabian Studies: Arabia, the Gulf, and the Red Sea* 1:1, 2011, pp. 69–79.
Tashkandi, A. A. and P. Rasheed. "Wife Abuse: A Hidden Problem—A Study Among Saudi Women Attending PHC Centres," *La Revue de Santé de la Méditerranée Orientale* 15: 5, 2009, pp. 1242–1253, at www.emro.who.int/emhj/1505/15_5_2009_1242_1253.pdf.
Taylor, Charles. "Nationalism and Modernity," in John Hall, ed., *The State of the Nation: Ernest Gellner and the Theory of Nationalism*, Cambridge: Cambridge University Press, 1998.
Teitelbaum, Joshua. *The Rise and Fall of the Hashimite Kingdom of Arabia*, New York: New York University Press, 2001.
Thomas, Katrina. "America as Alma Mater," *Saudi Aramco World*, Volume 30, Number 3, May/June 1979, pp. 2–11.
Trofimov, Yaroslav. *The Siege of Mecca: The Forgotten Uprising in Islam's Holiest Shrine and the Birth of Al Qaeda*, New York: Doubleday, 2007.
Tuncer, Hüner. *Yüzylda Osmanlı-Avrupa Ilişkileri, 1814–1914* [Ottoman–European relations between 1814 and 1914], Ankara: Umit Yayincılık, 2000.
Vassiliev, Alexei. *The History of Saudi Arabia*, London: Saqi Books, 1998.

Vitalis, Robert. *America's Kingdom: Mythmaking on the Saudi Oil Frontier*, Stanford, California: Stanford University Press, 2007.

Walker, Christopher J. *Armenia: The Survival of a Nation*, Revised Second Edition, New York: St. Martin's Press, 1980.

Waller, Maureen. *Sovereign Ladies: The Six Reigning Queens of England*, New York: St. Martin's Press, 2006.

Walsh, Elsa. "The Prince: How the Saudi Ambassador Became Washington's Indispensable Operator," *The New Yorker*, 24 March 2003, pp. 48–63.

Watt, William Montgomery. *Muhammad: Prophet and Statesman*, London and New York: Oxford University Press, 1961.

Woodward, Bob. *Veil: The Secret Wars of the CIA, 1981–1987*, New York: Simon & Schuster 1987.

"World Report 2012: Saudi Arabia," New York: Human Rights Watch, 2012, at http://www.hrw.org/world-report-2012/world-report-2012-saudi-arabia.

Yamani, Maha A. Z. *Polygamy and Law in Contemporary Saudi Arabia*, Reading, UK: Ithaca Press, 2008.

Yamani, Mai. "Some Observations on Women in Saudi Arabia," in Mai Yamani and Andrew Allen, *Feminism and Islam: Legal and Literary Perspectives*, London and New York: Ithaca Press, 1996, pp. 263–282.

Yamani, Mai, and Andrew Allen, *Feminism and Islam: Legal and Literary Perspectives*, London and New York: Ithaca Press, 1996.

Zahlan, Rosemarie Said. *Palestine and the Gulf States: The Presence at the Table*, London: Routledge, 2009.

Index

About the Author

Dr. Joseph A. Kéchichian is a Senior Fellow at the King Faysal Center for Research & Islamic Studies in Riyadh, Sa'udi Arabia, the CEO of Kéchichian & Associates, LLC, a consulting partnership that provides analysis on the Arabian/Persian Gulf region, specializing in the domestic and regional concerns of Bahrain, Iran, Iraq, Kuwait, Oman, Qatar, Sa'udi Arabia, the United Arab Emirates and the Yemen, as well as a Senior Writer at *Gulf News* in Dubai. Between 2006 and 2011 he served as the Honorary Consul of the Sultanate of Oman in Los Angeles, California.

Kéchichian received a doctorate in Foreign Affairs from the University of Virginia in 1985, where he also taught (1986–1988), and assumed the assistant deanship in international studies (1988–1989). In the summer of 1989 he was a Hoover Fellow at Stanford University (under the U.S. State Department Title VIII Program), and between 1990 and 1996 an Associate Political Scientist at the Santa Monica-based RAND Corporation as well as a lecturer at the University of California in Los Angeles (UCLA).

Between 1998 and 2001, Kéchichian was a fellow at UCLA's Gustav E. von Grunebaum Center for Near Eastern Studies, where he held a Smith Richardson Foundation grant (1998–1999) to compose *Succession in Saudi Arabia* (New York: Palgrave, 2001), translated into Arabic as *Al-Khilafah fil-'Arabiyyah al-Sa'udiyyah* in 2002, and reprinted in a second edition in 2003 (Beirut and London: Dar Al Saqi). In 2003–2004 he was the recipient of a Smith Richardson Foundation grant and held a Davenport fellowship at Pepperdine University in Malibu, California, to write *Power and Succession in Arab Monarchies* (Boulder, Colorado: Lynne Rienner Publishers, 2008), which was translated into Arabic as *Al-Sultah wa-Ta'aqub al-Hukm fil-Mamalikah al-'Arabiyyah*, 2 volumes (Beirut and London: Riad El-Rayyes Books, 2012).

Kéchichian published *Political Participation and Stability in the Sultanate of Oman* (Dubai: Gulf Research Center, 2005), *Oman and the World: The Emergence of an Independent Foreign Policy* (Santa Monica: RAND, 1995), and edited *A Century in Thirty Years: Shaykh Zayed and the United Arab Emirates* (Washington, D.C.: The Middle East Policy Council, 2000), as well as *Iran, Iraq, and the Arab Gulf States* (New York: Palgrave, 2001). In 2003 he co-authored (with R. Hrair Dekmejian) *The Just Prince: A Manual of Leadership* (London: Saqi Books), which includes a full translation of the *Sulwan al-Muta'* by Muhammad Ibn Zafar al-Siqilli, which appeared in a Turkish translation as *Adil Hükümdar,* translated by Bariş Doğru (Istanbul: Kırmızı Kedi Yayınevi, 2009). Among his more recent scholarly contributions are *Faysal: Saudi Arabia's King for All Seasons* (Gainesville, Florida: University Press of Florida, 2008), translated into Arabic as *Faysal: Al-Malik wal-Dawlah* (Beirut: Dar al-'Arabiyyah lil-Mawsu'at, 2012), and *Legal and Political Reforms in Sa'udi Arabia* (London: Routledge, 2012), translated into Arabic as *Al-Islahat al-Qanuniyyah wal-Siyasiyyah fil al-Mamlakah al-'Arabiyyah al-Sa'udiyyah* (Beirut, Lebanon: Riad El-Rayyes Books, 2014).

The author of over a dozen book chapters, close to fifty peer-reviewed academic essays, over 300 book reviews published in scholarly sources, and nearly 800 journalistic essays and opinion pieces, his latest two book manuscripts are *Qaboos: A Ruler who Revived the Sultanate of Oman* and *The Nationalist Al Sa'ud Consigliere: Shaykh Yusif Yassin of Sa'udi Arabia* (forthcoming).